RELIGION AND THE AMERICAN CONSTITUTIONAL EXPERIMENT

D1051789

RELIGION AND THE AMERICAN CONSTITUTIONAL EXPERIMENT

SECOND EDITION

JOHN WITTE JR.

Emory University

A Member of the Perseus Books Group

All rights reserved. Printed in the United States of America. No part of this publication may be reproduced or transmitted in any form or by any means, electronic or mechanical, including photocopy, recording, or any information storage and retrieval system, without permission in writing from the publisher.

Copyright © 2005 by Westview Press, A Member of the Perseus Books Group

Published in the United States of America by Westview Press, A Member of the Perseus Books Group, 5500 Central Avenue, Boulder, Colorado 80301–2877, and in the United Kingdom by Westview Press, 12 Hid's Copse Road, Cumnor Hill, Oxford OX2 9JJ.

Find us on the world wide web at www.westviewpress.com

Westview Press books are available at special discounts for bulk purchases in the United States by corporations, institutions, and other organizations. For more information, please contact the Special Markets Department at the Perseus Books Group, 11 Cambridge Center, Cambridge, MA 02142, or call (617) 252–5298, (800) 255–1514 or email special.markets@perseusbooks.com.

Library of Congress Cataloging-in-Publication Data

Witte, John, 1959-
 Religion and the American constitutional experiment : essential rights and liberties / John Witte, Jr—2nd ed.
  p. cm.
 Includes index.
 ISBN 0-8133-4232-5 (HC)
  1. Freedom of religion—United States—History. 2. Church and state—United States—History. 3. Freedom of religion—United States. 4. Church and state—United States. 5. United States. Constitution. 1st Amendment. I. Title.
  KF4783.Z9W58 2004
  342.7308'52—dc22

                                                                2004012100

The paper used in this publication meets the requirements of the American National Standard for Permanence of Paper for Printed Library Materials Z39.48–1984.

ISBN-10: 0-8133-4231-7 ISBN-13: 978-0-8133-4231-3 (PBK)

For Eliza Ellison,
my angel

CONTENTS

List of Tables and Figures   xi
Preface   xiii
Preface to the Second Edition   xv

Introduction   xix

    Notes, xxiv

1 The American Experiment in Historical Context   1

    The First Millennium, 3
    The Papal Revolution, 7
    The Protestant Reformation, 10
    Religious Establishment Versus Religious Freedom, 13
    Colonization and Experimentation, 15
    Notes, 17

2 The Theology and Politics of the Religion Clauses   21

    Puritan Views, 23
    Evangelical Views, 26
    Enlightenment Views, 29
    Republican Views, 33
    Notes, 36

3 The Essential Rights and Liberties of Religion   41

    Liberty of Conscience, 41
    Free Exercise of Religion, 45
    Religious Pluralism, 46
    Religious Equality, 48
    Separation of Church and State, 51

Disestablishment of Religion, 57
Interdependence of Principles, 61
Notes, 63

4   Forging the First Amendment Religion Clauses   71

Religion and the Continental Congress, 71
The 1787 Constitutional Convention, 76
Ratification and Proposed Amendments, 79
Drafting the First Amendment Religion Clauses, 80
The Final Text, 89
Summary and Conclusions, 100
Notes, 103

5   Religion and the States Before 1947   107

Liberty of Conscience and Free Exercise, 108
Religious Pluralism and Equality, 110
Separation of Church and State, 111
Disestablishment of Religion, 113
Faith, Freedom, and the Frontier, 117
Notes 121

6   Religion and the Supreme Court, 1815–1947   125

Review of Federal Laws Touching Religion, 126
Review of State Laws Touching Religion, 132
Fundamental Religious Liberty and Incorporation, 135
Notes, 140

7   Modern Free Exercise Law   143

Mapping Modern Free Exercise Doctrine, 144
The Multiple Principles of Modern Free Exercise Law, 152
Neutralizing the Free Exercise Clause, 163
Free Speech and Statutory Protections of Religion, 169
Conclusions, 176
Notes, 178

8   Modern Disestablishment Law   185

Mapping Modern Disestablishment Doctrine, 185

The Dominant Principle of Separation of Church and State, 201
Toward Multiple Principles of Disestablishment, 212
Conclusions, 224
Notes, 227

9   **Toward an Integration of Religious Liberty:
     The American Experiment in International Context**   **233**

Methods and Measures of Integration, 233
Religious Rights and Liberties in International Context, 236
International Norms and American Laws Compared, 241
Notes, 247

Concluding Reflections   **249**

Notes, 259

Appendix 1: Drafts of the Federal Religion Clauses (1787–1789)   261

Appendix 2: State Constitutional Provisions on Religion (as of 1947) 265
*Appendix 3: United States Supreme Court Decisions Relating to
               Religious Liberty*   271
Index   305

Tables and Figures

Tables

5.1 Proportional Numbers of Mainline Churches, 1780–1900   120

A.2 State Constitutional Provisions on Religion As of 1947   266
A.3 United States Supreme Court Decisions Relating to
    Religious Liberty   272

Figures

7.1 Trends in Modern Free Exercise law   148

8.1 Trends in Modern Disestablishment law   189

PREFACE

This volume is at once an introduction for students, a provocation for specialists, and an invitation for the public to view afresh the American experiment in religious rights and liberties. I combine historical, doctrinal, and comparative methods to tell the unique American story of religious freedom—from the formation of the First Amendment in 1789 to the Supreme Court's most recent interpretations of its guarantees of disestablishment and free exercise of religion.

This volume is calibrated to press uninitiated readers beyond simple incantation of Jefferson's wall of separation as the source and summary of the First Amendment. It is also calculated to lift seasoned readers above simple lamentation over the Supreme Court's recent First Amendment cases. I have sought to provide just enough historical, case law, and comparative analysis for readers to appreciate the ingenuity of the American founders and the intricacies of the experiment that they unleashed. I have also sought to provide just enough of an argument for the principled integration of religious liberty for readers to see the robust promise that the American experiment still holds.

This volume, however, deliberately sidesteps most of the thickets of casuistry in which First Amendment scholarship has become heavily entangled of late. Casuistry, of course, is essential for the constant reformation of the First Amendment. And *summae jurisprudentiae* are essential for the careful preservation of the best reforms to come from the same. But accessible condensation of this specialized material is also essential lest we become tempted to academic condescension. And a summary of our jurisprudence is essential lest we lose sight of the vigor and vitality of the American story of religious freedom. Such is the task of this volume.

I would like to express my appreciation to Spencer Carr, former executive editor at Westview Press, and his successor, Leo Wiegman at Westview Press, now an imprint of the Perseus Books Group, who commissioned this volume and worked so assiduously to bring it into print.

Several friends and colleagues lent liberally of their advice and criticisms. I would like especially to thank Thomas C. Arthur, Thomas C. Berg, Harold J. Berman, A. Morgan Cloud, Daniel L. Dreisbach, Frederick Mark Gedicks, T. Jeremy Gunn, and Douglas Laycock, who each read large portions of this volume and made numerous edifying suggestions and criticisms. I hope that the quality of this volume begins to approximate the quality of their advice.

A number of students at Emory Law School provided me with able and ample assistance in teaching my course on "American Constitutional Law: Church and State" over the past decade and in preparing this volume over the past few months. The names that come to mind are Scott Blevins, Blaine Bortnick, Bruce Frohnen, M. Christian Green, Jay Todd Hahn, Jeffrey Hammond, Heidi Hansan, David Hilts, Henry Kimmel, Tamara McCracken, Joel Nichols, Woodruff Polk, Audra Pontes, Stuart Poppel, Jeri Nazary Sute, Elizabeth Swinton, Jason Waite, and Gordon Young, all of whom I wish to thank. I owe a special word of thanks to Joel Nichols for his efforts in preparing the tables that appear in Appendices 2 and 3.

I would like to thank my friend and colleague, Dean Howard O. Hunter, for his unstinting support of me throughout my time at Emory and for his generosity in granting me a sabbatical leave this year to complete this volume, among other projects. I would also like to thank Will Haines, Holliday Osborne, and Rosalie Sanderson of the Emory Law Library for their impeccable library support, and Louise Jackson for her faithful secretarial services.

Prototypes of some of the material presented in this volume have appeared in print elsewhere. I express my gratitude to the publishers for permission to include revised excerpts from the following:

"Church and State," in *Encyclopedia of Religion,* ed. Mircea Eliade (New York: Macmillan and Free Press, 1987), 3: 489–505 (coauthored with Harold J. Berman);

"How to Govern a City on the Hill: The Early Puritan Contribution to American Constitutionalism," *Emory Law Journal* 39 (1990): 41–64;

"Law, Religion, and Human Rights," *Columbia Human Rights Law Review* 28 (1996): 1–31;

"Tax Exemption of Church Property: Historical Anomaly or Valid Constitutional Practice?" *Southern California Law Review* 64 (1991): 363–415;

"The Essential Rights and Liberties of Religion in the American Constitutional Experiment," *Notre Dame Law Review* 71 (1996): 371–445: and

"The Integration of Religious Liberty," *Michigan Law Review* 90 (1992): 1363–1383.

JOHN WITTE, JR.

PREFACE TO THE
SECOND EDITION

I intended the first edition of this volume to be an accessible introduction to the American story of religious liberty viewed in interdisciplinary and international perspective. Very few books of the sort were then on the market, and no book that I knew of sought to reach students and scholars of law, theology, history, ethics, political science, human rights, and American studies alike. It has been gratifying to see the generous adoption of this volume in classrooms and the generous reception of the book by scholars of many specialties over the past five years. The book seems to have filled a gap in the literature; given its success, I have retained much of the substance and style of the first edition in this second edition.

This new edition takes account of the latest chapters of the American story of religious liberty. Since the first edition of the volume went to press in 1999, the United States Supreme Court has issued seven major First Amendment cases on religious liberty. The White House and Congress have sponsored new initiatives supporting faith-based charities and protecting religious properties and prisoners. Several states have issued important new statutes on religious liberty, not least their own state religious freedom restoration acts. And questions of American compliance with international religious freedom standards have become more highly contested in the aftermath of September 11. Chapters 7–9 of this new edition analyze these new legal materials; Appendix 3 includes convenient summaries of all 161 Supreme Court cases on religious liberty, including the most recent cases.

This new edition also takes account of the latest scholarship on the American experiment in religious liberty. The new millennium has triggered a small avalanche of important new books and articles on the eighteenth-century founders, notably Thomas Jefferson and John Adams, on the Continental Congress and the Constitutional Convention, on the historical genesis and exodus of the metaphor of a wall of separation between church and state, and on the history of religion and theology in colonial and antebellum America. The revisions in Chapters 2–6 draw on some of the best of this new scholarship. The new millennium has done nothing to slow the ample flow of law review articles on recent religious liberty jurisprudence;

nearly 2,000 articles have been published since 2000, alongside scores of specialty monographs and humanities articles. I have drawn on this new scholarship to revise Chapters 7–9.

I have retained the structure and main argument of the first edition but have streamlined and shortened the text somewhat to enhance its utility as a classroom text and as an armchair paperback. I have pruned the notes to their essential core and have guided readers to these sources through index references rather than through a lengthy bibliography. I have dropped the long chapter from the first volume on tax exemption of church property, which many users found too detailed and specialized for an introductory text. I have added more cross-references to draw attention to common themes throughout and have highlighted those themes more prominently in the Concluding Reflections.

This new edition has been improved by the criticisms of several reviewers of the first edition. Some reviewers pointed out some of the Protestant biases in my analysis, particularly my failure to acknowledge the important contributions of early modern Catholics to the Western tradition of religious liberty and the sometimes virulent anti-Catholicism of nineteenth-century American Protestants. Chapters 1, 5, and 6 now take better account of this material. Other reviewers have criticized my characterizations of Roger Williams as an "Evangelical" and of James Madison as an "Enlightenment *philosophe*." I have been more careful in Chapters 2 and 3 to show that the Evangelical, Enlightenment, and other "models" of religious liberty are only heuristic types, and that various founders, Williams and Madison prominently among them, do not fit neatly into any of them. Still other reviewers have pressed me to consider more closely the interplay of American and international norms of religious liberty, not only today but throughout the twentieth century. I have used this lead to help revise Chapter 9.

Beyond that, I have stuck to my guns—with apologies to friends whose reviews called me to talk more about the Christian character of America and to talk less about principles of religious liberty. I still prefer to view America not as a Christian nation but as "a nation with the soul of a *sanctuary*"—both the sanctuary of churches and the sanctuary of consciences. And I still believe that the American experiment in religious liberty has endured because it was firmly built on founding principles, even if those principles have yielded confusing precepts and practices over the past two centuries and more.

I wish to thank my colleagues Amy Wheeler and Janice Wiggins for their dedicated work on the production of this second edition, and Will Haines and Kelly Parker of the Emory Law Library for their valuable library services. I also wish to thank Ashley Altenburger, Erin Englebrecht, Charles Hooker, and Sarah Pentz for their research assistance. And I appreciate the efforts of Steven Catalano and his colleagues at Westview Press for their efforts in bringing this new edition into press.

Finally, I wish to thank Craig Dykstra and his colleagues at the Lilly Endowment, Inc. in Indianapolis for their generous grant in support of my project on "Law, Religion, and the Protestant Tradition," which has provided research support for this and several other writing projects.

Several passages of this revised text are drawn from my recent publications, and are used herein with permission:

(1) Introduction to John Witte Jr. and Frank S. Alexander, eds., *Modern Christian Teachings on Law, Politics, Society, and Human Nature* (New York/London: Columbia University Press, 2004), 2 vols;

(2) "That Serpentine Wall of Separation," *Michigan Law Review* 101 (2003): 1869–1905;

(3) "'A Page of History Is Worth a Volume of Logic': Charting the Legal Pilgrimage of Public Religion in America," in Edith Blumhofer, ed., *Religion, Politics, and the American Experience: Reflections on Religion and American Public Life* (Tuscaloosa/London: University of Alabama Press, 2002), 44–61;

(4) *Law and Protestantism: The Legal Teachings of the Lutheran Reformation* (Cambridge/New York: Cambridge University Press, 2002), chaps. 1 and 3; and

(5) "A Dickensian Era of Religious Rights: An Update on *Religious Human Rights in Global Perspective*," *William and Mary Law Review* 42 (2001): 707–770.

JOHN WITTE, JR.
Emory Law School

INTRODUCTION

Thomas Jefferson once described the new religious liberty guarantees of 1776–1789 as a "fair" and "novel experiment."[1] These new state and federal constitutional guarantees defied the millennium-old assumptions inherited from Western Europe—that one form of Christianity must be established in a community and that the state must protect and support it against other religions. America would no longer suffer such prescriptions and proscriptions of religion by government, Jefferson declared. All forms of Christianity must now stand on their own feet and on an equal footing with all other faiths. Their survival and growth must turn on the cogency of their word, not the coercion of the sword, on the faith of their members, not the force of the law.

This bold constitutional experiment in granting religious liberty to all remains in place, and in progress, in the United States. From 1776 to 1940, principal governance of the experiment lay with the states. The First Amendment applied by its terms only to the federal government—"*Congress* shall make no law respecting an establishment of religion, or prohibiting the free exercise thereof." And these guarantees were only superficially enforced in the federal courts. Most questions of religious liberty were left to the states to resolve, each in accordance with its own state constitution. After 1940, principal control of the experiment shifted abruptly to the federal courts. In *Cantwell v. Connecticut* (1940) and *Everson v. Board of Education* (1947), the United States Supreme Court applied the First Amendment religion clauses to the states, reading its guarantees into the general liberty guarantee of the Fourteenth Amendment—"No state shall deprive any person of . . . liberty . . . without due process of law."[2] In more than 130 cases since 1940, the Court has sought to create a national law on religious liberty binding on all federal, state, and local officials.

The American experiment in religious liberty initially inspired exuberant rhetoric throughout the young republic and beyond. Preacher Elhanan Winchester declared proudly to a London audience in 1788:

> There is but one country in the world where liberty, and especially religious liberty, is so much enjoyed as in these kingdoms, and that is the United States of America: there religious liberty is in the highest perfection. All stand there on equal ground. There are no religious establishments, no preference of one

denomination of Christians above another. The constitution knows no difference between one good man, and another. A man may be chosen there to the
highest civil offices, without being obliged to give any account of his faith, sub-
scribe [to] any religious test, or go to the communion-table of any church.[3]

Yale President Ezra Stiles predicted robustly in 1783:

> The United States will embosom all the religious sects or denominations in
> christendom. Here they may all enjoy their whole respective systems of wor-
> ship and church government, complete. . . . All religious denominations will be
> independent of one another . . . and having, on account of religion, no superi-
> ority as to secular powers and civil immunities, they will cohabit together in
> harmony, and I hope, with a most generous catholicism and benevolence.[4]

Dozens of such enthusiastic endorsements of the American experiment can
be found among the founders' writings of the later eighteenth century.

Today, the American experiment inspires far more criticism than praise.
The United States does "embosom" all religious sects and denominations,
not only from Christendom but from around the world—more than 1,000
religious denominations, in which more than two-thirds of the American
population claims membership. American citizens and groups do enjoy remarkable freedom of religion. But the laboratory of the United States
Supreme Court, which has directed the American experiment since 1940,
no longer inspires confidence. The Court's holdings against Jews, Muslims,
and Native Americans have evoked withering attacks in the popular and
professional media. Indeed, the Court's recent record on religious rights
and liberties has become vilified for its lack of consistent and coherent principles, its uncritical use of mechanical tests and misleading metaphors, and
its massive farrago of divided opinions.

The United States Supreme Court is not the only body that is now "grap-
pling" with the experiment. In the past fifteen years, the testing ground
seems to be shifting away from the federal government to the states and
away from the courts to the legislatures—a trend encouraged by the generous nods toward federalism and separation of powers in a number of recent
Supreme Court cases on religious liberty and several other areas of constitutional law. Accordingly, state legislatures and courts of late have become
bolder in conducting their own experiments in religious liberty, which seem
calculated to revisit, if not rechallenge, prevailing Supreme Court interpretations of the disestablishment and free exercise clauses. At the same time,
Congress has issued a number of laws to defend the free exercise rights of
particular claimants—Native Americans, religious employers, religious
school groups, religious military personnel, religious property holders, and

religious prisoners, among others. The Supreme Court has responded with a barrage of widely discordant and divided opinions.

When an experiment becomes a "kind of wandering inquiry, without any regular system of operations," wrote Francis Bacon, the seventeenth-century "father" of the experimental method, "prudence commends three correctives."[5] First, said Bacon, we must "return to first principles and axioms," reassess them in light of our experience, and "if necessary refine them." Second, we must assess "our experience with the experiment" in light of these first principles, to determine where "the experiment should be adjusted." Third, we must "compare our experiments" and experiences with those of fellow scientists, and where we see in that comparison "superior techniques," we must "amend our experiments" and even our first principles accordingly.[6] Although Bacon offered these prudential instructions principally to correct scientific experiments that had gone awry, his instructions commend themselves to legal and political experiments as well—as he himself sought to demonstrate in seventeenth-century England.[7]

This volume applies Bacon's prudential instructions to the American constitutional experiment in religious rights and liberties—an experiment that today is indeed, as Bacon put it, "wandering, without any regular system of operations."

Applying Bacon's first instruction, Chapters 1–4 return to the "first principles" that inspired and informed the original American experiment. Looking backward from 1789, the year the First Amendment was drafted, these chapters survey the theological and political movements that were most critical to the formation of the new constitutional laws on religious liberty—the Puritan, Evangelical, Enlightenment, and Republican movements, each viewed in broader European context. These four groups of founders, I argue, while often independent and wide-ranging in their efforts, helped to forge the "first principles" of the American experiment in religious liberty.

Six principles stand out in these founders' writings: (1) liberty of conscience; (2) free exercise of religion; (3) religious pluralism; (4) religious equality; (5) separation of church and state; and (6) disestablishment of religion. These six principles were, in effect, "incorporated" into the First Amendment religion clauses as well as into a number of the other state constitutional bills of rights. They remain the guiding principles of the American experiment today—in their original form, and in provocative new constructions and combinations such as "religious accommodationism," "no religious coercion," "equal access," "equal treatment," and "substantive neutrality."

Applying Bacon's second instruction, Chapters 5–8 analyze the American constitutional experience in light of these first principles. I first review the plight of these principles in the state constitutions before 1940 and in the thirty-one cases on religious liberty that reached United States Supreme Court before 1940. I then analyze the 130-odd First Amendment cases on religious liberty issued since 1940. These modern cases have served both to enhance and to frustrate the American experiment, I argue—in part because these two lines of cases have not been effectively merged, in part because the Court has often dealt inconsistently with the first principles of the experiment.

In its free exercise cases from 1940 to 1980, the Court sought to incorporate the full range of first principles into its analysis—catalyzing great advances in the protection of religious rights and liberties. Since the mid-1980s, however, the Court has reduced the free exercise clause to a single principle of "neutrality," which has effectively neutralized the free exercise clause's protection of religious liberty. It is no small irony that today the free speech clause of the First Amendment affords considerably more protection to religion than the free exercise clause.

The trend in disestablishment law has been exactly the opposite. In its disestablishment cases from 1947 to 1982, the Court placed great emphasis on the principle of separation of church and state—sometimes yielding secularist dicta and decisions that seemed anomalous to a nation so widely devoted to a public religion and a religious public. Since the mid-1980s, however, the Court has opened its disestablishment calculus to a wider range of first principles, which the Court is now struggling mightily to integrate.

Applying Bacon's third instruction, Chapter 9 compares the principles and practices of the American experiment with prevailing international norms of religious rights and liberties. International human rights norms, I argue, are no panacea to the current constitutional confusion, but they do open promising new pathways toward a more integrated approach to the First Amendment religion clauses. The priority given to liberty of conscience, free exercise, and equality principles at international law might well serve as a prototype for the integration of the guarantees of free exercise and disestablishment. The firm insistence of international human rights instruments that state abridgments of religious rights be both "necessary" and "proportionate" encourages a stricter free exercise test than currently in vogue. The growing emphasis at international law on the rights of religious groups and on the need for affirmative state action toward them encourages greater protection of religious minorities in America and greater cooperation of religious and political officials on vital social tasks. The international doctrine of "a margin of appreciation" for local religious and political practices could be put to good use in our federalist system of government. The international debate over the "universalism versus relativism" of human rights has profound implications for the American debate concerning federal and state jurisdiction over religious rights.

The methodology at work in this volume is more expansionist than revisionist in intention. The argument that the First Amendment religion clauses reflect both the theology and the politics of the eighteenth century is not new. But I do give voice to some religious groups and theological sources that have not been conventionally included among the founders. Moreover, I argue that a more candid acknowledgment of the theological pedigree of the First Amendment is an instance of constitutional correction, not "religious correctness."[8] We cannot hold up as normative those eighteenth-century texts that happen to anticipate contemporary secular fashions and deprecate others that do not have modern forms. We cannot pretend that the First Amendment is a purely secular trope, or just another category of liberty and autonomy, and expect citizens to believe in it. It is better, in my view, to acknowledge the explicitly religious sources that helped to form the First Amendment and then seek to include more religious and nonreligious voices and values in the modern constitutional dialogue. It is better, in Judge John Noonan's words, for judges not "to pretend that they are neutrals somehow free from all prejudice when they decide intrachurch disputes, determine who has a religious claim, or balance the State's interest in relation to the First Amendment."[9]

The First Amendment, in both its formation and its enforcement, is predicated in part on theological visions and values. To insist that it is merely a neutral instrument, bleached of all religious qualities, only invites secular prejudices to become constitutional prerogatives. If we have learned anything from "postmodernism," it is that each narrative has its own nomos—its own beliefs, values, and ideals.[10] If we have learned anything from "legal realism," it is that judges in constitutional cases do not operate with mechanical logic but with feelings, passions, and prejudices. A more candid acknowledgment of these religious metasources of the First Amendment law on the books and in action enriches more than endangers our understanding.

The six principles of religious liberty analyzed and advocated herein are not new creations. But I have grounded these principles in several European legal traditions, eighteenth-century American texts, and modern human rights instruments that have not been part of the conventional literature. I have labeled and grouped them in a way that does not always follow current linguistic and conceptual fashions. And I have stripped them of some of the thick accretions of casuistry, which have tended to obscure their essential value and vigor in informing and integrating the twin religious liberty guarantees of the First Amendment.

In my view, the free exercise clause outlaws government *proscriptions* of religion—actions that unduly burden the conscience, restrict religious action and expression, discriminate on religious grounds, or invade the autonomy of churches and other religious bodies. The disestablishment clause outlaws government *prescriptions* of religion—actions that coerce the conscience, mandate forms of religious expression, discriminate in favor of religion, or improperly ally the state with churches or other religious bodies. Both the free exercise and the disestablishment clauses thereby provide complementary protections to the first principles of the American experiment—liberty of conscience, freedom of religious expression, equality of plural faiths before the law, and separation of church and state.

The call for a more integrated framework of religious liberty in America, built on these first principles, is also not new. But I warn against efforts to reduce the religion clause guarantees to one or two principles alone—even to such vaunted principles as coercion, neutrality, or accommodationism, currently in vogue. Religion is simply too vital and valuable a source of individual flourishing and social cohesion to be left to one or two legal defenses. As both the eighteenth-century American founders and twentieth-century international jurists have repeatedly argued, a variety of principles must be integrated into an interlocking and interdependent shield of religious liberties and rights for all. The principles of liberty of conscience, free exercise, pluralism, equality, separation, and disestablishment form the essential amalgam of the American shield.

Notes

1. Saul K. Padover, ed., *The Complete Jefferson, Containing His Major Writings* (1943), 538, 673–676, 1147; P. L. Ford, ed., *The Works of Thomas Jefferson*, 12 vols. (1904–1905), 11:7; Julian Boyd, ed., *The Papers of Thomas Jefferson*, 9 vols. (1950), 1:537–539. See analysis in Sidney E. Mead, *The Lively Experiment: The Shaping of Christianity in America* (1963), 55–71. The concept of an "experiment" in religious liberty goes back at least to John Locke and was used by American colonists Roger Williams and William Penn in the seventeenth century. See John Locke, "A Second Letter Concerning Toleration (c. 1690)," in *The Works of John Locke*, 12th ed. (1824), 5:59–138, at 63ff. See other early references in Chapter 1 herein and in Daniel L. Dreisbach, "A Lively and Fair Experiment: Religion and the American Constitutional Tradition," *Emory Law Journal* 49 (2000):223.

2. 310 U.S. 296 (1940); 330 U.S. 1 (1947).

3. Elhanan Winchester, "A Century Sermon on the Glorious Revolution (1788)," in *Political Sermons of the American Founding Era*, 1730–1805, ed. Ellis Sandoz (1991), 969, 988–989.

4. Ezra Stiles, *The United States Elevated to Glory and Honor* (1783), 54–55 (spelling modernized and original italics removed).

5. Francis Bacon, "The Great Instauration (1620)," preface, reprinted in id., *The New Organon and Related Writings*, ed. Fulton H. Anderson (1960), 3–30, at 11.

6. Francis Bacon, "The New Organon (1620)," *Aphorisms Book One*, 70, 82, 103, 104, reprinted in Bacon, *The New Organon and Related Writings*, 31–268, at 67–69, 78–80, 97–98.

7. See generally Barbara Shapiro, "Sir Francis Bacon and the Mid-Seventeenth Century Movement for Law Reform," *American Journal of Legal History* 24 (1980):331–362; Daniel Coquillette, *Francis Bacon* (1992).

8. Cf. Isaac Kramnick and R. Laurence Moore, *The Godless Constitution: The Case Against Religious Correctness* (1996).

9. John T. Noonan Jr., "The Tensions and the Ideals," in *Religious Human Rights in Global Perspective: Legal Perspectives,* ed. Johan D. van der Vyver and John Witte Jr. (1996), 593–606, at 604.

10. Cf. Robert M. Cover, "The Supreme Court 1982 Term—Foreword: Nomos and Narrative," *Harvard Law Review* 97 (1983):4–68.

1

THE AMERICAN EXPERIMENT

IN HISTORICAL CONTEXT

The American founders did not create their experiment on religious liberty out of whole cloth. They had more than a century and a half of colonial experience and more than a millennium and a half of European experience from which to draw both examples and counterexamples.

Historical examples and exemplars of religious liberty were amply at hand. Foremost among these sources was the Christian Bible, with its bracing aphorisms on freedom: "For freedom, Christ has set us free." "You were called to freedom." "Where the Spirit of the Lord is, there is freedom." "You will know the truth, and the truth will make you free." "You will be free indeed." You have been given "the glorious liberty of the children of God."[1] Equally important were the Bible's calls to believers to "render to Caesar the things that are Caesar's and to God the things that are God's" and to maintain a "wall of separation" against evil and worldly temptations."[2] For Christians are, at heart "strangers and foreigners on the earth"; their true "citizenship is in heaven."[3] Such biblical passages inspired hundreds of impassioned sermons in defense of religious liberty for Christian individuals and groups; indeed, political sermons constituted some 80 percent of all the American political literature published in the 1770s and 1780s.[4]

Beyond the Bible, the American founders also turned for inspiration to the martyred prophets of religious liberty in the West—Thomas Becket, John Wycliff, John Hus, and an ample number of early modern Continental Anabaptists, English Levellers, Quaker dissenters, and Catholic missionaries. They turned for instruction to a host of European theologians and philosophers, from the sixteenth-century Protestant reformers, Martin Luther and John Calvin, to early modern Catholic champions of rights, Francisco de Vitoria and Francisco Suarez, to later European voices, such as John Locke, Baron Montesquieu, William Blackstone, and a host of others.[5]

Historical counterexamples also came readily to mind, particularly as the founders prepared sermons, speeches, and pamphlets denouncing traditional religious establishments. In defending the novelty of the American experiment, the founders often dismissed their Western inheritance as a veritable "career of intolerance," in James Madison's apt phrase.[6] One pamphleteer wrote:

> No doubt, Constantine the Great, who first established christianity [in the fourth century], had a good intention in the same; but all the darkness that has since overspread the Christian church, the exorbitant power of the popes and church of Rome, all the oceans of blood that have been shed in the contests about religion, between different sects of Christians, the almost total cessation of the progress of christianity, the rise of Mahometanism, the rise and spread of deism, the general contempt in which christianity is fallen; all may fairly be laid at the door of that establishment.[7]

Thomas Jefferson concurred: "Millions of innocent men, women, and children, since the introduction of Christianity, have been burnt, tortured, fined, imprisoned; yet we have not advanced one inch towards uniformity."[8] Madison wrote similarly:

> During almost fifteen centuries has the legal establishment of Christianity been on trial. What has been its fruits? More or less in all places, pride and indolence in the Clergy, ignorance or servility in the laity, in both, superstition, bigotry and persecution. . . . Torrents of blood have been spilt in the old world, by vain attempts of the secular arm, to extinguish Religious discord, by proscribing all differences in Religious opinion. Time has at length revealed the True Remedy. . . . The American Theatre has exhibited proofs that equal and compleat liberty, if it does not wholly eradicate it, sufficiently destroys its malignant influence on the health and prosperity of the state.[9]

James Iredell of North Carolina reflected commonplaces of the day when he declared:

> Every person in the least conversant in the history of mankind, knows what dreadful mischiefs have been committed by religious persecutions. Under the color of religious tests the utmost cruelties have been exercised. Those in power have generally considered all wisdom centered in themselves, that they alone had a right to dictate to the rest of mankind, and that all opposition to their tenets was profane and impious. The consequence of this intolerant spirit had been, that each church has in turn set itself up against every

other, and persecutions and wars of the most implacable and bloody nature have taken place in every part of the world. America has [now] set an example to mankind to think more modestly and reasonably; that a man may be of different religious sentiments from our own, without being a bad member of society.[10]

Anyone who was still not convinced could turn to John Adams's massive three-volume *A Defense of the Constitutions of Government in the United States of America* (1788) for an exhaustive account of the "gory ecclesiastical or civil tyranny" of the Western tradition and the "glorious new experiment" of the American republic.[11]

To set the American experiment in historical relief and context, it is worth recounting briefly the main events and figures in the Western tradition of religious liberty. This story, even briefly told, bears out not only the genius of the eighteenth-century American experiment but also its genesis in texts and beliefs that antedate the American founding, sometimes by many centuries.

The American founders revolutionized the Western tradition of religious liberty. But they also remained within this Western tradition, dependent on its enduring and evolving postulates about God and humanity, authority and liberty, church and state. This Western pedigree of the American experiment in religious liberty might be a source of comfort to modern skeptics, who see in it a betrayal of the classic ideals of Western Christendom. This Western pedigree might also be a source of warning to modern enthusiasts, who see in it a universal formula of the good life and good society to be enforced throughout the world.

The First Millennium

In the first three centuries of its existence, the Christian church was largely isolated from official Roman society. It received virtually no support from the Roman political authorities and virtually no protection against oppression by them. Christians refused to acknowledge the divinity of the emperor, as required by Roman law, or to swear the oaths or to join the pagan rituals necessary for participation in Roman civic, political, or military life. Early Christians taught obedience to the authorities but only up to the limits of Christian conscience, following Christ's call to "render to Caesar the things that are Caesar's, and to God the things that are God's."[12] But they also sought to expand their faith and reform society, following Christ's call for them to "make disciples of all nations, teaching them to observe all that I have commanded you."[13] Both this nonconformity and agitation for reform by Christians brought reprisal from the Roman authorities. Even before the infamous reign of Emperor Nero (r. 54–68), the

Roman authorities began to repress Christians, departing from Rome's usual policy of indifferently tolerating all faiths that remained politically subservient and religiously sequestered. By the end of the first century, Rome declared Christianity to be an illicit religion and Christians to be guilty of treason unless they recanted their faith. Imperial edicts outlawed Christian worship, charity, and education, and instituted intermittent waves of brutal persecution against Christians.[14]

With the conversion of the Roman Emperor Constantine in 312, Christians came to enjoy an ample measure of religious toleration at Roman law. The imperial Edict of Milan (313) for the first time guaranteed to Christians alongside all other faiths "freedom to follow whatever religion each one wished"; "a public and free liberty to practice [or to "exercise"—from *exercere*] their religion or cult"; and a "free permission to follow their own religion and worship as befits the peacefulness of our times." The Edict of Milan also recognized the rights of Christian groups to property and places of worship, "which belonged by right to their body—that is, to the churches not to individuals," and the right to restitution of properties confiscated in earlier times of persecution. Such guarantees of individual and group religious rights were granted, the edict provides, "so that the supreme Divinity, whose religion we obey with free minds, may be able to show in all matters His accustomed favour and benevolence towards us."[15]

Had this law on the books remained the law in action, Rome would have instituted a regime of religious toleration that the West would not see again for more than a millennium. Even in Constantine's reign, however, and increasingly thereafter, the Roman emperors moved from a policy of open religious toleration of all to one of increasing preference for and control of Trinitarian Christianity. An imperial edict of 380 sealed this shift in policy, and for the first time legally established Trinitarian Christianity at law and declared all other faiths heretical:

> [T]here is one Godhead, Father, Son, and Holy Spirit, in an equal Majesty and Holy Trinity. We order that those who follow this doctrine to receive the title of Catholic Christians, but others we judge to be mad and raving and worthy of incurring the disgrace of heretical teaching, nor are their assemblies to receive the name of churches. They are to be punished not only by Divine retribution but also by our own measures.[16]

This formal establishment of Trinitarian Christianity as the official religion of the Roman Empire brought the church under both the support and the control of Roman political authorities. On the one hand, orthodox Christian clergy were given special military protection, legal privileges, and financial support to spread the faith, to educate the young, to care for the poor, and to build new churches, monasteries, schools, and charities. Heretics, pagans, and Jews, in turn, were subject to severe repression and legal disability, which Christian bishops sometimes led at the behest of the emperor.[17] On the other hand, the Roman emperors declared themselves to be the supreme rulers of both civil and religious affairs in the empire. The Roman emperors and their delegates convoked and presided over the major church councils, appointed and removed bishops and other clergy, and chartered and administered churches and monasteries. Numerous imperial laws regulated the internal activities of the church, the lives of its clerics and monks, the acquisition and disposition of church property, and the definition of church doctrine and liturgy. The great compilations of Roman law—the *Theodosian Code* (438), the *Corpus Iuris Civilis* (529–533), and *Novels* (c. 565)—were filled with literally thousands of new laws that governed the doctrine, liturgy, polity, and property of the church.

This radical new form of church-state relations drew to itself a variety of new Christian political theories. The most famous theory was developed by Augustine, Bishop of Hippo, who saw in this new arrangement not a betrayal of apostolic ideals of separatism but a better way of understanding the spiritual and temporal dimensions and powers of the earthly life. In his *City of God* (c. 413–427),[18] Augustine contrasted the city of God with the city of man that coexist on this earth. The city of God consists of all those who are predestined to salvation, bound by the love of God, and devoted to a life of Christian piety, morality, and worship led by the Christian clergy. The city of man consists of all the things of this sinful world, and the political and social institutions that God had created to maintain a modicum of order and peace on the earth. Augustine sometimes depicted this dualism as two walled cities separated from each other—particularly when he was describing the sequestered life and discipline of monasticism or the earlier plight of the Christian churches under pagan Roman persecution. But Augustine's more dominant teaching was that, in the Christianized Roman Empire, these two cities overlapped in responsibility and membership. Christians would remain dual citizens until these two cities were fully and finally separated on the Return of Christ and at the Last Judgment of God. A Christian remained bound by the sinful habits of the world, even if he aspired to greater purity of the Gospel. A Christian remained subject to the power of both cities, even if she aspired to be a citizen of the city of God alone. If the rulers of the city of man favored Christians rather than persecuting them, so much the better.

It was crucial, however, that the spiritual and temporal powers that prevailed in these two cities remain separate in their core functions. Even though Christianity became the one established religion of the Roman Empire, patronized and protected by the Roman authorities, Augustine and other Church Fathers insisted that political authorities not intrude upon core spiritual functions. All magistrates, even the Roman emperors, were not ordained clergy, but laity. They had no power to administer the sacraments or to mete out religious discipline. They were bound by the teachings of the Bible, the decrees of the ecumenical councils, and the traditions of their predecessors. They also had to accept the church's instruction, judgment, and spiritual discipline. Thus, for example, Ambrose, Bishop of Milan, excommunicated the powerful Emperor Theodosius for massacring the people of Thessalonica and readmitted him to communion only after he had done public penance for his immoral act. Pope Gelasius put the matter famously in 494 in a letter rebuking Emperor Anastasius:

> There are, indeed, most august Emperor, two powers by which the world is chiefly ruled: the sacred authority of the Popes and the royal power. Of these the priestly power is the more important, because it has to render account for kings of men themselves at [the Last Judgment]. For you know, our clement son, that although you have the chief place in dignity over the human race, yet you must submit yourself faithfully to those who have charge of Divine things, and look to them for the means of your salvation.[19]

This "two powers" passage became a *locus classicus* for many later theories of a basic separation between pope and emperor, clergy and laity, *regnum* and *sacerdotium*.[20]

This system of tempered imperial or royal rule within the church largely continued in the West after the fall of the Roman Empire in the fifth century. Before their conversion, many of the pagan Germanic kings and tribal rulers were considered to be divine and were the cult leaders as well as the military leaders of their people. Upon their conversion to Christianity, they lost their divinity, yet continued as sacral rulers of the church within their territories. They found in Christianity an important source of authority in their efforts to extend their rule over the diverse peoples that made up their regimes. The clergy not only supported the Germanic Christian kings in the suppression of tribal religions but also looked upon such leaders as the Frankish Emperor Charlemagne (r. 768–814) and the Anglo-Saxon King Alfred (r. 871–899) as their spiritual leaders. Those Germanic rulers who converted to Christianity, in turn, supported the clergy in their struggle against heresies and gave them military protection, political patronage, and material support. Feudal lords within these Germanic domains further patronized the church, by donating lands and other properties to the church in return for the power to appoint and control the priests, abbots, and abbesses who occupied these lands.

The Papal Revolution

This model of church-state relations was turned upside down after 1050. In the name of "freedom of the church" *(libertas ecclesiae),* Pope Gregory VII (1073–1085) and his successors threw off their political and feudal patrons, and declared the Catholic Church itself to be an independent and superior legal and political authority of Western Christendom.[21] In his revolutionary manifesto, *The Dictates of the Pope* (1075), Pope Gregory VII proclaimed that emperors and kings had no authority over the church, or over its clergy and polity. Only the pope, Gregory VII declared, had authority to ordain, discipline, depose, and reinstate bishops, to convoke and control church councils, and to establish and administer abbeys and bishoprics. Only the pope had authority "to enact new laws according to the needs of the time" that were binding on all. Only the papal court was "the court of the whole of Christendom" open and available to all Christians. The pope "may depose emperors," and "the pope is the only one whose feet are to be kissed by all princes."[22] Such a bold proclamation did not go unchallenged. For more than three generations thereafter, a good deal of Europe was locked in bitter religious and civil war, with the papacy and its supporters ultimately prevailing.

In the course of the twelfth and thirteenth centuries, the Roman Catholic Church made good on Gregory's grand claims. The pope and his clergy now claimed more than a spiritual and sacramental power over the church's affairs. They claimed a vast new jurisdiction, an authority to proclaim and enforce law, literally "to speak the law" *(jus dicere)* for Christendom. They claimed exclusive personal jurisdiction over clerics, pilgrims, students, heretics, Jews, and Muslims. They claimed subject matter jurisdiction over doctrine, liturgy, patronage, education, charity, inheritance, marriage, oaths, oral promises, and moral crimes. And they claimed concurrent jurisdiction with state authorities over secular subjects that required the church's special forms of Christian equity. A vast torrent of new church laws, called canon laws, issued by popes, bishops, and church councils came to govern Western Christendom. A vast network of church courts, headquartered in the papal court, enforced these laws throughout the West.[23] In the period from c. 1150–1350, the Roman Catholic Church ironically became "the first modern state" in the West.[24] The church's canon law became the first modern international law.

This high medieval system of church government and law was grounded in part in a new theory of the two swords that supplanted the traditional Gelasian formula of two powers. The two-swords theory taught that the pope is the vicar of Christ on earth, in whom Christ vested his whole authority.[25] This authority was symbolized in the "two swords" discussed in the Bible (Luke 22:38), a spiritual sword and a temporal sword. Christ had metaphorically handed these two swords to the highest being in the human world—the pope, the vicar of Christ. The pope and lower clergy wielded the spiritual sword, in part by establishing canon law rules for the governance of all Christendom. The clergy, however, were too holy to wield the temporal sword. They thus delegated this temporal sword to those authorities below the spiritual realm—emperors, kings, dukes, and their civil retinues, who held their swords "of" and "for" the church. These civil magistrates were to promulgate and enforce civil laws in a manner consistent with canon law. Under this two-swords theory, civil law was by its nature inferior to canon law. Civil jurisdiction was subordinate to ecclesiastical jurisdiction. The state answered to the church.[26] Pope Boniface VIII put this two-swords theory famously and forcefully in 1302:

> We are taught by the words of Gospel that in this Church and in its power there are two swords, a spiritual, to wit, and a temporal. . . . [B]oth are in the power of the Church, namely the spiritual and [temporal] swords; the one, indeed, to be wielded for the Church, the other by the Church; the former by the priest, the latter by the hand of kings and knights, but at the will and sufferance of the priest. For it is necessary that one sword shall be under another and that the temporal authority should be subjected to the spiritual. . . . If, therefore, the earthly power err, it shall be judged by the spiritual power; if the lesser spiritual power err, it shall be judged by the higher, competent spiritual power; but if the supreme spiritual power [i.e., the pope] should err, it could be judged solely by God, not by man.[27]

The church further predicated these jurisdictional claims on Christ's famous delegation of the keys to St. Peter (Matthew 16:18)—a key of knowledge to discern God's word and will, and a key of power to implement and enforce that word and will by law. And the church predicated its more specific subject matter jurisdiction on its traditional authority over the form and function of the Christian sacraments. By the fifteenth century, the church had gathered whole systems of law around the seven sacraments of baptism, eucharist, penance, orders, extreme unction, confirmation, and marriage.

The medieval church's law, called canon law, was based, in part, on the concept of individual and corporate rights. The canon law defined the rights of the clergy to their liturgical offices and ecclesiastical benefices, their exemptions from civil taxes and duties, their immunities from civil prosecution and compulsory testimony. It defined the rights of ecclesiastical organizations like parishes, monasteries, charities, and guilds to form and dissolve, to accept and reject members, to establish order and discipline, to acquire, use, and alienate property. It defined the rights of church councils and synods to participate in the election and discipline of bishops, abbots, and other clergy. It defined the rights of the laity to worship, evangelize, maintain religious symbols, participate in the sacraments, travel on religious pilgrimages, and educate their children. It defined the rights of the poor, widows, and needy to seek solace, succor, and sanctuary within the church. A good deal of the rich latticework of medieval canon law was cast, substantively and procedurally, in the form and language of rights.[28]

To be sure, such rights were not unguided by duties. Nor were they available to all parties. Only the Catholic faithful—and, notoriously, not Jews, Muslims, or heretics—had full rights protection, and their rights were to be exercised with appropriate ecclesiastical and sacramental constraints. But the basic medieval rights formulations of exemptions, immunities, privileges, and benefits, and the free exercise rights of religious worship, travel, speech, and education have persisted, with ever greater inclusivity, to this day. Many of the common formulations of religious rights and liberties that came to prevail in the eighteenth-century American experiment were first forged not by a James Madison or a Thomas Jefferson but by obscure Catholic theologians and canon lawyers four centuries and more before them.

In the course of the fourteenth century and thereafter, this intricate system of religious rights, and of church-state relations, began to break down. Strong monarchs began to increase their control over the church, and clerical authority began to wane—in part because of widespread corruption and compromise even at the highest levels of church government. In 1309, the papal seat was moved from Rome to Avignon and there came under increasing constraint and control by the kings of France. In 1377, the pope returned to Rome, only to have a rival pope appointed the next year in Avignon, claiming the same prerogatives as his Roman rival. In 1415, yet a third pope was appointed in Pavia, compounding the already widespread confusion and dissent within the church hierarchy.

In response, the German Emperor Sigismund convoked at Constance the first of a series of great church councils that declared their authority over church polity and canon law, despite papal disapproval. In the Pragmatic Sanction of Bourges (1438) and again in the Concordat of Bologna (1516), French kings banned various papal taxes, limited appeals to Rome, required French bishops to be elected by French church councils called by the king, subjected the clergy in France to royal discipline, and increased royal control over church property.[29] In Germany, strong princes and city councils began to pass "legal reformations" that placed limits on church property and taxation, disciplined wayward clergy, and curtailed the jurisdiction of church courts over crime, family, inheritance, and contracts. Fifteenth-century Spanish monarchs subordinated the ecclesiastical courts in Spain to the civil courts and assumed exclusive political and legal control, over the prosecution and execution of heretics, Jews, and Muslims, as well as the Inquisition

The Protestant Reformation

In retrospect, such developments could be seen as storm signals that announced the coming of the Protestant Reformation. The Reformation—inaugurated by Martin Luther's posting of the Ninety-Five Theses in 1517 and burning of the canon law books in 1520—began as a call for religious freedom. Luther, John Calvin, Thomas Cranmer, Menno Simons, and other sixteenth-century reformers all began their movements with a call for freedom of the individual conscience from intrusive canon laws and clerical controls, freedom of political officials from ecclesiastical power and privileges, freedom of the local clergy from central papal rule and oppressive princely controls. "Freedom of the Christian" became the rallying cry of the early Reformation.[30] It drove theologians and jurists, clergy and laity, princes and peasants alike to denounce canon laws and ecclesiastical authorities with unprecedented alacrity and to urge radical constitutional reforms. The reforms that they eventually instituted, however, often simply reestablished new forms of Christian faith, now again under civil control.

The Protestant Reformation broke the unity of Western Christendom and eventually laid the foundations for the modern Western system of religious pluralism. The Lutheran Reformation *territorialized* the faith. Luther replaced the two-swords theory of the Papal Revolution with a new two-kingdoms theory. The "invisible" church of the heavenly kingdom, Luther argued, is a perfect community of saints, where all stand equal in dignity before God, all enjoy perfect Christian liberty, and all govern their affairs in accordance with the Gospel. The "visible" church of this earthly kingdom, however, embraces saints and sinners alike. Its members still stand directly before God and still enjoy liberty of conscience, including the liberty to leave the visible church itself. But, unlike the invisible church, the visible church needs both the Gospel and human laws to govern its members' relationships with God and with fellow believers. The clergy must administer the Gospel. But the magistrate must administer the law. For the magistrate is God's vice-regent, called to appropriate and apply God's law in all aspects of earthly life.[31]

This Lutheran understanding of the role of the magistrate in religious affairs, predicated in part on Roman law precedents, was cast into enduring constitutional form. The Peace of Augsburg (1555) established the principle of *cuius regio eius religio* ("whose region, his religion") for much of Germany and surrounding polities.[32] Under this principle, princes, dukes, or city councils were authorized to establish by civil law the appropriate forms of religious doctrine, liturgy, charity, and education for their polities—with religious dissenters granted the right to worship privately in their homes or to emigrate peaceably from the polity. This new constitutional policy rendered Germany, with more than 350 distinct polities, a veritable honeycomb of religious pluralism.

The Anglican Reformation *nationalized* the faith. When the papacy denied him an annulment from his marriage with Catherine of Aragon, King Henry VIII ultimately severed all ties between the church in England and the pope. The Act of Succession (1534) denied papal authority over marriage and divorce, and granted Henry his annulment. Succeeding acts effectively divested the Catholic Church of all its remaining jurisdiction; banned tithes, annates, and appeals to Rome; dissolved the monasteries and guilds; and confiscated massive holdings of church property in England. The Supremacy Act (1534) declared the monarch to be "the only Supreme Head in Earth of the Church of England called *Anglicana Ecclesia.*"[33] The Church *in* England had become the Church *of* England.

As spiritual and temporal heads of the Church of England, Henry VIII and his successors, through their parliaments, established a uniform liturgy, doctrine, and administration of the sacraments, issued *The Book of Common Prayer* (1559) and *The Thirty-Nine Articles of Religion* (1571), and ordered the preparation of the Authorized Version of the Bible (1611) in English translation, which came to be known as the King James Version. The Crown and Parliament also claimed jurisdiction over poor relief, education, marriage, and other activities that had previously been carried on under Catholic auspices and had been subject to Catholic canon law. Communicant status in the Church of England was rendered a condition for citizenship status in the Commonwealth of England. Contraventions of royal religious policy were punishable both as heresy and as treason. Catholics and dissenting Protestants were subjected to severe repression, and untold hundreds of them were martyred.[34]

The Anabaptist Reformation *communalized* the faith by introducing what St. Paul had called a "wall of separation" between the redeemed realm of religion and the fallen realm of the world.[35] Anabaptist religious communities were ascetically withdrawn from the world into small, self-sufficient, intensely democratic communities. These ascetic religious communities were governed internally by biblical principles of discipleship, simplicity, charity, and hospitality. When such communities grew too large or too divided, they colonized themselves, eventually spreading the Anabaptist communities from Russia to Ireland to the furthest frontiers of North America—under such variant denominational labels as Amish, Hutterites, Mennonites, and Baptists.[36]

The Calvinist Reformation *congregationalized* the faith by introducing rule by a democratically elected consistory of pastors, elders, and deacons.

During John Calvin's tenure from 1541 to 1564, the Geneva consistory was still an appointed body and exercised wide legal authority within Geneva and surrounding rural areas. By the later sixteenth century, however, Calvinist consistories in many communities became elected, representative bodies with jurisdiction only within their congregations. These consistories featured separation among the offices of preaching, discipline, and charity, and a fluid, dialogical form of religious polity and policing centered around collective worship, the congregational meeting, and the regular election of church officers. This flexible form of ecclesiastical polity rendered the Calvinist churches and communities mobile and adaptable. They eventually spread throughout Europe under such labels as Scottish Presbyterians, English Puritans, Dutch Pietists, French Huguenots, and various Reformed groups.

The Protestant Reformation broke not only the unity of Western Christendom but also the primacy of corporate Christianity. Protestants gave new emphasis to the role of the individual believer in the economy of salvation and the individual rights that should attach thereto. The Protestant Reformation did not invent or discover the individual or the concept of individual rights; there were ample precedents for this in Greek, Roman, Patristic, and medieval sources. But the sixteenth-century Protestant reformers, more than most of their Catholic contemporaries, gave new emphasis to the (religious) rights and liberties of the individual at both religious law and civil law.[37]

The Anabaptist doctrine of adult baptism gave new emphasis to a voluntarist understanding of religion. The adult individual was called to make a conscientious choice to accept the faith through adult baptism—metaphorically, to scale the wall of separation between the fallen world and the realm of religion to come "within the perfection of Christ."[38] Later Free Church followers converted this cardinal image into a powerful platform of liberty of conscience and free exercise of religion—not only for Christians but eventually for all peaceable believers.

The Calvinist and Lutheran branches of the Reformation laid the basis for an even more expansive theory and law of (religious) rights. Classic Protestant theology teaches that a person is both saint and sinner. On the one hand, a person is created in the image of God and justified by faith in God. The person is called to a distinct vocation, which stands equal in dignity and sanctity to all others. The person is prophet, priest, and king, and responsible to exhort, minister, and rule in the community. Every person, therefore, stands equal before God and before his or her neighbor. Every person is vested with a natural liberty to live, to believe, to serve God and neighbor. Every person is entitled to the vernacular Scripture, to education, to work in a vocation. On the other hand, the person is sinful and prone to evil and egoism. He needs the restraint of the law to deter him from evil and to drive him to repentance. She needs the association of others to exhort, minister, and rule her with law and with love. Every person, therefore, is inherently a communal creature, a member of a family, a church, a political community.

Protestant groups in Europe and America cast these theological doctrines into democratic forms designed to protect religious rights. Protestant doctrines of the person and society were cast into democratic social forms. Since all persons stand equal before God, they must stand equal before God's political agents in the state. Since God has vested all persons with natural liberties of life and belief, the state must ensure them of similar civil liberties. Since God has called all persons to be prophets, priests, and kings, the state must protect their freedoms to speak, to preach, and to rule in the community. Since God has created persons as social creatures, the state must promote and protect a plurality of social institutions, particularly the church and the family.

Protestant doctrines of sin were cast into democratic political forms. The political office must be protected against the sinfulness of the political official. Political power, like ecclesiastical power, must be distributed among self-checking executive, legislative, and judicial branches. Officials must be elected to limited terms of office. Laws must be clearly codified and discretion closely guarded. If officials abuse their office, they must be disobeyed; if they persist in their abuse, they must be removed, even if by force. Such views would eventually have a monumental influence on the theories of inalienable rights and political revolution in early modern Europe and eighteenth-century America.[39]

Religious Establishment Versus Religious Freedom

The Reformation's splintering of Western Christendom into competing religious polities—each with its own preferred forms and norms of religious governance—was a recipe for religious warfare and persecution and for corresponding movements toward religious freedom.

In the 1570s, for example, the Spanish monarch Philip II, who was also Lord of the Netherlands, ordered a bloody inquisition against the growing population of Dutch Protestants, ultimately killing thousands of them and confiscating huge portions of private and church property. This sparked the revolt of the seven northern provinces on the strength of Calvinist principles of revolution. Presaging American developments two centuries later, the Dutch revolutionaries established a confederate government by the Union of Utrecht of 1579, which included a provision that "each person must enjoy freedom of religion, and no one may be persecuted or questioned about his religion." The confederacy led the revolutionary war against the Spanish monarch. In 1581, the confederacy issued a Declaration of Independence, invoking "the law of nature" and the "ancient rights, privileges, and liberties" of the people in justification of its revolutionary actions. When the war was settled, each of the seven Dutch provinces instituted its own constitution. These provincial constitutions embraced some of the most benign forms of religious toleration of the day and helped to render the Netherlands a haven for religious dissenters from throughout Europe—and a common point of departure for American colonists, from the Mayflower Pilgrims of 1620 onward.[40] When later comparing this sixteenth-century Dutch experience with the eighteenth-century American experience, John Adams wrote: "The originals of the two republics are so much alike, that the history of one seems but a transcript of that of the other."[41]

In the opening decades of the seventeenth century, much of northern Europe was locked in bitter religious warfare between and among Catholic and Protestant forces. This religious warfare finally ended with the Peace of Westphalia (1648).[42] Confirming and extending the principles of the 1555 Peace of Augsburg, this new treaty authorized each ruler to establish by civil law either Catholicism, Lutheranism, or Calvinism in his territory. Dissenting religious groups, though denied the right to worship publicly, were granted special privileges to assemble and to worship privately and to educate their children in their own faith, eventually in their own private religious schools. The spiritual jurisdiction of the canon law and papal authority over clergy and church property was guaranteed for Catholic territories. But canon law was barred from use in the Protestant territories, and Catholic clerics and groups were divested of any remaining privileges of forum, tax exemptions, and other civil immunities.

While this policy of balancing religious establishment with religious toleration proved effective to securing peace for a good deal of Europe for the remainder of the seventeenth century, it did not ultimately constrain France and England, the two main national powers of the day.

In France, the monarchy gradually abandoned its earlier policies of religious toleration—particularly as they had been set out in the Edict of Nantes (1598), which had granted modest toleration to Calvinist and other Protestant nonconformists.[43] Supported by the antipapalism of the revived Gallican party and by the new theories of absolute monarchy expounded by Jean Bodin and others on the strength of Roman law precedents, the French monarchs consolidated their control over a national Catholic Church. The French monarchy sharply curtailed remaining papal power over church property, ecclesiastical courts, and clerical nomination. King Louis XIV passed more than one hundred acts against Catholic and Protestant dissenters, confining their freedoms and imposing crushing taxes upon them. Finally, in the Edict of Fontainebleau (1685), Louis XIV ordered all Protestant churches and schools destroyed, proscribed all liturgies and theologies that deviated from officially sanctioned Gallicanism, and banished all dissenting clerics from France.[44] Protestants fled from France by the tens of thousands, many making their way to Belgium, the Netherlands, Switzerland, and Germany—and eventually to distant colonies in North America and southern Africa.

Similarly, in early seventeenth-century England, Kings James I and Charles I issued through their Parliaments a series of increasingly repressive laws against the few remaining Catholics and the growing numbers of Protestant dissenters in England. As official and unofficial persecution mounted in the 1620s and 1630s, tens of thousands of Puritans, Anabaptists, Lutherans, and other "sectaries," as English law called them, "flew out of England, as if out of Babylon" to make their way to the Continent, and often from there to North America.[45] When the English monarchy persisted in its abuse, the remaining Puritans led a revolutionary struggle against the English Crown. The revolutionaries ultimately deposed and executed King Charles I. In 1649, they passed a law "declaring and constituting the People of England to be a commonwealth and free state."[46] They further outlawed the establishment of the Church of England and granted toleration to all Protestants—though not to Catholics or to Jews. This experiment was short-lived. In 1660 royal rule was restored, Anglicanism was reestablished, and dissenters were again repressed. But when the dissenters again rose up in revolt and threatened a new civil war, Parliament ultimately passed the Toleration Act of 1689 that guaranteed freedom of association and worship to all Protestants dissenting from the Church of England.[47] Many of the remaining legal restrictions on the civil and political liberties of Protestants fell into desuetude in the following decades. Catholicism and Judaism, however, continued to be formally proscribed by criminal law until the Jewish and Roman Catholic Emancipation Acts of 1829 and 1833.[48]

Colonization and Experimentation

This checkerboard of rival religious and political groups in early modern Europe was projected in part onto the New World. European powers, eager to extend their political and religious regimes, issued charters and privileges to colonial companies that would establish themselves in the New World under the rule of the distant mother country and mother church. Thus, Spanish and Portuguese Catholic rulers from the early sixteenth century onward extended their regimes through much of Latin America, the Caribbean, Mexico, and modern-day Florida. From the later sixteenth century onward, Jesuits and other missionaries made frequent forays into the American frontier, reaching north to the Carolinas and Virginia, and more successfully west to modern-day Alabama, Louisiana, New Mexico, Arizona, and California. French Catholics sent colonists to Quebec and the Canadian Maritimes, many of whom migrated south into New England. By the eighteenth century, numerous Catholic families from Quebec had also settled in New York and Pennsylvania, and hundreds more had moved down the midwest corridor and the Mississippi River to Louisiana and westward. Dutch Protestant authorities chartered companies of Dutch Calvinists to New York (called New Amsterdam) and parts of New Jersey and Pennsylvania. These companies, though only modestly successful, were amply bolstered in the eighteenth century by new waves of Calvinist colonists from the German Palatinate. Swedish Lutheran monarchs sponsored scattered colonial companies to Delaware and eventually into Maryland, Pennsylvania, and New York as well.[49]

The most prominent colonizers of all, however, were the British, who established colonial companies all along the Atlantic seaboard—from the north in Ontario and the Maritimes to the southern colonies of Virginia, the Carolinas, and Georgia. Among the earliest and most influential colony was Virginia, which was founded as an Anglican "Christian colonie," to be populated by a "peculiar people, marked and chosen by the finger of God."[50] The British eventually assumed formal control of the Middle and New England colonies as well. The royal charters of all these colonies confirmed the rule of English laws and liberties, including its ecclesiastical laws. By the time of the American Revolution of 1776, there were Anglican churches in every American colony, and every American colony was formally under the jurisdiction of the Bishop of London and the Archbishop of Canterbury.

Colonial America was not only a frontier for European establishments but also a haven for European dissenters, many of whom introduced their own experiments in religious liberty. Both the Plymouth Colony of 1620 and the Massachusetts Bay Colony of 1629 were founded by Puritan dissenters from the Church of England and eventually became havens for Calvinist refugees from throughout Europe, though for few others until well into the eighteenth century. Providence Plantation was established in 1636 as "a lively experiment [for] full liberty in religious concernments," in the words of its founder, Roger Williams. The colony's policies of protecting "liberty of conscience" and "the free exercise and enjoyment of all their civil and religious rights" eventually attracted Anabaptists and other Christian dissenters from Europe and other North American colonies.[51]

Maryland, too, was founded by the Catholic leader Lord Baltimore in 1633 as an experiment in Catholic and Protestant coexistence. Its famous Act of 1649 provided that "noe person . . . professing to believe in Jesus Christ, shall from henceforth bee any waies troubled . . . for his or her religion nor in the free exercise thereof . . . nor any way compelled to the beliefe or exercise of any other Religion against his or her consent."[52] Though ultimately frustrated by persistent Catholic-Protestant rivalries and slowly eclipsed by new Anglican establishment policies of the 1660s onward, the Maryland experiment provided ample inspiration during the constitutional debates of the next century.

Equally inspirational was the Quaker leader William Penn's "holy experiment" in religious liberty instituted in Pennsylvania in 1681. The Great Law of 1682 captured Penn's cardinal convictions about Christian liberty:

> [N]o person now or at any time hereafter living in this province, who shall confess and acknowledge one almighty God to be the creator, upholder, and ruler of the world, and who profess[es] himself or herself to be obliged in conscience to live peaceably and quietly under the civil government, shall in any case be molested or prejudiced for his or her conscientious persuasion or practice. Nor shall he or she at any time be compelled to frequent or maintain any religious worship, place, or ministry whatever contrary to his or her mind, but shall freely and fully enjoy his, or her, christian liberty in that respect, without any interruption or reflection.[53]

The eighteenth-century American experiment in religious freedom was thus, at once, very old and very new. For a nation to contemplate the disestablishment of religion altogether and to grant religious liberty to all without obstruction was, indeed, a novel exercise. But legal precedents for such an experiment lay closely at hand in the constitutional example of sixteenth-century Holland and more distantly in the imperial edicts of fourth-century Rome. And firm legal principles to implement this experiment—liberty of conscience, freedom of religious exercise, separation of religious and political authorities, guarantees of religious group rights, and the like—were readily at hand in Catholic canon law, Protestant civil law, and European peace treaties alike. But, as James Madison put it, "[i]t remained for North America to bring the great & interesting subject to a fair, & finally, to a decisive test."[54]

Notes

1. Galatians 5:1, 13; 2 Corinthians 3:17; John 8:32, 36; Romans 8:21 (RSV).

2. Matthew 22:21; Mark 12:17; Luke 20:25; Romans 12:2; Ephesians 2:14; 2 Corinthians 6:14–18.

3. Hebrews 11:13, Philippians 3:20.

4. Donald S. Lutz, *The Origins of American Constitutionalism* (1988), 140–141. See Sandoz, ed., *Political Sermons*; J. W. Thornton, *The Pulpit of the American Revolution* (1860). See analysis in Nathan O. Hatch, *The Sacred Cause of Liberty* (1977); James H. Hutson, *Forgotten Features of the Founding: The Recovery of Religious Themes in the Early American Republic* (2003); Mark A. Noll, *America's God: From Jonathan Edwards to Abraham Lincoln* (2002).

5. See Lutz, *Origins*, 139–149: of all citations in these writings, those to the Bible constituted 34%, Montesquieu 8.3%, Blackstone 7.9%, and Locke 2.9%.

6. James Madison, "Memorial and Remonstrance Against Religious Assessments (1785)," sec. 9, in *The Papers of James Madison*, ed. W. T. Hutchinson, William M.E. Rachal, and Robert A. Rutland (1962), 8:298.

7. Winchester, "A Century Sermon," 989–990.

8. Thomas Jefferson, "Notes on the State of Virginia (1781–1785)," Query XVII, in *The Complete Jefferson*, 673–676.

9. Madison, "Memorial," secs. 8, 11.

10. North Carolina Ratification Debates, July 30, 1788, in Jonathan Elliot, ed., *The Debates in the Several State Conventions, on the Adoption of the Federal Constitution* (1854), 4:196–197 (hereafter cited as Elliot, ed., *Debates*).

11. In *The Works of John Adams*, ed. C. F. Adams (1850–1856), vols. 4–6; see further John Adams, "A Dissertation on the Canon and Feudal Law (1774)," in ibid., 3:447, 451ff.

12. Matthew 22:21; see also Romans 13:1–7.

13. Matt. 28:19–20; see also Acts 1:8.

14. Robert L. Wilken, *Christians as the Romans Saw Them* (1984); Charles Cochrane, *Christianity and Classical Culture* (2003 [1940]).

15. In Lactantius, *De Mortibus Persecutorum [c. 315]*, 48.2–12, ed. and trans. J. L. Creed (1984), 71–73.

16. In Sidney Z. Ehler and John B. Morrall, eds., *Church and State Through the Centuries: A Collection of Historic Documents with Commentaries* (1954), 7.

17. Harold A. Drake, *Constantine and the Bishops* (2000).

18. St. Augustine, *City of God*, trans. G. G. Walsh et al., ed. Vernon J. Bourke (1958), bk. 4.1–4; bk. 19.15–22; bk. 20.1–2, 30; bk. 21; see also *The Political Writings of St. Augustine*, ed. Henry Paolucci (1962).

19. In Ehler and Morrall, eds., *Church and State*, 10–11.

20. Karl F. Morrison, *The Two Kingdoms: Ecclesiology in Carolingian Political Thought* (1964); Ernst Kantorowicz, *The King's Two Bodies: A Study in Medieval Political Theology* (1957).

21. Harold J. Berman, *Law and Revolution: The Formation of the Western Legal Tradition* (1983).

22. In Ehler and Morrall, eds., *Church and State*, 43–44; see further Oliver O'-Donovan and Joan Lockwood O'Donovan, eds., *From Irenaeus to Grotius: A Sourcebook in Christian Political Thought* (1999), 231ff.

23. Berman, *Law and Revolution*, 199–254; R. H. Helmholz, *The Spirit of the Classical Canon Law* (1996).

24. F. W. Maitland, in Berman, *Law and Revolution*, 113–115.

25. Brian Tierney, *The Origins of Papal Infallibility, 1150–1350* (1972), 39–45, 82–121.

26. Otto von Gierke, *Political Theories of the Middle Age* F. W. Maitland, trans. (1958), 7–21; Ewart Lewis, *Medieval Political Ideas* (1954), 2:506–538; Lester L. Field, *Liberty, Dominion and the Two Swords: On the Origins of Western Political Theology* (1998).

27. In Ehler and Morrall, eds., *Church and State*, 89–92; Brian Tierney, *The Crisis of Church and State, 1050–1300* (1964), 180ff.

28. Brian Tierney, *The Idea of Natural Rights: Studies on Natural Rights, Natural Law, and Church Law, 1150–1625* (1997).

29. In Ehler and Morrall, eds., *Church and State*, 96–144.

30. Martin Luther, "Freedom of a Christian (1520)," in Jaroslav Pelikan et al., eds., *Luther's Works* (1955–1968), 31:327.

31. John Witte Jr., *Law and Protestantism: The Legal Teachings of the Lutheran Reformation* (2002).

32. In Ehler and Morrall, eds., *Church and State*, 164–173.

33. In Carl Stephenson and Frederick G. Marcham, eds., *Sources of English Constitutional History*, rev. ed. (1972), 311–312.

34. Joseph Lecler, *Toleration and the Reformation*, 4 vols. (1960).

35. See, e.g., *The Complete Writings of Menno Simons, c. 1496–1561*, trans. L. Verduin, ed. J. C. Wenger (1984), 29, 117–120, 158–159, 190–206.

36. Walter Klaassen, ed., *Anabaptism in Outline: Selected Primary Sources* (1981); George H. Williams, *The Radical Reformation*, 3d ed. (1992).

37. A notable exception was Francisco de Vitoria. See Tierney, *The Idea of Natural Rights*, 255ff.; O'Donovan and O'Donovan, *From Irenaeus to Grotius*, 609ff.

38. The phrase is from the Ur text of Anabaptists, the "Schleitheim Confession (1527)," in Howard J. Loewen, *One Lord, One Church, One Hope, and One God: Mennonite Confessions of Faith in North America* (1985), 79–84.

39. John Witte Jr., *The Reformation of Rights: Law, Religion, and Human Rights in the Calvinist Tradition* (forthcoming 2005).

40. E. H. Kossmann and A. Mellink, eds., *Texts Concerning the Revolt of the Netherlands* (1974).

41. In *New England Magazine* (n.s.) 10 (1894):517, 521.

42. In Ehler and Morrall, eds., *Church and State*, 193–198.

43. In ibid., 204–207.

44. In ibid., 208–213.

45. Harold J. Berman, *Faith and Order: The Reconciliation of Law and Religion* (1993), 104.

46. C. H. Firth and R. S. Rait, eds., *Acts and Ordinances of the Interregnum, 1642–1660* (1911), 2:18, 24, 120, 122.

47. In Stephenson and Marcham, *Sources*, 607–608.

48. Ibid., 678–679. See also the Quebec Act (1774), in ibid., 661–663, guaranteeing "free exercise" rights to Roman Catholics "subject to the King's supremacy."

49. See details in Edwin S. Gaustad and Philip L. Barlow, *New Historical Atlas of Religion in America* (2001), ch. 1.

50. William Strachey and John Rolfe, quoted and discussed in Frank Lambert, *The Founding Fathers and the Place of Religion in America* (2003), 46.

51. "Plantation Agreement of Providence (1640)" and "Charter of Rhode Island and Providence Plantations (1663)," in *The Federal and State Constitutions, Colonial Charters, and Other Organic Laws*, ed. F. Thorpe (1909), 6:3205–3206, 3211–3213. See further Edwin S. Gaustad, *Liberty of Conscience: Roger Williams in America* (1991).

52. In W. Browne, ed., *Archives of Maryland* (1883), 1:244, 246.

53. In J. T. Mitchell and J. Flanders, eds., *Statutes at Large of Pennsylvania* (1911), 1:107–109; see further *The Political Writings of William Penn*, ed. Andrew R. Murphy (2002); J. William Frost, *A Perfect Freedom: Religious Liberty in Pennsylvania* (1990).

54. James Madison, Letter to Rev. Adams (1833), in Daniel L. Dreisbach, *Religion and Politics in the Early Republic: Jasper Adams and the Church-State Debate* (1996), 117–121, at 118.

2

THE THEOLOGY AND POLITICS
OF THE RELIGION CLAUSES

The religion clauses of the state constitutions and of the First Amendment, forged between 1776 and 1789, express both theological and political sentiments. They reflect both the convictions of the religious believers of the young American republic and the calculations of their political leaders. They manifest both the certitude of such eighteenth-century theologians as Isaac Backus and John Witherspoon and the skepticism of such contemporaneous philosophers as Thomas Jefferson and Thomas Paine. A plurality of theological and political views helped to inform the early American experiment.

The American experiment in religious liberty cannot be reduced to the First Amendment religion clauses alone, nor can the understanding of the framers be determined simply by studying the debates on these clauses in the First Session of Congress in 1789. Not only is the record of these debates very slender—a mere three pages in the modern edition, as we shall see in Chapter 4—but the First Amendment religion clauses, by design, reflect only a part of the early constitutional experiment and experience. The religion clauses on their face define only the outer boundaries of appropriate governmental action respecting religion: Government may not prescribe ("establish") religion nor proscribe ("prohibit") its exercise. Precisely what governmental conduct short of outright prescription or proscription of religion is constitutionally permissible is left open for debate and development. Moreover, the religion clauses bind only the federal government ("Congress"), rendering prevailing state constitutional provisions and the sentiments of their drafters equally vital sources of the original understanding. Finally, the drafters of the religion clauses urged interpreters to look not to the drafters' intentions but, in James Madison's words, "to the text itself [and] the sense attached to it by the people in their respective State Conventions, where it received all the authority which it possesses."[1] The understanding of the state conventional delegates was derived from their own state constitutional experiments and experiences, which are reflected in contemporaneous pamphlets, sermons, letters, and speeches. A wide range of eighteenth-century textual and contextual materials must thus be consulted to come to terms with the prevailing sentiments on religious rights and liberties in the young American republic.

Within the ample eighteenth-century sources at hand, two theological views on religious liberty were critical to constitutional formation: those of congregational *Puritans* and those of Free Church *Evangelicals*. Two political views were equally influential: those of *Enlightenment* thinkers and those of *Civic Republicans*. Exponents of these four views often found common cause and used common language, particularly during the constitutional convention and ratification debates. Yet each group offered its own distinct teachings on religious liberty and had its own preferences for their implementation at law. Together, these groups held up the four corners of a wide canopy of opinion about religious liberty in the eighteenth century.

The image of a "canopy" of opinions—which swayed and stretched even while covering the same basic ground—underscores the notion that the founders' views on religious liberty defy easy description and classification. Many other views on religious liberty besides these four circulated, and many other labels besides Puritan, Evangelical, Enlightenment, and Republican can be used to describe even these four views. Moreover, the founders often moved freely between two or more perspectives, shifted their allegiances or alliances over time, or changed their tones and tunes as they moved from formal writing to the pulpit, letter desk, or political platform. Roger Williams, for example, though later adduced by Evangelical leader Isaac Backus as a champion of Evangelical views, espoused many traditional Puritan sentiments.[2] Isaac Backus himself, though a strong advocate for the religious liberty of Baptists and other Evangelicals, drew amply on Puritan and other Calvinist teachings.[3] John Adams moved freely between Puritan and Civic Republican views and eschewed denominational labels.[4] America's greatest eighteenth-century theologian, Jonathan Edwards, toed (and moved) the line between old light Puritan and new light Evangelical perspectives.[5] John Witherspoon, signer of the Declaration of Independence and president of Princeton, moved freely between Evangelical and Republican camps, even while maintaining a firm Presbyterian core.[6] Thomas Jefferson's strong Enlightenment views were sometimes voiced with thick Evangelical accents.[7] James Madison, born in an Anglican home, was attracted to the Puritan and Evangelical sentiments offered by John Witherspoon and his other teachers at Princeton; his political speeches both at home in Virginia and while serving in Congress often pulsed with Evangelical and Republican sentiments; his later writings, particularly after his presidency, were of increasingly firm Enlightenment stock.[8]

The Puritan, Evangelical, Republican, and Enlightenment perspectives that are described in this chapter are presented as heuristic models—typical clusters of argument and adherence, distinct and distinguishable contributions to eighteenth-century American debates about religious rights and liberties. The "original understanding"[9] of the founders respecting government and religion cannot be reduced to any one of these views. It must be sought in the tensions among them and in the general principles that emerged from their interaction. What follows in this chapter is a snapshot of these Puritan, Evangelical, Enlightenment, and Republican views on religious liberty. The next chapter provides a distillation of the first principles of religious liberty that they held in common.

Puritan Views

The Puritans of the New England states of Massachusetts, Connecticut, New Hampshire, Vermont, and Maine were heirs of the theology of religious liberty taught by European Calvinists.[10] They had refined this European legacy through the efforts of John Winthrop, John Cotton, Cotton Mather, and others in the seventeenth century. They had liberalized some of this legacy through the writings of John Wise, Charles Chauncy, Jonathan Mayhew, and others in the eighteenth century. They had propagated their views throughout colonial America through their relentless publications. But it was in New England, especially in the period from 1630 to 1730, that the Puritans had occasion to cast their Calvinist theological principles into constitutional practice.

The Puritans who wrote on religious liberty were concerned especially with the nature of the church, of the state, and of the relationship between them. They conceived of the church and the state as two separate covenantal associations, two seats of Godly authority in the community. Each institution, they believed, was vested with a distinct polity and calling. The church was to be governed by pastoral, pedagogical, and diaconal authorities who were called to preach the word, administer the sacraments, teach the young, and care for the poor and the needy. The state was to be governed by executive, legislative, and judicial authorities who were called to enforce law, punish crime, cultivate virtue, and protect peace and order.

In the New England communities where their views prevailed, the Puritans adopted a variety of rules designed to foster this basic separation of the institutions of church and state. Church officials were formally prohibited from holding political office, serving on juries, interfering in governmental affairs, endorsing political candidates, or censuring the official conduct of a statesman. Political officials, in turn, were prohibited from holding ministerial office, interfering in internal ecclesiastical government, performing sacerdotal functions of clergy, or censuring the official conduct of a cleric. To permit any such officiousness on the part of church or state officials, Governor John Winthrop averred, "would confound those Jurisdictions, which Christ hath made distinct."[11]

Although church and state were not to be confounded, they were still to be "close and compact."[12] For, to the Puritans, these two institutions were inextricably linked in nature and in function. Each was an instrument of Godly authority. Each did its part to establish and maintain the community. As one mid-eighteenth-century writer put it, "I look upon this as a little model of the gloriou[s] kingdom of Christ on earth. Christ reigns among us in the commonwealth as well as in the church, and hath his glorious interest involved and wrapped up in the good of both societies respectively."[13] The Puritans, therefore, countenanced both the coordination and the cooperation of church and state.

State officials provided various forms of material and moral aid to churches and their officials. Public properties were donated to church groups for meetinghouses, parsonages, day schools, and orphanages. Tax collectors collected tithes and special assessments to support the ministers and ministry of the congregational church. Tax exemptions and immunities were accorded to the religious, educational, and charitable organizations that they operated. Special subsidies and military protections were provided for missionaries and religious outposts. Special criminal laws prohibited interference with religious properties and services. Sabbath Day laws prohibited all forms of unnecessary labor and uncouth leisure on Sundays and holy days and required faithful attendance at worship services.

Church officials, in turn, provided various forms of material and moral aid to the state. Church meetinghouses and chapels were used not only to conduct religious services but also to host town assemblies, political rallies, and public auctions, to house the community school and library, to maintain census rolls and birth, marriage, and death certificates. Parsonages were used not only to house the minister and his family but also to harbor orphans, widows, the sick, the aged, and victims of abuse and disaster. Church officials preached obedience to the authorities and imposed spiritual discipline on parishioners found guilty of crime. They encouraged their parishioners to be active in political affairs and each year offered "election day sermons" on Christian political principles. They offered learned expositions on the requirements of Godly law and occasionally offered advice to legislatures and courts, particularly on heated questions of public morality and law, such as the execution of criminals.

Initially, the New England leadership left little room for individual religious experimentation. Despite their adherence to a basic separation of the offices of church and state, the New England authorities established a common Calvinist congregationalism for the community: Separatism for them did not connote disestablishment of one religion or the toleration of other religions. Already in the 1630s, dissidents from the established faith, such as Anne Hutchinson and Roger Williams, were summarily dismissed from the colony.[14] Immigration restrictions in Massachusetts Bay throughout the seventeenth century left little room for Catholics, Jews, "Familists, Antinomians, and other Enthusiasts"—especially Quakers.[15] Indeed, special laws in the late 1650s banned the Quakers and their teachings from the colony. Those Quakers who had newly arrived or newly converted were banished. Those who failed to leave were subject to flogging and the confiscation of their properties. The four Quakers who returned after banishment were hung in the Boston Common in 1659 and 1660.

Although Quakers remained unwelcome, Baptists, Anglicans, and other Protestant groups came to be tolerated in the New England colonies—partly on account of the Toleration Act (1689) passed by the English Parliament, which required all the colonies to be open to Protestant nonconformists.[16] Though tolerated, these non-Puritan groups enjoyed limited political rights and social benefits and were subject to various tithe rates and restrictions on their properties and professions.[17]

The growing presence of these religious nonconformists in New England, however, slowly shifted the Puritan understanding of liberty of conscience. Classic Calvinism taught that each person has the liberty to enter into a personal covenant relationship with God. Seventeenth-century Puritans had treated this covenant as something of a "divine adhesion contract."[18] God set the covenantal terms for salvation in the Bible; a person had the freedom only to accept or reject them. Such sentiments can be seen in a 1682 tract on "covenant liberty" by Samuel Willard, a leading Puritan systematizer of his day. Willard argued that every person has the "equal right," "title," "claim," "liberty," and "prerogative" "to enter and to enjoy every blessing of the covenant." But by the time Willard finished spelling out all the standard terms and conditions of the covenant, there seemed to be few at liberty to enter the covenant and little liberty left for those few who could.[19]

Confronted by the realities of religious pluralism, eighteenth-century Puritan writers began to view this covenantal relationship between God and persons in more open and voluntarist terms. The covenant was made more accessible to parties of various Christian faiths, and its terms were made more open to personal deliberation and innovation. Elisha Williams put the matter thus in 1744:

> Every man has an equal right to follow the dictates of his own conscience in the affairs of religion. Every one is under an indispensable obligation to search

the Scriptures for himself . . . and to make the best use of it he can for his own information in the will of God, the nature and duties of Christianity. And as every Christian is so bound; so he has the unalienable right to judge of the sense and meaning of it, and to follow his judgment wherever it leads him; even an equal right with any rulers be they civil or ecclesiastical.[20]

Such formulations became increasingly common among Puritan writers in the later eighteenth century.

It was only a short step from this formulation to the more generic and generous religious liberty guarantee of the 1780 Massachusetts Constitution, drafted principally by John Adams:

It is the right as well as the duty of all in society, publicly, and at stated seasons, to worship the Supreme Being, the great Creator and Preserver of the universe. And no subject shall be hurt, molested, or restrained, in his person, liberty, or estate, for worshipping God in the manner and season most agreeable to the dictates of his own conscience, or for his religious profession of sentiments; provided he doth not disturb the public peace or obstruct others in their religious worship.[21]

It was also a natural next step to find political, if not theological, virtue in the religious pluralism of the community. Zabdiel Adams put the prevailing opinion well in a sermon of 1782:

Modes and forms of religion; sentiments concerning doctrines, etc., people should be indulged in, without molestation. If coer[c]ion would bring mankind to a uniformity of sentiment, no advantage would result therefrom. It is on the contrary best to have different facts and denominations live in the same societies. They are a mutual check and spy upon each other, and become more attentive to their principles and practice. . . . [W]here Papists and Protestants live intermingled together, it serves to meliorate them both. . . . With madmen and enthusiasts there can be no agreement, except among people as distracted as themselves. But even such, where they put on a religious guise, and do not interrupt the peace of society, are not to be disturbed by the civil arm. . . . [Only] that part of religion which has an immediate aspect on the good of the community falls under the cognizance of the ruler.[22]

Evangelical Views

The eighteenth-century American Evangelical[23] tradition of religious liberty had its roots in sixteenth-century European Anabaptism and in the seventeenth-century "lively experiment" of Rhode Island that granted "full liberty in religious concernm[en]ts."[24] Evangelicals did not emerge as a strong political force in America, however, until after the Great Awakening of circa 1720–1780 expanded their membership and message exponentially. Numerous spokesmen for the Evangelical cause rose up in the course of the later eighteenth century all along the Atlantic seaboard—Isaac Backus, John Leland, John Wesley, Charles Wesley, George Whitfield, and a host of other preachers and pamphleteers. Numerous denominational labels began to be attached to their followers—Baptists, Anabaptists, Moravians, Methodists, Enthusiasts, among many others. Such labels sometimes signaled real differences in theological emphasis among these early groups, which later would harden into bitter denominational divisions. Despite these theological differences, early American Evangelicals were largely united in their insistence on liberty of conscience, disestablishment of religion, and separation of church and state. Although, outside of Rhode Island, the Evangelicals had fewer opportunities than the Puritans to institutionalize their views in the colonial era, their relentless preaching and pamphleteering had a formidable political influence on the early American experiment.

Like the Puritans, the Evangelicals advanced a theological theory of religious liberty. They likewise advocated the institutional separation of church and state—the construction of "a wall of separation between the garden of the Church and the wilderness of the world," as Roger Williams put it famously in 1643.[25]

Most Evangelicals, however, went beyond the Puritans—and battled with them in the New England states—both in their definition of the rights of religious individuals and groups and in their insistence on a fuller separation of the institutions of church and state. The Evangelicals sought to protect the liberty of conscience of every individual and the freedom of association of every religious group. Their preferred method for achieving these ends was to prohibit all legal establishments of religion and, indeed, all admixtures of religion and politics. John Leland, the fiery Baptist preacher, put it thus in a proposed amendment to the Massachusetts Constitution:

> To prevent the evils that have heretofore been occasioned in the world by religious establishments, and to keep up the proper distinction between religion and politics, no religious test shall ever be requested as a qualification of any officer, in any department of this government; neither shall the legislature, under this constitution, ever establish any religion by law, give any one sect a preference to another, or force any man in the commonwealth to part with his property for the support of religious worship, or the maintenance of ministers of the gospel.[26]

Later, Leland put the matter even more bluntly: "The notion of a Christian commonwealth should be exploded forever."[27]

Religious voluntarism lay at the heart of the Evangelical view. "[N]othing can be true religion but a voluntary obedience unto [God's] revealed will," declared Isaac Backus, the leading Baptist light of the eighteenth century.[28] God called the adult individual to make a conscientious choice to accept the faith. State coercion or control of this choice—either directly through persecution and repression or indirectly through withholding civil rights and benefits from those who made this choice—was an offense both to the individual and to God. A plurality of religions should coexist in the community. It was for God, not the state, to decide which of these religions should flourish and which should fade. "Religious liberty is a divine right," wrote the preacher Israel Evans, "immediately derived from the Supreme Being, without the intervention of any created authority. . . . [T]he all-wise Creator invested [no] order of men with the right of judging for their fellow-creatures in the great concerns of religion."[29]

Autonomy of religious governance also lay at the heart of this Evangelical view. Every religious body, Evangelicals argued, should be free from state control of their assembly and worship, state regulations of their property and polity, state incorporation of their society and clergy, state interference in their discipline and government, state collection of religious tithes and taxes. "I am as sensible of the importance of religion and of the utility of it to human society" as the Puritans are, Backus wrote. "And I concur with [them] that the fear and reverence of God and the terrors of eternity are the most powerful restraints upon the minds of men. But I am so far from thinking with [them] that these restraints would be broken down if equal religious liberty was established." Look at the long history of Christian establishment, where such forms of state intrusion on religious groups are countenanced. It has led not to pure religion. Instead, "tyranny, simony, and robbery came to be introduced and to be practiced under the Christian name." Look at communities with no religious establishments; there religion, state, and society all flourish without fail. Look at the principles of the American revolution; "all America [was] up in arms" against taxation without representation. But just as certainly as we Americans were not represented in the British Parliament, so we religious dissenters are not represented among the established civil authorities. Yet we are still subject to their religious taxes and regulations." Look at the principles of the Bible:

> God has expressly armed the magistrate with the sword to punish such as work ill to their neighbors, and his faithfulness in that work and our obedience to such authority, is enforced [by the Bible]. But it is evident that the sword is excluded from the kingdom of the Redeemer. . . . [I]t is impossible to blend church and state without violating our Lord's commands to both together. His command to the church is, Put away from among yourselves that wicked person. His command to the state is, Let both grow together until the harvest. But it has

appeared for these thousand years that pure Gospel discipline in the church is very little if at all known in state establishments of religion and that instead of letting conformists thereto, and dissenters therefrom, grow together or enjoy equal worldly privileges, the sword has been employed to root up, and to prepare war against all such as put not into the mouths of the established teachers who are the means of upholding such rulers as pervert all equity.[30]

Some Evangelicals extended the principle of church autonomy and disestablishment to argue against tax exemptions, civil immunities, property donations, and other forms of state support for all churches. Such Evangelicals feared state benevolence toward religion and religious bodies almost as much as they feared state repression. Those religious bodies that received state benefits would invariably become beholden to the state and distracted from their divine mandates. "[I]f civil Rulers go so far out of their Sphere as to take the Care and Management of religious affairs upon them," reads a 1776 Baptist Declaration, "Yea . . . Farwel to 'the free exercise of Religion.'"[31]

The chief concern of the Evangelicals was theological, not political. Having suffered as religious minorities for more than a century in colonial America and more than two centuries in Europe, Evangelicals sought a constitutional means to free all religion from the fetters of the law, to relieve all churches from the restrictions of the state. In so doing, most Evangelicals of the founding era—save Isaac Backus, building on his seventeenth-century hero, Roger Williams—developed only the rudiments of a political theory.[32] Most Evangelicals were content with a state that created a climate conducive to the cultivation of a plurality of religions and that accommodated all religious believers and religious bodies without conditions or controls.

Enlightenment Views

The Enlightenment movement in America provided a political theory that complemented the Evangelical theology of religious liberty. The Enlightenment was no single, unified movement, but a series of diverse ideological movements, in various academic disciplines and social circles throughout Europe and North America. Among its chief exponents were Montesquieu, Condorcet, and Voltaire in France, John Locke, Adam Smith, and David Hume in Great Britain, and a host of lesser-known writers. Among its leading lights in America were Thomas Jefferson and Thomas Paine, flanked on some causes by Benjamin Franklin and James Madison.[33] It was the American Revolution, especially, that catalyzed these American figures to convert Enlightenment ideals into constitutional imperatives.

The writings of English philosopher and theologian John Locke provided ample inspiration for this movement. In his famous *Letter Concerning Tol-*

eration (1689), Locke had distilled the liberal English and Dutch learning of the seventeenth century into an elegant plea for church and state to end their corrosive alliances and to end their corrupt abridgments of the liberty of conscience.[34] "[A]bove all things," Locke pleaded, it is "necessary to distinguish exactly the business of civil government from that of religion, and to settle the just bounds that lie between the one and the other." The church, Locke wrote, must be "absolutely separate and distinct from the commonwealth." For the church is simply "a voluntary society of men, joining themselves together of their own accord in order to the public worshipping of God in such manner as they judge acceptable to Him, and effectual for the salvation of their souls." Church members are free to enter and free to exit this society. They are free to determine its order and organization and arrange its discipline and worship in a manner they consider most conducive to eternal life. "Nothing ought nor can be transacted in this society relating to the possession of civil and worldly power. No force is to be made use of upon any occasion whatsoever. For force belongs wholly to the civil magistrate."

State force, in turn, cannot touch religion, Locke argued. The state exists merely to protect persons in their outward lives, in their enjoyment of life, liberty, and property. "True and saving religion consists in the inward persuasion of the mind," which only God can touch and tend. A person cannot be compelled to true belief of anything by outward force—whether through "confiscation of estate, imprisonments, [or] torments" or through mandatory compliance with "articles of faith or forms of worship" established by law. "For laws are of no force without penalties, and penalties in this case are absolutely impertinent, because they are not proper to convince the mind." "It is only light and evidence that can work a change in men's [religious] opinions: which light can in no manner proceed from corporal sufferings, or any other outward penalties" inflicted by the state. Every person "has the supreme and absolute authority of judging for himself" in matters of faith.

Locke did not press this thesis to radical conclusions. His *Letter Concerning Toleration* presupposed a magistracy and community committed to a common Christianity. State laws directed to the common good, he believed, would only "seldom" "appear unlawful to the conscience of a private person" and would only seldom run afoul of conventional Christian beliefs and practices. Catholics, Muslims, and other believers "who deliver themselves up to the service and protection of another prince" have no place in this community. Moreover, "those are not at all tolerated who deny the being of a God"—for "promises, covenants, and oaths which are the bonds of human society, can have no hold upon an atheist." Locke strengthened these qualifications even more in his theological writings—arguing in his volumes, *The Reasonableness of Christianity, Essays on the*

Law of Nature, and *Thoughts on Education* for the cogency of a simple biblical natural law and endorsing in his several commentaries on St. Paul's epistles the utility of a moderate Christian republicanism.[35]

A century later and an ocean away, American Enlightenment writers pressed Locke's theses into more concrete legal and political forms.[36] The state, they taught, should not give special aid, support, privilege, or protection to religious doctrines or groups—through special tax appropriations or collections of tithes, special donations of goods and realty, special laws of religious incorporation, or special criminal laws against blasphemy, sacrilege, and Sabbath-breaking. The state should not predicate its laws on explicitly religious premises nor direct them to exclusively religious purposes. The state should not draw on the services of religious officials to discharge its political tasks nor interfere in the order, organization, or orthodoxy of religious bodies. As Madison put it in 1822: "[A] perfect separation between ecclesiastical and civil matters" is the best course, for "religion and Government will both exist in greater purity, the less they are mixed together."[37]

Like Locke, Madison did not press this logic to absolutist conclusions—particularly when it came to the "unessentials" of church-state relations. In an 1833 letter to Rev. Jaspar Adams, he wrote:

> [I]t may not be easy, in every possible case, to trace the line of separation between the rights of Religion and the Civil authority, with such distinctness, as to avoid collisions & doubts on unessential points. The tendency to a usurpation on one side, or the other, or to a corrupting coalition or alliance between them, will be best guarded against by an entire abstinence of the Government from interference in any way whatever, beyond the necessity of preserving public order, & protecting each sect against trespasses on its legal rights by others.[38]

Such views were based on both a skepticism about organized religion and a fear of an autocratic state. To allow church and state to be unrestricted, it was thought, would be to invite arbitrariness and abuse. To allow them to combine would be to their mutual disadvantage—to produce, in Thomas Paine's words, "a sort of mule-animal, capable only of destroying, and not of breeding up."[39]

Such views were also based on the belief that a person is fundamentally an individual being and that religion is primarily a matter of private reason and conscience and only secondarily a matter of communal association and corporate confession. Every person, Madison wrote, has the right to form "a rational opinion" about the duty he owes the Creator and the manner in which that duty is to be discharged.[40] Whether that religious duty is to be discharged individually or corporately is of secondary importance.[41] Such views were also based on a contractarian political philosophy that called for the state to ensure the maximum liberty of citizens and their associations and to intervene only where one party's exercise of liberty intruded on that of the other.

Postrevolutionary Virginia proved to be fertile ground for political exponents of the Enlightenment tradition to cultivate these views.[42] Article 16 of the 1776 Virginia Bill of Rights, influenced in part by Madison, provided:

> That religion, or the duty which we owe to our Creator, and the manner of discharging it, can be directed only by reason and conviction, not by force or violence; and therefore, all men are equally entitled to the free exercise of religion, according to the dictates of conscience; and that it is the mutual duty of all to practise Christian forbearance, love, and charity, towards each other.[43]

This early Virginia constitutional text was one of the most influential formulations of religious liberty in the young republic and was echoed in many other early state constitutions' texts and ratification debates. Its appeal lay in part in its clever combination of Enlightenment and Evangelical accents on liberty of conscience, freedom of exercise, and equality of faiths, with Republican and traditional Christian emphases on the "Creator" God, and the mutual duties of all to practice "Christian forbearance, love, and charity" toward others.

The famous Virginia Statute for the Establishment of Religious Freedom, drafted by Thomas Jefferson in 1779 and enacted in 1786, provided less qualified Enlightenment language. The statute begins by celebrating that "Almighty God hath created the mind free; that all attempts to influence it by temporal punishment, or burthens, or by civil incapacitations, tend only to beget habits of hypocrisy and meanness, and are a departure from the plan of the Holy Author of our religion." The statute recounts the ravages of religious establishment and repression, and their resulting injuries to God, religion, churches, states, and individuals. It then guarantees:

> That no man shall be compelled to frequent or support any religious worship, place, or ministry whatsoever, nor shall be enforced, restrained, molested, or burthened, in his body or goods, nor shall otherwise suffer on account of his religious opinions or belief; but that all men shall be free to profess, and by argument to maintain, their opinions in matters of religion, and that the same shall in no wise diminish, enlarge or affect their civil capacities.[44]

These lofty protections of individual religious rights went hand in hand with the close restrictions on corporate religious rights that were also advocated by Enlightenment exponents. Before the turn of the nineteenth century, the Virginia legislature outlawed religious corporations, a prohibition still in place today in Virginia and West Virginia.[45]

The law of Virginia did not live entirely by the gospel of the Enlightenment, however. Even Governor Jefferson supported the revision of Virginia's postrevolutionary laws, which included A Bill for Punishing Disturbers of Religious Worship and Sabbath Breakers; A Bill for Appointing Days of Public Fasting and Thanksgiving; and A Bill Annulling Marriages Prohibited by the Levitical Law, and Appointing the Mode of Solemnizing Lawful Marriage [in Church].[46]

Republican Views

The Civic Republicans were an eclectic group of politicians, preachers, and pamphleteers who strove to cultivate a set of common values and beliefs for the new nation.[47] Their principal spokesmen were George Washington, John Adams, Benjamin Rush, Oliver Ellsworth, and other leaders—though the movement attracted considerable support among the spiritual and intellectual laity of the young republic as well. Many of the core ideas of this movement were grounded in earlier Anglican and Puritan ideals of a Christian commonwealth. By the later eighteenth century, Republican leaders found their most natural theological allies among the Puritans, just as most Enlightenment leaders found their most natural allies among the Evangelicals.

To be sure, Civic Republicans shared much common ground with Evangelical and Enlightenment exponents. They, too, advocated liberty of conscience for all and state support for a plurality of religions in the community. They, too, opposed religious intrusions on politics that rose to the level of political theocracy and political intrusions on religion that rose to the level of religious establishment. But, contrary to Evangelical and Enlightenment writers and consistent with Puritan writers, Republican writers sought to imbue the public square with a common religious ethic and ethos—albeit one less denominationally specific and theologically rigorous than that countenanced by the Puritans. Republicans stressed the utility of religion, particularly Christianity, for the prosperity and happiness of citizens, and the efficacy and efficiency of good government.[48]

"Religion and Morality are the essential pillars of Civil society," George Washington declared. "Of all the dispositions and habits which lead to political prosperity, religion and morality are indispensable supports."[49] "[W]e have no government," John Adams echoed, "armed with power capable of contending with human passions unbridled by morality and religion."[50] "Religion and liberty are the meat and the drink of the body politic," wrote Yale President Timothy Dwight.[51] According to Republican lore, society needs a fund of religious values and beliefs, a body of civic ideas and ideals, that are enforceable both through common law and communal suasion. This was what Benjamin Franklin in 1749 had called the "Publick Religion" (and what is now called the "civil religion") of America, which undergirded the plurality of sectarian religions.[52] This "Publick Religion" taught a creed of honesty, diligence, devotion, public spiritedness, patriotism, obedience, love of God, neighbor, and self, and other ethical commonplaces taught by various religious traditions at the time of the founding. Its icons were the Bible, the Declaration of Independence, the bells of liberty, and the Constitution. Its clergy were public-spirited ministers and religiously devout politicians. Its liturgy was the proclamations of prayers, songs, sermons, and Thanksgiving Day offerings by statesmen and churchmen. Its policy was government appointment of legislative and military chaplains, government sponsorship of general religious education and organization, and government enforcement of a religiously based morality through positive law.

These Republican views found favor in the Continental Congress, which authorized the appointment of tax-supported chaplains to the military, tax appropriations for religious schools and missionaries, diplomatic ties to the Vatican, and recitations of prayer at its opening sessions and during the day of Thanksgiving.[53] The Continental Congress also passed the Northwest Ordinance in 1787, which provided, in part: "Religion, morality and knowledge, being necessary to good government and the happiness of mankind, schools and the means of education shall forever be encouraged."[54]

These Republican views also found strong support among the states. Republicans countenanced state support and accommodation for religious institutions, for they were regarded as essential allies of good government and agents of the common good. "[R]eligion and its institutions are the best aid of government," declared Nathan Strong, "by strengthening the ruler's hand, and making the subject faithful in his place, and obedient to the general laws."[55] Similarly, Connecticut Senator Oliver Ellsworth declared: "Institutions for the promotion of good morals, are objects of legislative provision and support: and among these ... religious institutions are eminently useful and important."[56] Republicans, therefore, endorsed tax exemptions for church properties and tax support for religious schools, charities, and missionaries; donations of public lands to religious organizations; and criminal protections against blasphemy, sacrilege, and interruption of religious services.[57]

The 1780 Constitution of Massachusetts, which John Adams drafted, was an influential example of the Republican effort to balance the freedom of all private religions with the "mild and equitable establishment" of one public religion. We must certainly begin "by setting the conscience free,"

Adams wrote. For "[w]hen all men of all religions consistent with morals and property, shall enjoy equal liberty, . . . [and] security of property, and an equal chance for honors and power . . . we may expect that improvements will be made in the human character and the state of society." Moreover, a plurality of private religions in the community provides the best safeguard against religious persecution. "Checks and balances" in politics as well as religion, Adams wrote, "are our only Security, for the progress of Mind, as well as the Security of Body. Every Species of these Christians would persecute Deists, as [much] as either Sect would persecute another, if it had unchecked and unballanced Power. Nay, the Deists would persecute Christians, and Atheists would persecute Deists, with as unrelenting Cruelty, as any Christians would persecute them or one another."[58]

But just as certainly as we must guarantee the freedom of all private religions, Adams insisted, we must set a public "religion at the fore and floor of society and government." "Statesmen may plan and speculate for liberty, but it is religion and morality alone which can establish the principles upon which freedom can securely stand." "[R]eligion and virtue are the only foundations, not only of republicanism and of all free government, but of social felicity under all governments and in all the combinations of human society."[59]

The Massachusetts Constitution sought to balance the freedom of all private religions with what Adams called "a mild and equitable establishment" of a public religion. Article II provided: "It is the right as well as the duty of all men in society, publickly, and at stated seasons to worship the SUPREME BEING, the great Creator and preserver of the Universe." Article III stated the reason: "[T]he public worship of GOD and instructions in piety, religion, and morality . . . promote their happiness, and secure . . . the good order and preservation of their government."[60] The same constitution also insisted that all persons, particularly political leaders, maintain rigorous moral and religious standards, which they confirmed in their oaths of office. It also rendered these same moral qualities essential ingredients of education within the state, since "the encouragement of arts and sciences, and all good literature, tends to the honor of GOD, the advantage of the Christian religion, and the great benefit of this and the other United States of America."[61]

These four views—Puritan, Evangelical, Enlightenment, and Republican—helped to inform the early American experiment in religious rights and liberties. Each view was liberally espoused by federal and state leaders in the early American republic, informally in their letters and pamphlets, and formally in the constitutional convention and ratification debates. Each left indelible marks on the documents and developments of early American constitutionalism.

Notes

1. James Madison, Letter from James Madison to Thomas Richie (September 15, 1821), in *Letters and Other Writings of James Madison*, 4 vols. (1884), 3:228. See also the quote from Madison in *The Debates and Proceedings in the Congress of the United States, March 3, 1789–May 27, 1824*, ed. William W. Joseph (Gales and Seaton, 1834–1856), vol. 5, column 776 (hereafter cited as *Annals*): "As the instrument came from [the drafter] it was nothing more than the draft of a plan, nothing but a dead letter, until life and validity were breathed into it by the voice of the people, speaking through their several State conventions."

2. See Edmund S. Morgan, *Roger Williams: The Church and the State* (1967); Edwin S. Gaustad, *Liberty of Conscience: Roger Williams in America* (1991); Timothy Hall, *Separating Church and State: Roger Williams and Religious Liberty* (1998).

3. William G. McLoughlin, ed., *Isaac Backus on Church, State, and Calvinism: Pamphlets, 1754–1789* (1968); Peter J. Richards, "'A Clear and Steady Channel': Isaac Backus and the Limits of Liberty," *Journal of Church and State* 43 (2001):447.

4. Catherine Drinker Bowen, *John Adams and the American Revolution* (1950); Joseph J. Ellis, *Passionate Sage: The Character and Legacy of John Adams*, 2d ed. (2001); David McCullough, *John Adams* (2001).

5. George M. Marsden, *Jonathan Edwards: A Life* (2003).

6. L. Gordon Tait, *The Piety of John Witherspoon: Pew, Pulpit, and Public Forum* (2002); Martha L.L. Stohlman, *John Witherspoon: Parson, Politician, and Patriot* (1989 [1973]).

7. Edwin S. Gaustad, *Sworn on the Altar of God: A Religious Biography of Thomas Jefferson* (1996); Daniel L. Dreisbach, *Thomas Jefferson and the Wall of Separation Between Church and State* (2002).

8. See Garry Wills, *James Madison* (2002); Joseph LoConte, "Faith and the Founding: The Influence of Religion on the Politics of James Madison," *Journal of Church and State* 45 (2003):699.

9. Jack N. Rakove, *Original Meanings: Politics and Ideas in the Making of the Constitution* (1996), 3–22, 288–338, distinguishes the original "meaning," "intention," and "understanding" of the Constitution and urges a use of both "textual" and "contextual" material to comprehend the "original understanding" of the founders. I am using the generic term "founder" to describe the range of eighteenth-century figures who wrote on questions of religious liberty and/or participated in the formation of state and federal constitutional laws governing the same.

10. See sources and discussion in my *The Reformation of Rights*. For sample primary texts, see Edmund S. Morgan, *Puritan Political Ideas, 1558–1794* (2003 [1965]); Perry Miller and Thomas H. Johnson, *The Puritans*, rev. ed., 2 vols. (1963).

11. Quoted by Timothy Breen, *The Character of the Good Ruler* (1970), 42, n. 24. See samples in Max Farrand, ed., *The Book of the General Laws and Liberties Concerning the Inhabitants of Massachusetts (1648)* (1929), 18–20; "The Cambridge Synod and Platform (1648)," in *The Creeds and Platforms of Congregationalism*, ed. Williston Walker (1960), 234–237.

12. John Cotton, Letter from The Rev. John Cotton to Lord Say and Seal (1636), in Morgan, *Puritan Political Ideas*, 209–212.

13. Uriah Oakes, *New England Pleaded with, and Pressed to Consider the Things Which Concern Her* (1673), 49 (modern spelling and capitalization).

14. David D. Hall, *The Antinomian Controversy, 1636–1638*, 2d ed. (1968).

15. Nathaniel Ward, *The Simple Cobler of Aggawam in America*, 5th ed. (1713), 43.

16. In Stephenson and Marcham, *Sources*, 607–608.

17. William G. McLoughlin, *New England Dissent, 1630–1833*, 2 vols. (Cambridge, 1971).

18. The phrase is from Paul Ramsey, *Basic Christian Ethics* (1950), 371.

19. Samuel Willard, *Covenant-Keeping the Way to Blessedness* (Boston, 1682); id., *Morality Not to Be Relied on for Life* (1700); id., *Walking with God* (1701); see E. Brooks Holifield, *Theology in America: Christian Thought from the Age of the Puritans to the Civil War* (2003), 38ff.

20. Elisha Williams, *The Essential Rights and Liberties of Protestants* (1744), 7–8.

21. Massachusetts Constitution (1780), Pt. I, Art. II; see also Vermont Constitution (1793), Ch. I, Art. III.

22. Zabdiel Adams, An Election Sermon (1782), in Charles S. Hynemann and Donald S. Lutz, eds., *American Political Writing During the Founding Era, 1760–1805*, 2 vols. (1983), 1:539, 556 (capitalization and italics in original removed). See further Charles P. Hanson, *Necessary Virtue: The Pragmatic Origins of Religious Liberty in New England* (1998).

23. For the changing meaning of this label in American history, see Mark A. Noll, "Evangelicals in the American Founding and Evangelical Political Mobilization Today," in James H. Hutson, ed., *Religion and the New Republic: Faith in the Founding of America* (2000), 137.

24. Baptist leader Dr. John Clarke in c. 1662, quoted in Charles M. Andrews, *The Colonial Period in American History*, 2 vols. (1936), 2:42. The phrase recurs in the 1663 Charter of Rhode Island, which remained the state's constitutional text until 1843. Thorpe, ed. *Constitutions*, 6:3211.

25. Williams, *Writings*, 1:392. See other samples in Philip A. Hamburger, *Separation of Church and State* (2002), 38–50, 73–88.

26. Jack Nips [John Leland], "The Yankee Spy (1794)," in Hynemann and Lutz, eds., *American Political Writing*, 2:971–989, at 989.

27. *The Writings of the Late Elder John Leland* (1845), 118.

28. Isaac Backus, "A Declaration of the Rights, of the Inhabitants of the State of Massachusetts-Bay in New England (1779)," in *Isaac Backus on Church, State, and Calvinism*, 487.

29. Israel Evans, "A Sermon Delivered at Concord, Before the Hon. General Court of the State of New Hampshire at the Annual Election (1791)," in Sandoz, ed., *Political Sermons*, 1057, 1062–1063.

30. *Isaac Backus on Church, State, and Calvinism*, 351, 357–358, 373–375 (emphasis omitted).

31. "Declaration of the Virginia Association of Baptists (December 25, 1776)," in *The Papers of Thomas Jefferson*, ed. Julian P. Boyd (1950), 1:660–661.

32. Backus and a few other Evangelicals who did propound political views tended to agree with Puritans and Republicans that the political office should be restricted to Christians and that the state had a role to play in the cultivation of public morality through laws against blasphemy, theater-going, card-playing, and violations of the Sabbath day of rest. See William G. McLoughlin, *Soul Liberty: The Baptists' Struggle in New England, 1630–1833* (1991), 194–195, 267–268.

33. Henry May, *The Enlightenment in America* (1976).

34. John Locke, *Letter Concerning Toleration* (1689), in *The Works of John Locke*, 12th ed., 9 vols. (1824), 5:1–58. Locke wrote two subsequent such letters and had a fragment of a fourth letter underway on his death in 1704. It was the first letter of 1689 that was the best known in America.

35. John Locke, *The Reasonableness of Christianity*, in id., *Works*, 6:1–158, at 140–143; id., *Essays on the Law of Nature*, ed. W. von Leyden (2002 [c. 1662]); *The Educational Writings of John Locke*, ed. James Axtell (1968).

36. Jefferson took the lead in this, glossing Locke's *Letter Concerning Toleration* and incorporating a number of its most salient provisions in his famous "Bill for the Establishment of Religious Freedom" (1779). See his "Notes on Locke and Shaftesbury," in *The Papers of Thomas Jefferson*, 1:544–551. See Sanford Kessler, "Locke's Influence on Jefferson's 'Bill for Establishing Religious Freedom,'" *Journal of Church and State* 25 (1983):231; Noah Feldman, "The Intellectual Origins of the Establishment Clause," *New York University Law Review* 77 (2002):346, though Feldman exaggerates Locke's influence and underplays the diversity of founders' perspectives on religious liberty.

37. Letter to Edward Livingston (July 10, 1822), in *The Writings of James Madison*, ed. G. Hunt (1900–1910), 9:98–103, at 102.

38. James Madison, Letter to Rev. Adams (1833), in Dreisbach, *Religion and Politics*, 120. See Sidney E. Mead, "Neither Church nor State: Reflections on James Madison's 'Line of Separation,'" *Journal of Church and State* 10 (1968):349.

39. Thomas Paine, *The Rights of Man* (1791), in *The Complete Writings of Thomas Paine*, ed. P. S. Foner, 2 vols. (1945), 1:243–462, at 292.

40. Madison, "Memorial," sec. 1.

41. In his "Detached Memoranda" of c. 1817, Madison highlights his distaste for corporate organized religions by criticizing laws that allowed ecclesiastical bodies to incorporate, to be exempt from taxation, to accumulate property, and to gain political access through legislative chaplains and other means. See Elizabeth Fleet, "Madison's 'Detached Memoranda,'" *William and Mary Quarterly*, 3d ser., 3 (1946):534–568, at 554.

42. Thomas E. Buckley, *Church and State in Revolutionary Virginia, 1776–1787* (1977).

43. Madison, *Papers*, 1:175.

44. *The Statutes at Large . . . of Virginia*, 12:84–86.

45. Paul B. Kauper and Stephen B. Ellis, "Religious Corporations and the Law," *Michigan Law Review* 71 (1973):1499, 1529ff.

46. Daniel L. Dreisbach, "A New Perspective on Jefferson's Views on Church-State Relations: The Virginia Statute for Establishing Religious Freedom in Its Legislative Context," *American Journal of Legal History* 35 (1991):172–204.

47. Nathan O. Hatch, *The Sacred Cause of Liberty* (1977); Gordon S. Wood, *The Creation of the American Republic, 1776–1787* (1969); Paul Rahe, *Republics Ancient and Modern* (1992); Catherine L. Albanese, *Sons of the Fathers: The Civil Religion of the American Revolution* (1976).

48. See samples in Hutson, *Forgotten Features of the Founding*, 1–44; Noll, *America's God*, 53–92; Michael W. McConnell, "Establishment and Disestablishment at the Founding: Part I: Establishment of Religion," *William and Mary Law Review* 44 (2003):2105, 2181ff.

49. Letter to the Clergy of Philadelphia (March 3, 1797), in *The Writings of George Washington from the Original Manuscript Sources, 1745–1799*, ed. J. C. Fitzpatrick, 39 vols. (1931), 35:416; id., "Farewell Address (September 17, 1796)," in ibid., 35:214, 229.

50. Letter of John Adams to a Unit of the Massachusetts Militia (1798), in Adams, *Works*, 9:229.

51. Timothy Dwight, "The Duty of Americans at the Present Crisis, Illustrated in a Discourse Preached on the Fourth of July, 1798," in Sandoz, ed., *Political Sermons*, 1380.

52. Benjamin Franklin, "Proposals Relating to the Education of Youth in Pensilvania (1749)," quoted and discussed in Martin E. Marty, "On a Medial Moraine: Religious Dimensions of American Constitutionalism," *Emory Law Journal* 39 (1990):9–20, at 16–17. See below, pp. 253–257, on public religion today.

53. Derek H. Davis, *Religion and the Continental Congress, 1774–1789: Contributions to Original Intent* (2000).

54. Article III, 1 Stat. 50, 51–53, Ch. 8.

55. Nathan Strong, *Election Sermon* (1790), 15.

56. *The Public Records of the State of Connecticut*, ed. Christopher Collier (1967), 11:371, 373.

57. See below, pp. 113–119.

58. Letter to Thomas Jefferson (June 25, 1813), in *The Adams-Jefferson Letters*, 2 vols., ed. Lester J. Cappon (1959), 333, 334.

59. Adams, *Works*, 8:232; 9:635, 636; Letter to Abigail Adams (1775), quoted in Edwin S. Gaustad, *A Religious History of America* (1966), 127.

60. Massachusetts Constitution (1780), Pt. I, Arts. II and III; this language is retained in Amendment, Art. XI (1833), which replaced Pt. I, Art. III. See below, pp. 113–115.

61. Ibid., Pt. II, Ch. V.

3

THE ESSENTIAL RIGHTS AND LIBERTIES OF RELIGION

Puritans, Evangelicals, Republicans, and Enlightenment exponents—these four groups of founders held up the four corners of the wide and swaying canopy of opinion on religious liberty in eighteenth-century America. Beneath this canopy were gathered what they called the "essential rights and liberties" of religion: (1) liberty of conscience; (2) free exercise of religion; (3) religious pluralism; (4) religious equality; (5) separation of church and state; and (6) disestablishment of religion.[1]

These six principles appear regularly in the debates over religious liberty in the eighteenth century, though with varying definitions and priorities. They were also commonly incorporated into the original state and federal constitutions, though with different emphases and applications. They remain at the heart of the American experiment today—as central commandments of the American constitutional order and as cardinal axioms of a new American logic of religious liberty.

Liberty of Conscience

Liberty of conscience was the general solvent used in the early American experiment in religious liberty. It was almost universally embraced in the young republic—even by the most ardent proponents of continued religious establishments.[2] The phrase "liberty of conscience" is of ancient vintage, rooted in early Roman and Christian sources, and laden with multiple meanings in canon law, common law, and civil law alike.[3] The plasticity of the phrase was not lost on the American founders. Like their predecessors, they often conflated or equated the phrase with other favorite phrases, such as "free exercise of religion," "religious freedom," "religious liberty," "religious privileges," and "religious rights." James Madison, for example, simply rolled into one linguistic heap "religious freedom" or "the free exercise of religion according to the dictates of conscience."[4] In another passage, he spoke of "liberty of conscience" as the "religious rights and privileges . . . of a multiplicity of sects."[5] Such patterns of interwoven language appear regularly in writings of the day. One term often implicated and connoted several others.[6] To read the guarantee of liberty of conscience too dogmatically is to ignore its inherent elasticity.

That said, the founders did ascribe distinct content to the phrase "liberty of conscience," which won wide assent in the early republic.

First, for most founders, liberty of conscience protected *voluntarism*— "the unalienable right of private judgment in matters of religion," the unencumbered ability to choose and to change one's religious beliefs and adherences.[7] *The Westminster Confession* (1644), an anchor text for American ministers throughout the seventeenth and eighteenth centuries, emphasized the God-given qualities of this freedom: "God alone is Lord of the Conscience, and hath left it free from the Doctrines and Commandments of men."[8] *Cato's Letters* (1720–1723), which Benjamin Franklin helped to popularize, argued: "No man's belief is in his own power, or can be in the power of another. . . . Conviction is the province and effect of reason; when that fails nothing but the grace of God can supply it: And what has the power and penalties of men have to do either with reason or grace."[9] The Puritan Elisha Williams echoed these sentiments in 1744:

> Every man has an equal right to follow the dictates of his own conscience in the affairs of religion. Every one is under an indispensable obligation to search the Scripture for himself . . . and to make the best use of it he can for his own information in the will of God, the nature and duties of Christianity. And as every Christian is so bound; so he has the inalienable right to judge of the sense and meaning of it, and to follow his judgment wherever it leads him; even an equal right with any rulers be they civil or ecclesiastical.[10]

Every person must be "left alone" to worship God "in the manner and season most agreeable to the Dictates of his own conscience," John Adams echoed. For the rights of conscience are "indisputable, unalienable, indefeasible, [and] divine."[11] James Madison wrote more generically in 1785: "The Religion then of every man must be left to the conviction and conscience of every man; and it is the right of every man to exercise it as these may dictate."[12] The Evangelical leader John Leland echoed these sentiments in 1791:

> Every man must give an account of himself to God, and therefore every man ought to be at liberty to serve God in that way that he can reconcile it to his conscience. . . . It would be sinful for a man to surrender to man [that] which

is to be kept sacred for God. A man's mind should be always open to conviction, and an honest man will receive that doctrine which appears the best demonstrated; and what is more common for the best of men to change their minds?[13]

Puritan, Republican, Enlightenment philosopher, and Evangelical preacher alike could agree on this core meaning of liberty of conscience.

Second, and closely related, liberty of conscience *prohibited* religiously based *discrimination* against individuals. Persons could not be penalized for the religious choices they made nor swayed to make certain choices because of the civil advantages attached to them. Liberty of conscience, Ezra Stiles opined, permits "no bloody tribunals, no cardinal inquisitors-general, to bend the human mind, forcibly to control the understanding, and put out the light of reason, the candle of the Lord in man."[14] Liberty of conscience also prohibits more subtle forms of discrimination, prejudice, and cajolery by state, church, or even other citizens. "[N]o part of the community shall be permitted to perplex or harass the other for any supposed heresy," wrote a Massachusetts pamphleteer. "[E]ach individual shall be allowed to have and enjoy, profess and maintain his own system of religion."[15]

Third, in the view of some founders, liberty of conscience guaranteed "freedom and *exemption* from human impositions, and legal restraints, in matters of religion and conscience."[16] Persons of faith were to be "exempt from all those penal, sanguinary laws, that generate vice instead of virtue."[17] Such laws not only included the onerous criminal rules that traditionally encumbered and discriminated against religious nonconformists, and led to fines, whippings, banishments, and occasional executions of dissenting colonists. They also included more facially benign laws that worked injustice to certain religious believers—conscription laws that required religious pacifists to participate in the military, oath-swearing laws that ran afoul of the religious scruples of certain believers, tithing and taxing laws that forced believers to support churches, religious schools, and other causes that they found religiously odious.[18] Liberty of conscience required that persons be exempt or immune from civil duties and restrictions that they could not, in good conscience, accept or obey.[19] As pamphleteer Henry Cumings put it: "Liberty of conscience requires not [only] that persons are . . . exempt from hierarchical tyranny and domination, from the usurped authority of pope and prelates, and from every species of persecution on account of religion." It also requires that they "stand on equal ground, and behaving as good members of society, may equally enjoy their religious opinions, and without molestation, or being exposed to fines or forfeitures, or any other temporal disadvantages."[20]

It was commonly assumed in the eighteenth century that the laws of conscientious magistrates would not often tread on the religious scruples of their subjects.[21] As George Washington put it in a letter to a group of Quakers: "In my opinion the conscientious scruples of all men should be treated with great delicacy and tenderness: and it is my wish and desire, that the laws may always be as extensively accommodated to them, as a due regard for the protection and essential interests of the nation may justify and permit."[22] It was also commonly understood that the growing pluralization of American religious life might make such inherent accommodation of all religions increasingly difficult. Where general laws and policies did intrude on the religious scruples of an individual or group, liberty of conscience demanded protection of religious minorities through exemptions from such laws and policies. This was the heart of the meaning of religious toleration. Whether such exemptions should be accorded by the legislature or by the judiciary and whether they were per se a constitutional right or simply a rule of equity—the principal bones of much scholarly contention today—the eighteenth-century sources do not dispositively say.

All the early state constitutions included a guarantee of liberty of conscience for all. The Delaware Constitution had typical language:

> That all men have a natural and inalienable right to worship Almighty God according to the dictates of their own consciences and understandings; and that no man ought or of right can be compelled to attend any religious worship or maintain any religious ministry contrary to or against his own free will and consent, and that no authority can or ought to be vested in, or assumed by any power whatever that shall in any case interfere with, or in any manner controul the right of conscience and free exercise of religious worship.[23]

The Pennsylvania Constitution added a protection against religious discrimination: "Nor can any man, who acknowledges the being of a God, be justly deprived or abridged of any civil right as a citizen, on account of his religious sentiments or peculiar mode of religious worship." It also provided an exemption for conscientious objectors: "Nor can any man who is conscientiously scrupulous of bearing arms, be justly compelled thereto, if he will pay such equivalent."[24] The Constitution of New York addressed both state and church intrusions on conscience, endeavoring "not only to expel civil tyranny, but also to guard against that spiritual oppression and intolerance . . . wherewith the bigotry and ambition of weak and wicked priests have scourged mankind." It thus declared, "that the free exercise and enjoyment of religious profession and worship, without discrimination or preference, shall forever hereafter be allowed, within this State, to all mankind."[25] The Constitution of New Jersey provided exemptions from religious taxes, using typical language: "nor shall any person . . . ever be obliged to pay tithes, taxes, or any other rates, for the purpose of building or repairing any other church, . . . or ministry, contrary to what he believes to be right."[26]

The principle of liberty of conscience also informed some of the federal constitutional debates on religion. Article VI of the Constitution explicitly provides: "[N]o religious Test [oath] shall ever be required as a qualification" for public office, thereby protecting the religiously scrupulous against oath-swearing.[27] Early versions of the First Amendment religion clauses included such phrases as the following: "That any person religiously scrupulous of bearing arms ought to be exempted, upon payment of an equivalent to employ another to bear arms in his stead";[28] "[t]he civil rights of none shall be abridged on account of religious belief or worship . . . nor shall the full and equal rights of conscience be in any manner, or on any pretext, infringed";[29] "no State shall violate the equal rights of conscience";[30] and "Congress shall make no law . . . to infringe the rights of conscience."[31] Such phrases were ultimately abandoned (though not argued against in the extant records) for the more pregnant language: "Congress shall make no law . . . prohibiting the free exercise [of religion]." This language does not leave conscience unprotected, but more protected. Since Congress cannot "prohibit" the free exercise, the public manifestation, of religion, it follows that Congress cannot "prohibit" a person's private liberty of conscience and the precepts embraced therein.

Free Exercise of Religion

Freedom of conscience was tied to free exercise of religion. Liberty of conscience was the right to be left alone to choose, to entertain, and to change one's religious beliefs. Free exercise of religion was the right to act publicly on the choices of conscience once made—up to the limits of encroaching on the rights of others or the general peace of the community. This organic tie between religious conscience and religious exercise was well known in the Western tradition and was not lost on English and American writers.[32] Already in 1670, the Quaker leader William Penn had linked these two guarantees, insisting that in "plain English," religious liberty entails "not only a mere Liberty of the Mind, in believing or disbelieving" but equally "the free and uninterrupted exercise of our consciences, in that way of worship, we are most clearly persuaded, God requires us to serve Him in."[33] In the next century, this organic linkage was commonplace. Religion, Madison wrote, "must be left to the convictions and conscience of every man; and it is the right of man to exercise it as these may dictate."[34] For religion consists of both "the duties that we owe to our Creator, and the manner of discharging them."[35] For most eighteenth-century writers, religious belief and religious action went hand in hand, and each deserved legal protection.

Although no eighteenth-century writers or dictionaries offered a universal definition of "free exercise," the phrase generally connoted various forms of free public religious action—religious worship, religious speech, religious assembly, religious publication, religious education, among others. It also meant the right to engage in religious debate, expansion, and missionary work. But always peaceably; as the New York lawyer Henry Livingston put it: "I Believe, that to defend the Christian religion is one Thing, and to knock a Man in the Head for being of a different [faith], is another Thing."[36]

Free exercise of religion also embraced the right of the individual to join with like-minded believers in religious societies, which were free to devise their own modes of worship, articles of faith, standards of discipline, and patterns of ritual.[37] The founders did not speak of "religious group rights" or "corporate free exercise rights," as we do today. But they did speak of "ecclesiastical liberty," "the equal liberty of one sect . . . with another," and the right "to have the full enjoyment and free exercise of those purely spiritual powers . . . as may be consistent with the civil rights of society."[38]

Every early state constitution guaranteed "free exercise" rights of some sort—adding the familiar caveat that such exercise not violate the public peace or the private rights of others. Most states limited their guarantee to "the free exercise of religious worship" or the "free exercise of religious profession"—thereby leaving the protection of other forms of religious expression and action beyond worship to other constitutional protections, if any. A few states provided more generic free exercise guarantees. The Constitution of Virginia, for example, guaranteed "the free exercise of religion, according to the dictates of conscience"[39]—thereby expanding free exercise protection to cultic and noncultic religious expression and action, provided these were mandated by conscience. The Constitution of Georgia provided even more flatly: "All persons whatever shall have the free exercise of their religion; provided it be not repugnant to the peace and safety of the State."[40] The First Amendment drafters, too, chose the expansive language of "free exercise [of religion]"—without defining or delimiting the kinds of religious exercises that might be protected, as some of the states had done, and at the same time guaranteeing the freedom of speech, press, and assembly.

Religious Pluralism

The founders regarded "multiplicity," "diversity," or "plurality" as an equally important dimension of religious rights. Two kinds of pluralism were distinguished.

Evangelical and Enlightenment writers stressed the protection of *confessional pluralism*—the maintenance and accommodation of a plurality of forms of religious expression and organization in the community. Evangelical writers advanced a theological argument for this principle, emphasizing that it was for God, not the state, to decide which forms of religion should flourish and which should fade. "God always claimed it as his sole prerogative to determine by his own laws what his worship shall be, who shall minister in it, and how they shall be supported," Isaac Backus wrote.[41] "God's truth is great, and in the end He will allow it to prevail."[42] Confessional pluralism served to respect and reflect this divine prerogative.

Enlightenment writers advanced a rational argument for this principle. "Difference of opinion is advantageous in religion," Thomas Jefferson wrote. "The several sects perform the office of a *Censor morum* over each other. Is uniformity attainable? Millions of innocent men, women, and children, since the introduction of Christianity, have been burnt, tortured, fined, imprisoned; yet we have not advanced one inch towards uniformity. . . . Reason and persuasion are the only practicable instruments."[43] When Jefferson seemed to be wandering from these early sentiments, John Adams wrote to him: "Checks and balances, Jefferson"—in the political as well as the religious sphere—"are our only Security, for the progress of Mind, as well as the Security of Body. Every Species of these Christians would persecute Deists, as [much] as either Sect would persecute another, if it had unchecked and unbalanced Power. Nay, the Deists would persecute Christians, and Atheists would persecute Deists, with as unrelenting Cruelty, as any Christians would persecute them or one another. Know thyself, human Nature!"[44] Madison wrote similarly that "freedom arises from the multiplicity of sects, which pervades America, and which is the best and only security for religious liberty in any society. For where there is such a variety of sects, there cannot be a majority of any one sect to oppress and persecute the rest."[45] Other writers added that the maintenance of multiple faiths is the best protection of the core guarantee of liberty of conscience.[46]

Puritan and Republican writers, while sometimes endorsing confessional pluralism with comparable arguments, also urged the protection of *social pluralism*—the maintenance and accommodation of a plurality of associations to foster religion. Churches and synagogues were not the only "religious societies" that deserved constitutional protection. Families, schools, charities, and other learned and civic societies were equally vital bastions of religion and equally deserving of the special protections of religious liberty. These diverse social institutions had several redeeming qualities. They provided multiple forums for religious expression and action; important bulwarks against state encroachment on natural liberties, particularly religious liberties; and vital sources of theology, morality, charity, and discipline in the state and broader community.[47] John Adams put it thus:

> My opinion of the duties of religion and morality comprehends a very extensive connection with society at large. . . . The benevolence, charity, capacity

and industry which exerted in private life, would make a family, a parish or a town happy, employed upon a larger scale, in support of the great principles of virtue and freedom of political regulations might secure whole nations and generations from misery, want and contempt.[48]

Benjamin Rush concurred: "Religion is best supported under the patronage of particular societies." The differentiation of religion into multiple forums and forms "is as necessary to the perfection and government of the whole as regiments and brigades are in an army."[49] Another pamphleteer argued that not only "magistrates [but] ministers of the gospel and heads of families, all of who have a regard for the future happiness of their country . . . [ought] to use all possible means to destroy vice and immorality of every kind and to cultivate and promote the fear of God and a love of religion in the minds of our young people."[50]

Pluralism was thus not just a sociological fact for the founders. It was also a constitutional condition for the guarantee of religious liberty. This was a species and application of Madison's famous argument about the virtues of republican pluralism in *Federalist Papers No. 10* and *No. 51*. In a federalist republic, Madison had argued in *Federalist Paper No. 10*:

> The influence of factious leaders may kindle a flame within their particular States but will be unable to spread a general conflagration through the other States. A religious sect may degenerate into a political faction in a part of the Confederacy; but the variety of sects dispersed over the entire face of it must secure the national councils against any danger from that source.[51]

He summarized this general point crisply in *Paper No. 51:* "In a free government, the security for civil rights must be the same as that for religious rights; it consists in the one case in the multiplicity of interests, and in the other in the multiplicity of sects."[52]

Religious Equality

The efficacy of liberty of conscience, free exercise of religion, and religious pluralism depended on a guarantee of equality of all peaceable religions before the law. For the state to single out one pious person or one form of faith for either preferential benefits or discriminatory burdens would skew the choice of conscience, encumber the exercise of religion, and upset the natural plurality of faiths. Many of the founders therefore called for equality of all religions before the law. James Madison captured well the prevailing sentiment: "A just Government . . . will be best supported by protecting every Citizen in the enjoyment of his religion, with the same equal hand which protects his person and property; by neither invading the equal rights of any sect, nor suffering any sect to invade those of another."[53] John Adams concurred: "[A]ll men of all religions consistent with morals and property [must] enjoy equal liberty, . . . security of property . . . and an equal chance for honors and power."[54] Isaac Backus wrote similarly that religious liberty requires that "each person and each [religious] society are equally protected from being injured from others, all enjoying equal liberty to attend the worship which they believe is right."[55]

The founders' argument for religious equality became particularly pointed in their debates over religious test oaths as a condition for holding federal political office and positions of public trust. Oaths were commonly accepted in the early republic as "one of the principal instruments of government." They induce "the fear and reverence of God, and the terrors of eternity," one Puritan preacher put it, and thus impose "the most powerful restraints upon the minds of men."[56] Following colonial custom, eleven of the original thirteen states prescribed such oaths. These ranged in specificity from a general affirmation of belief in God or in (Protestant) Christianity to the Trinitarian confession required by Delaware: "I, A. B., do profess faith in God the Father, and in Jesus Christ His only Son, and in the Holy Ghost, one God, blessed for evermore; and I do acknowledge the holy scriptures of the Old and New Testament to be given by divine inspiration."[57] A number of Quakers, Moravians, Baptists, and other groups, before and after the Revolution, had condemned such oaths as a violation of the liberty of conscience and as an "invading of the essential prerogatives of our Lord Jesus Christ."[58] The few Jewish voices of the day protested oaths as a violation of their liberty of conscience and civil rights.[59] In response, most colonies and states exempted Quakers (and sometimes others with conscientious objections) from the oaths in deference to the principle of liberty of conscience.

The addition of an argument from religious equality proved particularly persuasive in outlawing religious test oaths. The argument first came to prominence in the federal Constitutional Convention of 1787 and in the ratification debates that followed within the states. Article VI of the Constitution provided that "no religious Test shall ever be required as a Qualification to any office or public Trust under the United States." James Iredell of North Carolina offered a quite typical defense of this provision: "This article is calculated to secure universal religious liberty, by putting all sects on a level."[60] Fellow Carolinian Richard Spaight elaborated the argument: "No sect is preferred to another. Every man has the right to worship the Supreme Being in the manner that he thinks proper. No test is required. All men of equal capacity and integrity are equally eligible to offices."[61] Such an argument for equality proved persuasive enough to convince the states to ratify the no religious test oath provision in Article VI of the Constitution. This argument also led several states to outlaw religious test oaths. Georgia (1789), Delaware (1792), and Vermont (1793) dropped their religious test oaths. Pennsylvania (1790) extended theirs to include Jews. The new state constitutions of Kentucky (1792) and Tennessee (1796) included no religious test oaths, although they still required that political officials be theists, if not Christians.[62]

Most founders extended the principle of equality before the law to all peaceable religions. A few founders pressed the principle even further, arguing for the equality of religions and nonreligions before the law—particularly on issues of test oaths and religious taxes. Luther Martin of Maryland grumbled about this solicitude for the nonreligious shown during the debates over religious test oaths during the Constitutional Convention:

> The part of the system which provides, that no religious test shall ever be required as a qualification to any office or public trust under the United States, was adopted by a great majority of the convention, and without much debate; however, there were some members so unfashionable as to think, that a belief of the existence of a Deity, and of a state of future rewards and punishments would be some security for the good conduct of our rulers, and that, in a Christian country, it would be *at least decent to hold out some distinction between the professors of Christianity and downright infidelity or paganism.*[63]

Similarly, James Madison, in protesting the proposed tax scheme for religious teachers in Virginia, wrote:

> Above all are they to be considered as retaining an "equal title to the free exercise of religion according to the dictates of conscience." While we assert for ourselves a freedom to embrace, to profess and to observe the religion which we believe to be of divine origin, *we cannot deny an equal freedom to those whose minds have not yet yielded to the evidence which has convinced us.* If this freedom be abused, it is an offence against God, not against man.[64]

These passages should not be overread, however. The founders' principal concern was directed to equality among religions before the law, not equality between religion and nonreligion. Benjamin Huntington indicated, during the House debates over the First Amendment, that "he hoped the amendment would be made in such a way to secure the rights of conscience, and a free exercise of the rights of religion but *not to patronize those who professed no religion at all.*"[65] In the same House debates about including conscientious objection among the rights of conscience, Representative Scott stated firmly, without rejoinder: "There are many sects I know, who are religiously scrupulous in this respect; I do not mean to deprive them of any indulgence. . . . *[M]y design is to guard against those who are of no religion.*"[66] Equality of faiths and believers before the law was the founders' principal concern; our modern concern of equality of religion and

nonreligion, of believers and nonbelievers, before the law was of little concern to the founders.

This principle of equality of all peaceable religious persons and bodies
before the law found its way into a number of early state constitutions.
New Jersey insisted that "there shall be no establishment of any one religious sect in ... preference to another."[67] Delaware guaranteed Christians
"equal rights and privileges"—a guarantee soon extended by judicial interpretation and later amendment to all religions.[68] Maryland insisted that
Christians "are equally entitled to protection in their religious liberty."[69]
Virginia guaranteed that "all men are equally entitled to the free exercise of
religion."[70] New York guaranteed all persons "free exercise and enjoyment
of religious profession and worship, without discrimination or preference."[71] Even Massachusetts, which maintained a Congregationalist establishment, nonetheless guaranteed that "all religious sects and denominations, demeaning themselves peaceably, and as good citizens of the
commonwealth, shall be equally under the protection of the law; and no
subordination of one sect or denomination to another shall ever be established by law."[72]

The principle of equality also found its place in early drafts of the First
Amendment religion clauses, yielding such phrases as: "nor shall the full
and equal rights of conscience be in any manner, or on any pretext, infringed";[73] "Congress shall make no law establishing One Religious Sect or
Society in preference to others";[74] and "Congress shall make no law establishing any particular denomination of religion in preference to another."[75]
Madison, in fact, regarded protection of the "equal rights of conscience" as
the "most valuable" guarantee for religious liberty, and he argued that it
should be guaranteed to apply both to the federal and to state governments.[76] These provisions and arguments were abandoned for the more
generic guarantees of disestablishment and free exercise at the federal
level—guarantees that presumably are to apply equally to all religions.

Separation of Church and State

While separation of church and state is often regarded as a distinctly modern American constitutional principle, it is in reality an ancient Western
teaching rooted in the Bible. The Hebrew Bible repeatedly enjoined the
chosen people of ancient Israel to remain separate from the Gentile world
around them and to separate the Levites and other temple officials from the
rest of the people. The Hebrew Bible also made much of building and re-
building "fortified walls" to protect the city of Jerusalem from the outside
world and to separate the temple and its priests from the commons and its
people—an ancient tradition still recognized and symbolized in the Jewish
rituals and prayers that take place at the Western (Wailing) Wall.[77] The

New Testament warned Christian believers "not [to] conform to the world" but to remain "separate," from worldly temptations and ever mindful that their true "citizenship is in heaven."[78] Echoing the Hebrew Bible, St. Paul spoke of a "wall of separation" *(paries maceriae)* between Christians and non-Christians interposed by the Law of God.[79]

These early biblical passages inspired a long history of speculation on the (wall of) separation between church and state among Western Catholics and Protestants alike. The archives hold a massive farrago of sermons and commentaries on the many biblical and apostolic passages that call for separation between the faithful and fallen, the religious and the political, the clergy and the laity, the spiritual and the temporal, the sacerdotal and the secular, the church and the state. The archives also hold a whole arsenal of legal and political provisions that churchmen and statesmen forged over the centuries to delimit their respective offices and powers and to determine their mutual responsibilities and rights.[80]

American Puritans and Evangelicals were drawn especially to early Protestant theological and legal formulations. Martin Luther, for example, had spoken of "a paper wall . . . between the spiritual estate [and] the temporal estate" and elaborated these views in his complex two-kingdoms theory.[81] John Calvin had argued that the "political kingdom" and "spiritual kingdom" must always be "considered separately." For there is "a great difference between the ecclesiastical and civil power" and it would be "unwise to mingle these two which have a completely different nature."[82] These early Protestant views were echoed in a number of New England Puritan writings and laws that called for a basic separation of the offices and officers of church and state.[83] Glossing the ample biblical passages on (a wall of) separation, European Anabaptist writers had also spoken of a "wall of separation" between the redeemed church of Christ and the fallen world that lay "beyond the perfection of Christ."[84] These early Free Church views recurred in a number of Baptist pamphlets that called for the church, as the "pure bride of Christ," to be free from "adulterous unions" with the state.[85] They recurred again in other American Evangelical writings that called for a "wall," "hedge," "line," or "fence" between church and state and an "absolute divorce" between the Christ and the state.[86]

The principle of separation of church and state also had solid grounding in political sources that appealed to American Enlightenment and Republican writers. John Locke, for example, had argued that the authority of the clergy, "since it is ecclesiastical, ought to be confined with the bounds of the church, nor can it in any manner be extended to civil affairs, because the church itself is a thing absolutely separate and distinct from the commonwealth. The boundaries on both sides are fixed and immovable."[87] James Burgh, a Scottish Whig who was popular among several American founders, pressed for the principle in his influential writings of the 1760s and 1770s.[88] Burgh lamented the "ill consequences" of the traditional "mixed-mungrel-spiritual-secular-ecclesiastical establishment." Such conflations of church and state, said Burgh, lead to "follies and knaveries" and make "the dispensers of religion despicable and odious to all men of sense, and will destroy the spirituality, in which consists the whole value, of religion." "Build an impenetrable wall of separation between sacred and civil," Burgh enjoined. "Do not send the graceless officer, reeking from the arms of his trull [i.e., prostitute], to the performance of a holy rite of religion, as a test for his holding the command of a regiment. To profane, in such a manner, a religion, which you pretend to reverence, is an impiety sufficient to bring down upon your heads, the roof of the sacred building you thus defile."[89]

The French revolutionary Marquis de Condorcet, who influenced Thomas Paine, put his case "to separate religion from the State," in the shriller anti-Catholic terms that would dominate the French Revolution. While it was important "to leave to the priests the freedom of sacraments, censures, [and] ecclesiastical functions," Condorcet conceded, the state must take steps to remove the traditional influence and privileges of the Catholic Church and clergy in society. The state was "not to give any civil effect to any of their decisions, not to give any influence over marriages or over birth or death certificates; not to allow them to intervene in any civil or political act; and to judge the lawsuits which would arise, between them and their citizens, for the temporal rights relating to their functions, as one would decide the similar lawsuits that would arise between the members of a free association, or between this association and private individuals."[90] Such anticlerical and anti-Catholic separationist sentiments were quite typical of the French revolutionaries. And, in the following decades, these kinds of sentiments inspired a devastating political and popular attack on the clergy and property of the Catholic Church.[91]

Such quotes, from theological and political sources, indicate the range of sentiments that surrounded the principle of separation of church and state in the early modern period. Sifting through this European and colonial legacy, the American founders adduced the principle of separation of church and state to press at least five concerns.

First, the principle of separation of church and state was invoked as means to protect the church from the state. This had long been a dominant motif in European Catholic and Protestant writings—captured in the Christian clergy's perennial call for "freedom of the church."[92] The concern was to protect church affairs from state intrusion, the clergy from the magistracy, church properties from state encroachment, ecclesiastical rules and rites from political coercion and control. This understanding of separation of church and state continued and grew in the eighteenth century. Elisha Williams spoke for many churchmen when he wrote: "[E]very church has

[the] right to judge in what manner God is to be worshipped by them, and what form of discipline ought to be observed by them, and the right also of electing their own officers" without interference from political officials.[93] George Washington wrote in 1789 of the need "to establish effectual barriers against the horrors of spiritual tyranny and every species of religious persecution" so that there was no threat "to the religious rights of any ecclesiastical Society."[94] A decade later, Tunis Wortman, a Jeffersonian, wrote:

> It is your duty, as Christians, to maintain the purity and independence of the church, to keep religion separate from politics, to prevent an union between the church and the state, and to preserve the clergy from temptation, corruption and reproach. . . . Unless you maintain the pure and primitive spirit of Christianity, and prevent the cunning and intrigue of statesmen from mingling with its institutions, you will become exposed to a renewal of the same dreadful and enormous scenes which have not only disgraced the annals of the church, but destroyed the peace, and sacrificed the lives of millions.[95]

This understanding of separation of church and state was captured especially in state and federal constitutional guarantees of freedom of association and the free exercise rights of religious groups.[96]

Second, the principle of separation of church and state was sometimes invoked as a means to protect the state from the church. Tunis Wortman, for example, wrote: "Religion and government are equally necessary, but their interests should be kept separate and distinct."[97] "Upon no plan, no system can they become united, without endangering the purity and usefulness of both—the church will corrupt the state, and the state pollute the church."[98] *Cato's Letters* gave readers no "small acquaintance with ecclesiastical history, and the history of the Turks and Saracens," to drive home this point: "Nor have churchmen, when they ruled states, had ever any other view; but having double authority, had generally double insolence and remarkably less mercy and regard to conscience or property, than others who had fewer ties to be merciful and just. And therefore the sorest tyrants have been they, who united in one person the royalty and priesthood."[99] In the same vein, John Adams devoted much of his *Dissertation on the Canon and the Feudal Law* (1774) to a lengthy history of the "tyrannous outrages" that the Catholic Church and the papacy had inflicted through its control of the state; this was "a wicked confederacy between two systems of tyranny."[100] Drawing on these historical lessons, John Jay urged his fellow constitutional conveners in New York: "by the benevolent principles of rational liberty not only to expel civil tyranny, but also to guard against that spiritual oppression and intolerance wherewith the bigotry and ambition of weak and wicked priests and princes have scourged mankind."[101]

This understanding of separation of church and state helped to inform the movement in some states to exclude ministers and other religious officials from participating in political office. Such exclusions had been commonplace among seventeenth-century Puritans, but they became attractive to some later Evangelicals and Enlightenment exponents as well. Ministers in political office, it was argued, could use the threat of spiritual reprisal to force their congregants, including fellow politicians who sat in their pews, to acquiesce in their political positions. Ministers would inevitably be conflicted over whose interests to represent and serve—the interests of their congregants or their constituents. Because they represented both religious congregants and political constituents, ministers would have disproportionate influence on the political process. Ministers who tried to serve both God and the state would be distracted from their fundamental callings of preaching and teaching, and tempted to train their religious messages toward political causes. Besides, ministers were often, as John Adams put it, "universally too little acquainted with the World, and the Modes of Business, to engage in civil affairs with any Advantage."[102] Finally, ministers could not enjoy both the benefit of exemption of taxation for themselves and the power to impose taxation on all others; this was even more odious than the great offense of taxation without representation.[103]

These kinds of arguments led seven of the original thirteen states to ban ministers from serving in political office.[104] The South Carolina Constitution (1778) had typical language: "And whereas, ministers of the Gospel are by their profession dedicated to the service of God and the cure of souls, and ought not to be diverted from their great duties of their function, therefore no minister of the Gospel or public preacher of any religious persuasion, while he continues in the exercise of his pastoral function, and for two years after, shall be eligible either as governor, lieutenant-governor, a member of the senate, house representative, or privy council in this State."[105]

Third, the principle of separation of church and state was invoked as a means to protect the individual's liberty of conscience from the intrusions of both church and state. This had been an early and enduring understanding of some Anabaptist writers in Europe and of some Evangelical and Quaker writers in colonial America.[106] This argument became more prominent in the young republic. "Every man has an equal right to follow the dictates of his own conscience in the affairs of religion . . . and to follow his own judgment wherever it leads him," Elisha Williams wrote in 1744. This is "an equal right with any rulers be they civil or ecclesiastical."[107] "Religion is altogether personal and the right of exercising it inalienable," reads a Presbyterian pamphlet of 1776; "it is not, cannot, and ought not to be, resigned to the will of the society at large" let alone to the authorities of church and state.[108] James Madison put the case more generically in 1785 in arguing for the maintenance of a "great barrier" between church and state to protect the rights of individuals:

> Their jurisdiction is both derivative and limited. It is limited with regard to the co-ordinate departments; more necessarily is it limited with regard to the constituents. The preservation of a free government requires not merely, that the metes and bounds which separate each department of power be invariably maintained; but more especially that neither of them be suffered to overleap the great barrier which defends the rights of the people.[109]

Thomas Jefferson's famous 1802 letter to the Danbury Baptist Association also tied the principle of separation of church and state directly to the principle of liberty of conscience:

> Believing with you that *religion is a matter which lies solely between a man and his God,* that he owes account to none other for his faith or his worship, that the [legitimate] powers of government reach actions only, and not opinions, I contemplate with sovereign reverence that the act of the whole American people which declared that their legislature should "make no law respecting an establishment of religion, or prohibiting the free exercise thereof," *thus building a wall of separation between church and State.* Adhering to this expression of the supreme will of the nation *in behalf of the rights of conscience,* I shall see with sincere satisfaction the progress of those sentiments which tend to *restore to man all his natural rights,* convinced he has no natural right in opposition to his social duties.[110]

In Jefferson's formulation, separation of church and state assured individuals of their natural, inalienable right of conscience, which could be exercised freely and fully to the point of breaching the peace or shirking social duties. Jefferson is not talking here of separating politics and religion altogether. Indeed, in the very next paragraph of his letter, President Jefferson performed an avowedly religious act of offering prayers on behalf of his Baptist correspondents: "I reciprocate your kind prayers for the protection and blessing of the common Father and Creator of man."[111]

Fourth, the principle of separation of church and state was occasionally used to argue for the protection of individual states from interference by the federal government in governing local religious affairs. As Daniel Dreisbach has shown, Thomas Jefferson sometimes used the principle of separation of church and state in this federalist jurisdictional sense as well.[112] Jefferson said many times that the federal government had no jurisdiction over religion; religion was entirely a state and local matter. As he put it in his Second Inaugural: "In matters of religion, I have considered that its free exercise is placed by the constitution independent of the general [federal] government. I have therefore undertaken, on no occasion, to prescribe the religious exercises suited to it; but have left them, as the constitution found them, under the direction and discipline of State or Church authorities."[113] The separation that Jefferson has in mind here was between local church-state relations and the federal government. The federal government could not interfere in the affairs of local churches. And the federal government could not interfere in the affairs of local states vis-à-vis these local churches. Under this federalist jurisdictional reading of separation, state governments were free to patronize and protect religion, or to establish or abridge religion, as their own state constitutions dictated. But the federal government was entirely foreclosed from the same. Thus while serving as governor of Virginia, Jefferson supported religion in a variety of ways, including making religious proclamations. But, when serving as president of the United States, Jefferson insisted more firmly on the separation of church and state, and refused to give Thanksgiving Day proclamations on behalf of the country.[114]

Fifth, the principle of separation of church and state was occasionally adduced as a means to protect society and its members from unwelcome participation in and support for religion. In the course of the eighteenth century, some religious dissenters used arguments of separation to argue against the established church policies of mandatory payments of tithes, required participation in swearing oaths, forced attendance at religious services, and compulsory registration of church properties.[115] At the close of the eighteenth century, the language of separation of church and state also began to fuel broader campaigns to remove traditional forms and forums of religion in law, politics, and society. This was the most novel, and controversial, understanding of separation of church and state in the young American republic, but it began to gain rhetorical currency. The first and most notorious instance came during the heated election of Thomas Jefferson in 1800. As Philip Hamburger has shown, in succeeding decades, separation of church and state became an increasingly useful rhetorical weapon in the battles over dueling, freemasonry, lotteries, drunkenness, Sunday laws, slavery and abolition, marriage and divorce reforms, women's suffrage, religious education, blasphemy prosecutions, enforcement of Christian morals, and more.[116]

Disestablishment of Religion

For some founders, particularly the New England Puritans who defended their "mild and equitable establishments," the roll of "essential rights and liberties" ended here. Many other founders, however, combined several of these principles into a call for the disestablishment of religion.

The term "establishment of religion" was an ambiguous phrase—in the eighteenth century, as much as today. In the dictionaries and common parlance of the founders' day, to "establish" meant "to settle firmly," "to fix unalterably," "to settle in any privilege or possession," "to make firm," "to ratify," "to ordain," "to enact," "to set up," "to build firmly."[117] Such was the basic meaning of the term, for example, when used in the 1787 Constitution—"We the people of the United States, in order to form a perfect union, to *establish* justice . . . do ordain and *establish* this Constitution" (preamble); Congress shall have power "[t]o *establish* an uniform rule of naturalization" and "[t]o *establish* post offices" (Art. I.8); governmental offices "shall be *established* by law" (Art. II.2); Congress may "ordain and *establish* . . . inferior courts" (Art. III.1); the ratification of nine states "shall be sufficient for the *establishment* of this Constitution" (Art. VI).[118]

Following this basic sense of the term, the founders understood the establishment of religion to mean the actions of government to "settle," "fix," "define," "ordain," "enact," or "set up" the religion of the community—its religious doctrines and liturgies, its religious texts and traditions, its clergy and property. To the founders, the most notorious example of religious establishment in this sense, was the establishment by law of Anglicanism. English ecclesiastical law formally required use of the Authorized (King James) Version of the Bible and of the liturgies, rites, prayers, and lectionaries of *The Book of Common Prayer.* It demanded subscription to the Thirty-Nine Articles of Faith and the swearing of loyalty oaths to the Church, Crown, and Commonwealth of England. When such ecclesiastical laws were rigorously applied—as they were in England in the early Stuart period of the 1610s–1630s, and again in the Restoration of the 1660s–1670s, and intermittently in the American colonies—they led to all manner of state controls of the internal affairs of the established church, and all manner of state repression and coercion of religious dissenters.

Many of the founders who called for the disestablishment of religion sought to outlaw this traditional form of religious establishment. To them, such an establishment of religion violated a number of first principles of religious liberty—notably liberty of conscience, equality and plurality of religion, and the separation of church and state.

Disestablishment of religion, under this understanding, served to protect the principle of liberty of conscience by foreclosing government from coercively prescribing mandatory forms of religious belief, doctrine, and practice. As both the Delaware and Pennsylvania Constitutions put it: "[N]o authority can or ought to be vested in, or assumed by any power whatever, that shall in any case interfere with, or in any manner controul, the right of conscience in the free exercise of religious worship."[119]

Disestablishment of religion further protected the principles of equality and pluralism by preventing government from singling out certain religious beliefs and bodies for preferential treatment. This concept of disestablishment came through repeatedly in both state and federal debates. In the Virginia Ratification Convention, for example, both Madison and Edmund Randolph stressed that religious pluralism would "prevent the establishment of any one sect in prejudice, to the rest, and will forever oppose all attempts to infringe religious liberty."[120] South Carolina conventioneer Francis Cummins likewise stated that it was "his duty and honor to oppose the ideas of religious establishments; or of states giving preference to any religious denomination."[121] The New Jersey Constitution provided "there shall be no establishment of any one religious sect . . . in preference to another."[122] Both the New York and the Rhode Island Ratification Conventions suggested amendments to the Constitution that "no religious sect or society ought to be favored or established by law in preference to others."[123] Two drafts of the religion clauses debated in the First Congress included a similar guarantee: "Congress shall make no law establishing one religious sect or society in preference to others"[124] and "Congress shall make no law establishing any particular denomination of religion in preference to another."[125]

Disestablishment of religion also served to protect the basic principle of separation of church and state. Disestablishment, in Jefferson's words, prohibited government "from intermeddling with religious institutions, their doctrines, discipline, or exercises" and from "the power of effecting any uniformity of time or matter among them. Fasting & prayer are religious exercises. The enjoining them is an act of discipline. Every religious society has a right to determine for itself the times for these exercises, & the objects proper for them, according to their own peculiar tenets."[126] To allow such governmental intermeddling in the affairs of religious bodies would inflate the competence of government. As Madison wrote, it "implies either that the Civil Magistrate is a competent judge of religious truth; or that he may employ religion as an engine of civil policy. The first is an arrogant pretension falsified by the contradictory opinions of rulers in all ages, and throughout the world, the second an unhallowed perversion of the means of salvation."[127] Governmental interference in religious affairs also compromises the pacific ideals of most religions. Thomas Paine, who is usually branded as a religious skeptic, put this well:

All religions are in their nature mild and benign, and united with principles of morality. They could not have made proselytes at first, by professing anything that was vicious, cruel, persecuting or immoral. . . . Persecution is not an original feature in any religion; but it is always the strongly marked feature of all law-religions, or religions established by law. Take away the law-establishment, and every religion reassumes its original benignity.[128]

The question that remained controversial—in the eighteenth century as much as in our own—was whether more gentle and generic forms of state support for religion could be countenanced. Did disestablishment of religion prohibit governmental support for religion altogether, or did it simply require that such governmental support be distributed nonpreferentially among all religions?

It takes a bit of historical imagination to appreciate this question in eighteenth-century terms, rather than in our own. In eighteenth-century America, government patronized religion in a variety of ways. Officials donated land and personalty for the building of churches, religious schools, and charities. They collected religious taxes and tithes to support ministers and missionaries. They exempted church property and their ministers from taxation. They had special forms of religious incorporation for churches, religious schools, charities, mission groups, and other religious bodies. They supported Christian education in schools and colleges. They outlawed blasphemy and sacrilege, unnecessary labor on the Sabbath and on religious holidays. They administered religious test oaths and foreclosed dissenters from political office.[129]

In earlier centuries, such forms of state patronage and protection of religion were reserved to one established church alone. All other faiths, if tolerated at all, were left to depend on their own resources. In the course of the later seventeenth and eighteenth centuries, the growth of religious pluralism in the colonies often entailed the gradual extension of these forms of state privilege and patronage to other churches besides the established churches—often in a piecemeal fashion: benefit by benefit, congregation by congregation, county by county, township by township. By the later eighteenth century, the hard constitutional question that faced the states became this: Should state patronage for religion end altogether? Or should state patronage be extended to all religions indiscriminately, rather than granted only in this piecemeal fashion? Given the overwhelmingly Christian, indeed Protestant, character of the new nation,[130] a policy of nonpreferential governmental support for all religions could be quite realistically envisioned—particularly if some special accommodation were made for Jewish sabbatarian beliefs and Quaker aversions to religious oaths. (No founder seriously thought of having to accommodate the African religions of the slaves or the traditional religions of the Native Americans.)

The question of whether disestablishment of religion outlaws all governmental support for religion or outlaws only preferential governmental support for some religions was not resolved in the eighteenth century. The founders were divided on the question. A number of Evangelical and Enlightenment writers viewed the principle of disestablishment as a firm bar on state support, particularly financial support, of religious beliefs, believers, and bodies.[131] James Madison, for example, wrote late in his life: "Every new & successful example . . . of a perfect separation between ecclesiastical and civil matters, is of importance. And I have no doubt that every new example, will succeed, as every past one has done, in shewing that religion & Govt. will both exist in greater purity, the less they are mixed together."[132] Similar sentiments can be found in contemporaneous Baptist tracts, particularly those of Isaac Backus and John Leland.[133] Puritan and Republican writers often viewed such principles only as a prohibition against direct financial support for the religious worship or exercise of one particular religious group. General governmental support for religion—in the form of tax exemptions to religious properties, land grants and tax subsidies to religious schools and charities, tax appropriations for missionaries and military chaplains, and similar general causes—were for them not only licit but necessary for good governance.

The state constitutions were likewise divided on the question. A number of states explicitly authorized such support for religion in their original constitutions, though they sometimes defined "religion" to mean Christianity (or even Protestantism).[134] The Constitution of Maryland (1776) was typical. It included strong guarantees of religious liberty that touched each of the principles of religious liberty we have rehearsed. "[A]ll persons, professing the Christian religion, are equally entitled to protection in their religious liberty." This includes freedom from "molestation" "on account of his religious persuasion or profession, or for his religious practice"; "nor ought any person to be compelled to frequent or maintain, or contribute, unless on contract [i.e., by agreement] to maintain any particular place of worship, or any particular ministry." But, the 1776 Maryland Constitution continued, without pause, to provide that "the Legislature may, in their discretion, lay a general and equal tax, for the support of the Christian religion; leaving to each individual the power of appointing the payment over of the money, collected from him, to the support of any particular place of worship or minister, or for the benefit of the poor of his own denomination, or the poor in general of any particular county."[135] A similar juxtaposition of provisions was included in the original constitutions of Massachusetts, New Hampshire, and Connecticut.[136] The other original state constitutions simply repeated the general principles of religious liberty, without touching the issue of whether government could support religion(s).

Similarly, none of the drafts nor the final version of the First Amendment addresses the question directly, beyond simply prohibiting "the" or "an" "establishment of religion."

Interdependence of Principles

For all the diversity of opinion one finds in the Constitutional Convention debates, and in pamphlets, sermons, editorials, and broadsides of the eighteenth century, most influential writers embraced this roll of "essential rights and liberties of religion"—liberty of conscience, free exercise of religion, religious pluralism, religious equality, separation of church and state, and disestablishment of religion. To be sure, many of these terms carried multiple meanings in the later eighteenth century. And to be sure, numerous other terms and norms were under discussion, often with widely discordant and confusing implications. But in the range of eighteenth-century sources at my disposal, these principles were the most commonly discussed and embraced.

On the one hand, eighteenth-century writers designed these principles to provide an interwoven shield against repressive religious establishments. Liberty of conscience protected the individual from coercion and discriminatory treatment by church or state officials and guaranteed unencumbered, voluntary choices of faith. Free exercise of religion protected the individual's ability to discharge the duties of conscience through religious worship, speech, publication, assembly, and other actions without necessary reference to a prescribed creed, cult, or code of conduct. Pluralism protected multiple forms and forums of religious belief and action, in place of a uniformly mandated religious doctrine, liturgy, and polity. Equality protected religious individuals and bodies from special benefits and from special burdens administered by the state or by other religious bodies. Separationism protected individual believers, as well as religious and political officials, from undue interference or intrusion on each other's processes and practices. Disestablishment precluded governmental prescriptions of the doctrine, liturgy, or morality of one faith and compromises of the principles of liberty of conscience, free exercise, equality, pluralism, or separationism.

On the other hand, eighteenth-century writers designed these principles to be mutually supportive and mutually subservient to the highest goal of guaranteeing "the essential rights and liberties of religion" for all. No single principle could by itself guarantee such religious liberty. Simple protection of liberty of conscience provided no protection of religious actions or organizations. Pure pluralism could decay into religious relativism and render the government blind to the special place of religion in the community and in the Constitution. Simple guarantees of the equality of religion could render governments indifferent to the widely divergent needs of different forms of religion. Pure separationism could deprive the church of all meaningful forms and functions and deprive states of an essential ally in government and social service. Pure nonestablishment could readily rob society of all common values and beliefs and the state of any effective religious role. Eighteenth-century writers, therefore, arranged these multiple principles into an interlocking and interdependent shield of religious liberties and rights for all. Religion was simply too vital and too valuable a source of individual flourishing and social cohesion to be left unguarded on any side. Religious liberty was simply too essential a foundation of other civil rights and liberties to be in any way deprecated. Religious liberty, as Thomas Jefferson put it, is "the most inalienable and sacred of all human rights."[137]

Notes

1. The term "essential rights and liberties" was quite common among the founders. This was the title of Elisha Williams, *The Essential Rights and Liberties of Protestants* (1744). The Virginia Ratifying Convention provided "that, among other essential rights, the liberty of conscience, and of the press, cannot be cancelled, abridged, restrained, or modified, by any authority of the United States." Elliot, ed., *Debates*, 1:327. James Madison spoke of "essential rights" of religious freedom and rights of conscience in his speech of August 17, 1789. See *Annals*, 1:784 and Madison, *Papers*, 11:404, 405. Likewise, John Adams included religion among "our most essential rights and liberties." See Adams, *Works*, 3:465. The Federal Farmer also saw "the free exercise of religion" as one of the "essential rights." Letter IV (October 12, 1787), in *The Anti-Federalist*, ed. Herbert J. Storing (1985), 58.

2. See prevailing sentiments collected in *The Palladium of Conscience, or, The Foundation of Religious Liberty Displayed, Asserted and Established, Agreeable to its True and Genuine Principles* (1773).

3. See sources and discussion in Brian Tierney, "Religious Rights: An Historical Perspective," in John Witte Jr. and Johan D. van der Vyver, eds., *Religious Human Rights in Global Perspective: Religious Perspectives* (1996), 17–45; Karl Schwarz, "Der Begriff Exercitium Religionis Privatum," *Zeitschrift der Savigny-Stiftung (Kan. Ab.)* 105 (1988):495–518. For biblical and patristic sources of the term "conscience" (*conscientia* in Latin, *suneidesis* in Greek), see David N. Freedman, ed., *Anchor Bible Dictionary*, 6 vols. (1992), 1:1128; Feldman, "The Intellectual Origins," 354ff.

4. Virginia Bill of Rights (1776), Art. 16.

5. Virginia Ratifying Convention (June 12, 1788), in Elliot, ed., *Debates*, 3:113–114; Madison, *Papers*, 11:130–131; Anson P. Stokes and Leo Pfeffer, *Church and State in the United States*, rev. ed. (1975), 61.

6. John Mellen, *The Great and Happy Doctrine of Liberty* (1795), 17–18; Amos Adams, *Religious Liberty an Invaluable Blessing* (1768), 39–40, 45–46; *A Manual of Religious Liberty*, 3d ed. (1767).

7. Williams, *Essential Rights and Liberties*, 42; John Lathrop, *A Discourse on the Peace* (1784), 29; Hugh Fisher, *The Divine Right of Private Judgment, Set in a True Light*, repr. ed. (1790).

8. Westminster Confession, chap. 20, sec. II, in *The Confession of Faith, Together with the Larger and Smaller Catechismes* (1658), 63; see also Feldman, "Intellectual Origins," 364–5.

9. John Trenchard and Thomas Gordon, *Cato's Letters, or Essays on Liberty, Civil and Religious, and Other Important Subjects*, ed. Ronald Hamowy (1995 [1720–1723]), 467–468.

10. Williams, *Essential Rights and Liberties*, 7–8.

11. Adams, *Works*, 3:452–456; Massachusetts Constitution (1780), Pt. I, Art. II.

12. Madison, "Memorial," para. 1.

13. John Leland, *The Rights of Conscience Inalienable* (1791), in Sandoz, ed., *Political Sermons*, 1079, 1085; Israel Evans, "A Sermon Delivered at Concord, Before the Hon. General Court of the State of New Hampshire at the Annual Election (1791)," in ibid., 1057, 1063ff.

14. Stiles, *The United States Elevated*, 56.

15. "Worcestriensis, Number IV (1776)," in Hynemann and Lutz, eds., *American Political Writing*, 1:449–450. The typical caveat follows: "provided it does not issue in overt acts of treason against the state undermining the peace and good order of society." Ibid.

16. Mellen, *The Great and Happy Doctrine of Liberty*, 17 (emphasis added).

17. Ibid., 20.

18. Parsons, *Freedom from Civil and Ecclesiastical Slavery*; Isaac Backus, *Appeal to the Public for Religious Liberty Against the Oppressions of the Present Day* (1773).

19. Henry Cumings, *A Sermon Preached at Billerica* (1797), 12–13; Thomas Jefferson, "Draft of Bill Exempting Dissenters from Contributing to the Support of the Church, 30 Nov. 1776," in Philip B. Kurland and Ralph S. Lerner, ed., *The Founders' Constitution* (1987), 5:74, arguing that dissenters be "totally free and exempt from all Levies, Taxes and Impositions whatever towards supporting and maintaining the [established Anglican] church" as a means of ensuring "equal Liberty as well religious as civil" to all "good People." These arguments were sometimes extended to claiming "exemptions" and "immunities" from the jurisdiction, discipline, and confessional statements of a local church. See, e.g., Isaac Foster, *A Defense of Religious Liberty* (1780) (a 192-page tract arguing for exemptions from compliance with the imposition of a new confession, the Saybrook Platform, in a local church).

20. Cumings, *A Sermon*, 12–13.

21. John Locke had made this point in his *Letter on Toleration* (1689): "But some may ask: 'What if the magistrate should enjoin anything by his authority that appears unlawful to the conscience of a private person?' I answer that, if government be faithfully administered and the counsels of the government be indeed directed to the public good, this will seldom happen." Locke, *Works*, 5:43–46.

22. Letter to the Religious Society Called Quakers, October, 1789, in Washington, *Writings*, 30:416; see also *George Washington on Religious Liberty and Mutual Understanding: Selections from Washington's Letters*, ed. Edward F. Humphrey (1932).

23. Delaware Declaration of Rights (1776), sec. 2.

24. Pennsylvania Declaration of Rights (1776), II, VIII.

25. Constitution of New York (1777), Art. XXXVIII.

26. Constitution of New Jersey (1776), Art. XVIII.

27. Joseph Story, *Commentaries on the Constitution* (1833), 3:703.

28. Virginia Version (June 27, 1788), in Elliot, ed., *Debates*, 1:327, and 3:591, 594.

29. James Madison's First Proposal, introduced in the House on June 8, 1789, in *Annals*, 1:451.

30. Ibid., 1:452.

31. Draft proposed by Fisher Ames of Massachusetts on August 20, 1789. Ibid., 1:796.

32. Schwarz, "Der Begriff Exercitium Religionis Privatum," 502ff.

33. William Penn, *The Great Case of Liberty of Conscience* (1670), in *The Political Writings of William Penn*, Andrew R. Murphy ed. (2002), 79, 81–82.

34. Madison, "Memorial," para. 1; Levi Hart, *Liberty Described and Recommended* (1775), 14–15.

35. Virginia Bill of Rights, Art. 16.

36. Quoted by Lambert, *The Founding Fathers*, 189.

37. Williams, *Essential Rights and Liberties*, 46ff.; *Isaac Backus on Church, State, and Calvinism*, 348ff.; Parsons, *Freedom from Civil and Ecclesiastical Slavery*, 14–15; Stiles, *The United States Elevated*, 55ff.; Amos Adams, *Religious Liberty*, 38–46.

38. Hart, *Liberty Described and Recommended*, 14; *Backus on Church, State, and Calvinism*, 348–349; "A Declaration of Certain Fundamental Rights and Liberties of the Protestant Episcopal Church in Maryland," quoted by Anson P. Stokes, *Church and States in the United States*, 3 vols. (1950), 1:741.

39. Virginia Declaration of Rights (1776), sec. 16.

40. Constitution of Georgia (1777), Art. LVI.

41. *Backus on Church, State, and Calvinism*, 317; *The Freeman's Remonstrance Against an Ecclesiastical Establishment* (1777), 13.

42. Isaac Backus, *Truth Is Great and Will Prevail* (1781); John R. Bolles, *A Brief Account of Persecutions, in Boston and Connecticut Governments* (1758), 47, 59. See also *George Washington on Religious Liberty*, 12.

43. Thomas Jefferson, "Notes on the State of Virginia," Query 17, in *The Complete Jefferson*, 673–676; Stiles, *The United States Elevated*, 55–56; Thomas Paine, *Common Sense and the Crisis* (1960 [1776]), 50.

44. Letter to Thomas Jefferson, June 25, 1813, in *The Adams-Jefferson Letters*, 333, 334.

45. Debates of June 12, 1788, in Elliot, ed., *Debates*, 3:313.

46. Williams, *Essential Rights and Liberties*, 40–42; Stiles, *The United States Elevated*, 55ff.; Comments of Governor Randolph (June 12, 1788), in Elliot, ed., *Debates*, 3:207–208; Max Farrand, ed., *The Records of the Federal Convention of 1787* (1911), 3:310.

47. *The Works of James Wilson*, ed. R. G. McCloskey (1967); W. C. McWilliams, *The Idea of Fraternity in America* (1973), 112–123; Clinton Rossiter, *The Political Thought of the American Revolution* (1963), 204.

48. Letter from John Adams to Abigail Adams (October 29, 1775), quoted by John R. Howe Jr., *The Changing Political Thought of John Adams* (1966), 156–157 (capitalization modernized).

49. Letter from Benjamin Rush to John Armstrong (March 19, 1793), in *The Founders' Constitution*, 5:78.

50. Hynemann and Lutz, eds., *American Political Writing*, 1:38–39. On the importance of the family as a "little commonweath" alongside the commonwealths of church and state to foster religion and morality, see my *From Sacrament to Contract: Religion, Marriage, and Law in the Western Tradition* (1997), ch. 4; John Demos, *A Little Commonwealth: Family Life in Plymouth County*, 2d ed. (2000); Thomas E. Buckley, *The Great Catastrophe of My Life: Divorce in the Old Dominion* (2002), ch. 1.

51. *The Federalist Papers: Alexander Hamilton, James Madison, John Jay*, ed. Clinton Rossiter (1961), 84.

52. Ibid., 324.

53. Madison, "Memorial," paras. 4, 8.

54. Letter to Dr. Price, April 8, 1785, in Adams, *Works*, 8:232; Frank Donovan, ed., *The John Adams Papers* (1965), 181.

55. *Backus on Church, State, and Calvinism*, 333.

56. Phillips Payson, "Election Sermon of 1778," in Hynemann and Lutz, eds., *American Political Writing*, 523, 529. A decade later, Payson apparently changed his mind, arguing in the Massachusetts Ratifying Convention that such religious tests were "attempts to erect human tribunals for the consciences of men, impious encroachments upon the prerogatives of God." Speech of January 30, 1788, in Elliot, ed., *Debates*, 2:120.

57. Delaware Constitution (1776), Art. XXII (outlawed by a 1792 amendment).

58. Speech of Isaac Backus (February 4, 1788), in Elliot, ed., *Debates*, 2:148; see also *The Founders' Constitution*, 4:633ff.

59. Petition of the Philadelphia Synagogue to the Council of Censors of Philadelphia (December 23, 1783), in *The Founders' Constitution*, 4:635; "Jonas Phillips to the President and Members of the Convention (September 7, 1789)," in Farrand, ed., *Records of the Federal Convention*, 3:78–79.

60. Speech of July 30, 1788, in ibid., 3:204. See also Governor Randolph in ibid., 3:207.

61. Speech of July 30, 1788, in Elliot, ed., *Debates*, 4:208.

62. Chester J. Antieau, Philip M. Carroll, and Thomas Carroll Burke, *Religion Under the State Constitutions* (1965), 101–107.

63. Luther Martin, *The Genuine Information* (1787), in Farrand, ed., *Records of the Federal Convention*, 3:227 (italics in original changed).

64. Madison, "Memorial," para. 4 (emphasis added).

65. House Debates, August 15, 1789, in *Annals*, 1:758 (emphasis added).

66. House Debates, August 20, 1789, in ibid., 1:796 (emphasis added).

67. Constitution of New Jersey (1776), Art. XIX.

68. Delaware Declaration of Rights (1776), Sec. 3.

69. Maryland Declaration of Rights (1776), Sec. XXXIII.

70. Virginia Declaration of Rights (1776), Art. 16.

71. Constitution of New York (1777), Art. XXXVIII.

72. Constitution of Massachusetts (1780), Part I, Art. 3, as amended by Art. XI.

73. James Madison's First Proposal, June 7, 1789, in *Annals*, 1:451.

74. Senate Version (September 3, 1789), in *Journal of the First Session of the United States of America* (1789) (Evans, First Series, No. 22207), 1:116.

75. Ibid., 1:117.

76. *Annals*, vol. 1, col. 784. See further below, pp. 81–82.

77. Exodus 34:11–16; Leviticus 20:24–25, 21:1–22:16; Numbers 8:14, 16:9; Deuteronomy 10:8, 32:8, 1 Chronicles 23:13; 1 Kings 3:1, 8:53; 2 Samuel 22:26–27; Ezra 6:21; 10:1; Nehemiah 3:1–32, 4:15–20, 9:1–15, 10:28–31, 12:27–43, 13:1–3; Jeremiah 1:18–19, 15:19–21; 1 Esdras 7–9.

78. Romans 12:2; 2 Corinthians 6:14–18; Philippians 3:20; see Michael W. McConnell, "Believers as Equal Citizens," in Nancy L. Rosenblum, ed., *Obligations of Citizenship and Demands of Faith: Religious Accommodation in Pluralistic Democracies* (2000), 90, 93ff.

79. Ephesians 2:14. See historical interpretation of this text in Markus Barth, *The Anchor Bible: Ephesians* (1974), 263–265, 283–287.

80. See examples above in Chap. 1 and in John Witte Jr. "That Serpentine Wall of Separation," *Michigan Law Review* 101 (2003):1869–1905.

81. Martin Luther, *To the Christian Nobility of the German Nation* (1520), in id., *Three Treatises*, 2d rev. ed. (1986), 12, 16; see my *Law and Protestantism*, 87–117.

82. John Calvin, *Institutes of the Christian Religion* (1559), bk. 3., chap. 19.15; bk. 4., chap. 11.3; bk. 4, chap. 20.1–2; see my *Reformation of Rights*, chap. 1.

83. See above, pp. 23–26, and my *Reformation of Rights*, chap. 6.

84. See above, pp. 11–12. See examples in *The Complete Writings of Menno Simons, c. 1496–1561*, L. Verduin, trans., J. C. Wenger, ed. (1984), 29, 117–120, 158–159, 190–206; *Biblical Concordance of the Swiss Brethren, 1540*, trans. C. A. Synder, ed. G. Fast and G. A. Peters (2001), 56–60 (a frequently reprinted volume listing all the biblical passages on separation that were subjects of Anabaptist sermons, devotions, and catechesis).

85. *The Freeman's Remonstrance*, 5–8, 12. The metaphor is drawn from the recurrent biblical image of the marriage between Christ and the Church, Yahweh and the elect nation of Israel. See esp. Ezekiel 16 and Ephesians 5:25–33.

86. See above, pp. 26–27, and Dreisbach, *Thomas Jefferson and the Wall of Separation*, 83–94; Hamburger, *Separation of Church and State*, 55.

87. Locke, *Works*, 5:82.

88. Dreisbach, *Thomas Jefferson*, 79–82.

89. James Burgh, *Crito, or Essays on Various Subjects* (1767), 2:117–119 (emphasis removed).

90. Condorcet's notes on Voltaire, in *Oeuvres Complètes de Voltaire*, 70 vols. (1784), 18:476, translated in Hamburger, *Separation of Church and State*, 60.

91. John T. Noonan, "The Tensions and the Ideals," in van der Vyver and Witte, eds., *Religious Human Rights*, 593; Russell Hittinger, "Introduction to Modern Catholicism," in John Witte Jr. and Frank S. Alexander, eds., *Modern Christian Teachings on Law, Politics, Society, and Human Nature* (2005), ch. 1.

92. See above, p. 7.

93. Williams, *Essential Rights and Liberties*, 46.

94. Quoted by Dreisbach, *Thomas Jefferson*, at 84–85.

95. Tunis Wortman, *A Solemn Address to Christians and Patriots* (1800), in Sandoz, ed., *Political Sermons*, 1477, 1482, 1487–1488.

96. See above, pp. 47–48, 55.

97. Wortman, *A Solemn Address*, 1488.

98. Ibid.

99. *Cato's Letters*, 2:469.

100. In Adams, *Works*, 3:447. See similar views in *Cato's Letters*, 2:797–803.

101. New York Constitution, Arts. XXXVIII–XXXIX.

102. Letter to Abigail Adams (September 17, 1775), quoted in Davis, *Religion and the Continental Congress*, 69. Adams was complaining about the Georgia delegate The Rev. John Zubly, whose stern Calvinist positions are ably described in Joel A. Nichols, "A Man True to His Principles: John Joachim Zubly and Calvinism," *Journal of Church and State* 43 (2001):297.

103. See John Witte Jr., "A Most Mild and Equitable Establishment of Religion: John Adams and the Massachusetts Experiment," *Journal of Church and State* 41 (1999):213, 242ff.; see also Hamburger, *Separation of Church and State,* 79–88, who also notes opposition to this exclusion of clergy among some Evangelicals, including John Leland.

104. Daniel L. Dreisbach, "The Constitution's Forgotten Religion Clause: Reflections on the Article VI Religious Test Ban," *Journal of Church and State* 38 (1996):261; Davis, *Religion and the Continental Congress,* 50–51, 73–94.

105. South Carolina Constitution, Art. XXI. See also New York Constitution, Arts. XXXVIII–XXXIX (1777); Delaware Constitution, Art. XXIX (1776), Maryland Constitution, Art. XXXVII (1776), North Carolina Constitution, Art. XXXI (1776). Among later constitutions, see Tennessee Constitution, Art. 8 (1796), struck down in *McDaniel v. Paty,* 436 U.S. 618 (1978).

106. See, e.g., *The Political Writings of William Penn,* 101, 112; Hutson, *Forgotten Features,* 133–153; Brian Tierney, "Religious Rights: A Historical Perspective," *Religious Human Rights: Religious Perspectives,* 38ff.

107. Williams, *Essential Rights and Liberties,* 7–8.

108. Charles James, ed., *Documentary History of Struggle for Religious Liberty in Virginia* (1971), 237–238.

109. Madison, "Memorial," para. 2.

110. *The Writings of Thomas Jefferson,* ed. H. Washington, 9 vols. (1853–1854), 8:113 (emphasis added). The Washington edition of the letter inaccurately transcribes "legitimate" as "legislative." See a more accurate transcription in Dreisbach, *Thomas Jefferson,* 148.

111. Ibid.

112. Ibid., 25–54.

113. Quoted in ibid., 152.

114. Ibid., 25–54, 129–133.

115. Lambert, *The Founding Fathers,* 207–235.

116. Hamburger, *Separation of Church and State,* 244–247, 262–267, 305–308, 355–357, 391–399, 414–417, 445–446.

117. See entries under "establish" and "establishment" in John Andrews, *A Complete Dictionary of the English Language,* 4th ed. (1789); John Ash, *A New and Complete Dictionary of the English Language* (1775); Samuel Johnson, *A Dictionary of the English Language,* 4th ed. (1773); William Perry, *The Royal Standard English Dictionary,* 1st Am. ed. (1788); Thomas Sheridan, *A Complete Dictionary of the English Language,* 2d ed. (1789).

118. See T. Jeremy Gunn, *A Standard for Repair: The Establishment Clause, Equality, and Natural Rights* (1992), 46–47, 71–73.

119. Delaware Declaration of Rights (1776), sec. 3; Pennsylvania Declaration of Rights (1776), II.

120. For Randolph, see Elliot, ed., *Debates,* 3:208; see also ibid., 3:431. For Madison, see ibid., 3:313.

121. Quoted in Chester J. Antieau, Arthur T. Downey, and Edward C. Roberts, *Freedom from Federal Establishment: Formation and Early History of the First Amendment Religion Clauses* (1964), 106. Cummins went on to say: "It would be impolite for a state to give preference to one religious order over any others in mat-

ters of state, and to dictate and prescribe in points of religion, in which men have from different modes of education and circumstances of one kind or other, will and must split in opinion." Ibid.

122. New Jersey Constitution (1776), Art. XIX.

123. Elliot, ed., *Debates*, 1:328, 334.

124. *Journal of the Senate of the United States* (1789–), 1:116.

125. Version rejected by the Senate on September 3, 1789. Ibid.

126. Thomas Jefferson, Letter to Rev. Samuel Miller (1808), in *The Founders' Constitution*, 5:98–99.

127. Madison, "Memorial," para. 5.

128. Thomas Paine, *Rights of Man* (1791), in *The Founders' Constitution*, 5:95–96.

129. See Antieau, Downey, and Roberts, *Freedom from Federal Establishment*, 1–92; Michael W. McConnell, "Establishment and Disestablishment at the Founding," *William and Mary Law Review* 44 (2003):2105–2181; Sanford H. Cobb, *The Rise of Religious Liberty in America: A History* (1902).

130. See Hutson, *Forgotten Features*, 111: "The white population of the United States in 1790 has been estimated at 3,173,000. Of this, a thousand or so were Jews who lived in cities along the Atlantic seaboard. Muslims, Hindus, and Buddhists, could be counted on the fingers of one hand." Citing Henry Gemery, "The White Population of the Colonial United States," in Michael R. Haines and Richard H. Steckel, eds., *A Population History of North America* (2000), 150.

131. See esp. sources and discussion in Leo Pfeffer, *Church, State, and Freedom*, rev. ed. (1967); Leonard W. Levy, *The Establishment Clause: Religion and the First Amendment* (1986). These debates began well before the American Revolution.

132. James Madison, Letter to Edward Livingston (1822), in *The Founders' Constitution*, 5:105–106. See also Madison, "Memorial," para. 9: "Distant as it may be in its present form from the Inquisition, it [i.e., the general assessment for religion] differs from it only in degree. The one is the first step, the other the last step in the career of intolerance."

133. See, e.g., *The Freeman's Remonstrance*, 5–11; Isaac Backus, *The Infinite Importance of the Obedience of Faith, and of a Separation from the World, Opened and Demonstrated* (1791), 15–31; id., *Policy as well as Honesty Forbids the Use of Secular Force in Religious Affairs* (1779).

134. See, e.g., Delaware Declaration of Rights (1776), sec. 3; Constitution of Maryland, Declaration of Rights, XXXIII (1776); Constitution of South Carolina (1778), XXXVIII.

135. Declaration of Rights, XXXIII. This was outlawed by amendment, Art. XIII (1810). See Thorpe, ed., *Federal and State Constitutions*, 3:1189, 1705.

136. See examples in my "A Most Mild and Equitable Establishment of Religion."

137. Thomas Jefferson, "Freedom of Religion at the University of Virginia (October 7, 1822)," in *The Complete Jefferson*, 958.

4

FORGING THE
FIRST AMENDMENT
RELIGION CLAUSES

Four views drove much of the early American experiment in religious liberty—Puritan, Evangelical, Enlightenment, and Republican. Six principles of religious liberty were held in common among them—liberty of conscience, free exercise of religion, religious pluralism, religious equality, separation of church and state, and disestablishment of religion. It is in the context of this plurality of opinions and panoply of principles that the First Amendment religion clauses should, in my view, be understood.

In an effort to come to terms with the range of original views on religious liberty, the two previous chapters have touched intermittently on speeches and acts made in the Continental Congress of 1774–1789, the Constitutional Convention of 1787, and the First Session of Congress of 1789. This chapter will digest more carefully the work of these federal bodies up to the final formulation of the First Amendment religion clauses on September 26, 1789. The federal record, in this early period, is rather spare. I shall quote extensively from what is said therein about religion and religious liberty, and then sketch the range of plausible meanings that can be assigned to the final text of the First Amendment: "Congress shall make no law respecting an establishment of religion, or prohibiting the free exercise thereof."

Religion and the Continental Congress

The Continental Congress, comprised of delegates from the colonies, met for the first time on September 5, 1774, to respond to the increasingly harsh economic measures imposed by the British mother country.[1] Its second session, commencing on May 10, 1775, was devoted to coordinating the Revolutionary War against Great Britain. During this session, the Congress also began to emerge as the provisional federal government of the budding nation, a status confirmed by the Articles of Confederation of 1781 and continued till 1789. The Congress's principal mandate was to deal with pressing issues of the military, interstate relationships, national commerce, foreign diplomacy, and the like. But in the course of its work from 1774 to 1789, the Continental Congress did issue a number of acts touching religion.

On the second day of its first session, September 6, 1774, the Continental Congress resolved to open its daily sessions with prayer; an Anglican priest began offering these prayers the next morning, along with Bible readings.[2] During the second session, on December 21, 1776, the Congress appointed two legislative chaplains, an Anglican priest and a Presbyterian divine, who served until 1784, until replaced by two other chaplains appointed by the Congress.[3]

On July 29, 1775, the Congress created the Chaplain Corps of the Continental Army, and appointed and paid chaplains to serve in it. Both as general and as first president, George Washington was a firm supporter of these military chaplains and issued several calls for Congress to increase the number of chaplains who served and several orders for military personnel to make ample use of these chaplains' services.[4]

On June 12, 1775, the Congress issued the first of its four fast-day proclamations, urging a "day of publick humiliation, fasting, and prayer; that we may, with united hearts and voices, unfeignedly confess and deplore our many sins"; that we may "be ever under the care and protection of a kind Providence, and be prospered"; and "that virtue and true religion may revive and flourish throughout our land."[5] On November 1, 1777, the Congress issued its first of what would become annual Thanksgiving Day proclamations. This first proclamation was an overtly Trinitarian Christian statement, providing that "it is the indispensable Duty of all men to adore the superintending Providence of Almighty God; to acknowledge with Gratitude their Obligation to him for Benefits received, and to implore such farther Blessings as they stand in need of." The proclamation set aside a day each year of "solemn thanksgiving and praise":

> That at one Time and with one Voice, the good People may express the grateful Feelings of their Hearts, and consecrate themselves to the Service of their Divine Benefactor; and that, together with their sincere Acknowledgements and Offerings, they may join the penitent Confession of their manifold Sins, whereby they had forfeited every Favour; and their humble and earnest Supplication that it may please God through the Merits of Jesus Christ, mercifully to forgive and blot them out of Remembrance: That it may please him graciously to afford his Blessing on the Governments of these States respectively, and

prosper the public Council of the whole: To inspire our Commanders, both by Land and Sea, and all under them, with that Wisdom and Fortitude which may render them fit instruments, under the Providence of Almighty God, to secure for these United States, the greatest of all human Blessings, Independence and Peace: That it may please him, to prosper the Trade and Manufactures of the People, and the Labour of the Husbandman, that our Land may yield its Increase: To take Schools and Seminaries of Education, so necessary for cultivating the Principles of true Liberty, Virtue and Piety, under his nurturing Hand; and to prosper the Means of Religion, for the promotion and enlargement of that Kingdom, which consisteth *"in Righteousness, Peace, and Joy, in the Holy Ghost."*[6]

Beyond issuing prayers, the Continental Congress took further steps to try to cultivate the moral and religious sentiments of the budding nation. In 1774, for example, Congress resolved to: "encourage frugality, economy, and industry, and . . . discountenance and discourage every species of extravagance and dissipation, especially all horse-racing, and all kinds of gaming, cockfighting, exhibition of shews, plays, and other expensive diversions and entertainments."[7]

During the Revolutionary War against Great Britain, the Continental Congress passed a resolution to protect the conscientious objections of pacifists to participation in war. Various Evangelical groups in the colonies—Quakers, Mennonites, Shakers, and Brethren most prominently—had professed pacifist scruples. The Congress accommodated them in a resolution of 1775 and urged them to assume noncombat duties instead: "As there are some people, who from religious principles, cannot bear arms in any case, this Congress intends no violence to their consciences, but earnestly recommend it to them, to contribute liberally in this time of universal calamity, to the relief of their distressed brethren, in the several colonies, and do all other services to their oppressed Country, which they can consistently [do] with their religious principles."[8]

The Continental Congress expressed ample concern about their Catholic neighbors to the north in Quebec. Initially, their views were hostile. In 1763, Quebec had come to be a British colony. In the Quebec Act of 1774, the British Parliament had guaranteed to these new subjects "free exercise of the religion of the Church of Rome, subject to the king's Supremacy."[9] The Congress denounced this act "for establishing the Roman Catholick religion." It expressed "astonishment that a British Parliament should ever consent to *establish* in that country a religion that has deluged your island in blood, and dispersed impiety, bigotry, persecution, murder and rebellion through every part of the world."[10] During the Revolutionary War with Britain, however, the Congress reversed its sentiments abruptly. Congress sent two letters to their Catholic neighbors in Quebec, urging them to cede from the British and to join the budding American union. In their over-tures, they guaranteed them, inter alia, religious freedom. To press their case, Congress also sent a distinguished delegation to the north with this in-struction:

> You are further to declare that we hold sacred the rights of conscience and may promise to the whole people, solemnly in our name, the free and undis-turbed exercise of their religion; and, to the clergy, the full, perfect, and peace-able possession and enjoyment of all their estates. That the government of everything relating to their religion and clergy, shall be left entirely in the hands of the good people of that province and such legislature as they shall constitute: provided, however, that all other denominations of Christians be equally entitled to hold offices and enjoy civil privileges and the free exercise of their religion and be totally exempt from the payment of any tythes or taxes for the support of any religion.[11]

Also during the Revolutionary War, the Congress sought to encourage defection of German mercenaries who were fighting for Great Britain. It of-fered would-be defectors guarantees of liberty, security, and property. It also ordered all states to receive these soldiers, and ensure that they "be protected in the free exercise of their respective religions."[12]

On September 11, 1777, a narrow majority of the Congress voted to im-port 20,000 Bibles for distribution in the new states. Absent sufficient funds and strong political support, no federal action to procure the Bibles was ever taken. Instead, the Congress resolved tepidly on October 26, 1780: "That it be recommended to such of the States who may think it con-venient for them that they take proper measures to procure one or more new and correct editions of the Old and New Testament to be printed and thus such states regulate their printers by law so as to secure effectively the said books from being misprinted."[13] Thereafter, the Congress also en-dorsed a privately funded translation of the Bible, directed the legislative and military chaplains to make use of it, and recommended "this edition of the Bible to the inhabitants of the United States."[14]

On November 15, 1778, the Congress approved the Articles of Confed-eration, which came to govern the body in 1781. An earlier draft of the ar-ticles, prepared principally by John Dickinson, had included a rather lengthy provision on religious liberty designed to bind the individual colonies and states:

> No person in any Colony living peaceably under the Civil Government, shall be molested or prejudiced in his or her person or Estate for his or her religious persuasion, Profession or practice, nor be compelled to frequent or maintain any religious Worship, Place of Worship, or Ministry, contrary to his or her

Mind, by any Law or ordinance hereafter to be made in any Colony different from the usual Laws & Customs subsisting at the Commencement of this War—provided, that such person frequent regularly some place of religious Worship on the Sabbath; & no religious Persuasion or practise for the Profession or Exercise of which, persons are not disqualified by the present Laws of the said Colonies respectively, from holding any offices Civil or military, shall by any Law or Ordinance hereafter to be made in any Colony, be rendered a Disqualification of any persons profession or exercising the same from holding such offices, as fully as they might have done heretofore: nor shall any further Tests or Qualifications concerning religious persuasion, Profession or Practise, than such have been usually administered in the said Colonies respectively, be imposed by any Law or Ordinance hereafter to be made in any Colony; and whenever on Election or Appointment to any Offices, or any other occasions, the Affirmation of persons conscientiously scrupulous of taking an Oath, hath been admitted in any Colony or Colonies, no Oath shall in any such Cases be hereafter imposed by any Law or Ordinance in any such Colony or Colonies, it being the full Intent of these united Colonies that all the Inhabitants thereof respectively of every Sect, Society, or religious Denomination shall enjoy under this Confederation, all the Liberties and Priviledges [sic] which they have heretofore enjoyed with the least abridgement of their civil Rights for or on Account of their religious Persuasion, profession or practise.[15]

Had this article passed, it would have been a remarkable step on the path toward creating a national law on religious liberty. The Congress, however, rejected this article as too intrusive on local regulation of religion. All that survived in the final Articles of Confederation was Article III, which bound the states to "assist each other, against all force offered to, or attacks made upon them, or any of them, on account of religion."[16]

Three treaties adopted by the Congress included religious liberty clauses. The Treaty with the Netherlands (1782) provided that "[t]here shall be an entire and perfect liberty of conscience allowed to the subjects and inhabitants of each party, and their families; and no one shall be molested in regard to his worship, provided he submits, as to the public demonstration of it, to the laws of the country."[17] The language recurs almost verbatim in a treaty with Sweden (1783). A 1785 treaty with Prussia provided: "The most perfect freedom of conscience and of worship is granted to the citizens or subjects of either party within the jurisdiction of the other, without being liable to molestation in that respect for any cause other than an insult on the religion of others."[18] The final peace treaty with England (1783) was also made "[i]n the name of the Most Holy and Undivided Trinity."[19]

The 1787 Northwest Ordinance, establishing a new territorial government for the midwestern frontier, set forth various "fundamental principles of civil and religious liberty," including: "No person, demeaning himself in a peaceable and orderly manner, shall ever be molested on account of his mode of worship, or religious sentiments"; and "Religion, morality and knowledge, being necessary to good government and the happiness of mankind, schools and the means of education shall forever be encouraged."[20]

The record of the Continental Congress also includes other scattered acknowledgments and endorsements of public worship, Christian thanksgiving, Sunday observance, and confession of sin. The record is also amply peppered with genial references to and invocations of God and Christianity. The most famous of these divine invocations was the Declaration of Independence of 1776, with its references to "the Laws of Nature and Nature's God," "the Creator," "the Supreme Judge of the world," and "a firm reliance on the protection of Divine Providence."[21]

The 1787 Constitutional Convention

The United States Constitution—debated and drafted by the Constitutional Convention from May 25 to September 17, 1787—was largely silent on questions of religion and religious freedom. The preamble to the Constitution speaks generically of the "Blessings of Liberty." Article I, section 7 recognizes the Christian Sabbath: "If any Bill should not be returned by the President within ten days (Sundays excepted) after it shall have been presented to him, the Same shall be a Law." Article VI provides "no religious Test shall ever be required as a Qualification to any Office or public Trust under the United States." A reference to "the Year of our Lord" sneaks into the dating of the instrument. But nothing more. The "Godless Constitution" has been both celebrated and lamented ever since.[22]

The seeming impiety of the work of the 1787 Constitutional Convention must be understood in political context. It was commonly assumed at the convention that questions of religion and of religious liberty were for the states and the people to resolve, not the budding federal government. By 1784, eleven of the thirteen states had already crafted detailed constitutional provisions on religious liberty. The two remaining states, Rhode Island and Connecticut, retained their colonial charters, which included religious liberty clauses. The mandate of the 1787 convention was to create a new national sovereign with enumerated powers and delineated procedures. What was not specifically given to this new federal sovereign was to be retained by the sovereign states and the sovereign people.

Federal power over religion was not considered part of this new constitutional calculus. As James Madison put it to the Virginia Ratification Convention: "There is not a shadow of right in the general government to intermeddle with religion. Its least interference with it, would be a most flagrant usurpation."[23] James Iredell concurred in the North Carolina Ratification

Convention, arguing that the federal branches of government "certainly have no authority to interfere in the establishment of any religion whatsoever, and I am astonished that any gentleman should conceive they have."[24]

Federal protection of religion was also considered beyond the mandate of the 1787 convention. Both the natural checks and balances inherent in the nation's religious pluralism and the new religious liberty provisions of the state constitutions were considered to be ample protection.[25] For the emerging federal constitution to guarantee religious and civil rights was viewed to be unnecessary, if not dangerous. James Wilson put the case famously in the Pennsylvania Ratification Convention:

> [A] bill of rights is neither an essential nor a necessary instrument in framing a system of government, since liberty may exist and be as well secured without it. But it was not only unnecessary, but on this occasion it was found impracticable—for who will be bold enough to undertake to enumerate all the rights of the people?—and when the attempt to enumerate them is made, it must be remembered that if the enumeration is not complete, everything not expressly mentioned will be presumed to be purposely omitted.[26]

Alexander Hamilton warned further in *Federalist Paper No. 84* that to specify federal rights was "not only unnecessary in the proposed Constitution, but would even be dangerous. They would contain various exceptions to powers not granted; and, on this very account, would afford a colorable pretext to claim more than was granted. For why declare that things shall not be done which there is no power to do?"[27]

Accordingly, the three weak attempts to introduce federal protections of religion and religious liberty into the new constitution were quickly quashed. Early in the convention debates, on May 29, 1787, Charles Pinckney of South Carolina submitted to the convention a draft constitution, which included a religion clause: "The Legislature of the United States shall pass no Law on the subject of Religion."[28] Although many of Pinckney's proposed provisions helped to shape the debates and the final form of the Constitution, his religious liberty clause was passed over without comment and died silently in committee. On September 12, five days before the conclusion of the convention, George Mason and Eldridge Gerry moved to designate a committee to attach a bill of rights to the largely completed Constitution. The motion failed 10–0.[29] On September 14, James Madison and Charles Pinckney sought to ascribe to Congress a power "to establish an University, in which no preferences or distinctions should be allowed on account of religion."[30] The motion failed 6–4.

Even Benjamin Franklin's motion to have the convention sessions open with prayer garnered virtually no support. On June 28, the elderly Franklin, exasperated by the casuistic debates in the convention to date, had issued a short sermon to his fellow delegates on the importance of prayer:

> [W]e have not hitherto once thought of humbly applying to the Father of lights to illuminate our understandings. In the beginning of the Contest with G. Britain, when we were sensible of danger we had daily prayer in this room for the divine protection. . . . And have we now forgotten that powerful friend? or do we imagine that we no longer need his assistance? I have lived, Sir, a long time, and the longer I live, the more convincing proofs I see of this truth—*that God governs in the affairs of men*. And if a sparrow cannot fall to the ground without his notice, is it probable that an empire can rise without his aid? We have been assured, Sir, in the sacred writings, that "except the Lord build the House they labour in vain that build it." I firmly believe this; and I also believe that without his concurring aid we shall succeed in this political building no better than the Builders of Babel: We shall be divided by our little partial local interests; our projects will be confounded, and we ourselves shall become a reproach and bye word down to future ages. And what is worse, mankind may hereafter from this unfortunate instance, despair of establishing Governments by Human Wisdom and leave it to chance, war and conquest.
>
> I therefore beg leave to move—that henceforth prayers imploring the assistance of Heaven, and its blessings on our deliberations, be held in this Assembly every morning before we proceed to business, and that one or more of the Clergy of this City be requested to officiate in that service.

Franklin's motion failed, the record reads, for fear it might "1. bring on it some disagreeable animadversions. & 2. lead the public to believe that the embarrassments and dissentions within the convention, had suggested this measure." Moreover, another delegate pointed out, there were no funds to pay for a chaplain to pray.[31]

The only proposal about religion to receive support was Charles Pinckney's proposal that religion not be considered a condition for federal office. On August 20, Pinckney had proposed a freestanding provision in the Constitution prohibiting religious tests or qualifications for federal office.[32] On August 30, he moved to amend a clause specifying the oath of office with the words that would eventually find their way into Article VI of the Constitution: "but no religious test shall ever be required as a qualification to any office or public trust under the authority of the U. States." Only one delegate objected to the motion—not because he favored religious test oaths but because he thought "it unnecessary, the prevailing liberality being a sufficient security against such tests." Pinckney's motion, however, was seconded and passed, with one dissent.[33]

During the ratification debates and thereafter, the no religious test provision of Article VI was sometimes denounced as an invitation to "Papists" and "Mahometans," and even "infidels" and "pagans," to hold federal office. It was defended, as we saw, on principles both of liberty of conscience and equality of faiths before the federal law.[34] But in the 1787 convention itself, the almost casual passage of the prohibition against religious tests for federal office was testimony to the commonality of the assumption that religion and religious liberty were beyond the pale of federal authority.

Ratification and Proposed Amendments

The Constitutional Convention completed its draft Constitution on September 17, 1787. The Continental Congress approved it by unanimous vote on September 28 and sent it on to the states for ratification. Article VII of the proposed Constitution required ratification by the "Conventions of nine States." The Constitution was ratified on July 2, 1788, when the ninth vote, from the New Hampshire Ratification Convention, was recorded.[35]

The absence of a bill of rights to the Constitution, however, was a point of considerable controversy in the state ratification debates. Despite the repeated assurances of the federalists that Congress could not exercise power over subjects like religion that were not specifically enumerated in the Constitution, only four states would ratify the instrument without a federal bill of rights. The remaining states ratified the Constitution only on the promise that the First Session of Congress would prepare a bill of rights to amend the Constitution. Seven states ultimately proposed provisions to be included in a federal bill of rights. Of these, six proposed religious liberty clauses, with some overlap in content. Four of these proposed amendments on religious liberty, tendered in the summer of 1788, were critical.[36]

On June 21, 1788, New Hampshire proposed the following religious liberty amendment:

[1] Congress shall make no laws touching religion, or to infringe the rights of conscience.[37]

On June 26, 1788, Virginia—stating its concern "that no right of any denomination" may be violated and "among other essential rights, the liberty of conscience, and of the press, cannot be cancelled, abridged, restrained, or modified, by any authority of the United States"—proposed the following amendment:

[2] That religion, or the duty which we owe to our creator, and the manner of discharging it, can be directed only by reason and conviction, not by force or violence, and therefore all men have an equal, natural and unalienable right to the free exercise of religion according to the dictates of conscience, and that no

particular religious sect or society ought to be favored or established by law in preference to others.[38]

On July 26, 1788, New York proposed:

[3] That the people have an equal, natural, and unalienable right freely and peaceably to exercise their religion, according to the dictates of conscience; and that no religious sect or society ought to be favored or established by law in preference to others.[39]

On August 1, 1788, North Carolina—resolving to protect the "great principles of civil and religious liberty"—repeated the Virginia provision (with only cosmetic changes in punctuation), prefaced by a conscientious objection clause:

[4] That any person religiously scrupulous of bearing arms ought to be exempted, upon payment of an equivalent to employ another to bear arms in his stead.[40]

Rhode Island repeated North Carolina's language in its proposed amendment, belatedly tendered on June 16, 1790.[41]

Drafting the First Amendment Religious Clauses

It was up to the First Session of Congress to cull from these proposals, and the broader traditions that they represented, a suitable amendment on religious rights and liberties. The record of the Congress's effort is considerably slimmer than is apt for such a momentous act. Neither the House nor the Senate kept an official record of its proceedings in this first year. The Senate met in closed session and merely kept a journal of brief minutes of its resolutions. The House debates were sometimes open to visitors; much of what appears in the *Annals of Congress* for the First Session of 1789 is drawn from the inexactly taken and transcribed notes of newspaper reporter Thomas Lloyd.[42] These minutes and notes do include several drafts of the religion clauses that were considered intermittently between June 8 and September 26, 1789. They also include summaries and paraphrases of a few of the House debates on August 15, 17, and 20. But for the critical stages of deliberation in late August and September 1789 when these various drafts and speeches were pressed into the final text of the First Amendment, the record is exceedingly cryptic and conclusory—leaving courts and commentators ever since with ample room for speculation and interpolation.

On June 8, 1789, James Madison, a newly elected representative from Virginia, proposed to the House of Representatives that they take up the task of preparing a bill of rights to the United States Constitution. He had reduced the multiple state proposals for rights provisions into a draft, which included two religion clauses. These he put to the House for consideration:

[5] The civil rights of none shall be abridged on account of religious belief or worship, nor shall any national religion be established, nor shall the full and equal rights of conscience be in any manner, or any pretext infringed.

[6] No state shall violate the equal rights of conscience, or the freedom of the press, or the trial by jury in criminal cases.[43]

The House agreed to give formal consideration to Madison's proposals in due course. But debate was postponed for several weeks as Congress devoted itself to the immediate task of organizing the new government.[44]

On July 21, again prompted by Madison, the House finally turned to Madison's proposals and appointed a committee comprised of one representative of each of the eleven states represented in the First Congress.[45] Madison, representing Virginia, was included. This committee of eleven put forward its proposed rights provisions on July 28, including three separate provisions on religion:

[7] no religion shall be established by law, nor shall the equal rights of conscience be infringed.

[8] no person religiously scrupulous shall be compelled to bear arms.

[9] no State shall infringe the equal rights of conscience, nor the freedom of speech or of the press, nor of the right of trial by jury in criminal cases.

The committee's report was tabled without any recorded discussion. On August 13, the House, sitting as a committee of the whole, took up the report, one provision at a time.

On August 15, the House reached the first of the three committee provisions on religion: "no religion shall be established by law, nor shall the equal rights of conscience be infringed." The House ultimately approved an amended version of the same. The full record of their debate, highlighting the amended provision, reads thus:

Mr. SYLVESTER had some doubts of the propriety of the mode of expression used in this paragraph. He apprehended that it was liable to a construction different from what had been made by the committee. He feared it might be thought to have a tendency to abolish religion altogether.

Mr. VINING suggested the propriety of transposing the two members of the sentence.

Mr. GERRY said it would read better if it was, that no religious doctrine shall be established by law.

Mr. SHERMAN thought the amendment altogether unnecessary, inasmuch as Congress had no authority whatever delegated to them by the constitution to make religious establishments; he would, therefore, move to have it struck out.

Mr. [Daniel] CARROLL. As the rights of conscience are, in their nature, of peculiar delicacy, and will little bear the gentlest touch of governmental hand; and as many sects have concurred in opinion that they are not well secured under the present constitution, he said he was much in favor of adopting the words. He thought it would tend more towards conciliating the minds of the people to the Government than almost any other amendment he had heard proposed. He would not contend with gentlemen about the phraseology, his object was to secure the substance in such a manner as to satisfy the wishes of the honest part of the community.

Mr. MADISON said, he apprehended the meaning of the words to be, that Congress should not establish a religion, and enforce the legal observation of it by law, nor compel men to worship God in any manner contrary to their conscience. Whether the words are necessary or not, he did not mean to say, but they had been required by some of the State Conventions, who seemed to entertain an opinion that under the clause of the constitution, which gave power to Congress to make all laws necessary and proper to carry into execution the constitution, and the laws made under it, enabled them to make laws of such a nature as might infringe the rights of conscience, and establish a national religion; to prevent these effects he presumed the amendment was intended, and he thought it as well expressed as the nature of the language would admit.

Mr. HUNTINGTON said that he feared, with the gentleman first up on this subject, that the words might be taken in such latitude as to be extremely hurtful to the cause of religion. He understood the amendment to mean what had been expressed by the gentleman from Virginia; but others might find it convenient to put another construction upon it. The ministers of their congregations to the Eastward were maintained by the contributions of those who belonged to their society; the expense of building meetinghouses was contributed in the same manner. These things were regulated by by-laws. If an action was brought before a Federal Court on any of these cases, the person who had neglected to perform his engagements could not be compelled to do it; for a support of ministers, or building of places of worship might be construed into a religious establishment.

By the charter of Rhode Island, no religion could be established by law; he could give a history of the effects of such a regulation; indeed the people were now enjoying the blessed fruits of it. He hoped, therefore, the amendment would be made in such a way as to secure the rights of conscience, and a free exercise of the rights of religion, but not to patronize those who professed no religion at all.

Mr. MADISON thought, if the word national was inserted before religion, it would satisfy the minds of honorable gentlemen. He believed that the people feared one sect might obtain a pre-eminence, or two combine together, and establish a religion to which they would compel others to conform. He thought if the word national was introduced, it would point the amendment directly to the object it was intended to prevent.

Mr. LIVERMORE was not satisfied with that amendment; but he did not wish them to dwell long on the subject. He thought it would be better if it was altered, and made to read in this manner, that [10] **Congress shall make no laws touching religion, or infringing the rights of conscience.**

Mr. GERRY did not like the term national, proposed by the gentleman from Virginia, and he hoped it would not be adopted by the House. It brought to his mind some observations that had taken place in the conventions at the time they were considering the present constitution. It had been insisted upon by those who were called antifederalists, that this form of Government consolidated the Union; the honorable gentleman's motion shows that he considers it in the same light. Those who were called antifederalists at that time complained that they had injustice done them by the title, because they were in favor of a Federal Government, and the others were in favor of a national one; the federalists were for ratifying the constitution as it stood, and the others not until amendments were made. Their names then ought not to have been distinguished by federalists and antifederalists, but rats and antirats.

Mr. MADISON withdrew his motion, but observed that the words "no national religion shall be established by law," did not imply that the Government was a national one; **the question was then taken on Livermore's motion, and passed in the affirmative,** thirty-one for, and twenty against it.[46]

On August 17, the House came to the second provision on religion in the committee report: "no person religiously scrupulous shall be compelled to bear arms." The record of their debate, which ended inconclusively, reads thus:

Mr. GERRY—This declaration of rights, I take it, is intended to secure the people against the mal-administration of the Government; if we could suppose that, in all cases, the rights of the people would be attended to, the occasion for guards of this kind would be removed. Now, I am apprehensive, sir, that this clause would give an opportunity to the people in power to destroy the constitution itself. They can declare who are those religiously scrupulous, and prevent them from bearing arms. . . . Now, if we give a discretionary power to exclude those from militia duty who have religious scruples, we may as well make no provision on this head. For this reason, he wished the words to be altered so as to be confined to persons belonging to a religious sect scrupulous of bearing arms.

Mr. JACKSON did not expect that all the people of the United States would turn Quakers or Moravians; consequently, one part would have to defend the other in case of invasion. Now this, in his opinion, was unjust, unless the constitution secured an equivalent: for this reason he moved to amend the clause, by inserting at the end of it, "upon paying an equivalent, to be established by law."

Mr. SMITH, of South Carolina, inquired what were the words used by the conventions respecting this amendment. If the gentleman would conform to what was proposed by Virginia and Carolina, he would second him. He thought they were to be excused provided they found a substitute.

Mr. JACKSON was willing to accommodate. He thought the expression was, "No one, religiously scrupulous of bearing arms, shall be compelled to render military service, in person, upon paying an equivalent."

Mr. SHERMAN conceived it difficult to modify the clause and make it better. It is well known that those who are religiously scrupulous of bearing arms are equally scrupulous of getting substitutes or paying an equivalent. Many of them would rather die than do either one or the other; but he did not see an absolute necessity for a clause of this kind. We do not live under an arbitrary Government, said he, and the States, respectively, will have the government of the militia, unless when called into actual service; besides, it would not do to alter it so as to exclude the whole of any sect, because there are men amongst the Quakers who will turn out, notwithstanding the religious principles of the society, and defend the cause of their country. Certainly it will be improper to prevent the exercise of such favorable dispositions, at least whilst it is the practice of nations to determine their contests by the slaughter of their citizens and subjects.

Mr. VINING hoped the clause would be suffered to remain as it stood, because he saw no use in it if it was amended so as to compel a man to find a substitute, which, with respect to the Government, was the same as if the person himself turned out to fight.

Mr. STONE inquired what the words "religiously scrupulous" had reference to: was it of bearing arms? If it was, it ought so to be expressed.

Mr. BENSON moved to have the words "but no person religiously scrupulous shall be compelled to bear arms," struck out. He would always leave it to the benevolence of the Legislature, for, modify it as you please, it will be impossible to express it in such a manner as to clear it from ambiguity. No man can claim this indulgence of right. It may be a religious persuasion, but it is no natural right, and therefore ought to be left to the discretion of the Government. If this stands part of the constitution, it will be a question before the Judiciary on every regulation you make with respect to the organization of the militia, whether it comports with this declaration or not. It is extremely injudicious to intermix matters of doubt with fundamentals.

I have no reason to believe but that the Legislature will always possess humanity enough to indulge this class of citizens in a matter they are so desirous of; but they ought to be left for their discretion.

The motion for striking out the whole clause being seconded, was put, and decided in the negative—22 members voting for it, and 24 against it.[47]

Later that same day of August 17, the House debated the third of the provisions recommended by the committee: "no State shall infringe the equal rights of conscience, nor the freedom of speech or of the press, nor of the right of trial by jury in criminal cases." It approved a slightly amended version:

Mr. TUCKER.—This is offered, I presume, as an amendment to the constitution of the United States, but it goes only to the alteration of the constitutions of particular States. It will be much better, I apprehend, to leave the State Governments to themselves, and not to interfere with them more than we already do; and that is thought by many to be rather too much. I therefore move, sir, to strike out these words.

Mr. MADISON conceived this to be the most valuable amendment in the whole list. If there was any reason to restrain the Government of the United States from infringing upon these essential rights, it was equally necessary that they should be secured against the State Governments. He thought that if they provided against the one, it was as necessary to provide against the other, and was satisfied that it would be equally grateful to the people.

Mr. LIVERMORE had no great objection to the sentiment, but he thought it not well expressed. He wished to make it an affirmative proposition; [11] "**the equal rights of conscience, the freedom of speech or of the press, and the right of trial by jury in criminal cases, shall not be infringed by any State.**"

This transposition being agreed to, and Mr. TUCKER's motion being rejected, the clause was adopted.[48]

Up to this point, the House had considered its rights amendments as individual provisions to be inserted at appropriate places in the body of the Constitution. On August 20, the House agreed to consolidate these multiple rights provisions, including those on religion, into a more systematic and uniform "supplement" to the Constitution—a separate bill of rights.[49] The three provisions on religion discussed to date were distilled into two provisions. The brief record of the debate on these two provisions on August 20, follows:

On motion of Mr. AMES, the fourth amendment was altered so as to read:

[12] "**Congress shall make no law establishing religion, or to prevent the free exercise thereof, or to infringe the rights of conscience.**" This being adopted, the first proposition was agreed to.

Mr. SCOTT objected to the clause in the sixth amendment, "No person religiously scrupulous shall be compelled to bear arms." He observed that if this becomes part of the constitution, such persons can neither be called upon for their services, nor can an equivalent be demanded; it is also attended with still further difficulties, for a militia can never be depended upon. This would lead to the violation of another article in the constitution, which secures to the people the right of keeping arms, and in this case recourse must be had to a standing army. I conceive it, said he, to be a legislative right altogether. There are many sects I know, who are religiously scrupulous in this respect; I do not mean to deprive them of any indulgence the law affords; my design is to guard against those who are of no religion. It has been urged that religion is on the decline; if so, the argument is more strong in my favor, for when the time comes that religion shall be discarded, the generality of persons will have recourse to these pretexts to get excused from bearing arms.

Mr. BOUDINOT thought the provision in the clause, or something similar to it, was necessary. Can any dependence, said he, be placed in men who are conscientious in this respect: or what justice can there be in compelling them to bear arms, when, according to their religious principles, they would rather die than use them? He adverted to several instances of oppression on this point, that occurred during the war. In forming a militia, an effectual defence ought to be calculated, and no characters of this religious description ought to be compelled to take up arms. I hope that in establishing this Government, we may show the world that proper care is taken that the Government may not interfere with the religious sentiments of any person. Now, by striking out the clause, people may be led to believe that there is an intention in the General Government to compel all its citizens to bear arms.

Some further desultory conversation arose, and it was agreed to insert the words "in person" to the end of the clause; after which it was adopted. (This yielded

[13] "No person religiously scrupulous shall be compelled to bear arms in person.")[50]

On August 22, these two provisions on religion, along with other amendments, were referred to a House style committee.[51] Two days later, the committee issued its final report. The report included the first religion provision, introduced by Fisher Ames on August 20, but slightly revised. It omitted the second provision without explanation. This final House version, sent to the Senate on August 25, reads thus:

[14] Congress shall make no law establishing religion, or prohibiting the free exercise thereof, nor shall the rights of conscience be infringed.[52]

On September 3, the Senate took up debate on this religion clause proposed by the House. No record of their debate survives. The *Journal of the Senate* reports that separate motions first to adopt and later to strike the House provision on religion were defeated.[53] The journal then reports that three alternative drafts of the religion clauses were proposed and defeated. These read seriatim:

[15] Congress shall make no law establishing One Religious Sect or Society in preference to others, nor shall the rights of conscience be infringed.[54]

[16] Congress shall not make any law, infringing the rights of conscience, or establishing any Religious Sect or Society.[55]

[17] Congress shall make no law establishing any particular denomination of religion in preference to another, or prohibiting the free exercise thereof, nor shall the rights of conscience be infringed.[56]

Although none of these versions passed, the Senate did agree to a fourth proposal on September 3:

[18] Congress shall make no law establishing religion, or prohibiting the free exercise thereof.[57]

Agreement on this clause, however, was short-lived. On September 9, the Senate passed a rather different version of the religion clause, now combined with clauses on free speech, press, and assembly.

[19] Congress shall make no law establishing articles of faith or a mode of worship, or prohibiting the free exercise of religion, or abridging the freedom of speech, or the press, or the right of the people peaceably to assemble, and petition to the Government for the redress of grievances.[58]

That same day, September 9, the Senate sent this final version to the House for approval.

The House rejected this version. A joint committee, composed of three representatives and three senators was appointed to forge a consensus draft. Representing the House were three members of the original committee of eleven that had prepared the draft religion clauses of July 28—Madison; Roger Sherman, a Puritan from Connecticut; and John Vining, a Republican from Delaware. Representing the Senate were Oliver Ellsworth, a Connecticut Republican; William Patterson, an Evangelical from New Jersey; and Charles Carroll, a Catholic from Maryland.[59] No record of their debate survives. On September 24, 1789, they reported the final text that came to be the First Amendment:

[20] Congress shall make no Law respecting an establishment of Religion, or prohibiting the free exercise thereof.[60]

On September 25, the Senate concurred in the House resolution to send the draft Bill of Rights, including this religion clause, to President Washington. It was sent the following day, and the president sent it to the states for ratification. The final vote needed for ratification, from Virginia, was recorded on December 15, 1791, rendering the amendments effective from that day forward.

The Final Text

Determining the original understanding of the First Amendment has been the perennial challenge of the American experiment ever since. The final text has no plain meaning. The congressional record holds no Rosetta Stone for easy interpretation. Twenty separate drafts of the religion clauses (highlighted and numbered above) came under Congress's consideration— four tendered by the states, ten debated in the House, five more debated in the Senate, and the final draft forged by the joint committee of the House and Senate. The congressional record holds no dispositive argument against any one of the nineteen interim drafts and few clear clues on why the sixteen words that comprise the final text were chosen.

A Thinner Reading

One plausible reading is that the final text is a compromise agreement only on the outer boundaries of appropriate congressional action on religion. *Congress* may not *prescribe* religion. *Congress* may not *proscribe* religion. Nothing more—and to try to impute more to the text is to overread the unreliable record of debates in the First Congress.

On this reading, the First Amendment leaves open to later discussion and development which governmental bodies, besides Congress, might be bound. Earlier drafts of the religion clauses had bound the states by name—"no state may infringe [or "violate"] the equal rights of conscience" (Draft Nos. 6, 9, 11). Other drafts had been written in the passive voice and were thus potentially applicable to all government officials—"no religion shall be established by law, nor shall the equal rights of conscience be infringed"; "the people have an equal, natural, and unalienable right freely and peaceably to exercise their religion according to the dictates of conscience" (Nos. 2–5, 7, 8, 13). But in the final text, Congress alone is singled out for special limitation in a way that no other amendment in the Bill of Rights seeks to do.

On this reading, the First Amendment also leaves open to later discussion and development what conduct short of prescribing or proscribing religion is outlawed. Earlier drafts of the disestablishment clause had included much more sweeping language: Congress was not to "touch" or "favor" religion; not to give "preference" to any religious sect society, or denomination; not to "establish" any articles of faith or mode of worship (Nos. 1–3, 10, 15–17, 19). Such provisions were left aside for the more blunt provision that Congress should simply not do anything that would point to ("respect") an establishment of religion. It is an open question whether congressional conduct favorable toward religion, but not of a sort traditionally associated with an established religion, is outlawed by the instrument.

Likewise, the first seventeen drafts of the free exercise clause had included much more sweeping guarantees: Congress was not to "touch," "infringe," "abridge," "violate," "compel" or "prevent" the exercise of religion or the rights and freedom of conscience. Again, such provisions were left aside for a more blunt provision: Congress should simply not "prohibit" the free exercise of religion. It is an open question whether governmental conduct short of outright prohibition of religious exercise is outlawed.

Such a thin reading of the religion clauses comports with the eighteenth-century ideal that the new Constitution is a blueprint of government, not a code of governmental conduct. The First Amendment simply sets the outer boundaries to appropriate congressional action—no prescription and no proscription of religion. But it leaves the middle way between these outer boundaries open to constitutional discussion and development. The founders knew that this middle way was not uncharted and that the discussion was not unprincipled. After all, the nineteen earlier drafts of the religion clauses included five of the six main principles of religious liberty regularly discussed in the founding era. Concern for the liberty (or rights or scruples) of conscience appear in fifteen drafts. Free exercise appears in nine drafts, religious equality in nine, religious pluralism in six, disestablishment in twelve. (Conspicuously absent from all the drafts is the principle of separation of church and state.)

It is instructive, on this thinner reading, that Congress chose the terms "free exercise" and "establishment" to define the outer boundaries of proper congressional conduct. As we saw, these were the broadest terms at hand to describe the principles and province of religious liberty. "Free exercise" was at once a source, summary, and synonym for "liberty of conscience," "religious equality," "religious pluralism," and "separation of church and state." "Non-" or "disestablishment" was broadly defined as a general guarantee of "religious equality," "liberty of conscience," and "separation of church and state."[61] The religion clauses, therefore, set only outside limits to Congress's action respecting religion. But the guarantees of disestablishment and free exercise together had embodied—incorporated—within them the full range of first principles of religious liberty prized by the founders. And these first principles would help set the metes and bounds of the proper constitutional way between these two outer boundaries.

Thicker Readings

The record of the debates over the religion clauses can also support some-what more nuanced interpretations. The temptation to self-serving present-mindedness, of course, increases as one thickens the interpretation. But even a cautious reading of the spare record suggests a bit more about the original understanding of some of the words and phrases.

"Congress". The specification of "Congress" underscored the founders' general agreement that the religion clauses were binding not on the states but on the most dangerous branch of the new federal government. This was the strong sentiment already in the Continental Congress, and it continued in the 1787 Constitutional Convention and the state ratification debates. It was repeated in the surviving speeches of Representatives Sherman, Liver-more, Gerry, and Tucker in the House.

The first draft of the religion clauses, submitted by New Hampshire, had specified "Congress" (No. 1). The three other state drafts submitted in the summer of 1788 included general guarantees of religious liberty that could be read to bind both federal and state governments. In his June 8, 1789, consolidated draft, Madison had sought to accommodate both readings—by outlawing a "national" establishment and by prohibiting states from in-fringing on conscience (Nos. 5, 6). This construction failed, despite Madi-son's two arguments for it in the August 15 debate. The original New Hampshire focus on "Congress" (No. 1) became the norm.

In his same June 8 draft, Madison had also included generic guarantees of religious liberty without specifying the government entity bound thereby—"the full and equal rights of conscience shall not be infringed" and "the civil rights of none shall be abridged on account of religion" (No. 5). Such provisions, too, died without explanation. By August 20, Fisher Ames's draft (No. 12) specified Congress alone, and the Senate held to this.

"Shall Make". The phrase "shall make no law" is rather distinctive—written in a future active imperative voice, as our grammar teachers would say. In eighteenth-century parlance, "shall," as opposed to "will," is an im-perative; it is an order, rather than a prediction, about what Congress does in the future. "Shall" is so used fifteen times in the Bill of Rights alone. But why the construction "shall make no law," which is a phrasing unique to the First Amendment? Could it be that Congress could make no new laws on religion but could confirm laws that had already been made—before the First Amendment was passed, or by the Continental Congress before it?

Such a reading seems fanciful until one notes the exchange in the House, on September 25, 1787, the very day the House approved the final text of the religion clauses. Elias Boudinot of New Jersey, who chaired the recorded House debates on the religion clauses, announced that "he could not think of letting the session pass over without offering an opportunity to all the citizens of the United States of joining, with one voice, in returning to Almighty God their sincere thanks for the many blessings he had poured down upon them." He then moved that both houses of Congress request the president to set aside a day of "public thanksgiving and prayer, to be observed by acknowledging . . . the many signal favors of Almighty God." Aedanus Burke of South Carolina thought this too redolent of a military European custom, which made "a mere mockery of thanksgiving." Thomas Tucker, also of South Carolina, objected that "it is a business with which Congress ha[s] nothing to do; it is a religious matter, and, as such, is proscribed to us. If a day of thanksgiving must take place, let it be done by the authority of the several States; they know best what reason their constituents have to be pleased with the establishment of the Constitution." Roger Sherman countered that the tradition of offering such public prayers was "laudable," and after citing a few biblical precedents for it, declared the practice "worthy of Christian imitation on the present occasion." Boudinot defended his motion on grounds that it was "a measure both prudent and just" and quoted "further precedents from the practice of the late [Continental] Congress" to drive home his point. The motion passed in the House, and later also in the Senate.[62] President Washington set aside a Thanksgiving Day and gave a robust proclamation on October 3, 1789.

This was not the only such inherited tradition touching religion that the First Congress confirmed and continued. On April 15, 1789, before deliberating the religion clauses, the Congress voted to appoint "two Chaplains of different denominations" to serve Congress, one in each house.[63] On April 27, the Congress ordered, relevant to the pending inauguration of President Washington: "That after the oath shall have been administered to the President, he, attended by the Vice President, and members of the Senate, and House of Representatives, proceed to St. Paul's Chapel, to hear divine service, to be performed by the Chaplain of Congress already appointed."[64] These chaplains served the Congress throughout the period of the debates on the religion clauses. On September 22, 1789, just as the joint committee was polishing the final draft of the religion clauses, Congress passed an act confirming their appointment and stipulating that the chaplains were to be paid a salary of $500 per annum.[65] Similarly, on August 7, 1789, after the committee of eleven had put to the House its three proposed religion clauses (Nos. 7–9), the Congress reenacted without issue the Northwest Ordinance, with its two religion clauses: "No person, demeaning himself in a peaceable and orderly manner, shall ever be molested on account of his mode of worship, or religious sentiments"; and "Religion, morality and knowledge, being necessary to good government and happiness of mankind, schools and other means of education shall forever be encouraged."[66]

One cannot lean too heavily on this construction of the phrase "shall make no law." First, the congressional record is too blunt and cryptic to decide whether such a subtle play on words was deliberate. Second, it must be remembered that the First Congress served as both a legislature and a constitutional drafter in 1789. Its legislative acts were driven by the fleeting necessities of the time, its constitutional amendments by the enduring needs of the nation. And the two kinds of acts should not be conflated.

Nonetheless, it is rather clear that the First Congress had little compunction about confirming and continuing the Continental Congress's tradition of supporting chaplains, prayers, Thanksgiving Day proclamations, and religious education. And, in later sessions in the 1790s and 1800s, the Congress also continued the Continental Congress's practice of including religion clauses in its treaties, condoning the American edition of the Bible, funding chaplains in the military, and celebrating religious services officiated by congressional chaplains—all with very little dissent or debate. The ease with which Congress passed such laws does give some guidance on what forms of religious support the First Congress might have condoned.

"Respecting an Establishment". The phrase *"respecting an establishment of religion"* has long been the most hotly contested phrase of the First Amendment. We certainly cannot resolve all the modern contests on a reading of the congressional record alone. But at least three plausible lines of interpretation that speak to perennial questions of the relationship of religion and government can be made out.

Thirteen of the nineteen drafts of the religion clauses included disestablishment clauses. The only recorded debate is that of August 15 on the formulation: "no religion shall be established by law" (No. 7). Although all the words of the final text of the disestablishment clause appear and recur in earlier drafts, the word "respecting" is new. It is a studiously ambiguous term, variously defined in the day as: "to look at, regard, or consider"; to "heed or pay attention to"; "to regard with deference, esteem, or honor"; to "expect, anticipate, look toward."[67]

One plausible reading of the final text is that Congress shall make no laws "respecting" a *state establishment* of religion. In 1789, six states still had some form of religious establishment, which both their state legislatures and constitutional conventions defined and defended, often against strong opposition from religious dissenters. Moreover, Virginia had just passed Jefferson's bill "for the *establishment* of religious freedom," also against firm opposition by defenders of the traditional establishment of Anglicanism. Having just defended their state establishments (of whatever sort) at home, the new members of Congress were not about to relinquish control of them to the new federal government. There was special concern to prevent Congress, the lawmaking body, from passing laws that might interfere in such religious matters—particularly through the "necessary and proper clause" of Article I, which Madison in the August 15 debate signaled as the danger point. There was also some concern—reflected both in Representative Huntington's second intervention on August 15 and in Representative Benson's intervention on August 17—about state actions on religion being adjudicated in "federal courts."

To be sure, the First Congress had already quite explicitly rejected those drafts of the religion clauses that bound the states directly and those that were cast in general terms and thus potentially binding on the states. And to be sure, the Tenth Amendment (which was under discussion in the Congress at the same time) guaranteed generally: "The powers not delegated to the United States by the Constitution . . . are reserved to the States respectively, or to the people." But perhaps on so sensitive an issue as religion, it was best to be triply sure—and explicitly outlaw any congressional interference in the states' establishments of religion or of religious freedom. Perhaps, in the final House-Senate committee of six, it was the hard political issue of federal versus state power that was resolved by adding the curious phrase "respecting an establishment." Congress could simply make no law that "looked at," "regarded," or "paid attention to" a state establishment of religion—whether benignly or unfavorably.

This reading of the disestablishment clause would be considerably easier to press if the final draft said "a *state* establishment," rather than "*an establishment.*" But since reference to "state establishments" had not appeared before in the drafts, perhaps the final committee thought it prudent to avoid introducing a new contested term so late in the debate—particularly given the squabbling over the term "*national* establishment" in the August 15 House debate.

A second plausible reading is that Congress could neither establish religion outright nor make laws that would "point toward," "anticipate," or "reflect" such an establishment. On this reading, Congress could not pass a comprehensive new religion law defining the texts, doctrines, and liturgies of the nation's faith and/or governing religious polity, clergy, and property. Such a law, reflective of prevailing English ecclesiastical laws, would clearly be unconstitutional. But that was not the founders' only fear, according to this reading. Congress could also not make more discrete laws that might "respect"—that is, point toward, anticipate, or reflect—such an establishment. The First Congress's concern was to prevent not only a single comprehensive law that established a national religion but also piecemeal laws that would move incrementally toward the same.

The disestablishment clause, on this reading, was not necessarily a prohibition against all laws "touching" religion, as some earlier drafts had indicated. After all, Congress had already passed several such laws (supporting chaplains, prayers, religious education, and Thanksgiving Day proclamations). Such laws presumably did not point toward or reflect an established religion but simply reflected commonplaces of the day about what was proper for the young nation. But the disestablishment clause was a rather firm barrier against a large number of laws touching religion that might move toward an establishment.

This reading turns on a crucial judgment about why the First Congress had rejected earlier drafts that were more specific about defining a religious establishment. On August 15, the House debated whether to outlaw "religious establishment" per se (No. 7). There seemed to be consensus on this, as Roger Sherman said early in the debate. The moment that the representatives began to specify what they meant by religious establishment, however, the conversation broke down: Gerry was concerned about establishing religious doctrines, Huntington about forced payments of religious tithes, Madison about compulsory worship of God and giving preeminence to one sect—all of which were features of a traditional establishment of religion. The initial compromise was Livermore's clause that sought "no law touching religion" at all (No. 10). By August 20, the House had returned to the language that opened the August 15 debate: "no law establishing religion" (No. 12). That was the language sent to the Senate. The Senate also could not nuance this "no establishment" formulation—failing to reach agreement on clauses that would outlaw the establishment of "one Religious Sect or Society" or of "articles of faith or a mode of worship" or that would outlaw the preference of one religious sect, society, or denomination (Nos. 15–17, 19). On this second reading of the disestablishment clause, the word "respecting," therefore, becomes something of an umbrella term for these and other features of a religious establishment. Congress could not agree on what specifics of religious establishment to outlaw—and so they simply outlawed the establishment of religion altogether and anything that "pointed to" or "moved toward" the same.

On the first reading, the disestablishment clause is a limited prohibition against congressional interference with state controls of religion. This leaves little guidance for what Congress might do at the federal level respecting (an establishment of) religion. On the second reading, the disestablishment clause is a comprehensive prohibition against any congressional inclination toward establishing religion. This leaves a little room for Congress to pass laws "touching religion," but not much. Between these two readings of "respecting an establishment" of religion, one can find in the literature a whole host of alternatives.

Among the more popular of such intermediate readings is that of "nonpreferentialism." The disestablishment clause, on this reading, simply outlaws preferential support for a "national religion" but allows for "nonpreferential" support for multiple religions. On this reading, the feature of "establishment" that concerned Congress most was not a grand scheme of ecclesiastical law as prevailed in England; that was clearly beyond the pale, and no one was seriously advocating this for America in the 1780s. Congress's real concern was to avoid official "preferences" for certain religious sects, denominations, doctrines, or modes of worship. Six drafts of the religion clauses, including the penultimate one, sought to formulate this directly by outlawing various types of "preferential" establishments by name (Nos. 2, 3, 15–17, 19). None of these drafts passed muster. But Congress accomplished its goal of outlawing preferential support more efficiently by simply prohibiting laws against "an" establishment of this sort—rather than prohibiting laws against "the" establishment of religion altogether. On this formulation, Congress could certainly "touch religion"—rather generously in fact—so long as it did so in a way that would not prefer one religious sect or society above another. And Congress demonstrated what such nonpreferential support meant by appointing and funding chaplains from different denominations, supporting general "religious education," and condoning pious but nondenominational prayers and Thanksgiving Day proclamations.

This "nonpreferential" reading of the disestablishment clause, while certainly plausible, relies heavily on Madison's rejected concern about "national establishment." It does rather little to explain the insertion of the curious word "respecting." It also relies heavily on a clever distinction between "an" and "the" establishment of religion—words on which the sloppy congressional record slipped more than once.[68]

"Prohibiting Free Exercise". Although the origins of the disestablishment clause have long occupied commentators, the origins of the free exercise clause have only recently come into prominent discussion. A modern controversy has driven much of the new interest—the weakening of the free exercise clause, culminating in the Supreme Court case of *Employment Division v. Smith* (1990) and Congress's various attempts to restore a more rigorous free exercise test. Here, too, as in the case of the disestablishment clause, the record does not resolve all modern questions. Indeed, in the case of the free exercise clause, the congressional record raises as many questions as it answers.

First, as we noted in the "thinner" reading above, the free exercise clause merely outlaws congressional acts that "prohibit" the free exercise of religion. Earlier drafts had included much more embracive protections, outlawing laws that would "touch," "infringe," "abridge," "violate," "compel" or "prevent" the same. All this is replaced by the seemingly minimalist guarantee that Congress not "prohibit" the free exercise of religion.

Second, the free exercise clause is not matched by a liberty of conscience clause. The first seventeen drafts of the religion clauses had included a provision protecting the liberty or rights of conscience, sometimes generally, sometimes specifically with respect to religious scruples against bearing arms. The final recorded House debates on August 20 show agreement on both such protections: "Congress shall make no law establishing religion, or to prevent the free exercise thereof, or to *infringe the rights of conscience*" (No. 12). And again, "no person *religiously scrupulous* shall be compelled to bear arms in person" (No. 13). The Senate included such a guarantee in its first three drafts but then abruptly dropped it for good at the end of September 3 (No. 18). We are left with the final spare free exercise clause.

Third, it must be remembered that while formulating the free exercise clause, Congress was also formulating the free speech, free press, and free assembly clauses. The House had combined the speech, press, and religion clauses already on July 28 (Nos. 9, 11). The Senate combined these and the assembly clause on September 9 (No. 19), and thereafter, they were considered together. The House debates on these other First Amendment provisions make rather clear that religious speech, religious press, and religious assembly were covered by these three clauses.[69] The free exercise clause could not be merely redundant of these attendant clauses. So what is protected by the free exercise clause beyond free religious speech, free religious press, and free religious assembly?

To read the free exercise clause too minimally is hard to square with the widespread solicitude for rights of conscience and free exercise reflected in the First Congress's debates. All four state drafts of the religion clauses included such protections. The Virginia and North Carolina drafts, as we saw, went on at length: "That religion, or the duty which we owe to our creator, and the manner of discharging it, can be directed only by reason and conviction, not by force or violence, and therefore all men have an equal, natural and unalienable right to the free exercise of religion according to the dictates of conscience" (No. 2). New York's draft was also effusive: "That the people have an equal, natural, and unalienable right freely and peaceably to exercise their religion, according to the dictates of conscience" (No. 3).

These favorable sentiments are reflected in the August House debates that have survived. Daniel Carroll, as we saw, spoke eloquently that "the rights of conscience are, in their nature of such peculiar delicacy, and will little bear the gentlest touch of government." Benjamin Huntington warned against anything "hurtful to religion" and hoped the "amendment would be made in such a way as "to secure the rights of conscience and a free exercise of the right of religion." Elias Boudinot gave the final resounding word of the House on August 20: "I hope that in establishing this Government, we may show the world that proper care is taken that the Government may not interfere with the religious sentiments of any person."

How does all this enthusiasm in the First Congress for the rights of conscience and freedom of exercise square with the seemingly crabbed guarantee that "Congress shall make no law ... prohibiting the free exercise" of religion?

The free exercise clause is somewhat less crabbed when read in eighteenth-century terms, rather than ours. The word "prohibiting," in eighteenth-century parlance, was as much a synonym as a substitute for the terms "infringing," "restraining," or "abridging." As Michael McConnell has shown, both dictionaries and political tracts of the day conflated these terms. To flip from one to the other, particularly in the charged political rhetoric of the First Congress, might well have been driven more by aesthetics and taste than by substantive calculation.[70]

One can see this conflation of terms in the original draft submitted by the Virginia Ratification Convention in the summer of 1788. In the preface to its proffered amendments, the convention cites its main concern—"that essential rights, the liberty of conscience, and of the press, cannot be cancelled, abridged, restrained, *or* modified, by any authority." Commenting on this passage in 1800, Madison argued that the point of listing all these verbs was simply to underscore "that the liberty of conscience and the freedom of press were equally and completely exempted from all authority whatever of the United States." And such rights, in Madison's view, were equally and completely protected by the First Amendment, despite its use of the alternative terms, "prohibiting" and "abridging." To read the First Amendment otherwise would lead to silly results:

> [I]f Congress may regulate the freedom of the press, provided they do not abridge it, because it is said only "they shall not abridge it," and is not said, "they shall make no law respecting it," the analogy of reasoning is conclusive that Congress may regulate and even abridge the free exercise of religion, provided they do not prohibit it; because it is said only "they shall not prohibit it," and is not said "they shall make no law respecting, or no law abridging it."[71]

One cannot lean too heavily on this construction, since the primary meaning of "prohibit" in the eighteenth century was still to "forbid," "prevent," or "preclude." But awareness both of the elasticity of the term in the day and of the inexactitude of the congressional record helps to explain what the First Congress may have been about.

Moreover, the phrase "free exercise," in eighteenth-century parlance, was both a source and a summary of a whole range of principles of religious rights and liberties. "Free exercise" did have a distinct meaning in the eighteenth century, as we saw.[72] It was conventionally understood to protect the religious speech, press, assembly, and other activities of individuals, and the actions respecting the religious property, polity, discipline, and clergy of religious groups.[73] But, as we also saw, "free exercise" was just as much an umbrella term that connoted protections of liberty of conscience, religious equality and pluralism, and (in some formulations) separation of church and state. In earlier drafts of the religion clauses, Congress sought to spell out these various principles separately—listing liberty of conscience fifteen times, free exercise and religious equality nine times each, and religious pluralism six times. Perhaps in an attempt to avoid giving priority to any particular construction, Congress thought it best to use the generic term "free exercise" and leave its specific province open to ongoing constitutional development and application. This is a speculative reading, but plausible even on the thin congressional record.

The record of the First Congress does give a better indication of why the clause on conscientious objection to bearing arms might have been excluded. The Continental Congress had included such a provision, as we saw, and several state constitutions did so as well. The North Carolina Ratification Convention had suggested in 1788 that such a provision be included (No. 4). The House committee of eleven had repeated it on July 28 (No. 8). The House debated the clause on August 17 and 20. It was clearly controversial—passing only 24–22 in the full House on August 20, before being silently dropped by the House style committee four days later. Both Representatives Gerry and Scott objected because such an open-ended clause might well be abused, with the military and the nation thereby imperiled. Both Representatives Scott and Jackson thought it unfair that "one part" of the nation "would have to defend the other in case of invasion." Chairman Boudinot ultimately carried the slender majority with an impassioned speech: "[W]hat justice can there be in compelling them to bear arms, when, according to their religious principles, they would rather die than use them?"

But three of the representatives had suggested a legislative alternative that may have ultimately led to the quiet disappearance of this clause after August 20. Sherman hinted at this by saying the clause was not "absolutely necessary." Scott said more explicitly that conscientious objection status was not a constitutional but a "legislative right." Benson elaborated this view, advising that such questions be left "to the benevolence of the Legislature," to the "discretion of the Government." "If this stands part of the constitution," Benson reasoned, "it will be before the Judiciary on every regulation you make with respect to the organization of the militia." Such a reading has proved prophetic. The contentious issue of conscientious objection status in the military has remained almost consistently subconstitutional ever since—handled by statute and regulation, rather than by direct free exercise inquiry.[74]

"Religion". "What is religion?" is today a recurrent refrain that echoes through much First Amendment law as well as in statutory law. The issue is as intractable at modern law as it is in modern theology, philosophy, sociology, and anthropology. At law, a claim or claimant must be deemed religious to seek the protection of the free exercise clause. A government action must be deemed religious to trigger the limitations of the disestablishment clause. With the remarkable pluralism of modern America, featuring more than 1,000 denominations, charting the course between religion and nonreligion can be a hazardous exercise.

The issue was a good bit simpler in the eighteenth century. The founders recognized and celebrated a plurality of Protestant Christian faiths. The issue was how much further to extend the pale of recognized religion and thus of constitutional protection. Some set the legal line at Protestantism. Others set the legal line at Christianity, thereby including Catholics and Eastern Orthodox. Others set the legal line at theism, thereby including Jews, Muslims, and Deists. No founders writing on religious rights and liberties argued seriously about setting the line any further—to include African or Native American religions, let alone nontheistic faiths from the East, such as Buddhism.

The First Congress did little more than repeat this conventional lore. The House debates repeated the general endorsement of a plurality of sects, societies, and denominations but touched by name only Quakers and Moravians. They also alluded to a distinction between religion and nonreligion, seeking to reserve the protections of constitutional religious rights to the former. In the House debates, Representative Sylvester expressed concern about "abolishing religion altogether" by crafting too broad a disestablishment clause. Huntington wished "to secure the rights of conscience, and a free exercise of the rights of religion, but not to patronize those who professed no religion at all." Scott wanted to prevent misuse of the conscientious objection clause by "those who are of no religion." But precisely what constituted religion and nonreligion and where the line was to be drawn between them, the congressional record simply does not say.

Summary and Conclusions

In the foregoing four chapters, we have taken our stand with the founders in 1789 and looked backward to appreciate both the genesis and the genius of the American experiment in religious liberty. James Madison tells us what the founders saw and what they initially had in mind:

> In most of the governments of the old world, the legal establishment of a particular religion and without any, or with very little toleration of others, makes a pa[c]t of the political & civil organization; & there are few of the most en-

lightened judges who will maintain that the system has been favourable either to Religion or to government. Until Holland ventured on the experiment of combining a liberal toleration, with the establishment of a particular creed, it was taken for granted that an exclusive & intolerant establishment was essential, and notwithstanding the light thrown on the subject by the experiment, the prevailing opinion in Europe, England not excepted, has been that Religion could not be preserved without the support of Government, nor Government be supported witht. an established Religion, that there must be at least an alliance of some sort between them. It remained for North America to bring the great & interesting subject to a fair, & finally, to a decisive test.[75]

The "decisive test" of the American founders was to press the earlier European and colonial experiments with religious toleration and disestablishment to their theological and political conclusions. Theologians and jurists, believers and skeptics, churchmen and statesmen all participated in this exercise—Puritans, Evangelicals, Republicans, and Enlightenment exponents most prominently and consistently. Their efforts, while often independent and wide-ranging, collectively yielded several "first principles" to guide the new American experiment—liberty of conscience, free exercise of religion, religious equality, religious pluralism, separation of church and state, and disestablishment of religion. These first principles, some of ancient Western vintage, were collectively called "the essential rights and liberties of religion."

These essential rights and liberties of religion came to fullest expression and experimentation in the eleven new state constitutions forged between 1776 and 1784. No state constitution embraced all six of these principles equally, nor did they institute them without the kind of qualifications we would regard as improper, if not unconstitutional, today. Most states still retained some semblance of a traditional religious establishment—usually by favoring certain religious ceremonies and moral codes; sometimes by instituting religious tithes, taxes, and test oaths; occasionally by condoning only certain modes and manners of religious worship and organization. Most of the states still retained ample constraints on the free exercise of religion—usually by prohibiting breaches of the peace and public morality; sometimes by curbing religious speech that was deemed blasphemous, religious assemblies that were considered dangerous, or religious allegiances that were judged unpatriotic, if not treasonous.

These essential rights and liberties of religion were also incorporated into the First Amendment to the United States Constitution. The founders regarded religion as special and assigned it a distinct place in the Bill of Rights, with its own unique protections. Today, the First Amendment is taken as the source and summary of much of the nation's law on religious liberty. We have thus taken the time to watch its birth carefully and to parse its words closely, for they will be our principal occupation for much of the remainder of the volume.

It must be stressed, however, that in the founding era, the First Amendment religion clauses were only a small part of the American experiment. The religion clauses bound only the national government ("Congress"). They set only hazy outer boundaries to constitutional congressional conduct respecting religion. These religion clauses were designed in part to legitimate, and to live off, the state constitutional guarantees of religious rights and liberties. The twin guarantees of disestablishment and free exercise depended for their efficacy both on each other and on other religious rights and liberties that the founders regarded as "essential." The guarantees of disestablishment and free exercise standing alone—as they came to be during the 1940s when the Supreme Court "incorporated" these two guarantees into the due process clause of the Fourteenth Amendment—could legitimately be read to have multiple principles incorporated within them.

Indeed, it might not be too strong to say that the "first incorporation" of religious rights and liberties was engineered not by the Supreme Court in the 1940s but by the First Congress in 1789 when it drafted the First Amendment religion clauses. This "first incorporation"—if it can be so called—had two dimensions. First, the pregnant language that "Congress shall make no law *respecting an establishment* of religion" can be read as a confirmation and incorporation of prevailing state constitutional precepts and practices. Such state practices included "the slender establishments" of religion in New England and the Carolinas, which nonetheless included ample guarantees of liberty of conscience, free exercise, religious equality, religious pluralism, and separation of church and state. Such practices also included the "establishment of religious freedom" that had prevailed in Virginia since 1786. The First Amendment drafters seem to have contemplated and confirmed a plurality of constitutional constructions "respecting" religion and its establishment.

Second, the embracive terms "free exercise" and "establishment" can be read to incorporate the full range of "essential rights and liberties" discussed in the eighteenth century. The founders often used the term "free exercise" synonymously with liberty of conscience, religious equality, religious pluralism, and separation of church and state. They similarly regarded "nonestablishment" or "disestablishment" as a generic guarantee of liberty of conscience, religious equality, and separation of church and state. Read in historical context, therefore, the cryptic religion clauses of the First Amendment can be seen to "embody"—to "incorporate"—multiple expressions of the essential rights and liberties of religion.

Notes

1. See Davis, *Religion and the Continental Congress*, with summaries in Stokes, *Church and State*, 1:447–182; Pfeffer, *Church, State, and Freedom*, 106–109, 119–121. For the record, see *Journals of the Continental Congress, 1774–1789*, 34 vols., ed. Worthing C. Ford et al. (1904–1937).

2. Davis, *Religion and the Continental Congress*, 73–75.

3. Ibid., 76.

4. *Journals of the Continental Congress*, 2:220; Davis, *Religion and the Continental Congress*, 80–83.

5. *Journals of the Continental Congress*, 2:87.

6. Ibid., 9:855 (emphasis in original).

7. Ibid., 1:3; see Davis, *Religion and the Continental Congress*, 67, 175–198.

8. *Journals of the Continental Congress*, 2:18.

9. 14 Geo. III, c. 83.

10. *Journals of the Continental Congress*, 1:72, 88; see T. Jeremy Gunn, *A Standard for Repair: The Establishment Clause, Equality, and Natural Rights* (1992), 73–78.

11. *Journals of the Continental Congress*, 4:217.

12. Ibid., 5:654.

13. Ibid., 18:979.

14. Ibid., 23:574.

15. Ibid, 5:547; see also Davis, *Religion and the Continental Congress*, 160–161.

16. *Journal of the Continental Congress*, 19:214.

17. Ibid., 24:67–80, quoted by Stokes, *Church and State*, 1:475.

18. Ibid., 30:269–285; Stokes, *Church and State*, 1:476.

19. Quoted by Pfeffer, *Church, State, and Freedom*, 120.

20. *Journals of the Continental Congress*, 32:340.

21. See various examples in Davis, *Religion and the Continental Congress*, 57–72, 95–116.

22. See Isaac Kramnick and R. Laurence Moore, *The Godless Constitution: The Case Against Religious Correctness* (1996).

23. Elliot, ed., *Debates*, 3:313.

24. Ibid., 4:197.

25. Ibid., 3:207–208, 313, 431.

26. Farrand, ed., *Records of the Federal Convention*, 3:143–144.

27. Catherine Drinker Bowen, *Miracle at Philadelphia: The Story of the Constitutional Convention, May to September, 1787* (1966), 243–253.

28. Farrand, ed., *Records of the Federal Convention*, 1:23; reprinted in ibid., 3:595–609, at 599.

29. Ibid., 2:587–588. The motion makes no express mention of religious liberty, however; when Mason later specified what rights he had in mind, he mentioned only liberty of press, jury trial, and protection against the military in peacetime. Ibid., 2:640.

30. Ibid., 2:616.

31. Ibid., 1:451–452. For recollections of this speech by other convention members, see documents in ibid., 3:471–472, 479, 499, 531. See also Franklin's own reflections on this motion in ibid., 3:296–297.

32. Ibid., 2:342.

33. Ibid., 2:468. A constitutional text proposed by Alexander Hamilton at the conclusion of the 1787 convention, but apparently never considered, had included a more expansive clause: "Nor shall any Religious Sect, or denomination, or religious test for any office or place, be ever established by law." Ibid., 3:617–630, at 628.

34. See above, pp. 41–45, 48–51, and Elliot, ed., *Debates*, 2:44, 119, 148–149, 199, 215; 3:207–208; 4:195–199.

35. Elliot, ed., *Debates*, 1:332.

36. I am omitting from analysis the repeated attempt of South Carolina, in the ratification and congressional debates, to have Article VI amended to read "no other religious test shall ever be required." Such an amendment would have allowed for introduction of religious oaths through the prior clause of Article VI binding all federal officials "by Oath or Affirmation to support the Constitution." The proposal received no support each time it was raised. See Elliot, ed., *Debates*, 1:325; *Annals*, 1:807; *Journal of Senate*, 1:122.

37. Elliot, ed., *Debates*, 1:326.

38. Ibid., 1:327; 3:591, 594.

39. Ibid., 1:328.

40. Ibid., 1:331, 4:244.

41. Ibid., 1:333–335.

42. See Marion Timling, "Thomas Lloyd's Reports of the First Federal Congress," *William and Mary Quarterly*, 3d ser., 18 (1961):519; James H. Hutson, "The Creation of the Constitution: The Integrity of the Documentary Record," *Texas Law Review* 65 (1986):1.

43. *Annals*, 1:451, 452.

44. Ibid., 1:468.

45. The committee included John Vining of Delaware, Abraham Baldwin of Georgia, Roger Sherman of Connecticut, Aedanus Burke of South Carolina, Nicholas Gilman of New Hampshire, George Clymer of Pennsylvania, Elias Boudinot of New Jersey, and George Gales of Maryland.

46. Ibid., 1:757–759.

47. Ibid., 1:778–780.

48. Ibid., 1:783–784.

49. Ibid., 1:795–796.

50. Ibid., 1:796.

51. Ibid., 1:808.

52. Linda DePauw et al., eds., *Documentary History of the First Federal Congress of the United States of America*, 14 vols. (1972), 3:159, 166.

53. *Journal of Senate*, 1:116–117.

54. Ibid., 1:116.

55. Ibid.

56. Ibid., 1:117.

57. Ibid.

58. Ibid., 1:129.

59. For biographical materials on these and other founders, see, e.g., Stokes, *Church and State*, 1:292ff., 507ff.; Stephen A. Marini, "Religion, Politics, and Ratification," in *Religion in a Revolutionary Age*, ed. Ronald Hoffman and Peter J. Albert (1994), 184–217; Morton Borden, "Federalists, AntiFederalists, and Religious Freedom," *Journal of Church and State* 21 (1979):469; M. E. Bradford, *Founding Fathers: Brief Lives of the Framers of the United States Constitution*, 2d rev. ed. (1994).

60. *Journal of Senate*, 1:145, 148; *Annals*, 1:948.

61. See above, pp. 57–61.

62. *Annals*, 1:949–950, 958–959.

63. Ibid., 1:18–19. See also *Journal of Senate*, 16 (reporting that the Senate voted for its chaplain on April 25, 1789); *Annals*, 1:233 (recording that the House voted for its chaplain on May 1, 1789).

64. *Journal of Senate* (April 27, 1789), as reported in *Annals*, 1:25. A slightly reworded version was passed in the House on April 29, 1789. Ibid., 1:241.

65. Ibid., 2:2237; 1 Stat. 71.

66. Statutes, 1789, C. VIII, in *Documents of American History*, ed. Henry Steele Commager, 5th ed. (1949), 130, 131. However, this does not appear in the *Annals* for August 7, 1789. See *Annals*, vol. 1:59–62, 710–714.

67. See the dictionaries listed in Chap. 3, note 117, under "respect." See also the early modern sources quoted in *Oxford English Dictionary* (1971) under "respect."

68. See, e.g., *Annals*, 1:948, transcribing the final Senate version of the free exercise clause: "prohibiting *a* free exercise thereof." See also *Annals*, 1:451, 778–780, variously quoting Madison's call for disestablishment of "*any*" and "*a*" religion.

69. *The Founders' Constitution*, 5:111–208.

70. McConnell, "Origins and Historical Understanding," 1486–1488. See entries under "prohibit" in dictionaries listed in Chap. 3, note 117.

71. Report on the Virginia Resolutions (January 1800), in *The Founders' Constitution*, 5:141, 146–147.

72. See above, pp. 45–46.

73. The Congressional Record of 1790 includes an instructive anecdote illustrating the Congress's presumption of the free exercise rights of the church and clergy. Medieval canon law had granted to clergy "privilege of forum" or "benefit of clergy"—the right of an ordained cleric to have any criminal case against him heard in a church court, rather than in a civil court. This practice continued after the Reformation, in Catholic and in some Anglican polities alike, and was a familiar feature of American colonial law. See Richard Burn, *Ecclesiastical Law*, 6th ed., 4 vols. (1797), 1:185–192; and George W. Balzell, *Benefit of Clergy in America and Related Matters* (1955). In an act of 1790, Congress provided: "That the benefit of clergy shall not be used or allowed, upon conviction of any crime, for which, by any statute of the United States, the punishment is or shall be declared to be death." Stokes, *Church and State*, 1:492.

74. See cases below, pp. 129–131.

75. Letter to Rev. Adams (1833), in Daniel L. Dreisbach, *Religion and Politics in the Early Republic: Jasper Adams and the Church-State Debate* (1996), 117–121, at 118 (paragraph breaks omitted).

5

RELIGION AND THE

STATES BEFORE 1947

For the first 150 years of the republic, principal responsibility for the American experiment in religious rights and liberties lay with the states. The First Amendment religion clauses applied only to Congress, and Congress made rather little law respecting an establishment of religion or prohibiting the free exercise thereof. Various attempts to develop a national law on religious liberty applicable to the states and enforceable in the federal courts—most notably the agitation in 1875–1876 for Congress to pass the Blaine Amendment to the United States Constitution—were defeated.[1] Most questions of religious liberty were left to the states to resolve, each in accordance with its own state constitution. This remained the norm until the landmark cases of *Cantwell v. Connecticut* (1940) and *Everson v. Board of Education* (1947) applied the First Amendment religion clauses to state and local governments—thereby catalyzing the development of a national law on religious liberty, enforceable in the federal courts.

The making of state constitutions was a brisk business in the period from 1787 to 1947—with 135 different state constitutions featured. Each of the thirteen original states, save Massachusetts and New Hampshire, adopted at least one new constitution in this period—Georgia leading the way with eight new constitutions, the last in 1945. Thirty-five new states joined the union in this period, each adding its own new constitution. Seventeen of these thirty-five new states retained their original constitutions; eighteen adopted at least one replacement constitution before 1947—Louisiana leading the way with ten, the last in 1921.[2] Every such constitution empowered the state courts to hear constitutional cases from its own citizens or subjects. Literally thousands of state cases came before these courts raising questions of state power over religious matters or of religious liberties from this exercise of state power.

A comprehensive analysis of this state constitutional law on religious liberty—both on the books and in action—could easily fill several dozen thick volumes. For our purposes, we shall focus primarily on the patterns of religious rights and liberties protected formally in the state constitutions until 1947.[3] Our particular concern will be to watch the treatment of the six main principles of religious liberty forged in the founding period. A table in Appendix 2 summarizes each state's treatment of these and related principles.

Liberty of Conscience and Free Exercise

Forty-two of the forty-eight state constitutions in effect before 1947 had a general clause explicitly protecting the liberty and/or right of conscience. Sometimes the language was direct and efficient, as in the 1851 Constitution of Indiana:

> All men shall be secured in the natural right to worship Almighty God according to the dictates of their own consciences. No law shall, in any case whatever, control the free exercise and enjoyment of religious opinions, or interfere with the rights of conscience. No preference shall be given, by law, to any creed, religious society or mode of worship; and no man shall be compelled to attend, erect or support any place of worship, or to maintain any ministry, against his consent. No religious test shall be required as a qualification for any office of trust or profit. . . . No person shall be rendered incompetent as a witness, in consequence of his opinion on matters of religion.[4]

Sometimes the language was more florid, as was the 1843 Rhode Island Constitution's paraphrase of Jefferson's Bill for the Establishment of Religious Freedom:

> Whereas Almighty God hath created the mind free; and all attempts to influence it by temporal punishments or burdens, or by civil incapacitations, tend to beget habits of hypocrisy and meanness; and whereas a principal object of our venerable ancestors, in their migration to this country and their settlement of this state, was, as they expressed it, to hold forth a lively experiment, that a flourishing civil state may stand and be best maintained with full liberty in religious concernments: We, therefore, declare that no man shall be compelled to frequent or to support any religious worship, place, or ministry whatever, except in fulfillment of his own voluntary contract; nor enforced, restrained, molested, or burdened in his body or goods; nor disqualified from holding any office; nor otherwise suffer on account of his religious belief; and that every man shall be free to worship God according to the dictates of his own conscience,

and to profess and by argument to maintain his opinion in matters of religion; and that the same shall in no wise diminish, enlarge or affect his civil capacity.[5]

Six constitutions lacked an express liberty or rights of conscience clause—those of Alabama, Iowa, Maryland, Oklahoma, South Carolina, and West Virginia. Of these six constitutions, however, four expressly outlawed compulsory participation in, or support for, religion. Three added a clause protecting those with religious scruples against bearing arms—this being a day where state involvement in the military was still commonly assumed. The Constitution of Oklahoma (1907), though lacking both a conscientious objection and a compulsory support clause, nonetheless provided: "Perfect toleration of religious sentiment shall be secured, and no inhabitant of the State shall ever be molested in person or property on account of his or her mode of religious worship; and no religious test shall be required for the exercise of civil or political rights."[6]

Only twenty-five state constitutions included an explicit free exercise clause. Of these, nine couched this as "the free exercise" or the "(free) enjoyment" of "religious profession," "religious sentiment," or "religious worship." Delaware and Vermont spoke of "the free exercise of religious worship" alone. Oregon and Indiana spoke of "the free exercise of religious opinion." Idaho spoke of "the free exercise of religious faith and worship." The remaining state constitutions had more open-ended free exercise clauses.

The relative rarity and restrictiveness of these free exercise clauses is explained in part by the detail of most state constitutional provisions on religion. Rather than using the umbrella term "free exercise," as the First Amendment does, most state constitutions spelled out the meaning of religious freedom in some detail. Twenty-nine state constitutions outlawed state coercion or compulsion in matters of religion, particularly compulsory attendance at religious worship or in religious exercises. Twenty-two state constitutions had explicit provisions exempting those with religious scruples from bearing arms.[7] Nineteen state constitutions explicitly outlawed mandatory payments of religious tithes, taxes, or other forms of compulsory support for religion; none, after 1833, required such support. Fifteen state constitutions provided in more general terms that a person's civil and political rights could not be affected or comprised by his or her religious beliefs or affiliations. Three states, Colorado, New Jersey, and Kentucky, specifically outlawed religious discrimination within public schools.

Religious test oaths for holding political office remained a highly contested issue among the states—and, indeed, would remain so until outlawed by the United States Supreme Court in *Torcaso v. Watkins* (1961).[8] Twenty-four states explicitly banned religious test oaths for political or public office altogether; but of these states, six required that political officers must believe in God. Seven state constitutions provided explicitly that the guarantees of religious freedom did not foreclose the state from administering religious test oaths. In practice, these latter six states plus the remaining states that lacked constitutional provisions on political test oaths generally continued to administer religious test oaths, of varying rigor, at least for the governor.[9]

Controversies over the application of religious tests and oaths spilled over into other areas of public involvement as well. Twenty-four state constitutions banned such oaths and tests as a condition for sitting on juries and/or testifying in criminal and civil cases; two states insisted that such tests could continue. Eight states also banned religious tests as a condition for voting in political elections.

A number of state constitutions, following eighteenth-century precedents, set firm limits on the rights of conscience and free exercise of religion. Seventeen constitutions indicated that these guarantees would not excuse "licentious" actions or conduct that violated the peace, safety, order, and/or security of the state. Two other states added "morals" to this list. Four states added that one person's exercise of religious rights could not violate "the natural, civil, or religious rights" of others.[10] The Connecticut Constitution (1818) spelled out in some detail the relative rights of religious groups and religious individuals in an instance of dispute.

The constitutions of five Western states, Arizona, Montana, New Mexico, Idaho, and Utah, following congressional mandates, explicitly foreclosed religious liberty protection to bigamy or polygamy—Idaho aggressively so. Every other state had criminal laws against polygamy, but their constitutions did not touch on the religious liberty implications of these laws.

Religious Pluralism and Equality

In the eighteenth century, explicit guarantees of religious pluralism were considered critical to ensuring religious liberty. Religious pluralism, in the founders' view, served as a natural check both on the monopolistic inclination of any church and on the establishment tendencies of any state. In the state constitutions of the nineteenth and early twentieth centuries, religious pluralism was more a sociological fact than a constitutional condition of religious liberty. Most state constitutions included clauses that simply acknowledged the existence of confessional pluralism—the multiplicity of religious sects, societies, and/or denominations within the community. Most also included clauses that acknowledged the existence of social pluralism—the multiple "institutions," "societies," "associations," and/or "corporations" that religious groups operated besides places of worship: lower schools, colleges, seminaries, charities, cemeteries, hospitals, asylums, poorhouses, mission societies, religious clubs, and other such voluntary religious associations.

Thirty-six state constitutions included affirmative guarantees of equality for these multiple religious institutions. Of these, thirty-two constitutions formulated this as a general "no preference" clause. The Constitution of Arkansas (1874) had typical language: "Religion, morality and knowledge being essential to good government, the General Assembly shall enact suitable laws to protect every religious denomination in the peaceable enjoyment of its own mode of public worship . . . and no preference shall be given, by law, to any religious establishment, denomination or mode of worship above any other."[11] Seven state constitutions couched this as a guarantee of "equality of faiths" before the law or "equal protection under the law" for all faiths. Eight state constitutions included compacts with the United States that guaranteed "a perfect toleration" of all religious sects and sentiments. The constitutions of New Hampshire (1784) and Connecticut (1818) were alone in restricting their equality guarantee to "every denomination of Christians"—though in practice these provisions were extended to all theistic religious groups.[12]

Few state constitutions went much beyond these general guarantees of equality to specify the affirmative constitutional rights of religious groups. The Delaware Constitution guaranteed the "rights, privileges, immunities, and estates of religious societies."[13] Kansas included a right of religious groups to incorporate and to hold corporate property. Louisiana and Maryland protected the rights of religious trusts and charities to receive donations. Maine and Massachusetts provided that religious societies had freedom to enter contracts with their ministers. New Mexico explicitly protected the church authority's right to acquire and use sacramental wines. But most states left the issue of particular religious group rights to statutory, rather than constitutional, formulation.[14]

Two pairs of state constitutions imposed explicit disabilities on religious bodies. Virginia and West Virginia banned the right of religious groups to organize themselves as corporations, thereby foreclosing to them the property, liability, inheritance, and tax advantages that attached to corporate status. Maryland and Tennessee both expressly prohibited clergy from holding political office—prohibitions that remained on the books in Tennessee until outlawed by the United States Supreme Court in *McDaniel v. Paty* (1978).[15]

Separation of Church and State

While today the principle of separation of church and state is regarded as essential to American religious liberty, historically the principle was considered more dispensable. None of the twenty drafts of the First Amendment religion clauses in 1788 and 1789 had included the principle, as we saw in Chapter 4. This trend continued among the state constitutional drafters. Only the Constitution of Utah (1896) included a general guarantee: "There shall be no union of Church and State, nor shall any church dominate the State or interfere with its functions"—a provision on which Congress had insisted before admitting the heavily Mormon territory of Utah to statehood.[16]

Although they did not use the language of separation of church and state, a number of state constitutions adopted at least a measure of this principle in the context of education and state funding. Thirty-five state constitutions insisted that state and local governments grant no funds to religious schools. Fifteen state constitutions insisted that state schools remain free from "sectarian influence" or from the control of religious officials and institutions. These provisions were motivated, in part, by the growing bias against emerging Catholic primary and secondary schools in the nineteenth century.[17] These provisions also testified to the growing number and power of Baptists and Methodists who, following their eighteenth-century forebears, urged a greater separation of church and state.[18] And they were also part and product of the effort in the nineteenth century to create a "nonsectarian" "common school" movement.[19]

A few constitutions included affirmative guarantees for religious education. The Constitution of Missouri (1945) required that the Bible be taught in public schools. The constitutions of New York (1895) and New Jersey (1947) provided that "the legislature may provide for the transportation of children to or from any school or institution of learning."[20] Six other states repeated the platitudes of the Northwest Ordinance without comment— "Religion, morality, and knowledge being necessary for good government and the happiness of mankind, schools and the means of education shall forever be encouraged."

Twenty-nine state constitutions broadened their rule of "no state funding for religion" to apply not only to religious schools but to all religious causes and institutions. The Nevada Constitution (1864), for example, provided briefly: "No public funds of any kind or character whatever, State, county, or municipal, shall be used for sectarian purpose[s]."[21] Several states echoed the strong language of the 1870 Illinois Constitution:

> Neither the General Assembly nor any county, city, town, township, school district or other public corporation shall ever make any appropriation or pay from any public fund whatever, anything in aid of any church or sectarian purpose, or to help support or sustain any school, academy, seminary, college, university or other literary or scientific institution, controlled by any church or sectarian denomination whatever; nor shall any grant or donation of land,

money or other personal property ever be made by the State or any such public corporation to any church or for any sectarian or religious purpose.[22]

Today, these state constitutional provisions against funding of religion are often called "state-Blaine" or "mini-Blaine" amendments, in reference to Representative Blaine's proposed amendment to the Constitution that was narrowly defeated in the Congress in 1875.[23] A number of these state constitutional provisions against religious funding, however, antedated Blaine's efforts by more than a decade, and often used language quite different from the proposed federal amendment.

Today, these state constitutional provisions are also often described as the products of a growing anti-Catholic, and anticlerical, campaign by sundry nineteenth-century "nativist" groups—the American Protestant Association, the Know-Nothing Party, the Ku Klux Klan, the American Protective Association, the National Liberal League, the American Secular Union, the National Reform Association, and others.[24] While these and other anti-Catholic groups certainly gained ample rhetorical currency in the nineteenth century, their legal influence on these state constitutional reforms should not be exaggerated. A number of the state constitutional delegates who sought to outlaw government aid to religion used familiar eighteenth-century Evangelical and Enlightenment arguments for separation of church and state that had little to do with anti-Catholicism or anticlericalism. Indeed, they were often made by clerics themselves.[25] Moreover, their separationist arguments against government funding of religion were often coupled with separationist arguments for religious tax exemptions that would aid all religions. Thirty-three state constitutions exempted from general taxation all properties devoted to religious worship, religious charity, and religious education.[26] These new tax exemption provisions were not just Pyrrhic victories—attempts by religious bodies to seize indirect funding now that they lacked the political power to command direct funding. Tax exemption provisions were often described as a better way to ensure nonpreferential state support to all religious organizations, rather than preferential state support to those religious groups that had power to extract funding from the legislatures.

Disestablishment of Religion

In the eighteenth century, as we saw, disestablishment of religion was a broad, multilayered guarantee. At its core, this principle prohibited government from defining by law the religious doctrines, liturgies, texts, and traditions of a community. But as an umbrella term, disestablishment outlawed governmental violations of a number of other principles of religious liberty—particularly liberty of conscience, religious equality, and separation of church and state.[27]

Only seven of the state constitutions before 1947 included an explicit disestablishment clause. The constitutions of New Jersey and Maine cast the clause thus: "[N]o subordination nor preference of any one sect or denomination shall ever be established by law." The constitutions of Iowa, Louisiana, South Carolina, and Utah simply emulated the First Amendment: "The General Assembly shall make no law respecting an establishment of religion." Only the Alabama Constitution of 1901 had a direct and general guarantee: "[N]o religion shall be established by law."

This relative rarity of state disestablishment clauses is explained in part by the pervasive religious pluralism among most of the states. Pluralism made the establishment of one state religion too remote a prospect to outlaw. In the new, thinly populated Western states, however, the threat of such a religious establishment was quite real. These states sought to avert this threat not by adopting a disestablishment clause but by entering a compact with the United States that guaranteed a "perfect toleration" among all religious sects and sentiments.[28]

This relative rarity of state disestablishment clauses is also explained in part by the detail of state religious freedom guarantees. Most state constitutions, as we have seen, had lengthy provisions on liberty of conscience, free exercise of religion, and religious pluralism and equality. Most also respected the separation of church and state at least to the point of granting religious institutions their autonomy and equality, and in a number of states, also barring them from interfering in state education and from receiving state funds. With the express outlawing of these features of a traditional established religion, a general disestablishment clause was often considered unnecessary, if not dangerous.

The danger was that a general prohibition against establishment might conflict with a number of other provisions in the state constitutions favorably touching religion. A good illustration of this comes from Massachusetts.[29] Massachusetts is usually described as the last state to disestablish religion—by passage of its famous Amendment XI of 1833. But this 1833 amendment said nothing about disestablishment. It simply replaced Article III of the original 1780 constitution, which had mandated the payment of tithes and supports for religion. The 1833 amendment, in fact, commended theistic religion, even while confirming the principles of religious equality and freedom of exercise. The full text of Amendment XI reads thus:

> As the public worship of GOD and instructions in piety, religion, and morality, promote the happiness and prosperity of a people, and the security of a republican government; therefore, the several religious societies of this common-

wealth, whether corporate or incorporate, at any meeting legally warned and holden for that purpose, shall ever have the right to elect their pastors or religious teachers, to contract with them for their support, to raise money for erecting and repairing houses for public worship, for the maintenance of religious instruction, and for the payment of necessary expenses. And all persons belonging to any religious society shall be taken and held to be members, until they shall file with the clerk of such society, a written notice declaring the dissolution of their membership, and thenceforth shall not be liable for any grant or contract which may be thereafter made, and denominations, demeaning themselves peaceably, and as good citizens of the Commonwealth, shall be equally under the protection of the law; and no subordination of one sect or denomination to another shall ever be established by law.

The 1833 amendment left untouched many provisions in the Massachusetts Constitution, still in place today, that commend religious ceremony and morality. The preamble, for example, refers to the constitution as "a covenant" or "compact" between the people and God:

[T]he people of Massachusetts, acknowledging, with grateful hearts, the goodness of the great Legislator of the universe, in affording us, in the course of His providence, an opportunity, deliberately and peaceably, without fraud, violence, or surprise, of entering into an original, explicit, and solemn compact with each other; and of forming a new constitution of civil government for ourselves and Posterity; and devoutly imploring His direction in so interesting a design, do agree upon, ordain and establish the following *Declaration of Rights and Frame of Government.*

This is a classic covenant ceremony, rooted in the Hebrew Bible and in a New England tradition going back to the Mayflower Compact of 1620.[30]

The moral implications of this covenant are set out elsewhere in the Massachusetts Constitution. Article II of the Declaration of Rights states: "It is the right as well as the duty of all men in society, publicly, and at stated seasons to worship the SUPREME BEING, the great Creator and Preserver of the Universe." Article XVIII rendered adherence to moral duties integral to the character of public offices and public officials:

A frequent recurrence to the fundamental principles of the constitution, and a constant adherence to those of piety, justice, moderation, temperance, industry, and frugality, are absolutely necessary to preserve the advantages of liberty, and to maintain a free government. The people ought, consequently, to have a particular attention to all those principles, in the choice of their officers and representatives: and they have a right to require of their lawgivers and magistrates an exact and constant observance of them, in the formation and execution of the laws necessary for the good administration of the commonwealth.

For, as Article VII put it: "Government is instituted for the common good; for the protection, safety, prosperity, and happiness of the people."

Such moral qualities were also regarded as essential ingredients of state-funded public education. Chapter V of the Frame of Government provides:

> Wisdom, and knowledge, as well as virtue, diffused generally among the body of the people, [are] necessary for the preservation of their rights and liberties. . . . [It is thus] the duty of Legislatures and magistrates in all future periods of this commonwealth to cherish the interests of literature and sciences, and all seminaries of them; . . . to encourage private societies and public institutions, rewards and immunities, for the promotion of [education]; . . . to countenance and inculcate the principles of humanity and general benevolence, public and private charity, industry and frugality, honesty and punctuality in their dealings; sincerity, good humor, and all social affections, and generous sentiments among the people.

The same Chapter V confirmed and commended the incorporation of Harvard College, since "the encouragement of arts and sciences, and all good literature, tends to the honor of GOD, the advantage of the Christian religion, and the great benefit of this and the other United States of America." All these constitutional provisions remain in place in the Massachusetts Constitution still today.[31]

To be sure, the 1780 Massachusetts Constitution was unusual in the rigor and detail of its continued endorsement of religion. And the thick religious language, crafted in the days of Puritan hegemony, might well have been more tempered had the Massachusetts Constitution been reissued by a more religiously heterogeneous nineteenth-century state convention. Nonetheless, this language attests to a pervasive understanding among the states about the salutary, even necessary, role of religion in public life.

Like Massachusetts, forty-three of the forty-eight state constitutions in place before 1947 included in their preambles some ceremonial expression of gratitude to "Almighty God" (or the "Supreme Legislator" or "Supreme Being" or "Supreme Ruler of the Universe" or "Sovereign Ruler of Nations"). Most of these preambles were a brief line or two, but several went on for a paragraph. The New Jersey Constitution of 1947, for example, which was the last constitution ratified in this period, provided: "We, the people of New Jersey, grateful to Almighty God for the civil and religious liberty which He hath so long permitted us to enjoy, and looking to Him for a blessing upon our endeavors to secure and transmit the same unimpaired to succeeding generations, do ordain and establish this Constitution."

Endorsements of religious morality also appear in some of the state constitutions. Connecticut, Delaware, and Maryland followed Massachusetts in providing that it was the right as well as the duty of the person to worship Almighty God. The 1902 Constitution of Virginia retained its original 1776 religious liberty clause with its concluding admonition that "it is the mutual duty of all to practice Christian forbearance, love, and charity towards each other."[32] Six state constitutions repeated the language that "religion, morality, and knowledge" are necessary for good government and the happiness of mankind. Three state constitutions made provisions for chaplains in prisons and the legislatures, two others for observance of the Christian Sabbath and of religious holidays.

Faith, Freedom, and the Frontier

The constitutional law on the books, of course, does not describe the law in action. But the foregoing provisions of the state constitutions of 1787–1947 do give some indication of the prevailing pattern of religious rights and liberties among the states in the nineteenth century. The dominant pattern was that states sought to balance the general freedom of all private religions with the general patronage of one common public religion—increasingly relying on the frontier as a release valve for the tensions between this private religious freedom and public religious patronage.

On the one hand, state and local governments granted basic freedoms of conscience, exercise, and equality to most religious groups and religious practices, at least those that conformed with common culture and average temperament. Most religious individuals were granted rights to assemble, speak, publish, parent, educate, travel, and the like on the basis of their religious beliefs. Most religious groups were generally afforded the rights to incorporate, to hold property, to receive private donations, to enforce religious laws, and to maintain buildings, schools, and charities for their voluntary members.

Many states, however, still dealt discriminately with religious minorities, particularly those of high religious temperature or low cultural conformity. The New England states, for example, continued to resist the missionizing efforts of Quakers, Baptists, and Methodists, routinely delaying delivery of their corporate charters, tax exemptions, and educational licenses. New York, New Jersey, and Pennsylvania were similarly churlish with Unitarians, Adventists, and Christian Scientists, often turning a blind eye to private abuses against them. Virginia and the Carolinas tended to be hard on conservative Episcopalians and upstart Evangelicals alike. Many of the

Southern states were notorious in their resistance to Catholic churches, schools, missions, and literature. Few legislatures and courts, outside of the main cities on the Eastern seaboard, showed much respect for the religious rights of the few Jews or Muslims about, let alone the religious rights of Native Americans or enslaved African Americans.

On the other hand, state and local governments patronized a "public" religion that was generally Christian, if not Protestant, in character. A "mass of organic utterances," as the Supreme Court later put it, attest to the typical features of this system.[33]

State and local governments endorsed religious symbols and ceremonies. "In God We Trust" and similar confessions appeared on governmental seals and stationery. The Ten Commandments and favorite Bible verses were inscribed on the walls of courthouses, public schools, and other public buildings. Crucifixes were erected in state parks and on statehouse grounds. Flags flew at half mast on Good Friday. Christmas, Easter, and other holy days were official holidays. Sundays remained official days of rest. Government-sponsored chaplains were appointed to the state legislatures, military groups, and state prisons, asylums, and hospitals. Prayers were offered at the commencement of each session of many state legislatures and at city council meetings. Thanksgiving Day prayers were offered by governors, mayors, and local officials. Election Day sermons were offered, especially in rural and town churches, throughout the nineteenth century.

State and local governments also afforded various forms of aid to religious groups. Subsidies were given to Christian missionaries on the frontier. States and municipalities occasionally underwrote the costs of Bibles and liturgical books for poorer churches and donated land and services to them. Property grants and tax subsidies were furnished to Christian schools and charities. Special criminal laws protected the property, clergy, and worship services of the churches. Tax exemptions were accorded to the real and personal properties of many churches, clerics, and charities. Tax revenues supported the acquisition of religious art and statuary for state museums and other public buildings.

State and local governments predicated some of their laws and policies on biblical teachings. Many of the first public schools and state universities had mandatory courses in the Bible and religion and compulsory attendance in daily chapel and Sunday worship services. Employees in state prisons, reformatories, orphanages, and asylums were required to know and to teach basic Christian beliefs and values. Polygamy, prostitution, pornography, and other sexual offenses against Christian morals and mores were prohibited. Blasphemy and sacrilege were still prosecuted. Gambling, lotteries, fortune-telling, and other activities that depended on fate or magic were forbidden. In many jurisdictions, these and other laws were predicated on explicitly religious grounds. It was a commonplace of nineteenth-century American legal thought that "Christianity is a part of the common law."[34]

This prevalent pattern of balancing the freedom of all private religions with the patronage of one public religion worked rather well for the more religiously homogeneous times and towns of the early republic. The established public religion confirmed and celebrated each community's civic unity and confessional identity. It also set natural limits on both political action and individual freedom—limits that were enforced more by communal reprobation than by constitutional litigation.

One of the saving assumptions of this system was the presence of the frontier, and the right to emigrate thereto. Religious minorities who could not abide a community's religious restrictions or accept its religious patronage were not expected to stay long to fight the local establishment as their European counterparts had done. They moved—sometimes at gunpoint—to establish their own communities on the frontier, often on the heels of missionaries and schoolmasters who had preceded them. Mormons moved from New York to Ohio, to Missouri, to Illinois, before finally settling in Utah and thereafter colonizing Nevada, California, Idaho, and Wyoming. Catholics moved to California, the Dakotas, Illinois, Louisiana, Montana, Nevada, and New Mexico. Baptists and Methodists poured into the Southern states from Georgia and Tennessee to Mississippi and Texas. Free spirits escaped to the mountainous frontiers of Wyoming, Montana, Washington, and Oregon.[35]

The right—sometimes the duty—to emigrate was a basic assumption of the American experiment in religious liberty. Many first-generation Americans had left their European faiths and territories to gain their freedom. Accordingly, they embraced the right to leave—to exit their faith, to abandon their blood and soil, to reestablish their lives, beliefs, and identities afresh—as a cardinal axiom of religious freedom. Escape to the frontier provided the release valve for the common state system of balancing freedom for all private religions with patronage of one public religion.

As the American populace became more pluralized and the American frontier more populated, however, this system became harder to maintain. The Second Great Awakening of 1820–1860 introduced to the American scene a host of newly minted faiths—Adventists, Christian Scientists, Disciples, Holiness Churches, Jehovah's Witnesses, Mormons, Pentecostals, Unitarians, and Universalists. The Second Great Awakening also fueled what Edwin Gaustad has aptly called "the reconquest" of the original Eastern seaboard states by Evangelical Baptists and Methodists as well as by Roman Catholics.[36] The American Civil War (1861–1865) permanently divided Lutherans, Presbyterians, and other denominations into northern and southern branches. The Thirteenth, Fourteenth, and Fifteenth Amendments (1865–1870) not only outlawed slavery but also liberated a host of long-

TABLE 5.1 Proportional Numbers of Mainline Churches, 1780–1900

	Anglican *percent*	Calvinist *percent*	Evangelical *percent*	Lutheran *percent*	Catholic *percent*
1780	14.8	50.2	16.7	8.7	2.1
1820	5.5	30.1	49.4	7.3	1.1
1860	4.1	18.6	61.2	4.1	4.9
1900	3.8	14.3	63.7	6.6	6.3

cloaked African beliefs and rituals, some in pure African forms, many inculturated with various Christian traditions. After the 1840s, the great waves of European emigration brought new concentrations and forms of Catholicism and Protestantism from Ireland, Germany, and Great Britain, joined by a number of Catholic emigrants from Mexico. After the 1880s, fresh waves of emigrants from Eastern Europe and Russia brought new forms and concentrations of Catholicism, Judaism, and Orthodox Christianity. At the same time, a growing number of emigrants from across the Pacific introduced Buddhism, Confucianism, Hinduism, and other Eastern religions to the Western states.

These movements of new inspiration, immigration, and invention radically recast the American religious map in the course of the nineteenth century—with the traditional Calvinist and Anglican strongholds of the early republic giving way, especially to precocious new forms of Evangelical Baptists and Methodists.

Table 5.1 shows the change over time in the relative numbers of the main founding churches: (1) Anglican (later called Episcopalian); (2) Calvinist (Congregationalist, Presbyterian, and Reformed); (3) Evangelical (mostly Methodist and Baptist); (4) Lutheran (Swedish, German, and Swiss); and (5) Roman Catholic.[37] Note the huge percentage increase in Evangelical churches and the corresponding drop in Calvinist and Anglican churches between 1780 and 1860. Throughout this period, Quakers remained a consistent minority, attracting between 1 to 2 percent of the population. By 1850, and increasingly thereafter, new religious groups became prominent—notably, Adventists, Christian Scientists, Holiness Churches, Mormons, Pentecostals, Unitarians, and Universalists.

This radical reconfiguration of the American religious map in the nineteenth century eventually challenged state constitutional patterns of religious liberty. In particular, state policies of patronizing a public religion became increasingly difficult to maintain with the growing plurality of the populace and the growing political strength of groups that opposed such policies. Many Evangelical churches, both Baptist and Methodist, insisted that states adhere more firmly to principles of disestablishment and separatism; in a number of states, they gained the political power to revise the constitutions accordingly. Religious minorities in many communities— whether Protestant, Catholic, Orthodox, Jewish, Adventist, or Mormon— also began to ally themselves in opposition to this system, particularly the patronage of a common Protestantism within the public schools. Some of these minority religious communities refused to conform or to assimilate. Others refused to live or leave quietly. Still others began to crusade actively against the system.

When neither assimilation nor accommodation policies proved effective, state and local legislatures began to clamp down on these dissenters. At the turn of the twentieth century and increasingly thereafter, local officials began routinely denying Roman Catholics their school charters, Jehovah's Witnesses their preaching permits, Eastern Orthodox their canonical freedoms, Jews and Adventists their Sabbath-day accommodations, non-Christian pacifists their conscientious objection status. As state courts and legislatures turned an increasingly blind eye to their plight, religious dissenters began to turn to the federal courts for relief.

Notes

1. The proposed Blaine Amendment read: "No state shall make any law respecting an establishment of religion, or prohibiting the free exercise thereof; no money raised by taxation in any state for the support of public schools, or derived from any public fund therefor nor any public lands devoted thereto, shall ever be under control of any religious sect or denomination; nor shall any money so raised or lands so devoted be divided between religious sects or denominations." The amendment proposed by Rep. Blaine in 1875 passed the House but was narrowly defeated in the Senate. 4 *Congressional Record* 5190 (1876). A furious lobbying effort in the 1880s and 1890s sought to resurrect this amendment, but in vain. See Alfred W. Meyer, "The Blaine Amendment and the Bill of Rights," *Harvard Law Review* 64 (1951):939–945; F. William O'Brien, "The Blaine Amendment, 1875–1876," *University of Detroit Law Journal* 41 (1963):137–205; id., "The States and 'No Establishment': Proposed Amendments to the Constitution Since 1789," *Washburn Law Journal* 4 (1965):183–210 (listing 21 failed attempts to introduce such amendments to the United States Constitution). On the modern usages of the amendment, see Steven K. Green, "The Blaine Amendment Reconsidered," *American Journal of Legal History* 36 (1992):38 and sources below at notes 17, 19, 23.

2. See *The Book of the States* (1972), 21; and Cynthia E. Browne, *State Constitutional Conventions* (1973), xxviii–xxix, for convenient tables. For multiple editions of these state constitutions, see Thorpe, ed., *The Federal and State Constitutions*.

3. The provisions here under review are from the following state constitutions: Alabama (1901), I.3, IV.73, XI.217, XII.229, XIV.263; Arizona (1912), II.7, 12, IX.2, 10, XI.7; Arkansas (1874), II.24–26, XVI.5, XIX.1; California (1879), I.4,

IV.22, 30, IX.8, 9, XIII.1.5; Colorado (1876), II.4, V.34, IX.7, 8, X.5, XVII.5; Connecticut (1818), I.3, 4, VII.1, 2, VIII.2; Delaware (1897), I.1, 2, VIII.1, IX.4, X.3, 4; Florida (1887), Decl., sec. 5; IX.1, XII.13, XIV.1; Georgia (1945), I.12–14, VII.4; Idaho (1890), I.4, VI.3, IX.5, 6, XIV.1, XXI.19; Illinois (1870), II.3, IX.3, XII.6; Indiana (1851), I.1–8, X.1, XII.6; Iowa (1857), I.3, 4, VI.2; Kansas (1861), Rights, sec. 7; VI.8, VIII.1, XI.1, XII.2, 3; Kentucky (1891), Rights, secs. 1, 5; Revenue, sec. 170; Education, sec. 189; Militia, sec. 220; Louisiana (1921), I.4, IV.8, 16, X.4, 8, XII.13, XIV.15; Maine (1820), I.3, VII.5, IX.1; Maryland (1867), Rights, Arts. 36–39; III.11; Massachusetts (1780), Part I, Arts. II, III, XVIII; Amendment XI (1833), XLVI (1917); Michigan (1890), II.3, 17; V.26, XI.1, XV.1; Minnesota (1857), I.16, 17, VIII.3, IX.1; Mississippi (1890), III.18, IV.66, VIII.208, XIV.265; Missouri (1945), I.5–7, III.38, IX.8, X.6; Montana (1889), III.4, V.35, XI.8, 9, XII.2, XIII.1; Nebraska (1875), I.4, VII.11, VIII.2; Nevada (1864), I.4, II.2, VIII.2; New Hampshire (1784), Part I, 4–6, 13; Part II, 83, 84; New Jersey (1947), I.3, 4, VIII.2; New Mexico (1912), II.11, IV.31, VII.3, VIII.2, IX.14, XII.3, XX.13, XXI.1, 4; New York (1895), I.3, 11, VII.8, VIII.1, XI.4, XVI.1; North Carolina (1868), I.26, V.5, VII.8, IX.1, XII.1; North Dakota (1889), I.4, VIII.147, 149, 152, IX.159, XI.176, XII.185, XIII.188, XVI.203, XVII.211; Ohio (1851), I.7, VI.1, 2, VII.2; Oklahoma (1907), I.2, 5, II.5, X.6, 15, XI.5; Oregon (1859), I.1–6, X.2; Pennsylvania (1874), I.3, 4, III.17, 18, IX.1, X.2, XI.1; Rhode Island (1843), I.3; South Carolina (1895), I.4, X.1, 4, XI.9, XIII.1, XVII.4; South Dakota (1889), VI.3, VIII.16, XI.6, XV.7, XXII, XXVI.18; Tennessee (1870), I.3, 4, 6, 28, II.28, VIII.3, IX.1, 2, XI.15; Texas (1876), I.4–7, III.51, VII.5, VIII.2, XVI.47; Utah (1896), I.1, 4, III.1, 4, X.1, 12, 13, XIII.2; Vermont (1793), Rights, III, IX; II.64; Virginia (1902), I.16, IV.58, 59, 67, IX.141, XIII.183; Washington (1889), I.11, IX.4, X.6, XXVI.1, 4; West Virginia (1872), III.11, 15, VI.47, X.1; Wisconsin (1848), I.18, 19, X.3, 6; Wyoming (1890), I.18, 19, III.36, VII.8, 12, XV.12, XVI.6, XVII.1, XXI.25, 28.The table in Appendix 2 summarizes these provisions. See analysis in Antieau, Carroll, and Burke, *Religion Under the State Constitutions;* Carl Zollman, *American Church Law,* repr. ed. (1933); Michael S. Ariens and Robert A. Destro, *Religious Liberty in a Pluralistic Society* (1996), 99–203.

4. Constitution of Indiana (1851), I.2–7 (deleting section numbers).

5. Constitution of Rhode Island (1843), Art. I.3.

6. Constitution of Oklahoma (1907), Art. I.2.

7. In addition, the Constitution of Florida (1887), Art. XIV.1 explicitly put questions of conscientious objection to the legislature. The rest of the states were silent on the subject.

8. 367 U.S. 488 (1961).

9. See details in Antieau, Carroll, and Burke, *Religion and the State Constitutions,* 100–119.

10. Constitution of Maryland (1867), Rights, Art. 36.

11. Constitution of Arkansas (1874), Art. II.24, 25.

12. Constitution of New Hampshire (1784), Part I, Art. 6, and Constitution of Connecticut (1818), Art. I.4, both repeating Constitution of Massachusetts (1780), Part I, Art. III. By Amendment XI (1833), the Massachusetts Constitution rendered this as "all religious sects and denominations."

13. Constitution of Delaware (1897), Art. IX.4.

14. See generally Paul G. Kauper and Stephen B. Ellis, "Religious Corporations and the Law," *Michigan Law Review* 71 (1973):1499.

15. 435 U.S. 618 (1978).

16. Constitution of Utah (1896), Art. I.4. See below, pp. 126–129.

17. See John C. Jeffries Jr. and James E. Ryan, "A Political History of the Establishment Clause," *Michigan Law Review* 100 (2001):279, 297ff.; Hamburger, *Separation of Church and State*, 219–229, 321–322, 340–341, 412–418.

18. See below, pp. 119–120, on the numbers.

19. Noah Feldman, "Non-Sectarianism Reconsidered," *Journal of Law and Politics* 18 (2002):65, 81ff.

20. Constitution of New York (1895), Art. XI.4. See similarly Constitution of New Jersey (1947), Art. VIII. sec. IV.3. Such policies of furnishing transportation to religious school children on public school buses were upheld as constitutional in *Everson v. Board of Education*, 330 U.S. 1 (1947).

21. Constitution of Nevada (1864), Art. XI.10.

22. Constitution of Illinois (1870), Art. VIII.3.

23. See above note 1. See Joseph Viterriti, "Blaine's Wake: School Choice, The First Amendment and State Constitutional Law," *Harvard Journal of Law and Public Policy* 21 (1998):657, 672ff.

24. See Hamburger, *Separation of Church and State*; id., "Separation and Interpretation," *Journal of Law and Politics* 18 (2002):7.

25. See Thomas E. Buckley, "After Disestablishment: Thomas Jefferson's Wall of Separation in Antebellum Virginia," *Journal of Southern History* 61 (1995):445; id., "'A Great Religious Octopus': Church and State at Virginia's Constitutional Convention, 1901–1902," *Church History* 72 (2003):333; and my "Tax Exemption of Church Property: Historical Anomaly or Valid Constitutional Precept," *Southern California Law Review* 64 (1991):363, upated in the first edition of this volume, ch. 9.

26. Twenty-seven of the thirty-three state constitutions that explicitly outlawed state funding of religion also explicitly authorized such exemptions, and the remaining seven states had strong statutory provisions in effect providing for the same. See Appendix 2.

27. See above, pp. 57–61.

28. These western states were Arizona, Idaho, Montana, New Mexico, North Dakota, South Dakota, Washington, and Wyoming. Congress generally included these religious liberty clauses, among others, in the enabling acts that allowed new states into the union. Such clauses were irrevocable without the consent of the Congress and the people of the states, and they remain in place still today, albeit sometimes in new forms. See, e.g., 1953 amendment to the New Mexico compact, consented to by Congress, 67 Stat. 586, chap. 506.3. See further Robert F. Williams, *State Constitutional Law*, 2d ed. (1993), 76ff.

29. See my "A Most Mild and Equitable Establishment of Religion."

30. Lutz, *The Origins of American Constitutionalism*; David A. Weir, *Church Covenanting in New England* (2004).

31. Reprinted, with modernized spelling and capitalization in Thorpe, ed., *Federal and State Constitutions*, 3:1888.

32. Constitution of Virginia (1902), Article I.16 (retained in the 1971 Constitution).

33. *Church of the Holy Trinity v. United States*, 143 U.S. 457, 478 (1892).

34. The phrase was coined by Sir Matthew Hale in *Taylor's Case*, 1 Vent. 293, 86 English Reports 189 (K.B. 1676), and is repeated in several American tracts and cases. See, e.g., McCloskey, ed., *The Works of James Wilson*, 2:671; and *Vidal v. Girard's Executors*, 43 U.S. (2 How.) 127, 198 (1844); see Stuart Banner, "When Christianity Was Part of the Common Law," *Law and History Review* 16 (1998):27–62.

35. Edwin S. Gaustad, *Historical Atlas of Religion in America*, rev. ed. (New York, 1976).

36. Ibid., 42.

37. The figures are drawn from the tables in ibid., 4, 42–44, which include actual numbers of churches. In calculating these percentages, I have simply totaled the number of churches in each table and divided the number of churches listed under each category against the total.

6

RELIGION AND THE
SUPREME COURT, 1815–1947

The United States Supreme Court has long held the power to review federal and state laws. Article III of the United States Constitution provides: "The judicial power shall extend to all Cases, in Law and Equity, arising under this Constitution." In the landmark case of *Marbury v. Madison* (1803), the Court ruled that this provision empowered it to review and invalidate *federal* laws that violated any provision of the Constitution.[1] In a trio of cases from 1810 to 1821, the Court ruled further that it had similar power to review and overturn state laws.[2]

Before 1940, however, the Supreme Court made only modest use of this power to review laws touching religion. The first application of the free exercise clause to federal law came in *Reynolds v. United States* (1879), the first application of the disestablishment clause in *Bradfield v. Roberts* (1899). In both these cases, and in the dozen federal cases to follow before 1940, the Court found no First Amendment violation. It held for Congress in each instance, often employing rudimentary analysis of the religion clauses in so holding.

Before 1940, the Supreme Court did review a number of state and local laws touching religion—but not under the First Amendment religion clauses. The First Amendment, by its terms, governed "Congress," and in its earliest cases on point, the Court insisted that this language be read literally: "The Constitution makes no provision for protecting the citizens of the respective states in their religious liberties; this is left to the state constitutions and laws."[3] The Court did have power to review state laws touching religion under other provisions of the Constitution or under general principles of law and fairness. Particularly determined parties, therefore, who exhausted their remedies at state law, could appeal to the Supreme

Court for final relief. The Court heard seventeen such cases from the states from 1815 to 1939.

Ironically, it was these early cases arising from the states, not the early First Amendment cases reviewing congressional laws, that provided the more sophisticated analysis of religious rights and liberties. The cases from 1815 to 1914 developed the principles of free exercise of religion, religious pluralism and equality, and separation of church and state in a manner that would be critical to later First Amendment law. The cases from 1923 to 1939 also cast the concept of religious liberty as a fundamental liberty to be protected against both federal and state action. These latter cases laid the foundation for *Cantwell v. Connecticut* (1940) and *Everson v. Board of Education* (1947) that incorporated the First Amendment religion clauses into the due process clause of the Fourteenth Amendment, and thereby applied them to the states.

Review of Federal Laws Touching Religion

Polygamy

The Court's first application of the free exercise clause came in *Reynolds v. United States* (1879).[4] In that case, and in a pair of cases in 1890, the Court offered an extremely narrow reading of the free exercise clause to uphold congressional restrictions on the preaching and practice of polygamy.

Each of the cases involved the Church of Jesus Christ of Latter-Day Saints.[5] This was one of numerous new churches to emerge during the Second Great Awakening of 1820–1860. Its founder, Joseph Smith, had developed, under divine inspiration, a new Scripture to supplement the Bible— the *Book of Mormon,* which he published in 1830. He had further developed a separate *Book of Commandments* in 1833, which described followers of the *Book of Mormon* as a new chosen people. The Mormon faith prescribed the formation of new communities centered on a temple, devoted to a common "Law of Consecration and Stewardship," and committed especially to mission. This faith also featured a number of novel teachings, such as the efficacy of proxy baptism for the dead, the preexistence of man, and a metaphysical materialism that stood in tension with the traditional biblical story of the creation *ex nihilo.* Such novel teachings and practices, and the ardent advocacy of them by missionaries, soon led to severe repression of the Mormon Church. The church was driven first from New York to Ohio, then to Missouri and Illinois. After severe rioting and the murder of Joseph Smith and his brother in 1844, the Mormon members escaped to the frontier under the new leadership of Brigham Young, establishing themselves in what became in 1850 the Territory of Utah.

Far on the frontier, the Mormon Church may well have been left to itself, like many other new religious communities born of the Second Great Awakening. But in 1852, the church leadership issued a manifesto commending polygamy. For one man to have several wives, the church taught, was an appropriate and biblical form of communal living. It also increased the opportunities for women to enjoy the spiritually salutary steps of marriage and motherhood. To set an example for the reticent, the church's leaders took several wives. They further reported that Joseph Smith and other church leaders had done the same in the 1830s and 1840s.[6]

When word of this policy of polygamy reached Washington, D.C., it prompted instant denunciation and a mounting political crusade against the Mormon Church. Since Utah and some of the other Western areas where the Mormons settled were still United States territories, Congress had general authority to pass laws that touched on issues of marriage, family, and sexuality, and Congress exercised this authority with increasing sternness. An 1862 law made polygamy a federal crime in United States territories.[7] An 1882 law disqualified polygamists, as well as men cohabiting with more than one woman, from holding political office, voting in elections, and sitting on juries, among other rights.[8] Related statutes required parties to swear oaths denying any practice or advocacy of polygamy and subjected them to close scrutiny for suspected participation or even belief in the same.[9] An 1887 law called for the forfeiture of the Mormon Church's property altogether if it persisted in its preaching and practice of polygamy.[10]

Three main cases challenged these congressional laws as violations of the free exercise clause. In *Reynolds v. United States* (1879), a Mormon appealed a conviction under the criminal law against bigamy. In *Davis v. Beason* (1890), a Mormon appealed a conviction for false swearing of a mandatory oath renouncing polygamy.[11] In *Church of Jesus Christ of Latter Day Saints v. United States* (1890), the Mormon Church challenged the government's dissolution of its corporate charter and confiscation of its property.[12]

The Supreme Court upheld congressional law in each instance and would hear nothing of the Mormons' free exercise arguments. In *Reynolds,* Chief Justice Waite took Jefferson's adage of "building a wall of separation between church and State . . . almost as an authoritative declaration of the scope and effect of the [first] amendment thus secured." The free exercise clause protects religious beliefs, not religious actions, he argued. "Congress was deprived of all legislative power over mere opinion, but was left free to reach [religious] actions which were in violation of social duties and subversive of good order."[13] This congressional "freedom," the Court continued in *Davis* (1890), could not be compromised by judicial creations of a free exercise exemption from general antipolygamy legislation. To exempt Mormons, particularly from criminal prohibitions against polygamy, Justice Field thundered for the Court, would be "to shock the moral judgment of the community . . . [and] offend the common sense of mankind."[14]

Justice Bradley drove home these sentiments in the Court's opinion in *Latter Day Corporation:* "The organization of a community for the spread and practice of polygamy is, in a measure, a return to barbarism. It is contrary to the spirit of Christianity and of the civilization which Christianity has produced in the Western world." It is a "sophistical plea" to claim free exercise protection for this "nefarious doctrine." For the Court to grant free exercise protection in this case would invite all manner of specious evasions of the criminal law—even religious excuses for human sacrifice and suicide. "The state has a perfect right to prohibit polygamy, and all other open offenses against the enlightened sentiment of mankind, notwithstanding the pretense of religious conviction by which they may be advocated and practiced."[15]

Confronted by these realities in 1890, Wilford Woodruff, the presiding officer of the Mormon Church, issued a manifesto disavowing any further participation in polygamy and urging church members to follow. On October 6, 1890, a Mormon Church conference accepted the manifesto, although a group that insisted on traditional doctrine split off from the main church and relocated, quietly maintaining their polygamous practices to this day.[16] Congress returned the church's property in 1894. Utah became a state in 1896, its new constitution prohibiting polygamy and featuring the only explicit clause on separation of church and state to appear among the state constitutions before 1947.[17] In time, the church began to develop its distinctive ethical code, featuring abstinence from tobacco, alcohol, and caffeine and strict codes for dress, diet, hygiene, and sexual practice. It also routinized its theology and practice of mission, becoming one of the fastest-growing faiths in twentieth-century America.[18]

These early cases did little to embellish the meaning of the free exercise clause. The Court had effectively reduced the free exercise clause to a minimalist guarantee of liberty of conscience alone—and even that was now cast as a mere freedom to have one's opinion, not as a protection against being forced on demand to swear oaths, to give testimony about one's religious opinion, or to have one's right to vote denied if associated with Mormonism. The Court gave short shrift to free exercise arguments that individuals are entitled to preach or practice polygamy peaceably and privately, or even to associate with those who were suspected of the same. The free exercise clause protected religious opinions about polygamy; it gave no protection to actions taken upon such beliefs by individuals or groups. Congress had power to regulate all such religious actions, and it had declared all such actions related to polygamy to be dangerous and criminal.

Congress had power to incorporate the Mormon Church; it also had power to dissolve this corporation if it persisted in its crime. For the Court, this was the end of the matter. Very little in the text or the history of the free exercise clause supported such a narrow reading.

Pacifism

In a series of cases from 1918 to 1945, the Court used similar logic to address the free exercise claims of pacifists to conscientious objection to war. Belief in pacifism was constitutionally protected; actions or omissions taken upon those beliefs were not. Congress had full power to decide whether and which pacifists might be excused from military preparation or participation, or oaths attesting to the same. And it was simply not "within the province of the courts to make bargains" with individuals whose religious scruples were not sufficiently respected by Congress.[19]

In *Arver v. United States* (1918), a pacifist challenged the 1917 Selective Draft Act in which Congress had granted conscientious objector status only to ordained ministers and theology students and to members of "any well recognized religious sect or organization whose existing creed or principles forbids its members to participate in war."[20] The petitioner contended that the Selective Draft Act violated both the free exercise and the disestablishment clauses by privileging religious pacifists over nonreligious and by preferring some religious pacifists over others. The Court dismissed this argument out of hand: "We pass without anything but statement the proposition that an establishment of a religion or an interference with the free exercise thereof repugnant to the First Amendment resulted from the exemption clauses . . . because we think its unsoundness is too apparent to require us to do more."[21]

In *United States v. Schwimmer* (1929) and *United States v. Macintosh* (1931), the Court denied relief to parties who were denied naturalized citizenship status solely because of their failure to swear an oath that they would take up arms in defense of the country. Schwimmer was a forty-nine-year-old, well-educated Hungarian woman who wrote and lectured on pacifism. Macintosh was a Baptist divinity professor at Yale and former military chaplain in the Canadian armed forces. Both were ineligible for the military under then current draft laws. Both were otherwise eligible for citizenship. Both were willing to swear full allegiance to the nation but could not swear they could bear arms in defense of the same because of their religious beliefs in pacifism. Both were denied citizenship and appealed to the Supreme Court. Both lost.

In *Schwimmer,* Justice Butler defended the military power of Congress as "a fundamental principle of the Constitution" and described pacifism as a danger to the same. "The common defense was one of the purposes for which the people ordained and established the Constitution," he wrote for the Court. "It empowers the Congress to provide for such defense, to declare war, to raise and support armies, to maintain a navy, to make rules for the government and regulation of the land and naval forces, to provide for organizing, arming and disciplining the militia." Pacifists can be dangerous, for they are "apt to be more detrimental than their mere refusal to bear arms. The fact that, by reason of sex, age, or other cause, they may be unfit to serve does not lessen their purpose or power to influence others."[22]

In *Macintosh,* Justice Sutherland, speaking for the Court, added that conscientious objection status was a legislative privilege, not a natural right. The status "comes not from the Constitution, but from the acts of Congress. That body may grant or withhold the exemption as in its wisdom it sees fit." Moreover, it was for Congress, not for the individual subject, to judge the religious and moral propriety of the nation's military policy and the role of its citizens therein:

> We are a Christian people according to one another the equal right of religious freedom, and acknowledging with reverence the duty of obedience to the will of God. But, also, we are a nation with the duty to survive; a nation whose Constitution contemplates war as well as peace; whose government must go forward upon the assumption, and safely can proceed upon no other, that unqualified allegiance to the nation and submission and obedience to the laws of the land, as well those made for war as those made for peace, are not inconsistent with the will of God.[23]

Chief Justice Hughes wrote a strong dissent in *Macintosh,* arguing that the Court had trespassed even the narrow view of liberty of conscience set out in the Mormon polygamy cases as well as the policy reflected in the "no religious test oath" in Article VI. This argument failed to convince the *Macintosh* Court. It also failed to convince three subsequent Courts that heard comparable cases on the rights of pacifism.[24] Fifteen years later, however, in *Girouard v. United States* (1946), Chief Justice Hughes's argument, particularly his rendering of the no religious test oath clause, convinced a slender majority of the Court to outlaw such military test oaths as part of the application for naturalized citizenship status.[25]

Though perhaps harsh, the Court's reading of the free exercise clause in these pacifism cases stood on somewhat firmer historical ground. As we saw,[26] three drafts of the First Amendment religion clauses had included an explicit conscientious objection clause, following in part precedents from the Continental Congress. But the proposal for the Bill of Rights to include a conscientious objection clause was perennially controversial and eventually dropped. The most persuasive argument against it came from Representative Benson in the House debate of August 17, 1789: Questions of conscientious objection to military service must be left "to the benevolence of the Legislature" and to the "discretion of the Government," he declared. "If this stands part of the constitution, it will be before the Judiciary on every regulation you make with respect to the organization of the militia."[27] Although the Court made no reference to this history, its dismissive treatment of the claim of a constitutional right to pacifism seemed to be driven in part by this concern. It was for the legislature, not the Court, to decide the rights and limits of the pacifist.

In these early cases, the Court was firm in maintaining Congress's strict limits on pacifism. In a series of cases in the 1960s and 1970s, arising from the Vietnam War, the Court was equally firm in enforcing to the fullest extent possible Congress's generous extension of conscientious objector status to anyone who was a pacifist "by reason of religion and belief."[28]

Funding

Bradfield v. Roberts (1899) was the Court's first disestablishment clause case. In *Bradfield,* Congress had made available some $30,000 to build two new hospital buildings in the District of Columbia. The funding was given to a nonprofit hospital, properly incorporated in 1864. The hospital, though open to the public, was operated by an order of nuns under the auspices of the Roman Catholic Church. A taxpayer and citizen of the district challenged the funding as a violation of the disestablishment clause. The Court rejected the challenge out of hand. On the one hand, the Court stated, "a law respecting a religious establishment" is not necessarily "a law respecting an establishment of religion." Moreover, in this instance, the recipient hospital was not a religious establishment but simply a hospital devoted to medical services that happened to be run by people of faith.

> [T]he fact that its members . . . are members of a monastic order or sisterhood of the Roman Catholic [Church], and the further fact that the hospital is conducted under the auspices of the said church, are wholly immaterial. . . . Whether the individuals who compose the corporation under its charter happen to be all Roman Catholics, or all Methodists, or Presbyterians, or Unitarians, or members of any other religious organization, or of no organization at all, is not of the slightest consequence with reference to the law of its incorporation, nor can the religious beliefs upon religious matters of the various incorporators of the religious body be inquired into.[29]

The Court used similar reasoning in *Quick Bear v. Leupp* (1908). In treaties with the Sioux Indians, Congress had agreed to hold money in trust to be used later for the Indians' education—as partial consideration for the tribal lands that the federal government had confiscated. The treaties entitled the Sioux to designate the schools for which the money should be spent. When the Sioux requested that the funds be spent on Catholic schools that would serve their communities, however, taxpayers objected. Such payments were alleged to violate both a governing statute and the "spirit of the Constitution" that required that government must "always be undenominational [and] never act in a sectarian capacity." Citing *Bradfield,* the Court dismissed this argument, saying that Congress was not establishing religion or prohibiting its free exercise but discharging its treaty obligations to pay for the Sioux's education—a patently secular governmental function.[30]

Review of State Laws Touching Religion

Before 1940, the United States Supreme Court did not apply the First Amendment religion clauses to the states. But the Court did review (or at least issue federal common law respecting) state and local laws touching religion under other provisions of the Constitution as well as under general principles of law and equity. Seventeen such cases reached the Court.

Church Property and Polity

Nine of these seventeen cases involved disputes over church property. In *Terrett v. Taylor* (1815), its first case touching religion, the Supreme Court declared null and void an 1801 Virginia act that rescinded the corporate charter of the Episcopal Church issued in 1776 and required the church to sell its vacant glebe lands and turn over the proceeds to the poor. The act, even if consistent with the Constitution of Virginia, Justice Story wrote for the Court, violated "fundamental principles of natural justice." Religious groups, like all other legal associations, must be allowed to retain a corporate charter once lawfully given and to use their properties in any lawful manner they deem apt, without undue interference by the state.[31]

In a trio of cases in 1852, 1856, and 1887, the Court upheld the corporate property rights of a communitarian Christian group against the claims of defecting members. The Harmony Society, an intensely communitarian sect of German Anabaptist origin and orientation, professed and practiced a policy of holding all property in common. Members were expected to give up their private properties and to accept a new ethic and practice of communal sharing and caring. Most parties signed a document to this effect upon joining the group. In each of the three cases that reached the Court, members who defected from the Harmony Society sought to recover the private property that they had contributed—in two cases alleging fraud on the part of the religious leadership in acquiring and retaining the once-private property. The Court held for the Harmony Society in each instance, resolving each case using basic laws of contract and association.[32]

The Court distilled the rationale of these cases in *Order of St. Benedict v. Steinhauser* (1914).[33] There, a monastic order that practiced community property claimed title to the estate of a deceased lifelong member. The Court upheld the order's right to the property on the strength of these earlier Harmony Society cases and set out its basic method of adjudication:

> We are not concerned in the present case with any question of ecclesiastical requirement or monastic discipline. The question is solely one of civil rights. The claim in suit rests upon the constitution of the complainant corporation, and the obligations inherent in membership. . . . [T]he question here is not one of canon law or ecclesiastical polity. The requirement of complainant's constitution [respecting community property] must be read according to its terms, and its validity must thus be determined.[34]

The Court extended this logic in another trio of cases in 1853, 1871, and 1872, each involving disputes over property between two factions within a church. "Religious organizations come before us in the same attitude as other voluntary associations for benevolent or charitable purposes," Justice Miller wrote for the Court in *Watson v. Jones* (1871), "and their rights of property, or contract, are equally under the protection of the law, and the actions of their members subject to its restraints."[35] State courts could thus hear such intrachurch dispute cases and grant equitable or legal relief as was apt.[36] But in determining which of the two factions is entitled to the property, a civil court should defer to the judgment of the highest religious authority:

> [W]e think the rule of action which should govern the civil courts, founded in a broad and sound view of the relations of church and state . . . is, that whenever the questions of discipline, or of faith or ecclesiastical rule, custom, or law have been decided by the highest of these church judicatories to which the matter has been carried, the legal tribunals must accept such decisions as final and binding on them, in their application of the case before them.[37]

In *Watson v. Jones,* Justice Miller offered a crisp rendition of the basics of individual and corporate religious rights and liberties that supported these holdings:

> In this country the full and free right to entertain any religious belief, to practice any religious principle, and teach any religious doctrine which does not violate the laws of morality and property, and which does not infringe personal

rights, is conceded to all. The law knows no heresy, and is committed to the support of no dogma, the establishment of no sect. The right to organize voluntary religious associations to assist in the expression and dissemination of any religious doctrine, and to create tribunals for the decision of controverted questions of faith within the association . . . is unquestioned.[38]

Justice Strong amplified the principles of liberty of conscience and separation of church and state in *Bouldin v. Alexander* (1872), stating for the Court: "[W]e have no power to revise or question ordinary acts of church discipline, or of excision of church membership. . . . [W]e cannot decide who ought to be members of the church, nor whether the excommunicated have been regularly or irregularly cut off."[39]

Although they did not involve application of the First Amendment, these early Supreme Court cases reviewing state laws on religion underscored the principles of religious equality and pluralism and separation of church and state: First, religion is both individual and corporate in character, and both these forms of religious identity and expression are deserving of legal protection. Second, religious groups are entitled to acquire, use, maintain, and alienate their properties in accordance with their own internal religious strictures, so long as these abide by general laws of property that prevail within the state. Third, religious groups are entitled to govern their own internal affairs, at least with respect to property, without interference by secular courts. These holdings helped to lay an important foundation for later developments of religious group rights in matters of property, education, employment, and discipline.[40]

Cummings v. Missouri (1866) was the only nonproperty case touching religion to come to the Court from the states in the nineteenth century. A state statute, adopted in the aftermath of the American Civil War, required various licensed professionals, including clergy, to swear an oath disavowing support or sympathy for the cause of the Confederate states against the United States. A Roman Catholic priest was fined $500 for preaching without having sworn the oath. On appeal, a sharply divided Court held that the law violated Article I, section 10 of the United States Constitution that no state shall "pass any Bill of Attainder, ex post facto Law, or Law impairing the Obligation of Contracts." The majority said nothing of the oath violating the priest's religious liberty, save one line: "It would be strange, indeed, if a minister of the Gospel, whose sympathies are with all the children of men—the good, the sinful, the happy, and the sorrowing—might not manifest such sympathy by an act of charity or a word of consolation."[41] The dissenting justices saw the case as a specious attempt to impose First Amendment values onto the states, even though nothing in the Constitution "interposes any such protection between the State governments and their own citizens."[42]

Fundamental Religious Liberty and Incorporation

In several cases in the 1920s and 1930s, the Supreme Court began to review state and local laws touching religion under an emerging standard of "fundamental religious liberty." These cases first stated the concept of fundamental religious liberty in the abstract, then tied it to the Fourteenth Amendment guarantee that no state shall "deprive any person of life, liberty, or property, without due process of law." The Supreme Court began to outlaw state laws touching religion because they violated the liberty guarantee of the Fourteenth Amendment.

The first reference to this standard of religion as a "fundamental liberty" came in *Meyer v. Nebraska* (1923). The state of Nebraska, like several other states in the aftermath of World War I, began to clamp down on German Protestants, exposing them to a number of increasingly onerous registration and taxation policies and often turning a blind eye to private violence against them. At issue in *Meyer* was a new state law that mandated English instruction in all grade schools. Teachers in private Protestant grade schools were convicted under this statute for allowing the reading of Bible stories in German. The Supreme Court reversed the conviction, mostly on grounds of the rights of the parents to direct the education of their children. But the Court noted in a passing dictum that such an action also violated the Fourteenth Amendment due process clause that protected, among others, the defendant's right "to worship God according to the dictates of his own conscience."[43]

The Court touched on this standard again in *Pierce v. Society of Sisters* (1925). Oregon had passed a law mandating that all eligible students must attend public schools. The Oregon law, like that of many states at the time, was enacted, in part, to drive out of existence emerging Catholic and other private religious schools and to give new impetus to the development of public schools. The Society of Sisters, which owned and operated several private Catholic schools that were jeopardized by the new Oregon law, challenged this law as a violation of the right of the parents, children, schools, and schoolteachers alike. The Court struck down the Oregon law and upheld the rights of the parents and of the religious schools. Again, the Court offered a suggestive dictum about protecting the fundamental liberty interests at stake: "[R]ights guaranteed by the Constitution may not be abridged by legislation which has no reasonable relation to some purpose within the competency of the state. The fundamental theory of liberty upon which all governments in this Union repose excludes any general power of the state to standardize its children by forcing them to accept instruction from public teachers only." It also forecloses "unwarranted compulsion . . . over present and future patrons" of the religious schools.[44] These principles were echoed in two subsequent cases.[45]

In *Hamilton v. Board of Regents* (1934), the Court stated this principle of fundamental liberty more explicitly. State university students objected to mandatory R.O.T.C. training in violation of their conscientious scruples to participation in war, or preparation for the same. One basis of their challenge was the explicit guarantee of liberty in the Fourteenth Amendment due process clause. Although the Court rejected the students' appeal, they did accept this constitutional basis for review. As Justice Butler put it for the Court: "There need be no attempt to enumerate or comprehensively to define what is included in the 'liberty' protected by the due process clause [of the Fourteenth Amendment]. Undoubtedly it does include the right to entertain the beliefs, to adhere to the principles, and to teach the doctrines" of a faith.[46] Justice Cardozo concurred in the result but added even more directly: "I assume for present purposes that the religious liberty protected by the First Amendment against invasion by the nation is protected by the Fourteenth Amendment against invasion by the states."[47]

Three years later, in *Palko v. Connecticut* (1937), Justice Cardozo sharpened this view of fundamental liberty. The due process clause of the Fourteenth Amendment, he argued, requires that all state and local governments must adhere to the "fundamental principles of liberty and justice which lie at the base of all our civil and political institutions." An authoritative definition of these principles of liberty and justice is set forth in the Bill of Rights attached to the United States Constitution. The first eight amendments of the Bill of Rights, by their terms, bind the federal government. But, as authoritative statements of fundamental principles of liberty, they might also be understood to bind the states. The Court, in interpreting and applying the "liberty" provision of the Fourteenth Amendment due process clause may thus selectively apply various provisions of the federal Bill of Rights to test state and local ordinances.[48]

In *Lovell v. City of Griffin* (1938) and *Schneider v. Town of Irvington* (1939), the Court selectively applied the free speech and free press clauses of the First Amendment to invalidate a series of municipal ordinances that prohibited the distribution of religious literature. Freedoms of speech and press, Chief Justice Hughes declared for the *Lovell* Court, are "among the fundamental personal rights" that neither federal nor state officials have power to abridge.[49]

In *Cantwell v. Connecticut* (1940), the Court for the first time applied the free exercise clause to a local ordinance. In *Cantwell,* Jehovah's Witnesses appealed their conviction under a city licensing law, among others. The law required all parties who wished to solicit for "any alleged religious, charitable or philanthropic cause" to procure a license in advance. Local administrators could deny a license to those whose cause did not seem to be in good faith. The Witnesses were convicted for preaching and soliciting without having procured such a license. They appealed, arguing, in the Court's words, that the statute "was offensive to the due process clause of the Fourteenth Amendment because, on its face and as construed and applied, it denied them freedom of speech and prohibited their free exercise of religion."[50]

With matter-of-fact simplicity, the Court applied the free exercise clause to the local ordinance and held for the Witnesses. Justice Roberts wrote for the Court:

> We hold that the statute, as construed and applied to the appellants, deprives them of their liberty without due process of law in contravention of the Fourteenth Amendment. The fundamental concept of liberty embodied in that Amendment embraces the liberties guaranteed by the First Amendment. The First Amendment declares that Congress shall make no law respecting an establishment of religion or prohibiting the free exercise thereof. The Fourteenth Amendment has rendered the legislatures of the states as incompetent as Congress to enact such laws.[51]

The Court went on to soften the wooden belief-action distinction of its earlier free exercise cases and to restate a number of basic principles of religious liberty that were at work in its earlier cases reviewing state laws touching religion:

> The constitutional inhibition of legislation on the subject of religion has a double aspect. On the one hand, it forestalls compulsion by law of the acceptance of any creed or the practice of any form of worship. Freedom of conscience and freedom to adhere to such religious organization or form of worship as the individual may choose cannot be restricted by law. On the other hand, it safeguards the free exercise of the chosen form of religion. Thus the Amendment embraces two concepts,—freedom to believe and freedom to act. The first is absolute but, in the nature of things, the second cannot be. Conduct remains subject to regulation for the protection of society. The freedom to act must have appropriate definition to preserve the enforcement of that protection. In every case the power to regulate must be so exercised as not, in attaining a permissible end, unduly to infringe the protected freedom.[52]

Seventeen cases over the next six years drove home the lessons of *Cantwell*—that the free exercise clause applied as readily to the states as to the federal government and that the clause required states to respect the principles of liberty of conscience and the equality of a plurality of faiths before the law.[53] Most of these early free exercise cases, as we shall see in the next chapter, simply adjusted the American experiment by protecting the rights of newly emergent religious groups against recalcitrant local officials. Jehovah's Witnesses, the Court held repeatedly, could not be denied licenses to preach, parade, or pamphleteer just because they were unpopular. Public school students could not be compelled to salute the flag or recite the pledge if they were conscientiously opposed. Other parties, with scruples of conscience, could not be forced to swear oaths before receiving citizenship status, property tax exemptions, state bureaucratic positions, social welfare benefits, or standing in courts. Such free exercise remedies are often condemned as a corruption of the federalism inherent in the religion clauses. But read more charitably, they can be seen as an effort to make the traditional state systems of religious governance more "mild and equitable" for the many new private religions on the American scene.

In *Everson v. Board of Education* (1947), the Court signaled a more radical change to the American experiment. *Everson* formally incorporated the First Amendment disestablishment clause into the Fourteenth Amendment due process clause and applied it to the states. After a long recitation of the history and purpose of the religion clauses, Justice Black declared for the Court:

> The meaning and scope of the First Amendment, preventing [an] establishment of religion or prohibiting the free exercise thereof, in light of its history and the evils it was designed forever to suppress, have been several times elaborated by the decisions of this Court prior to the application of the First Amendment to the states by the Fourteenth. The broad meaning given the Amendment by these earlier cases has been accepted by this Court in its decisions concerning an individual's religious freedom [of exercise].... There is every reason to give the same application and broad interpretation to the "establishment of religion" clause.[54]

Like the *Cantwell* Court, the *Everson* Court went on to state a preliminary standard of review for future disestablishment cases. But the *Everson* Court, unlike the *Cantwell* Court, did not have a brace of earlier Supreme Court cases on which to call—only *Bradfield* and *Quick Bear*, neither of which offered much guidance. The disestablishment standard that the Court chose in this opening case was the strong separationist standard already in place in some of the state constitutions and initially proposed in the defeated Blaine Amendment of 1875. In Justice Black's famous words:

> The "establishment of religion" clause of the First Amendment means at least this: Neither a state nor the Federal Government can set up a church. Neither can pass laws which aid one religion, aid all religions, or prefer one religion over another. Neither can force nor influence a person to go or to remain away

from church against his will or force him to profess a belief or disbelief in any religion. No person can be punished for entertaining or professing religious beliefs or disbeliefs, for church attendance or non-attendance. No tax in any amount, large or small, can be levied to support any religious activities or institutions, whatever they may be called, or whatever form they may adopt to teach or practice religion. Neither a state nor the Federal Government can, openly or secretly, participate in the affairs of any religious organizations or groups, or vice versa. In the words of Jefferson, the clause against establishment of religion by law was intended to erect "a wall of separation between church and state." . . . That wall must be kept high and impregnable. We could not approve the slightest breach.[55]

Justice Black, and Justice Rutledge in dissent in *Everson,* described these sentiments as the "original intent of the eighteenth century framers."[56] But in determining the intent of the framers, they turned only to Enlightenment writers—principally Jefferson and Madison—and read primarily the constitutional history of Virginia, where these writers had their greatest influence. The justices did not consider the multiple opinions of Puritans, Evangelicals, or Republicans, nor the constitutional experiments or experiences of other early states besides Virginia. The justices also did not consider the nuances of even the sternest Enlightenment writers on religion, who were concerned with other "essential rights and liberties" besides separation of church and state. The disestablishment clause, the Court declared, demanded a strict separationism. Henceforth, all federal and state laws would be held to this strong principle or struck down as unconstitutional.

By so incorporating the First Amendment religion clauses into the Fourteenth Amendment due process clause, the Court set in motion the creation of a new national law on religious liberty, governed by the federal courts and enforceable against federal, state, and local governments alike.[57] Viewed in isolation, this development might seem to be a rather remarkable attack on the basic principle of federalism built in the text of the First Amendment ("*Congress* shall make no law. . . . "). But this development was of a piece with other movements of the day—the growing federalization of the society and the economy through the New Deal legislation and case law, the pressing need for national solidarity in the face of World War II and in the Cold War to follow, the grim lessons about religious and cultural bigotry learned through the Holocaust and the gulag.

The incorporation doctrine was a small part of an emerging constitutional nationalism that insisted on the guarantees of fundamental liberty and rule of law for all and that would brook neither local bigotry nor local favoritism even in the name of federalism. Before 1940, a number of other provisions of the Bill of Rights had already been selectively incorporated into the Fourteenth Amendment due process clause and applied to the states.[58] Given the grim lessons about unchecked religious bigotry taught by the death camps of World War II, it was almost culturally inevitable, even if not constitutionally ineluctable, that the religion clauses be incorporated as well. This move brought fundamental change to the American experiment in religious liberty.

Notes

1. 5 U.S. (1 Cranch) 137 (1803).

2. *Fletcher v. Peck* 10 U.S. (6 Cranch) 87 (1810); *Martin v. Hunter's Lessee*, 14 U.S. (1 Wheat) 304 (1816); and *Cohens v. Commonwealth of Virginia*, 19 U.S. (6 Wheat) 264 (1821).

3. *Permoli v. Municipality No. 1 of New Orleans*, 44 U.S. (3 How.) 589, 609 (1845). See also *Barron v. Baltimore*, 32 U.S. (7 Pet.) 243 (1833) (holding that the Bill of Rights in general, and the Fifth Amendment in particular, applied only to the national government); see also Joseph Story, *Commentaries on the Constitution*, 2d ed. (1851), 2:597.

4. 98 U.S. 145, 164 (1879).

5. See detailed study in Sarah Barringer Gordon, *The Mormon Question: Polygamy and Constitutional Conflict in Nineteenth-Century America* (2002); Edwin B. Firmage and Richard Collin Mangrum, *Zion in the Courts: A Legal History of the Church of Jesus Christ of Latter-Day Saints, 1830–1900* (2001).

6. See Leonard J. Arrington and Davis Bitton, *The Mormon Experience: A History of the Latter-Day Saints* (1979); Klaus J. Hansen, *Mormonism and the American Experience* (1981); Jan Shipps, *Mormonism: The Story of a New Religious Tradition* (1984).

7. 12 Stat. 501–502 (1862).

8. 22 Stat. 30–32 (1882). In *Cannon v. United States*, 116 U.S. 55 (1885), the Court held that proof of sexual intercourse between the man and the multiple women with whom he cohabited was not required for a bigamy conviction.

9. The most pertinent laws, and attendant regulations, are quoted and analyzed in *Murphy v. Ramsey*, 114 U.S. 15 (1885).

10. 18 *Congressional Record* 585–593 (January 1887).

11. 133 U.S. 333, 341–342 (1890).

12. 136 U.S. 1 (1890) and the companion case *Romney v. United States*, 136 U.S. 1 (1890). *Murphy v. Ramsey*, 114 U.S. 15, 45 (1885) upheld various laws disenfranchising known and suspected bigamists against challenges that the laws violated "constitutional rights and liberties." In defense of the laws, Justice Matthews wrote: "For, certainly, no legislation can be supposed more wholesome and necessary in the founding of a free, self-governing commonwealth . . . than that which seeks to establish it on the basis of the idea of the family, as consisting in and springing from the union for life of one man and one woman in the holy estate of matrimony; the sure foundation of all that is stable and noble in our civilization; the best guarantee of that reverent morality which is the source of all beneficent progress in social and political improvement." See also *Cleveland v. United States*, 329 U.S. 14 (1946).

13. *Reynolds*, 98 U.S. at 164.

14. *Davis*, 133 U.S. at 336–337, 341–342.

15. *The Late Corporation of the Church of Jesus Christ of Latter-Day Saints*, 136 U.S. 1, 48–50 (1890).

16. Kenneth Driggs, "After the Manifesto: Modern Polygamy and Fundamentalist Mormons," *Journal of Church and State* 32 (1990):367.

17. Constitution of Utah (1896), Art. I, sec. 4; Art. III.

18. See Dallin H. Oaks and Lance B. Wickman, "The Mission Work of the Church of Jesus Christ of Latter Day Saints," in *Sharing the Book: The Rights and Wrongs of Mission*, ed. John Witte Jr. and Richard C. Martin (1999), ch. 12.

19. *United States v. Macintosh*, 283 U.S. 605, 626 (1931).

20. 40 Stat. 76, 78 (1917).

21. 245 U.S. 366, 389–390 (1918). See similar results in *Eagles v. Samuels*, 329 U.S. 304 (1946); *Eagles v. Horowitz*, 329 U.S. 317 (1946).

22. *United States v. Schwimmer*, 279 U.S. 644, 650–651 (1929).

23. *Macintosh*, 283 U.S. at 624–625 (1931).

24. See *United States v. Bland*, 283 U.S. 636 (1931); *Hamilton v. Regents of the University of California*, 293 U.S. 245 (1934); *In re Summers*, 325 U.S. 561 (1945).

25. 328 U.S. 61 (1946).

26. See above, pp. 99–100.

27. See above, p. 87.

28. See *United States v. Seeger*, 380 U.S. 163 (1965); *Welsh v. United States*, 398 U.S. 333 (1970).

29. 175 U.S. 291, 298 (1899).

30. 210 U.S. 50, 81 (1908).

31. 13 U.S. (9 Cranch) 43 (1815).

32. *Goesele v. Bimeler*, 55 U.S. (14 How.) 589 (1852); *Baker v. Nachtrieb*, 60 U.S. (19 How.) 126 (1856); *Speidel v. Henrici*, 120 U.S. 377 (1887) (also holding that the defecting member should not be granted relief because of the doctrine of "laches," a party's undue delay in seeking equity relief).

33. 234 U.S. 640 (1914).

34. Ibid., 642, 648.

35. *Watson v. Jones*, 80 U.S. (13 Wall.) 679, 714 (1871).

36. *Smith v. Swormstedt*, 57 U.S. (16 How.) 288 (1853).

37. *Watson v. Jones*, 80 U.S. at 727.

38. Ibid., 728–729.

39. *Bouldin v. Alexander*, 82 U.S. (15 Wall.) 131, 139–140 (1872); see further Justice Strong's *Two Lectures upon the Relations of Civil Law to Church Polity, Discipline, and Property* (1875).

40. See William W. Bassett, *Religious Organizations and the Law*, 2 vols. (1999–); Ira C. Lupu and Robert Tuttle, "The Distinctive Place of Religious Entities in Our Constitutional Order," *Villanova Law Review* 47 (2002):37. Among early cases, see *Church of the Holy Trinity v. United States*, 143 U.S. 457 (1892); *Ponce v. Roman Catholic Apostolic Church*, 210 U.S. 296 (1908); *Gonzalez v. Roman Catholic Archbishop of Manila*, 280 U.S. 1 (1929) described further in Appendix 3.

41. 71 U.S. (4 Wall.) 277, 285 (1866).

42. Dissent attached to *Ex parte Garland*, 71 U.S. (4 Wall.) 397 (1866).

43. 262 U.S. 390, 399 (1923).

44. 268 U.S. 510, 535 (1925).

45. *Farrington v. Tokushige,* 273 U.S. 284 (1927); *Cochran v. Louisiana State Board of Education,* 281 U.S. 370 (1930).

46. *Hamilton v. Board of Regents,* 293 U.S. at 262.

47. Ibid., 265 (Cardozo, J., concurring).

48. 302 U.S. 319, 328 (1937).

49. 303 U.S. 444, 450 (1938).

50. 310 U.S. 296, 297, 300 (1940).

51. Ibid., 303.

52. Ibid., 303–304.

53. See Appendix 3.

54. 330 U.S. 1, 14–15 (1947).

55. Ibid., 15–16, 18.

56. Ibid., 8–15, 33–43.

57. See Chap. 5, note 1.

58. See John E. Nowak and Ronald B. Rotunda, *Constitutional Law,* 6th ed. (2000), secs. 10.2, 11.6.

7

MODERN FREE EXERCISE LAW

The incorporation of the First Amendment religion clauses into the Fourteenth Amendment due process clause shifted final authority over the American experiment from the states to the United States Supreme Court. In the first 150 years of the republic, the Court issued thirty-one cases on religious liberty—none of them applying the First Amendment religion clauses to state and local governments. Since 1940, the Court has issued more than 130 cases on religious liberty—most of them applying the First Amendment to state and local governments.

The incorporation doctrine has not foreclosed the states from participation in the American experiment on religious liberty. State and local legislatures have continued to issue numerous laws touching religion—from prison regulations governing the religious exercises of state inmates, to regulations of religious expression in public schools and the public square, to criminal laws prohibiting violations of life, limb, and property in the name of religion, among many other laws. State courts have kept an ample docket of religion cases, adjudicating them under their own state constitutional and statutory provisions on religion.

From the 1940s to 1990s, however, most laws in America that touch religion have become subject to First Amendment influence, if not scrutiny. And most judicial interpretations of religious liberty—both by lower federal courts and by state courts—have generally followed the precedents laid down by the United States Supreme Court. Every major Supreme Court case on religious liberty produces numerous lower court progeny. And every major shift in prevailing Supreme Court law on religious liberty has taken years to trickle down into the constitutional calculus of the lower courts.

It is no small challenge to master the Supreme Court's modern First Amendment cases. Not only are some of the Court's opinions rife with casuistry and contradiction. But particularly in the cases of the past fifteen years, a bitterly divided Court has issued a barrage of lengthy concurring and dissenting opinions—often bristling with long historical and jurisprudential debates and disquisitions that go far beyond the constitutional issues at hand. No amount of summarizing can ultimately substitute for sitting down and reading the cases for oneself. A table summarizing all these Supreme Court cases is provided in Appendix 3 herein. Several good indices and collections of cases are at hand.[1]

Two tasks are before us in this chapter on modern free exercise law and in the following chapter on modern disestablishment law. First, I shall map the main shifts in doctrine in the Supreme Court cases since the 1940s. Under both clauses, the Court has developed various doctrinal approaches or tests that are driven, in part, by broader constitutional concerns over federalism, judicial review, and separation of powers. To provide some guidance to these broader constitutional dimensions of First Amendment law, this chapter, and the next, will open by mapping the main doctrinal issues and tests at work before analyzing various groups of cases touching religion. Second, in analyzing these cases, I shall review especially the Supreme Court's treatment of the first principles of the American experiment—not only the principles of free exercise and disestablishment per se but also the allied principles of liberty of conscience, religious equality, religious pluralism, and separation of church and state.

Mapping Modern Free Exercise Doctrine

Government Power Versus Free Exercise Rights

At the heart of a modern free exercise case is a basic conflict between the exercise of governmental power and the exercise of a private party's religion. The private party challenges the exercise of governmental power as a violation of its rights protected by the free exercise clause.

The challenged governmental entity can be at any level—federal, state, county, or municipal. The governmental action that is challenged can be executive, legislative, or regulatory in nature. But it must be governmental, not private, conduct that is at issue. When private entities or individuals violate another private party's religious rights, such conduct is addressed by civil suits and/or criminal prosecution, not by free exercise litigation.

The claimant in a free exercise case can be a religious individual or a religious group. Their claim is that the law at issue somehow "prohibits" the freedom of their religious exercise. The law infringes upon their beliefs of conscience. It inhibits their acts of worship or of religious speech, press, or association. It commands them to do something, or to forgo something, that conflicts with the demands of their individual consciences or collective faiths. It discriminatorily singles out their activities or properties for duties or exclusions that are not imposed on other individuals or groups similarly situated. In brief, government unduly "burdens" their religion.[2]

Free exercise claimants must meet the usual requirements for pressing any constitutional case against the government. The claimants must state an actual "case or controversy"—not an issue that has become moot or requests only an advisory opinion from the Court. They must have standing to bring the suit—showing an actual injury to themselves. They must raise a constitutional issue on which a court may sit—not a "political question" that is better addressed by other branches of government.[3]

In addition, free exercise claimants must demonstrate that it is their *religious* exercise that has been improperly burdened. In many instances, the religious qualities of the claim are easy enough to make out. A Jehovah's Witness is discriminately denied a license to preach.[4] An atheist is indiscriminately required to swear an oath reciting his belief in God.[5] A Jewish officer is forbidden from wearing his yarmulke on an Air Force base.[6] A Muslim prisoner is kept from prayer at the appointed hour of the day or from collective Friday worship.[7] These are core free exercise cases involving religious individuals. A religious school is required to hire a teacher who does not share its faith.[8] A religious crusader is fined for selling religious articles without collecting sales and use taxes.[9] A bishop is denied his *cathedra* and cathedral because a state religious incorporation law does not recognize the foreign religious authority that appoints him and governs his church.[10] These are core free exercise cases involving religious groups.

In a number of cases, however, the free exercise interest can appear more attenuated. An applicant for a temporary agency refuses a job because it might require him to work on Sunday, his day for rest, though not for worship. He claims unemployment compensation, is denied, and appeals alleging free exercise violations.[11] A furniture store owner, who is a strict Saturday sabbatarian, opens his store on Sunday in violation of Sunday blue laws that prohibit all but "necessary labor." He is fined, and appeals, claiming that the law burdens his free exercise rights to observe his Saturday Sabbath.[12] A religious university discriminates against African American employees and students on the understanding that the Bible requires that races be kept separate. The school is stripped of its federal tax exempt status, and appeals, claiming that its free exercise rights have been violated just because its beliefs are not popular.[13] A manufacturing company, owned and operated by devout religious believers, requires all its employees to participate in regular devotional activities on company time. The federal Equal Employment Opportunity Commission forbids them from imposing this requirement on a recalcitrant employee. The company owners appeal, alleging violations of their free exercise rights to practice a holistic faith.[14] In each of these cases, from the internal claimant's perspective, the religious interests may be no less central and sincere. But from the external legal perspective, the religious interests at stake may be viewed as more penumbral and attenuated. Sometimes they will not prove sufficient to meet threshold requirements to press a free exercise claim.

The Supreme Court has generally allowed individuals to press free exercise claims that are "sincere"—even if they are inconsistent, incoherent, idiosyncratic, or newly acquired.[15] In some cases, this sincerity test "cannot completely escape the distinctly bad aroma of an inquisition," in Ira Lupu's apt phrase.[16] It can lead judges or juries to inquire intrusively into the faith of a person or a group or to play to their prejudices against unpopular or exotic religions.[17] But, if the Court is to be protected from fraudulent or sham claims under the free exercise clause, some measured inquiry into the claims of faith is unavoidable.

The Court has provided less guidance to decide the free exercise standing of religious groups. It is easy enough when a church, synagogue, mosque, or temple alleges free exercise violations. But what if the group deliberately mixes religious and secular functions and forms?[18] What if the group's religiosity seems thin, transient, or contrived? What if the claimant is a large family that describes itself as a naturalist faith and wishes to have tax exemptions for farmland, which it calls a religious shrine?[19] Absent Supreme Court direction, lower courts have developed a range of tests to decide the free exercise standing of such religious groups.[20]

Resolving the Conflict

Assuming that the claimant can meet the threshold requirements to press a free exercise claim, how does the Court resolve this basic conflict between government power and religious rights, both anchored in the Constitution? Two principal methods seem to be at work in the Court's free exercise cases since 1940: (1) "case-by-case balancing," which has led to clusters of free exercise cases; and (2) "definitional balancing," which has led to shifting standards of judicial review under the free exercise clause.

One way to read the Court's free exercise cases is that they reflect a method of case-by-case balancing of these conflicting constitutional interests. Thin lines and then clusters of cases have slowly emerged as the Court has adjudicated cases with comparable fact patterns and built on its immediate precedents. Accordingly, today there are clusters of cases upholding free exercise rights to engage in proselytism, worship, and other forms of religious expression; to receive unemployment compensation when discharged from work for religious reasons; to gain equal access to public schools, public forums, and public benefits. There are also clusters of cases dealing with failed free exercise claims to exemptions from military, prison, and taxation laws. A relatively consistent internal logic governs each cluster

of cases, and the Court will sometimes reach back several decades to re-
trieve or distinguish a precedent in that cluster.[21] But it is harder to make
out a common free exercise logic that applies across these clusters of cases.
Under this reading, proper categorization of the dispute in advance is critical to locking one's position into the cluster of cases most advantageous to
one's cause.[22]

A second, more complicated, way to read these cases is that they represent a series of shifting definitions of how the free exercise clause is to be
applied across the board in all cases. In a few cases, the Court has said explicitly, as it did in *Prince v. Massachusetts* (1944): "Our ruling does not
extend beyond the facts the case presents."[23] But in other cases, the Court
has defined a standard of review to be used to adjudicate future free exercise cases, even with decidedly different facts. Subsequent cases have applied this same standard of review until the Court determines that the experiment requires a new standard. What sometimes seems to trigger a
change in the standard of review is an extreme application of the prior
standard by an overreaching litigant or by an overindulgent Court.[24]

Defining general standards of review to resolve constitutional conflicts
between powers and rights is not unique to the free exercise clause. The
Supreme Court has engaged in this exercise in many cases arising under the
Bill of Rights and the Fourteenth Amendment. Particularly in the past half
century, the Court has developed a whole spectrum of standards of review,
from low-level to high-level scrutiny of the law that is challenged.

Under *low-level scrutiny*, the Court will uphold the challenged law if: (1)
it is in pursuit of a *legitimate* governmental interest, and (2) it is *reasonably
related* to that interest. This test, often called the *rational basis test,* involves high judicial deference to the legislature. It provides a loose safety
net to protect parties against governmental caprice and abuse by allowing a
court to strike down patently discriminatory and arbitrary laws.

Under *high-level scrutiny*, a court will uphold the challenged law only if:
(1) it is in pursuit of a *compelling* or overriding *governmental interest,* and
(2) it is *narrowly tailored* to achieve that interest, not intruding on the
claimant's rights any more than is absolutely necessary. This test, often
called the *compelling state interest test,* involves close judicial inquiry into
the purposes and provisions of the law—though the justices are divided
whether and how to read the legislative history alongside the actual text of
the challenged law. This strict scrutiny test empowers a court to strike
down the law altogether or to tailor it in a manner that will cause less harm
to the claimant.

Between these forms of review, the Court has developed a category of
"heightened" scrutiny. Under this standard, the Court will uphold the challenged law if: (1) it is in pursuit of an *important* or significant *governmental
interest,* and (2) it is *substantially related* to that interest. This test, often

FIGURE 7.1   Trends in Modern Free Exercise Law

Low Scrutiny	**Heightened Scrutiny**	**Strict Scrutiny**
legitimate interest	*significant interest*	*compelling interest*
rational link	*substantial link*	*narrowly tailored*
Reynolds (1879)		
	Cantwell (1940)	
		Sherbert (1963)
Smith (1990)		
		RFRA (1993)
Boerne [state laws] (1997)		RFRA/*Boerne* [federal laws] (1997)

called the *intermediate scrutiny test,* is neither as deferential to the legislature as the rational basis test nor as penetrating in its scrutiny as the compelling state interest test.

These standards of review can be easily contracted or conflated. A strong rational basis test can slide into an intermediate scrutiny test.[25] A strong intermediate scrutiny test can fold into a compelling state interest test. The three "tests" are not so much insular modes of analysis as general stopping points on a continuum. Viewed as such, they guide a court in resolving the constitutional conflict before it, and they help litigants predict the outcome of a case. The lower the level of scrutiny, the more likely it is that government will win. The higher the scrutiny, the more likely it is that the rights claimant will win.

This spectrum of standards of review helps us to gain another picture of the Supreme Court's free exercise doctrine. Since its first free exercise case in 1879, the United States Supreme Court has ranged across this entire spectrum of review. Although not all free exercise cases fit on this spectrum, a number of the main cases do. By plotting them (see Figure 7.1), we can at least get a rough picture of the main shifts in the Court's application of the free exercise clause.

In *Reynolds v. United States* (1879), the Court applied a very low level of scrutiny. The Court's only stated concern was whether the laws outlawing polygamy were "authorized," "reasonable," and "general" and whether they properly reached the actions of the parties.[26] This standard of review recurred in the pacifism cases from *Arver v. United States* (1918) onward, where the Court several times upheld military oaths and training as "legitimate," "authorized," and "necessary and proper" exercises of congressional power over national security and the military.[27] Every early religious liberty case that applied this standard of review found for the government.

In *Cantwell v. Connecticut* (1940), the Court for the first time applied a heightened level of scrutiny in its application of the free exercise clause. The Court cordoned off areas of religion that government could not regulate unless they were clearly criminal: religious beliefs, worship, and assembly. Regulation of other religious conduct was "permissible" so long as it was by "general and non-discriminatory legislation" and did not "unduly infringe" upon this exercise.[28] Later *Cantwell* progeny stated that government could not infringe on religious conduct on "such slender grounds" as "rational basis" or other "modest estimates of governmental competence." The law at issue, as the Court later put it, must "serve a significant governmental interest" to withstand free exercise scrutiny.[29] More than two dozen cases in the next two decades—often combining free exercise and free speech analysis—generally applied this intermediate standard of review. The cases were roughly evenly divided in holding for government and for the free exercise claimant.

In *Sherbert v. Verner* (1963), the Court for the first time applied a strict scrutiny standard of review in applying the free exercise clause. Not only was the law at issue to be general, as the rational basis test required. Not only was the law to be nondiscriminatory on religious grounds and not touch religious beliefs, as the intermediate scrutiny test required. The law was now also (1) to serve a compelling state interest, and (2) to be narrowly tailored to achieve that interest with the least possible intrusion on free exercise rights.[30] Under this standard, the *Sherbert* Court reviewed both the general law and its particular application to this free exercise claimant. Finding no compelling reason to apply the general law to this claimant, the Court ordered her exempt from the general law and entitled to receive the state unemployment compensation benefits that had been withheld from her. The Supreme Court used this strict scrutiny test of free exercise in ten cases after 1963, six times finding for the religious claimant, four times for the government.[31]

In *Employment Division v. Smith* (1990), the Court formally rejected the strict scrutiny test of free exercise and adopted a lower-level scrutiny test. Building on a series of cases in the prior decade that had avoided application of the *Sherbert* strict scrutiny test, the *Smith* Court held that "the right of free exercise does not relieve an individual of the obligation to comply with a 'valid and neutral law of general applicability on the ground that the law proscribes (or prescribes) conduct that his religion prescribes (or proscribes).'"[32] If a law is neutral and generally applicable, it is constitutional, even if it burdens a central aspect of the claimant's religion.[33] But if a law is not neutral or not generally applicable, it must be justified by a compelling governmental interest and narrowly tailored to achieve that interest. This latter caveat rendered the *Smith* test somewhat more protective of religious interests than the original *Reynolds* test. The Court in *Reynolds* and its progeny had readily upheld patently discriminatory laws that targeted the Mormons. In 1993, the Supreme Court used the *Smith* test to strike down discriminatory criminal laws that transparently targeted the ritual slaughtering practices of Santerians.[34] But in 2004, the Court refused to read the *Smith* test to require strict scrutiny of a state scholarship program that was open to all gifted post-secondary students, except those who pursued theology degrees.[35]

The weakening of free exercise scrutiny introduced by *Smith* was widely denounced as a travesty to religious liberty. In reaction, Congress passed the Religious Freedom Restoration Act (RFRA) in 1993. The stated purpose of the act was to "restore the compelling state interest test" of *Sherbert* and progeny—which the act called "a workable test for striking sensible balances between religious liberty and competing prior governmental interests." The act provided: "(a) In General [—] Government shall not substantially burden a person's exercise of religion even if the burden results from a rule of general applicability, except as provided in subsection (b). (b) Exception [—] Government may substantially burden a person's exercise of religion only if it demonstrates that application of the burden to the person (1) is in furtherance of a compelling governmental interest; and (2) is the least restrictive means of furthering that compelling governmental interest."[36]

In *City of Boerne v. Flores* (1997), however, the Supreme Court declared the Religious Freedom Restoration Act unconstitutional, at least as applied to the states. Congress had passed RFRA on the strength of section 5 of the Fourteenth Amendment, which empowered Congress to "enforce" the liberty provisions of the amendment, using "appropriate legislation." In the Court's judgment: "Legislation which alters the meaning of the Free Exercise Clause cannot be said to be enforcing the Clause."[37] The act, in the Court's judgment, fundamentally changed the free exercise law and was thus unconstitutional. With respect to free exercise claims against state and local laws, the *Smith* lower-level scrutiny test is again the law. Several states have responded to *Boerne* by passing their own religious freedom acts, modeled on RFRA and grounded in their own state constitutions. This has encouraged at least some religious litigants to sue local officials in state courts and receive the higher scrutiny of the local religious freedom restoration act—rather than sue in federal courts and receive the lower scrutiny mandated by *Smith* for the First Amendment free exercise clause.[38]

The *Boerne* case left the Religious Freedom Restoration Act standing as applied to judicial review of federal laws. Some lower federal courts have continued to apply RFRA, particularly in cases challenging the new application of federal laws of bankruptcy to religious parties.[39] In 2000, Congress passed a narrower statute, the Religious Land Use and Institutionalized Persons Act (RLUIPA). This law requires federal and state courts to apply strict scrutiny in cases involving substantial burdens on the free exercise rights of persons in prisons, hospitals, nursing homes, and other institutions. It also requires strict scrutiny of zoning and landmark laws that impose substantial burdens on the free exercise rights of religious property owners or that discriminate against or exclude religious properties and organizations in the implementation of these laws.[40] This act, too, has triggered new litigation by free exercise litigants against both federal and state officials. It remains to be seen whether RLUIPA will pass constitutional muster as applied to state claims. Unlike RFRA, RLUIPA targets only very specific free exercise claims, and it is grounded not only in section 5 of the Fourteenth Amendment but also in Congress's Article I powers over commerce and over taxing and spending. Even so, some lower courts question whether *Boerne* allows RLUIPA to be applied to the states.[41]

For now, *Boerne* might be best viewed as a step along the way to the creation of a two-track understanding of the free exercise clause. The federal government will be held to the stricter free exercise standard of RFRA and RLUIPA. State and local governments will be held to the looser free exercise standard of *Smith*. In its current form, this two-tracked approach to free exercise rights is not a reversal of *Cantwell's* incorporation doctrine. But it is something of a revival of the federalism values built into the text of the First Amendment. It is an open, and heated, question whether this neofederalist approach to religious freedom is wise or even warranted today. But *Boerne* is consistent with the Court's new concern for federalism in several other areas of constitutional law, most notably in its recent interpretation of the commerce clause of Article I of the Constitution and of section 5 of the Fourteenth Amendment.[42]

The two foregoing readings give us two pictures of the Court's modern free exercise doctrine—one as a collection of case clusters, a second as a series of shifting standards of review. Both readings account for most of the free exercise cases of the modern era, but not all. Occasionally, the Court has defied the common logic of a factual cluster—as it did in the *Smith* case, which was after all just another unemployment compensation case in the *Sherbert* cluster. Occasionally, the Court has wandered from a general standard of review—as it did in several cases holding against protections of

Jewish Sabbath Day observance, Muslim Friday worship, and Native American religious rites and sites. Occasionally, the Court has simply decided a case categorically—as it did in holding that pacifism is a statutory privilege and not a free exercise right or that religious oaths impugn religious beliefs and are thus categorically prohibited.

The Multiple Principles of Modern Free Exercise Law

The Supreme Court's modern free exercise cases are, in part, small skirmishes in great constitutional battles over principles of federalism, judicial review, and separation of powers. The Court's free exercise opinions thus sometimes reflect and project grand constitutional causes and conundrums that seem far removed from a litigant's simple petition for protection of the sources, sanctions, or sanctuaries of faith.

The Supreme Court's modern free exercise cases are also, however, small laboratories for carrying on the great American experiment in religious liberty. It is thus apt to read the Court's main free exercise cases not only in light of broader constitutional movements but also in terms of the founding principles of the American tradition of religious liberty. Such a reading produces a rather different picture of modern free exercise law. The main cases fall into clusters around the four main founding principles that are incorporated into the free exercise clause—principles that have, since 1980, been slowly reduced to a single concern for neutrality.

The eighteenth-century founders, as we saw, regarded the principle of free exercise as a basic protection for religious speech, press, and assembly—what is today called freedom of religious expression. They also regarded "free exercise" as an umbrella term that incorporated the principles of liberty of conscience, separation of church and state, and equality of a plurality of faiths.[43]

In its first modern case on point, *Cantwell v. Connecticut* (1940), the Court effectively read each of these principles into the free exercise clause, as well as the free speech clause as applied to religion. This First Amendment guarantee, the *Cantwell* Court declared, protects "[f]reedom of conscience and freedom to adhere to such religious organization or form of worship as the individual may choose." It "safeguards the free exercise of the chosen form of religion," the "freedom to act" on one's beliefs. It protects a "plurality of forms and expressions" of faith, each of which deserves equal protection under the law. "In the realm of religious faith, and in that of political belief," the Court wrote, "sharp differences arise."

> But the people of this nation have ordained in light of history that, in spite of the probability of the excesses and abuses, these liberties are, in the long view, essential to enlightened opinion and right conduct on the part of the citizens of

the democracy. The essential characteristic of these liberties is that under their shield, many types of life, character, opinion, and belief can develop unmolested and unobstructed. Nowhere is this shield more necessary than in our own country for a people composed of many races and of many creeds.[44]

In a number of free exercise cases from the early 1940s onward, the Supreme Court elaborated each of these founding principles of religious liberty.

Freedom and Equality of Religious Expression

The *Cantwell* Court gave clear guidance as to the meaning and measure of the freedom of religious expression. All religious expression, Justice Roberts wrote for the Court, "remains subject to regulation for the protection of society."

> In every case the power to regulate must be so exercised as not, in attaining a permissible end, unduly to infringe the protected freedom. No one would contest the proposition that a State may not, by statute, wholly deny the right to preach or to disseminate religious views. Plainly such a previous and absolute restraint would violate the terms of the guarantee. It is equally clear that a State may by general and non-discriminatory legislation regulate the times, the places, and the manner of [religious expression] . . . without unconstitutionally invading the liberties protected by the Fourteenth Amendment. . . . No one would have the hardihood to suggest . . . that religious liberty connotes the privilege to exhort others to physical attack upon those belonging to another sect. When clear and present danger of riot, disorder, interference with traffic upon the public streets, or other immediate threat to public safety, peace, or order appears, the power of the State to prevent or punish is obvious. Equally obvious is it that a State may not unduly suppress free communication of views, religious or other, under the guise of conserving desirable conditions.[45]

These were the keys to adjudicating free exercise cases on religious expression: (1) outright prohibitions and prior restraints on religious expression that effectively foreclosed it were forbidden; (2) discriminatory regulations of religious expression were also forbidden; but (3) general regulations that properly protected public safety and security were permissible. The Court elaborated on these sentiments in a long series of cases following *Cantwell*. Most of these cases were raised by the indefatigable Jehovah's Witnesses—a newly prominent Christian missionary group, for whom strong religious preaching, proselytism, pamphleteering, and public demonstrations of biblical beliefs were vital exercises of faith.[46]

The Court readily struck down outright prohibitions on religious proselytism and other forms of religious expression. In *Cantwell* itself, the Court held that merely unpopular preaching on the public streets of a religious neighborhood could not be prohibited or punished as a breach of the peace. In *Jamison v. Texas* (1943) and *Martin v. Struthers* (1943), the Court struck down ordinances that prohibited distribution of religious pamphlets in the public square and door to door. "The state may prohibit the use of the streets for the distribution of purely commercial leaflets," Justice Black declared for the *Jamison* Court. But "they may not prohibit the distribution of handbills in pursuit of a clearly religious activity merely because the handbills invite the purchase of books for the improved understanding of the religion or because the handbills seek in a lawful fashion to promote the raising of funds for religious purposes."[47] Three years later, the Court extended this ruling to company- and government-owned towns: Per se prohibitions and criminal penalties levied on such religious expression violate the free exercise and free speech clauses.[48]

The Court also struck down taxing schemes on religious preaching as "prior restraints" on the freedom of religious expression. In the leading case, *Murdock v. Pennsylvania* (1943), a Jehovah's Witness challenged the constitutionality of a city ordinance that required all persons soliciting or selling goods to procure a license for a day or for a one-, two-, or three-week period. Each license required payment of a fee: from $1.50 for a day to $20 for three weeks—more than nominal fees by 1943 standards. Jehovah's Witnesses were convicted and fined for soliciting, distributing religious literature, and collecting donations in the town without a license. They appealed, arguing that this was a tax laid specifically on the exercise of their religion.

The *Murdock* Court agreed. "The hand distribution of religious tracts is an age-old form of missionary evangelism," Justice Douglas wrote for the Court. It "occupies the same high estate under the First Amendment as do worship in the churches or preaching from the pulpits. It has the same claim to protection as the more orthodox and conventional exercises of religion." The freedom to engage in such religious activity is "available to all, not merely to those who can pay their own way." The tax imposed by the city "is a flat license tax, the payment of which is a condition for the exercise of these constitutional privileges. The power to tax the exercise of a privilege is the power to control or suppress its enjoyment. Those who can tax the exercise of this religious practice can make its exercise so costly as to deprive it of the resources necessary for its maintenance."[49] The *Murdock* Court thus struck down this licensing scheme. Three other early cases struck down comparable schemes, even with more nominal fees, that taxed the solicitation, distribution, and sale of religious literature and articles by Jehovah's Witnesses.[50]

Consistent with the dicta of *Cantwell,* the Court did allow general "time, place, and manner" regulations of religious expression—so long as they did not target religious expression per se, and so long as local officials implementing the statute had clear standards for implementation and no discretion to discriminate on religious grounds. In *Cantwell* itself, the city licensing regulation failed because it targeted religion and gave officials discretion to deny licenses to unpopular religious applicants. In *Kunz v. New York* (1951), the denial of a license to a Baptist minister to preach in a public park was struck down because local officials had open discretion to deny the licenses.[51] In *Niemotko v. State of Maryland* (1951), the denial of a permit to use a public park for "Bible talks" was struck down because the statute lacked clear criteria for such denials.[52] In *Fowler v. Rhode Island* (1953), an ordinance that prohibited religious speech but allowed for religious services in a public park was struck down because it was religiously discriminatory.[53]

In *Poulos v. New Hampshire* (1953), the Court upheld a municipal regulation of religious expression, and it used the case to underscore the kinds of regulation of religious expression that were permissible under the free exercise and free speech clauses. In this case, a New Hampshire town provided what the Court considered a properly "uniform, non-discriminatory, and consistent administration of . . . licenses for public meetings." Any parties intending to use public streets or parks for "theatrical or dramatic representation," "parades or processions," or "open air public meetings" were required to procure a license by written application in advance. A sliding fee of up to $300 would be charged for the license to pay for police protection, crowd control, and cleanup. Officials had no discretion to deny an application based on the nature of the applicant's activities. Parties would be charged with a set fine of $20 if they failed to procure a license for such an occasion.

A group of Jehovah's Witnesses seeking to use the public park for a religious meeting challenged the statute. The Court upheld it as a valid regulation of religious expression. What impressed the Court was that "the state left to the licensing officials no discretion as to granting permits, no power to discriminate, no control over speech. . . . The ordinance merely calls for the adjustment of unrestrained exercise of religions with the reasonable convenience and comfort of the whole city." This was licit even in the face of strong claims to religious expression. Justice Reed wrote for the Court:

> The principles of the First Amendment are not to be treated as a promise that everyone with opinions or beliefs to express may gather around him at any public place and any time a group for discussion or instruction. It is a non sequitur to say that First Amendment rights may not be regulated because they hold a preferred position in the hierarchy of the constitutional guarantees of the incidents of freedom. This Court has never so held and indeed has definitely indicated the contrary. It has indicated approval of reasonable non-dis-

criminatory regulation by government authority that preserves peace, order and tranquillity without deprivation of the First Amendment guarantees of free speech, press and the exercise of religion. . . . There is no basis for saying that freedom and order are not compatible. That would be a decision of desperation. Regulation and suppression are not the same, either in purpose or result, and courts of justice can tell the difference.[54]

Several subsequent cases have upheld this standard, on both free exercise and free speech grounds.[55] Most recently, in *Watchtower Bible and Tract Society of New York Inc. v. Village of Stratton* (2002),[56] the Court struck down under both the free speech and free exercise clauses an ordinance requiring all door-to-door solicitors and canvassers, including Jehovah's Witnesses, to obtain a permit containing the licensee's name. The *Watchtower* majority recognized the "legitimate interests" a town may have to regulate solicitation, including the prevention of crime and fraud and the protection of privacy. However, the Court stressed that "our precedent is clear that there must be a balance between these interests and the effect of the regulations on First Amendment rights." The *Watchtower* Court struck the balance in favor of the Jehovah's Witnesses. The Court recognized the Witnesses' religiously motivated desire for anonymity, and it found no evidence of crime or fraud in the record. Moreover, in the Court's judgment, the ordinance would have little to no effect on criminals who registered under a false name or knocked on doors for reasons not covered by the ordinance. The Court thus held that the ordinance was too broad in scope and insufficiently tailored to the government's stated interests to justify this burden on the Witnesses' free speech and free exercise rights.

The Court has long upheld regulations of religious expression even more readily when such expression threatened the life and limb of others or violated criminal law. In the leading case, *Prince v. Massachusetts* (1944), the Court upheld a state criminal law against a Jehovah's Witness, who with her nine-year-old ward distributed religious literature on the public streets in the evening. This was in technical violation of a state criminal law against the use of child labor after certain set hours. The woman was arrested and fined for violation of the statute. She appealed, claiming violation of both her and her ward's free exercise rights, as well as her parental rights to raise her ward in her own faith. She claimed further that the distribution of religious literature was not "labor" under the applicable statute but a form of religious exercise under the First Amendment. Given the gravity of the state interest in protecting children, who had historically been abused in the workplace, the Court applied the child labor statute literally and held for the state. Justice Rutledge stated the "delicate balance" struck by the Court:

On one side is the obviously earnest claim for freedom of conscience and religious practice. With it is allied the parent's claim to authority in her own household and in the rearing of her children. The parent's conflict with the state ... is serious enough when only secular matters are concerned. It becomes the more so when an element of religious conviction enters. Against these sacred private interests, basic in a democracy, stand the interests of society to protect the welfare of children. ... [N]either rights of religion nor rights of parenthood are beyond limitation. Acting to guard the general interest in youth's well being, the state as *parens patriae* may restrict the parent's control by requiring school attendance, regulating or prohibiting the child's labor, and in many other ways. Its authority is not nullified merely because the parent grounds his claims to control the child's course of conduct on religion or conscience. ... The right to practice religion freely does not include liberty to expose the community or the child to communicable disease or the latter to ill health or death.[57]

The Court thus held for the state. With this precedent, it was very easy for the Court, a few years later, to affirm a lower court decision that a child of Jehovah's Witness parents could receive a blood transfusion, despite the religious objection of conscientiously opposed parents.[58]

Liberty of Conscience

This brings us to the second main principle protected by the free exercise clause—the individual's liberty of conscience. At the heart of this principle is what the founders had called "the unalienable right of private judgment in matters of religion."[59] Liberty of conscience, as understood at American law today, embraces the freedom of the person to choose or to change religious beliefs or practices without coercion or control by government and without facing discrimination or penalties for the religious choices once made.

The Supreme Court came only gradually to this understanding of liberty of conscience in its interpretation of the free exercise clause. The Court's dicta in early cases, issued long before *Cantwell,* were promising enough. In *Watson v. Jones* (1871), Justice Miller had declared for a unanimous Court: "In this country the full and free right to entertain any religious belief, to practice any religious principle, and to teach any religious doctrine which does not violate the laws of morality and property, and which does not infringe personal rights, is conceded to all. The law knows no heresy, and is committed to the support of no dogma, the establishment of no sect."[60] Eight years later, in *Reynolds v. United States* (1879), the Court had underscored this principle by declaring that "Congress was deprived of all legislative power over mere [religious] opinion."[61]

Although it endorsed the liberty of conscience, the Court did little to protect it in these early free exercise cases. The polygamy cases from 1879 to
1890 upheld congressional laws that penalized Mormons for their practices,
as well as their beliefs in polygamy, and demanded from them all manner of
confessions and exculpatory oaths.[62] The early pacifism cases from 1918 to
1934 would hear nothing of a party's constitutional right to be protected
from swearing oaths to, or training for service in, the military—no matter
how devout and developed a party's conscientious scruples.[63]

This discordance of principle and practice continued in the early years after *Cantwell*. In *Cantwell* itself, Justice Roberts had declared confidently
for the Court that the free exercise clause was "absolute" in forestalling
"compulsion by law of the acceptance of any creed or the practice of any
form of worship."[64] But in its very next case, *Minersville School Board v.
Gobitis* (1940), decided two weeks later, the Court betrayed this very principle. The children of a Jehovah's Witness were expelled from a public
school because they refused to salute the American flag or recite the pledge
of allegiance. The Bible, in their understanding and that of their coreligionists, prohibited such acts as forms of false worship. To compel them to such
acts, their parents argued, was a violation of the liberty of conscience. The
Supreme Court disagreed. The purpose of the school policy was to promote
national unity and loyalty, said the Court, not to institute a false form of
worship. "To stigmatize legislative judgment in providing for this universal
gesture of respect for the symbol of our national life in the setting of the
common school as a lawless inroad on that freedom of conscience which
the Constitution protects," Justice Frankfurter wrote for a divided Court,
"would amount to no less than the pronouncement of pedagogical and psy-
chological dogma in a field where courts possess no marked and certainly
no controlling competence."[65]

Three years later, in *West Virginia State Board of Education v. Barnette*
(1943), the Court overruled *Gobitis* and read the First Amendment to exempt parties from mandatory participation in rituals to which they were
conscientiously opposed. *Barnette* raised similar facts to those of *Gobitis*:
Jehovah's Witness children were again expelled from public school for their
failure to salute the flag and recite the pledge of allegiance, and now faced
fines if they persisted in their recalcitrance. While acknowledging the importance of teaching national loyalty and unity in public schools, the Court
held that the compulsory participation in such civic ceremonies violated the
liberty of conscience. As Justice Jackson wrote for the Court:

> If there is any fixed star in our constitutional constellation, it is that no official,
> high or petty, can prescribe what shall be orthodox in politics, nationalism, re-
> ligion, or other matters of opinion or force citizens to confess by word or act

their faith therein. If there are any circumstances which permit an exception, they do not now occur to us.[66]

Although in a pair of cases immediately thereafter the Court again stumbled on this principle of liberty of conscience, *Barnette* soon became the rule.[67] The Court has since held that government officials cannot require a party who is conscientiously opposed to swear an oath before receiving citizenship status[68] or a property tax exemption.[69] In *Torcaso v. Watkins* (1961), the Court extended this principle to say that a professed atheist could not be required to swear an oath attesting to his belief in God as part of his initiation into a state bureaucratic position.[70] "The Free Exercise Clause categorically forbids government from regulating, prohibiting, or rewarding religious beliefs as such," the Court later put it in summary of the case.[71]

In *Sherbert v. Verner* (1963), the Court widened this liberty of conscience reading of the free exercise clause. Not only could the free exercise clause exempt conscientious parties from participation in oath swearing and other ceremonies that ran afoul of their conscientious beliefs, but the free exercise clause could also exempt them from adherence to other general laws and regulations that unduly burdened their consciences.

Sherbert posed a conflict between the right of religious conscience and the right to a state benefit. A Seventh-day Adventist was discharged from employment, and foreclosed from reemployment, because of her conscientious refusal to work on Saturday, her Sabbath Day. She was denied unemployment compensation from the state, for she had been, according to the applicable statute, discharged "for cause" and was thus disqualified from the benefit. She appealed, arguing that the disqualifying provisions of the statute "abridged her right to the free exercise of her religion." If she exercised her religious right to Saturday sabbatarianism, she would lose her civil right to a state benefit. If she was to receive her civil right to a state benefit, she would have to forgo her religious right to Saturday sabbatarianism. Such a conflict, she argued, violated her free exercise rights.

The Supreme Court agreed. As Justice Brennan put it for the Court: "To condition the availability of [state] benefits upon this appellant's willingness to violate a cardinal principle of her religious faith effectively penalizes the free exercise of her constitutional liberties."[72] The Court ordered Ms. Sherbert exempt from the general strictures on payment and entitled to unemployment compensation benefits.

In a trio of cases, the Court extended the technical *Sherbert* holding. One case involved a Jehovah's Witness who had individual scruples, not shared by fellow Witnesses, against production of hardware that would be used for military tanks.[73] Another case involved a new convert to Seventh-day

Adventism who began to insist on the right to observe her Saturday Sabbath.[74] A third case involved a Christian party who refused a temporary position because it might require him to work on his Sabbath.[75] Each of these parties lost their employment. Each was denied unemployment compensation benefits on the general rule that he or she had been discharged for cause. Each successfully appealed to the Court for a free exercise exemption from this general rule and was found entitled to unemployment compensation. Neither the novelty nor the idiosyncrasy of a religious belief changed the core violation of the liberty of conscience. As Chief Justice Burger put it for the Court in *Thomas v. Review Board* (1981): "Where the state conditions receipt of an important benefit upon conduct proscribed by a religious faith, or where it denies such a benefit because of conduct mandated by religious belief, thereby putting substantial pressure on an adherent to modify his behavior and to violate his beliefs, a burden upon religion exists." This violates the liberty of conscience values of the free exercise clause and entitles the claimant to an exemption.[76]

In *McDaniel v. Paty* (1978), the Court extended this analysis to the political sphere. The original Constitution of Tennessee (1796) prohibited clergy from holding political office in the state. The purpose of this prohibition was "to assure the success of a new political experiment, the separation of church and state."[77] With the growing religious pluralism of their societies, other states had eventually struck such clauses from their constitutions. Tennessee alone retained it. An otherwise qualified Baptist minister was enjoined from running for a political position. He appealed, arguing that this prohibition violated his free exercise rights. It posed a direct conflict between his religious rights to ministry and his civil rights to run for political office. The Court agreed. Quoting both *Sherbert* and James Madison, the Court held that "the State is 'punishing a religious profession with the privation of a civil right.'"[78] The state constitutional prohibition was struck down as a violation of the free exercise clause.

Separation of Church and State

The heart of the principle of liberty of conscience is the individual's "right of private judgment" in matters of faith. The heart of the principle of separation of church and state is a religious group's right to define for itself what *Cantwell* had called its "religious organization and form of worship." Separation of church and state, as we shall see in the next chapter, has been a critical principle for interpretation of the disestablishment clause. But it has also been a valuable principle for interpretation of the free exercise clause: It protects a religious group's rights to organize its worship, property, and polity without interference from the state.

Before *Cantwell,* the Court had issued more than a dozen cases that protected the general common law rights of religious groups to acquire, use, and alienate property without confiscation or undue interference by the state. It had also upheld the common law rights of religious groups to organize their own internal polities, to regulate the internal activities of their religious officials, and to set standards for the entrance and exit of their voluntary members.[79]

After *Cantwell,* the Court converted some of these early common law rules into constitutional principles protected by the free exercise clause.[80] A trio of cases held that religious groups must have autonomy to decide their own internal disputes, and courts must defer to the judgment of the highest religious authorities among such disputants.

In *Kedroff v. Saint Nicholas Cathedral* (1952), the Court struck down a New York religious corporation law, passed in the Cold War era, that rejected the authority of the Moscow Patriarch to appoint a bishop in a local Russian Orthodox church. Justice Reed declared for the Court:

> Here there is a transfer by statute of control over churches. This violates our rule of separation between church and state.... [It also violates] a spirit of freedom for religious organizations, an independence from secular control or manipulation, in short, power to decide for themselves, free from state interference, matters of church government as well as those of faith and doctrine. Freedom to select the clergy, where no improper methods of choice are proven, we think, must now be said to have federal constitutional protection as a part of the free exercise of religion against state interference.[81]

In *Presbyterian Church of the United States v. Hull Presbyterian Church* (1969), the Court reversed the Georgia Supreme Court, which had resolved an internal church dispute over property by inquiring whether either party had departed from orthodox doctrine. In outlawing such a "departure-from-doctrine" test, Justice Brennan put the matter firmly for a unanimous Court:

> First Amendment values are plainly jeopardized when church property litigation is made to turn on the resolution by civil courts of controversies over religious doctrine and practice. If civil courts undertake to resolve such controversies in order to adjudicate the property dispute, the hazards are ever present of inhibiting the free development of religious doctrine and of implicating secular interests in matters of purely ecclesiastical concern.[82]

In *Orthodox Diocese v. Milivojevich* (1976), the Court outlawed even "marginal review" by a civil court of an ecclesiastical decision that might appear "arbitrary or collusive." Justice Brennan again spoke for the Court:

"Indeed, it is the essence of religious faith that ecclesiastical decisions are reached and are to be accepted as matters of faith whether or not rational or acceptable by objective criteria." The Constitution allows "religious organizations to establish their own rules and regulations for internal discipline and government, and to create tribunals for adjudicating disputes over these matters. When this choice is exercised and ecclesiastical tribunals are created to decide disputes . . . the Constitution requires that civil courts accept their decisions as binding."[83]

The Court also extended this concern for religious group rights in other contexts. Already in *Pierce v. Society of Sisters* (1925), the Court had upheld the "fundamental right" of religious schools to exist and to educate children in the faith without undue interference by the state.[84] In *National Labor Relations Board v. Catholic Bishop* (1979), the Court used this same principle to deny the NLRB jurisdiction over a Catholic school's teachers.[85] In the same vein, *Corporation of the Presiding Bishop v. Amos* (1987) upheld the exemption provision of the Civil Rights Act, which allowed a religious employer to discriminate on religious grounds in the selection or retention of its employees.[86]

In *Wisconsin v. Yoder* (1972), the Court extended this concern for religious group identity and autonomy even further. The Court required that Old Order Amish parents and communities be exempted from full compliance with compulsory school attendance laws for their children, in order to preserve their ascetic, agrarian religious communitarianism. What seemed to impress the Court was that the Amish "lifestyle" was "not merely a matter of personal preference, but one of deep religious conviction, shared by an organized group, and intimately related to daily living" and that these "religious beliefs and attitudes towards life, family and home . . . have not altered in fundamentals for centuries." In the Court's view, compliance with the compulsory school attendance law "carries with it a very real threat of undermining the Amish community and religious practice as they exist today; they must either abandon belief and be assimilated into society at large, or be forced to migrate to some other and more tolerant region."[87]

Religious Pluralism

The point of all these protections of individual and corporate free exercise was to encourage and protect a plurality of religions before the law. "The essential characteristic of these liberties" of the free exercise clause, Justice Roberts wrote in *Cantwell*, "is, that under their shield many types of life, character, opinion and belief can develop unmolested and unobstructed. Nowhere is this shield more necessary than in our own country for a people composed of many races and of many creeds."[88]

Even Justice Frankfurter and Justice Black, whose interpretations of the First Amendment religion clauses have often been criticized, earnestly defended the principle of religious pluralism. "Propagation of belief—or even disbelief in the supernatural—is protected, whether in church or chapel, mosque or synagogue, tabernacle or meetinghouse," wrote Justice Frankfurter wisely in his otherwise unwise *Gobitis* opinion. "Likewise the Constitution assures generous immunity to the individual from imposition of penalties for offending, in the course of his own religious activities, the religious views of others, be they a minority or those dominant in government."[89] The free exercise clause, Justice Black echoed, mandates that government "cannot exclude individual Catholics, Lutherans, Mohammedans, Baptists, Jews, Methodists, Non-believers, Presbyterians, or the members of any faith, *because of their faith, or lack of it,* from receiving the benefits of public welfare legislation."[90]

Justice Douglas underscored the difficulty of living up to these constitutional mandates as the nation's religions had pluralized and its welfare laws had proliferated. He wrote in concurrence in *Sherbert v. Verner:*

> Religious scruples of Moslems require them to attend a mosque on Friday and to pray five times daily. Religious scruples of a Sikh require him to carry a regular or a symbolic sword. Religious scruples of a Jehovah's Witness teach him to be a colporteur, going from door to door, from town to town, distributing his religious pamphlets. Religious scruples of a Quaker compel him to refrain from swearing [an oath] and to affirm instead. Religious scruples of a Buddhist may require him to refrain from partaking of any flesh. The examples could be multiplied . . . to show that many people hold beliefs alien to the majority of our society—beliefs that are protected by the First Amendment but which could easily be trod upon under the guise of "police" or "health" regulations reflecting the majority's views.[91]

Neutralizing the Free Exercise Clause

From 1940 to the early 1980s, the Supreme Court read the free exercise clause in expansive terms. The clause not only protected the freedom of religious expression. It also protected the attendant principles of liberty of conscience, separation of church and state, and equality of plural faiths before the law. The rigor and range of the Court's free exercise inquiry did not always bring victory to religious claimants. Free exercise claimants lost as many cases as they won in this period, particularly when their religious exercise touched on fundamental issues of public policy or criminal law. But the free exercise clause provided what *Cantwell* had called for: "a multilayered shield" to protect many forms and forums of individual and corporate religious life.

In the course of the 1980s, the Supreme Court slowly reduced the free exercise clause to a single and simple principle of neutrality. The Court's earlier concerns to protect the conscience of the religious individual and the autonomy of the religious group from state intrusions slowly fell aside. The Court's earlier decisions to strike down laws that imposed taxes or discriminatory restrictions on religious expression also fell aside. In a series of cases culminating in *Employment Division v. Smith* (1990), the Court systematically read each of these constitutive principles out of the free exercise clause, reducing it to a single and simple principle of neutrality.

The Court's first step on the path to neutrality came already in *Jones v. Wolf* (1979). This was another intrachurch dispute case. Three years before, in *Milivojevich,* the Court had confirmed, in strong terms, its century-long sentiment that religious groups must be left to resolve their own internal disputes over polity and property without state interference. The Court had ordered lower courts to defer to the resolution offered by the highest religious authority and to forgo even "marginal review" of that religious authority's decision. Since the *Kedroff* case of 1952, the Court had said that this deferential approach to religious groups was mandated by the First Amendment.

In *Jones v. Wolf,* however, the Court held that intrachurch disputes could be resolved on the basis of "neutral principles of law." With little attempt to distinguish these earlier cases, Justice Blackmun declared for the Court: Nothing in "the First Amendment requires States to adopt a rule of compulsory deference to religious authority in resolving church property disputes." In most instances, courts can resolve these cases without reference to the religious sources or dimensions of the dispute.

> The primary advantages of the neutral principles approach are that it is completely secular in operation, and yet flexible enough to accommodate all forms of religious organization and polity. The method relies exclusively on objective, well-established concepts of trust and property law familiar to lawyers and judges.[92]

Since *Jones v. Wolf* was issued, intrachurch disputes over everything from consecrated sanctuaries and cemeteries to church storage sheds and campgrounds have been resolved under the simple "neutral principles" approach.[93]

In *Goldman v. Weinberger* (1986), the Court took a further step down this neutrality path. The Court held that the free exercise clause permitted the Air Force to prohibit a rabbi from wearing his yarmulke as part of his military uniform. The Court so held even though the petitioner served as a psychologist in the mental health clinic of a military base (not on the front lines), even though for three years earlier he was accorded this "privilege," and even though numerous other exemptions for religious garb, including crucifixes, were accorded by the 190-page military dress code. The requirements for military discipline and uniformity, in the Court's view, outweighed the countervailing religious interests—however deep-seated and essential they were to the petitioner.[94]

In *Bowen v. Roy* (1986), the Court pressed this concern for uniformity and neutrality from the military context to the regulatory context. A Native American objected to having a Social Security number assigned to his daughter, arguing, in the Court's words, that "he must keep her person and spirit unique and that the uniqueness of the Social Security number as an identifier, coupled with the other uses of the number over which she has no control, will 'rob the spirit' of his daughter and prevent her from attaining greater spiritual power." He requested an exemption for his daughter, until she reached sufficient spiritual maturity at the age of sixteen. Although it acknowledged the sincerity and substance of the parent's claim, the Court found for the government. Chief Justice Burger's opinion for the Court was in striking contrast to his highly solicitous tone in *Wisconsin v. Yoder* (1972):

> Never to our knowledge has the Court interpreted the First Amendment to require the Government *itself* to behave in ways that the individual believes will further his or her spiritual development or that of his or her own family. The Free Exercise Clause simply cannot be understood to require the Government to conduct its own internal affairs in ways that comport with the religious beliefs of particular citizens.... Government meets its burden when it demonstrates that a challenged requirement for governmental benefits, neutral and uniform in its application, is a reasonable means of promoting a legitimate public interest.[95]

In *O'Lone v. Estate of Shabazz* (1987), the Court extended this logic to prison officials, holding that a change in prison policy that deprived Muslim inmates from attending Jumu'ah, their Friday collective worship service, did not violate their free exercise rights. Here the requirements for security, protection of other prisoners, and other "reasonable penological objectives," in the Court's view, outweighed the free exercise rights of the Muslim prisoners. Moreover, said the Court quoting *Bowen v. Roy* and other precedents, it is wrong to impose a "special burden on prison officials to prove 'that no reasonable method exists by which [prisoners'] religious rights can be accommodated.'" So long as the prison's regulations are "neutral and reasonable," they pass constitutional muster.[96]

In *Lyng v. Northwest Indian Cemetery Protective Association* (1988),[97] the Court extended this neutrality logic to the actions of the United States Forest Service. The Court held that the free exercise clause does not prohibit the Forest Service's construction of a road through a sacred site used for centuries by Indians—notwithstanding the protective policy of the American Indian Religious Freedom Act[98] and the Court's recognition that this construction "will have severe adverse effects on the practice of their religion."[99] Citing *Roy* and *O'Lone,* Justice O'Connor defended this holding with blunt literalism:

> The crucial word in the constitutional text is "prohibit": "For the Free Exercise Clause is written in terms of what the government cannot do to the individual." . . . However much we might wish that it were otherwise, government simply could not operate if it were required to satisfy every citizen's religious needs and desires. A broad range of government activities—from social welfare programs to foreign aid to conservation policies—will always be considered essential to the spiritual well-being of some citizens, often on the basis of sincerely-held religious beliefs. Others will find the very same activities deeply offensive, and perhaps incompatible with their own search for spiritual fulfillment and with the tenets of their religion. The First Amendment must apply to all citizens alike, and it can give to none of them a veto over public programs that do not prohibit the free exercise of religion. The Constitution does not, and courts cannot, offer to reconcile the various competing demands on government, many of them rooted in sincere religious belief, that inevitably arise in so diverse a society as ours.[100]

The following term, in *Jimmy Swaggart Ministries v. Board of Equalization of California* (1990), the Court pressed this logic further and upheld the retroactive imposition of sales and use taxes on the sales of religious articles by a religious ministry. Swaggart Ministries argued that the imposition of such taxes was a prior restraint on the exercise of its religion—which the Court had explicitly outlawed in *Murdock v. Pennsylvania* (1943) and its progeny. The Court rather speciously distinguished these earlier cases: These earlier cases, Justice O'Connor wrote for the Court, dealt with "prior" restraints on free exercise, not post hoc collections of taxes. (The Court said nothing about the effect of future collection of such taxes on Swaggart Ministries.) They addressed specific flat taxes on religious solicitation, not general state taxes imposed on all sales of goods. (The Court ignored that the earlier tax schemes were imposed on all solicitors, not just religious ministers, and in some schemes had sliding fee scales depending on the number of days the license was to be used.) By contrast, the state's tax challenged in this case is not "a flat tax, represents only a small fraction of any retail sale, and applies neutrally to all retail sales of tangible personal property." To drive home her point, Justice O'Connor also questioned whether Swaggart Ministries really had much of a free exercise burden: "There is no evidence in this case that collection and payment of the tax violates appellant's sincere religious beliefs. . . . The only burden on appellant is the claimed reduction in income."[101]

The foregoing cases had, in effect, written out of the free exercise clause the multiple principles that had earlier informed the Court's free exercise opinions. *Bowen v. Roy* and *O'Lone v. Estate of Shabazz* undercut the Court's earlier solicitude for liberty of conscience. *Jones v. Wolf* and *Lyng* undercut the Court's concerns for the rights of religious groups captured in the principle of separation of church and state. *Lyng, O'Lone,* and *Goldman v. Weinberger* undercut the Court's earlier solicitude for the equality of plural religious faiths, particularly the needs of religious minorities to be protected against general legislation. All these cases, most notably *Lyng* and *Swaggart Ministries,* reduced the Court's nuanced interpretations of the freedom of religious expression to a blunt inquiry into simple neutrality.

While these cases may have been isolated to their facts, *Employment Division v. Smith* (1990) wove their holdings into a new and narrow understanding of the free exercise clause.[102] Smith, a Native American, ingested peyote as part of the sacramental rite of the Native American church of which he was a member. Discharged from employment at a drug rehabilitation center because of this practice, he applied for unemployment compensation from the State of Oregon. Such compensation was denied on grounds that peyote ingestion was disqualifying criminal misconduct. Smith appealed, ultimately to the Supreme Court, claiming a violation of his free exercise rights.

The *Smith* Court rejected his argument, even though the case fell within the holdings of unemployment compensation cases from *Sherbert v. Verner* (1963) to *Frazee v. Illinois Employment Security Department* (1989). More important, the Court denied the validity of the *Sherbert* "compelling state interest" test altogether and explained away its application in subsequent cases. Henceforth, Justice Scalia wrote for the majority, "the right of free exercise does not relieve an individual of the obligation to comply with a 'valid and neutral law of general applicability.'"[103] Such laws, when promulgated under proper procedures, must prevail—regardless of the nature of the state's interest and regardless of any intrusion on the interest of a religious believer or body. Religious petitioners whose beliefs or practices are burdened by such neutral, generally applicable laws must seek redress in the legislatures, not the courts.

Smith effectively reduced the free exercise guarantee to the single principle of neutrality. This is not an entirely toothless provision, as the Court showed in its next free exercise case, *Church of Lukumi Babalu Aye, Inc. v. City of Hialeah* (1993).[104] The *Hialeah* case posed a free exercise challenge to a city ordinance that singled out local followers of the Santerian faith for special restrictions and penalties for engaging in the ritual slaughter of animals—a central practice of their faith. Even using the *Smith* test, the Court struck down the statute in question, for it was neither a general law nor neutrally applied. It transparently targeted Santerian believers and practices for special prohibitions, in pursuit of no compelling state interest.

The weakness of the *Smith* neutrality test, however, can be seen in *Locke v. Davey* (2004).[105] The State of Washington established a "Promise Scholarship" program for its gifted college-bound students. The program required students to meet clear academic and financial need criteria. Students were free to use the scholarship at any accredited college. But the program's regulations stated that the student could not pursue a degree in theology, for that would violate the state constitutional prohibition on funding of religion. Davey met all the eligibility criteria and received a Promise Scholarship. He chose to attend Northwest College, an accredited college affiliated with the Assemblies of God that teaches a liberal arts curriculum from a decidedly Christian perspective. Davey declared a double major in business and in pastoral ministry. Because of his pastoral ministry major, the state withdrew his scholarship.

Davey appealed, arguing that such targeting of religion majors for special exclusions violates the principle of equal treatment and neutrality demanded by both the free exercise and the disestablishment clause. Moreover, it forces him to choose between two rights: if he accepts the scholarship, he may not pursue a theology degree; if he pursues a theology degree, he must give up his scholarship. The State of Washington countered that it was not obstructing Davey's free exercise rights but merely refusing to subsidize his exercise of them in violation of its state constitution.

The Supreme Court agreed with the State of Washington and found no violation of Davey's free exercise rights. Writing for a 7–2 majority, Chief Justice Rehnquist characterized this as a case that involves the "play in the joints" between the free exercise and disestablishment clauses.[106] The free exercise clause does not require the state to pay for Davey's scholarship, nor does the disestablishment clause prevent the state from doing so. Distribution of scholarship money was a state legislative decision, and the state's decision to exclude theology majors from funding cast only "a relatively minor burden on Promise Scholars." Eligible students could still go to any accredited college, including a religious college. They could still take any courses, including religion courses. They simply could not be theology majors. This is not the kind of facial discrimination, the Court concluded, that requires inquiry into a compelling state interest or least restrictive alternative. It is a sensible, neutral, and generally applicable law that states are and must be fully empowered to make.

Only Justice Scalia, the author of the *Smith* test, and Justice Thomas dissented. For them, Washington's program was transparently discriminatory against religion on its face, and this required the state to demonstrate a compelling state interest for excluding theology majors.

As we saw in our mapping of free exercise doctrine, *Smith* remains the law, at least for all free exercise challenges to state and local laws. But virtually all the earlier free exercise cases that had offered a more multiprincipled reading of the free exercise clause also remain good law. A few of these cases were distinguished by *Smith* and its predecessors, but none was overturned. This collection of cases will provide a formidable arsenal of free exercise protections if and when redeployed. But, for now, these earlier free exercise cases have been effectively set aside in favor of the prevailing neutrality test.

Free Speech and Statutory Protections of Religion

With the neutralization of the free exercise clause, religious claimants have sought other forms and forums of protection. Two forums have been particularly important—the First Amendment free speech clause and new federal and state statutes.

Free Speech and Religion

It is no small irony that today the free speech clause affords considerably more protection to religious liberty than the free exercise clause. But it must be noted that the free speech clause has long been invoked for the protection of religious liberty. The free speech clause has been used to review state and local laws since 1925.[107] Before *Cantwell v. Connecticut* (1940), both the Supreme Court and lower federal courts used the free speech clause to outlaw patently discriminatory laws that closed local public squares to religious preaching and pamphleteering.[108] In *Cantwell* and in several cases thereafter, religious claimants seeking protection of their religious expression used both the free exercise and free speech clauses to assert their rights. The two clauses afforded comparably rigorous standards of review, and it often proved safer, even if sometimes redundant, to predicate one's claim on both clauses. To be sure, there were dimensions of free exercise protection—notably claims of conscience and of church autonomy—that the free speech clause did not and could not reach. But at least on questions of freedom of religious expression, claimants often sought free speech and free exercise protection simultaneously.

With the gradual weakening of the free exercise clause in the course of the 1980s and 1990s, religious claimants have turned increasingly to the free speech clause alone for protection. Several of these free speech cases have reinvigorated the doctrine of equality by requiring that religious individuals and groups must be given "equal access" to facilities and benefits generally afforded to nonreligious groups.[109]

The opening case in this sequence was *Widmar v. Vincent* (1981). The state university in Missouri at Kansas City had a policy of opening its facilities to voluntary student groups. More than 100 student groups organized themselves in the year at issue. A voluntary student group, organized for private religious devotion and charity, sought access to the university facilities that year. The group was denied access, in application of the university's written policy that its buildings and grounds were not to be used "for purposes of religious worship or religious teaching." The student group appealed, arguing that this policy of exclusion violated their free exercise, free speech, and equal protection rights. The university countered that it had a compelling state interest in maintaining the "strict separation of church and state" as both the First Amendment and the state constitution required.

The *Widmar* Court found for the religious student group. Drawing on free speech precedents, the Court held that where a state university creates a limited public forum open to voluntary student groups, religious groups must be given "equal access" to that forum. Justice Powell wrote for the Court that the university "has discriminated against student groups and speakers based on their desire to use a generally open forum to engage in religious worship and discussion. These are forms of speech and association protected by the First Amendment. In order to justify discriminatory exclusions from a public forum based on the religious content of the group's intended speech" the university must show that "its regulation is necessary to serve a compelling state interest and that it is narrowly drawn to achieve that end." In the Court's view, a general desire to keep a strict separation of church and state was not a sufficiently compelling state interest. The religious groups would enjoy only "incidental benefits" from this ruling. The values of "equal treatment and access" for religious groups outweighed the hypothetical dangers of a religious establishment.[110]

In *Lamb's Chapel v. Center Moriches Union Free School District* (1993), the Court extended the "equal access" principle of the free speech clause to other religious groups besides students. A local school board, pursuant to state policy, opened its school facilities, during nonschool time, for various "social, civic, recreational, and political uses" by voluntary groups in the community. The school board policy stated explicitly, however, that the "school premises shall not be used by any group for religious purposes." An evangelical church twice applied for use of the facilities to show a film series that discussed traditional family values from a Christian perspective. Their application was denied. Lamb's Chapel appealed, arguing that this exclusion violated their free speech rights.

The *Lamb's Chapel* Court agreed. Relying on *Widmar* and other free speech cases, the Court found that Lamb's Chapel had been discriminatorily denied access to this limited public forum. As Justice White put it for the Court:

The film series involved here no doubt dealt with a subject otherwise permissible, . . . and its exhibition was denied solely because the film series dealt with the subject from a religious standpoint. The principle that has emerged from our cases "is that the First Amendment forbids the government to regulate speech in ways that favor some viewpoints or ideas at the expense of others."[111]

Again, the school district's concern for protecting against the establishment of religion was not considered a sufficient reason for denying equal access to this religious group.

In *Rosenberger v. Rector and Visitors of the University of Virginia* (1995), a sharply divided Court extended this equal access principle to hold that a voluntary group of religious students in a state university was entitled to the same funding made available to nonreligious student groups. The University of Virginia encouraged student groups to organize themselves for extracurricular activities. Each student group was required to petition for the right to be recognized as such a group, to pledge that it would not discriminate in its membership, and to include in all communications a disclaimer that the group and its activities were independent of the university. In the year in question, 343 such voluntary student groups were organized.

Properly registered student groups were permitted to apply for funding from a general student activity fund to facilitate their activities. The funds could be used for a variety of purposes, including the costs of printing and distributing the group's literature. All such funds were to be paid to outside contractors. Of the 343 properly registered student groups, 118 received funds, and fifteen were denied funds.

One of the groups denied funds was a religious student group that was properly registered at the university. The group printed an overtly religious newspaper, called *Wide Awake: A Christian Perspective at the University of Virginia*. The group's request for funds to defray printing costs was denied, on grounds that the student activity fund could not be used for "religious activities." Such activities were defined in the school's regulations as "any activity 'that primarily promotes or manifests a particular belief in or about a deity or an ultimate reality.'" The group appealed, arguing that such discriminatory treatment violated, among other things, their free speech rights.

The *Rosenberger* Court agreed and held that the University of Virginia had violated these students' free speech rights. The state university policy, Justice Kennedy wrote for the Court, improperly "selects for disfavored treatment those student journalistic efforts with religious editorial viewpoints." The denial of funding to this otherwise qualified student group "is based upon viewpoint discrimination not unlike the discrimination the

school district relied upon in *Lamb's Chapel* and that we found invalid."
The principle of equal access applied as much to state university funding as
to state university facilities.

Justice Kennedy elaborated:

> Vital First Amendment speech principles are at stake here. The first danger to
> liberty lies in granting the State the power to examine publications to deter-
> mine whether or not they are based on some ultimate idea and if so for the
> State to classify them [as religious]. The second, and corollary, danger is to
> speech from the chilling of individual thought and expression. That danger is
> especially real in the University setting, where the State acts against a back-
> ground and tradition of thought and experiment that is at the center of our in-
> tellectual and philosophic tradition. . . . For the University, by regulation, to
> cast disapproval on particular viewpoints of its students risks the suppression
> of free speech and creative inquiry in one of the vital centers for the nation's
> intellectual life, its college and university campuses.[112]

In a sharply worded dissent, Justice Souter, joined by three others, argued
that the Court had used the equal access principle of the free speech clause
to undermine a cardinal principle of the disestablishment clause. "Using
public funds for the direct subsidization of preaching the word is categorically forbidden under the Establishment Clause, and if the Clause was
meant to accomplish nothing else, it was meant to bar this use of public
money."[113]

In *Good News Club v. Milford Central School* (2001),[114] the Court again
upheld the equal access principle in the face of countervailing establishment
concerns. Authorized by a New York statute, the Milford Central School
District enacted a policy for local residents to use local public school facilities after school hours, among other things, for "instruction in any branch
of education, learning, or the arts" and for "social, civic and recreational
meetings. . . . " The policy, however, prohibited use of the facilities by any
group "for religious purposes" lest the school district violate federal and
state prohibitions on the establishment of religion.

Local representatives of the Good News Club, a private Christian organization that instructed children aged 6–12 in Christian morality and practice, sought permission from the Milford School District to hold the club's
weekly after-school meetings in the cafeteria of an elementary school. The
lesson plans indicated that these meetings would involve adult-led prayers,
the collective singing of religious songs, and the children's recitation of
Bible verses, among other activities. The Milford superintendent concluded
that such intended activities would constitute use of the public school facilities for overtly "religious purposes" and denied the application for access
to the school facilities. Good News appealed, arguing that Milford's policy

of excluding the club's meetings from this limited public forum was religious viewpoint discrimination in violation of its free speech rights.

The *Good News* Court agreed. Writing for a plurality, Justice Thomas declared that while the State may restrict its forum to and for certain purposes, "[t]he State's power to restrict speech" within such a forum "must not discriminate against speech on the basis of viewpoint." The school district was not obliged to create this "limited public forum," but once it did, any restriction had to be viewpoint-neutral and reasonable in light of the forum's purpose. The Good News Club's intended use of the forum fit easily within this public forum's stated purpose of facilitating "instruction in any branch of education, learning, or the arts," Justice Thomas reasoned. "[S]peech discussing otherwise permissible subjects cannot be excluded from a limited public forum on the ground that the subject is discussed from a religious viewpoint." That a program of instruction might be "quintessentially religious" in inspiration or "decidedly religious in nature" does not prohibit it from being characterized as a proper teaching of morals and sound cultivation of character. The Court noted that the Good News Club's storytelling and prayers were no more religious in content than the *Wide Awake* articles protected in *Rosenberger* or the family values film protected in *Lamb's Chapel*. The Court noted further that "for purposes of the Free Speech Clause . . . we can see no logical difference in kind between the invocation of Christianity by the Club and the invocation of teamwork, loyalty, or patriotism by other associations to provide a foundation for their lessons." Accordingly, the Court held that the denial of Good News's application violated its equal access rights guaranteed under the free speech clause.

The *Good News* Court held further that this free speech protection of equal access rights outweighed the school district's concerns to avoid an establishment of religion. "The Good News Club seeks nothing more than to be treated neutrally and given access to speak about the same topics as are other groups. Because allowing the Club to speak on school grounds would ensure neutrality and not threaten it, Milford [School District] faces an uphill battle in arguing that the Establishment Clause compels it to exclude the Good News Club." Both Justice Thomas writing for the plurality and Justice Scalia writing in concurrence found unpersuasive the school's arguments that the club's use of their facilities would constitute a form of coercion, endorsement, or indoctrination of religion that violated the disestablishment clause.

Three dissenting justices argued that the Good News Club's activities constituted overt "religious proselytizing" rather than simple moral instruction from a "religious viewpoint." Justice Souter, joined by Justice Ginsburg, accused the majority of ignoring the reality that Good News intends to use the public school forum for an "evangelical service of worship calling children to commit themselves in an act of Christian conversion" and not for mere discussion of secular subjects from a Christian point of view. The Court's holding effectively "stand[s] for the remarkable proposition that any public school opened for civic meetings must be opened for use as a church, synagogue, or mosque."

The Court's recent line of equal access cases, predicated largely on the free speech clause, have provided an important counterweight to some of the corrosive effects of the *Smith* case. These equal access cases have a close parallel in the Court's recent line of equal treatment cases, which, as we shall see, have been developed largely under the establishment clause.[115] Whether these two lines of cases will eventually be brought together to yield a new era of free exercise protection remains to be seen. The Court's recent decision in *Locke v. Davey* (2004) will, if nothing else, postpone any such move toward integration of the free speech, free exercise, disestablishment, and equal protection clauses around the principles of equal access and equal treatment.[116]

Statutes and Religion

The Court's recent "equal access" cases point to a second way in which religious liberty has come to be protected—through federal and state statutes. The Court has repeatedly upheld statutes that protect vital religious interests, terming these a proper governmental accommodation, rather than an improper governmental establishment, of religion.[117]

Some legislative accommodations of vital religious interests have long enjoyed constitutional protection. Already in *Arver v. United States* (1918), the Court rejected a disestablishment clause challenge to the Selective Service Act that exempted clergy, seminary students, and members of certain faiths from military service. This legislative accommodation of pacifism has continued to this day, and the Court has rebuffed disestablishment clause challenges to the same.[118] In *Zorach v. Clauson* (1952), the Court upheld a public school program allowing religious students release time to attend religious classes off the school's premises—calling this a "suitable accommodation . . . to spiritual needs" rather than an establishment of religion.[119] In *Walz v. Tax Commission* (1970), the Court sustained a state tax exemption of church property against a taxpayer challenge that this was an establishment of religion.[120] In *Transworld Airlines v. Hardison* (1977), the Court upheld Title VII provisions that required employers to make "reasonable accommodations" to their employees' religious needs.[121] In *Presiding Bishop v. Amos* (1987), the Court sustained a 1972 amendment to the Civil Rights Act that exempted religious organizations from the general prohibition against religious discrimination.[122] Several lower federal courts have sustained, against disestablishment clause challenges, provisions in the federal Fair Housing Act that allow religious organizations to favor their own coreligionists and state laws that allow religious schools and charities to favor their own coreligionist pupils and patrons.

Furthermore, the Court has repeatedly said in dicta from *Sherbert* in 1963 to *Good News* in 2001 (where it used the free exercise or free speech clauses to create exemptions for religious interests) that a statute could have included such an accommodation of religion without running afoul of the disestablishment clause.

Since the early 1980s, Congress and state legislatures have seized upon these precedents with new vigor in an effort to offset the narrowing of free exercise protections. The most dramatic example of this trend is provided by the "equal access" principle itself. A week after the 1981 *Widmar v. Vincent* case, the Court declined to review a case in which a lower court denied that a voluntary group of public high school students organized for religious devotions must have equal access to school facilities.[123] Congress responded in 1984 with the Equal Access Act that effectively imposed the *Widmar* principle on public high schools:

> It shall be unlawful for any public secondary school which receives Federal financial assistance and which has a limited open forum to deny equal access or a fair opportunity to, or discriminate against, any students who wish to conduct a meeting within that limited open forum on the basis of the religious, political, or other content of the speech at such meetings.[124]

In *Westside Community Schools v. Mergens* (1990), the Court upheld the Equal Access Act against charges that it was an establishment of religion.[125]

Other statutes have undone the results of some of the Court's more controversial free exercise cases. Following *Goldman v. Weinberger* (1986), for example, Congress in 1988 amended the military dress code such that it would allow the wearing of a yarmulke: "[A] member of the armed forces may wear an item of religious apparel while wearing the uniform of the member's armed force."[126] Similarly, following *Employment Division v. Smith* (1990), the State of Oregon amended its criminal code to allow for the ingestion of peyote as part of a Native American religious ceremony. Subsequent challenges of these new statutes as forms of religious establishment have failed.

Not all such legislative accommodations of religion have been sustained or have proven equally effective.[127] For example, in an attempt to grant protections to the religious rights of Native Americans which had fared poorly in the lower courts to date, Congress passed the American Indian Religious Freedom Act (AIRFA) in 1978. The act was only a resolution—not a statute with specific rights and duties set forth. Nonetheless, AIRFA provided, in pertinent part: "It shall be the policy of the United States to protect and preserve for American Indians their inherent right of freedom to believe, express, and exercise the traditional religions of the American Indians ... including but not limited to access to sites, use and possession of sacred objects, and the freedom to worship through ceremonials and traditional rites."[128] The Native American claims at issue in *Bowen v. Roy, Lyng v. Protective Association,* and *Employment Division v. Smith* all fell easily within the preferred policy of AIRFA. The Court could have used the language of the act as a basis for extending free exercise protections to these claims, without undue worry of creating precedents for numerous new non-Native American claims. The Court chose instead to dismiss the act with wooden language, declaring in *Lyng:* "Nowhere in the law is there so much as a hint of any intent to create a cause of action or any judicially enforceable individual rights."[129]

In 1993, Congress passed a statute that did "create a cause of action and judicially enforceable individual rights"—the Religious Freedom Restoration Act (1993) designed to offset the *Smith* Court's narrow neutrality reading of the free exercise clause. But in the *City of Boerne v. Flores* (1997), as we saw, the Court struck down RFRA as a violation of section 5 of the Fourteenth Amendment.[130] Congress has responded with the Religious Land Use and Institutionalized Persons Act (2000), which is much narrower in scope and more broadly based not only on Congress's section 5 power but also on its power over commerce, taxing, and spending in Article I. RLUIPA has been challenged both as an illegitimate encroachment by Congress on state power and as an establishment of religion. The former challenge might well succeed. The latter challenge, however, has little merit. The Court has said repeatedly that the disestablishment clause leaves ample room for legislative accommodation of religion, and the *Boerne* case said nothing to change this.[131]

Conclusions

It must be said in conclusion that neither free speech nor statutory protections of religious liberty can ultimately substitute for a more rigorous free exercise clause. To be sure, the development of these doctrines testifies both to the ingenuity of litigants and legislators and to the flexibility of the constitutional process to accommodate the pressing spiritual needs of citizens. And to be sure, the development of these doctrines has provided some religious minorities with forms and forums of relief hitherto foreclosed to them.

These can only be temporary refuges for religious liberty, however. Speech is only one form of religious exercise; equality is only one principle that the free exercise clause protects. Even generously defined, "speech" cannot embrace many forms of individual and corporate religious exercise—from the silent meditations of the sages to the noisy pilgrimages of the saints, from the corporate consecration of the sanctuary to the ecclesiastical discipline of the clergy.[132] Even expansively interpreted, "equality" cannot protect the special needs of religious individuals and religious groups. These needs were traditionally protected by the principles of liberty of conscience and separation of church and state and traditionally reflected in the exemptions and exclusions countenanced and created by the free exercise clause.[133]

Likewise, statutory provisions cannot substitute for constitutional principles of free exercise. It is an elementary, but essential, political reality that statutes generally privilege the views of the majority, not the minority. They are passed by elected officials who must be as vigilant in reflecting popular opinion as protecting constitutional imperatives. The free exercise clause, by contrast, is designed to protect the needs of the minority as much as the majority. Its provisions are enforced by appointed officials who must be more vigilant about protecting constitutional imperatives than reflecting popular opinion. The free exercise clause is designed to provide remedies for individuals and groups with insufficient political strength to have their religious views or practices reflected in or protected by statutes.[134]

The original vision of the founders was that religion was special and that it was deserving of special protection. The founders thus placed the free exercise clause alongside the free speech, press, and assembly clauses to provide religious claimants with a special pathway to relief. They incorporated within this free exercise clause the principles of liberty of conscience, freedom of religious expression, religious equality and pluralism, and separation of church from the state. Both individuals and groups were thus protected in their most fundamental religious rights.

One need not necessarily endorse a jurisprudence of originalism to embrace this multiprincipled reading of the free exercise clause. This was, after all, the vision articulated by the Supreme Court in *Cantwell v. Connecticut* (1940), the case that opened the modern era of free exercise jurisprudence. And this was the Court's vision of the free exercise clause for more than forty years thereafter.

The majority of the Supreme Court has to date shown little willingness to overturn the 1990 *Smith* case that sealed the Court's rejection of this multiprincipled reading of the free exercise clause. In *Church of Lukumi Babalu Aye v. Hialeah* (1993), which applied the free exercise clause, a six-member majority applied the *Smith* test, with only Justices Souter, O'Connor, and Blackmun objecting thereto.[135] In *City of Boerne v. Flores* (1997), which outlawed the Religious Freedom Restoration Act, again only three justices argued that the *Smith* test should be reconsidered.[136] A solid majority of the Court has shown little indication that it will change its position any time soon.[137]

Therefore, further free speech and statutory protections of religious liberty must be vigilantly pursued in the short term, along with more rigorous state constitutional laws. But, at the same time, religious claimants must continue to press their free exercise cases in federal courts, inviting the Supreme Court slowly to draw the sting from *Smith* and to isolate it, if not overturn it.

Notes

1. See, e.g., *Religious Freedom Reporter* (1981–); *Church Law and Tax Report* (1987–). See comprehensive collection in Robert T. Miller and Ronald B. Flowers, eds., *Toward Benevolent Neutrality: Church, State, and the Supreme Court*, 5th ed., 2 vols. (1996), with more recent material sampled in Michael W. McConnell, John Garvey, and Thomas C. Berg, *Religion and the Constitution* (2002); Michael S. Ariens and Robert A. Destro, *Religious Liberty in a Pluralistic Society*, 2d ed. (2000); John T. Noonan Jr. and Edward M. Gaffney, *Religious Freedom*, 2d ed. (2001).

2. See Ira Lupu, "Where Rights Begin: The Problem of Burdens on the Free Exercise of Religion," *Harvard Law Review* 102 (1989):933.

3. Nowak and Rotunda, *Constitutional Law*, secs. 2.12–2.15. For application, see *Bender v. Williamsport Area School District*, 475 U.S. 534 (1986) (school board member has no standing, in his capacity as a parent, to appeal a board decision affecting the religious rights of his child in the school). See also *Cooper v. Pate*, 378 U.S. 546 (1964) (Muslim prisoner entitled to hearing on the merits that he was denied access to religious publications); *Catholic Conference v. Abortion Rights Mobilization*, 487 U.S. 72 (1988) (a nonparty witness held in contempt given standing to challenge federal court's jurisdiction over case).

4. *Cantwell v. Connecticut*, 310 U.S. 296 (1940).

5. *Torcaso v. Watkins*, 367 U.S. 488 (1961).

6. *Goldman v. Weinberger*, 475 U.S. 503 (1986).

7. *O'Lone v. Estate of Shabazz*, 482 U.S. 342 (1987); *Cruz v. Beto*, 405 U.S. 319 (1972).

8. *National Labor Relations Board v. Catholic Bishop of Chicago*, 440 U.S. 490 (1979); *Corporation of the Presiding Bishop v. Amos*, 483 U.S. 327 (1987).

9. *Jimmy Swaggart Ministries v. California Board of Equalization*, 493 U.S. 378 (1990).

10. *Kedroff v. St. Nicholas Cathedral*, 344 U.S. 94 (1952).

11. *Frazee v. Illinois Employment Security Department*, 489 U.S. 829 (1989).

12. *Braunfeld v. Brown*, 366 U.S. 599 (1961). See also *McGowan v. Maryland*, 366 U.S. 420 (1961); *Gallagher v. Crown Kosher Super Market of Massachusetts*, 366 U.S. 617 (1961).

13. *Bob Jones University v. United States*, 461 U.S. 574 (1983).

14. *E.E.O.C. v. Townley Engineering* (9th Cir., 1988).

15. See, e.g., *United States v. Seeger*, 380 U.S. 163, 175 (1965); *Thomas v. Review Board of Indiana Employment Security Division*, 450 U.S. 707 (1981); *Hob-*

bie v. Unemployment Appeals Commission of Florida, 480 U.S. 136 (1987); *Frazee v. Illinois Department of Employment Security*, 489 U.S. 829 (1989).

16. Lupu, "Where Rights Begin," 954.

17. See *United States v. Ballard*, 322 U.S. 78 (1944) (allowing for jury instruction questioning the sincerity of claimant's "I Am" religion).

18. See, e.g., *Alamo Foundation v. Secretary of Labor*, 471 U.S. 290 (1985).

19. *Golden Writ of God v. Department of Revenue*, 300 Or. 479 (1986).

20. See Lupu and Tuttle, "The Distinctive Place of Religious Entities"; Bassett, "Religious Organizations"; Frederick Mark Gedicks, "Toward a Constitutional Jurisprudence of Religious Group Rights," *Wisconsin Law Review* (1989):99.

21. See, e.g., *Swaggart Ministries*, 493 U.S. at 385ff. distinguishing at length *Murdock v. Pennsylvania*, 319 U.S. 105 (1943) and *Follett v. McCormick*, 321 U.S. 573 (1944) to uphold collection of taxes on sales of religious articles. See also *Employment Division v. Smith*, 494 U.S. 872, 879–880 (1990), reaching back to *Reynolds v. United States*, 98 U.S. 145 (1879) and *Prince v. Massachusetts*, 321 U.S. 158 (1944) to uphold application of a criminal law against free exercise objection.

22. See, e.g. *Swaggart Ministries* (1990): The free exercise claimant argued that this was a religious group rights case, which would have provided ample protection; the Court characterized it as a tax exemption case. See also *Employment Division v. Smith* (1990): The free exercise claimant argued that this was simply an unemployment compensation case where the Court had consistently found for the discharged employee; the Court characterized it as a case seeking free exercise exemption from criminal laws.

23. 321 U.S. at 171.

24. The cases right before the introduction of the *Sherbert* strict scrutiny test in 1963 were the Court's cavalier dismissal of Jewish claims to protection from Sunday blue laws. See cases in Chap. 7, note 12. The case right before the introduction of the *Smith* lower scrutiny standard was the application of the technical *Sherbert* holding to an applicant for a temporary secretarial post, who rejected proffered employment because it might require work on Sunday. *Frazee v. Illinois Department of Employment Security* (1989). The *Smith* case, however, was also a culmination of other cases that had slowly reduced the free exercise clause to a principle of neutrality. See discussion below, pp. 164–168.

25. See, e.g., *City of Cleburne v. Cleburne Living Center*, 473 U.S. 432 (1985).

26. *Reynolds v. United States*, 98 U.S. 145, 166–167 (1879); *Davis v. Beason*, 133 U.S. 333, 345–348 (1890).

27. *Arver v. United States*, 245 U.S. 366 (1918).

28. 310 U.S. 296, at 303–304.

29. *West Virginia State Board v. Barnette*, 319 U.S. 624, 639 (1943); *Heffron v. International Society for Krishna Consciousness*, 452 U.S. 640, 649 (1981), quoting, in part, *Virginia State Board of Pharmacy v. Virginia Citizens Consumer Council*, 425 U.S. 748 (1976).

30. 374 U.S. 398 (1963).

31. For cases using the strict scrutiny test and finding for the religious claimant, see *Wisconsin v. Yoder*, 406 U.S. 205 (1972); *McDaniel v. Paty*, 435 U.S. 618 (1978); *Widmar v. Vincent*, 454 U.S. 263 (1981); *Thomas v. Review Board* (1981);

Hobbie v. Unemployment Commission (1987); and *Frazee v. Illinois Department of Employment Security* (1989). For cases using the strict scrutiny test and finding for government, see *Gillette v. United States,* 401 U.S. 437 (1971); *United States v. Lee* (1982); *Bob Jones University v. United States* (1983); *Hernandez v. Commissioner of Internal Revenue,* 490 U.S. 680 (1989). See summaries of holdings in Appendix 3.

32. *Smith,* 494 U.S. at 879, quoting in part, *United States v. Lee* (Stevens, J., concurring). For prior cases, see *Bowen v. Roy,* 476 U.S. 693, 707–708 (1986) ("Government meets its burden when it demonstrates that a challenged requirement for governmental benefits, *neutral* and *uniform* in its application, is a *reasonable* means of promoting a *legitimate* public interest.") (emphasis added). This language is repeated in *Estate of Shabazz,* 482 U.S. at 349–351; and *Lyng v. Northwest Indian Cemetery Protective Association,* 485 U.S. 439, 448–451 (1988).

33. *Smith,* 494 U.S. at 886–887.

34. *Lukumi Babalu Aye v. Hialeah,* 508 U.S. 520 (1993). See Douglas Laycock, "The Supreme Court and Religious Liberty," *Catholic University Law Review* 40 (2000):25; Richard F. Duncan, "Free Exercise Is Dead, Long Live Free Exercise: *Smith, Lukumi,* and the General Applicability Doctrine," *University of Pennsylvania Journal of Constitutional Law* 3 (2001), 850.

35. *Locke v. Davey,* 124 S.Ct. 1307 (2004); see also *Watchtower Bible and Tract Society v. Village of Stratton,* 122 S.Ct. 2080 (2002).

36. 42 U.S.C. secs. 2000bb to 2000bb–4.

37. 117 S.Ct. 2157, 2164 (1997).

38. These new state laws on religious liberty have been controversial. See Symposium, "State and Federal Religious Liberty Legislation: Is It Necessary? Is It Constitutional? Is It Good Policy?" *Cardozo Law Review* 21 (1999):415; Symposium, "Restoring Religious Liberty in the States," *University of California at Davis Law Review* 32 (1999):515; Mark J. Austin, "Holier Than Thou: Attacking the Constitutionality of State Religious Freedom Legislation," *Loyola Los Angeles Law Review* 33 (2000):1183; Stanley H. Friedelbaum, "Free Exercise in the States: Belief, Conduct, and Judicial Benchmarks," *Albany Law Review* 63 (2001):1059. See further summary of other literature and cases in *Religious Freedom Reporter,* secs. 1–520–520 (1998–).

39. See analysis in Thomas C. Berg, "The Constitutional Future of Religious Freedom Legislation," *University of Arkansas Law Journal* 20 (1998):715, 727ff. See Gregory P. Magarian, "How to Apply the Religious Freedom Restoration Act to Federal Law Without Violating the Constitution," *Michigan Law Review* 99 (2001):1903.

40. 42 U.S.C.A. secs. 2000cc–2000cc5.

41. See Marci Hamilton, "Federalism and the Common Good: The True Story Behind the Religious Land Use and Institutionalized Persons Act," *Indiana Law Journal* 78 (2003):311.

42. See John T. Noonan Jr., *Narrowing the Nation's Power: The Supreme Court Sides with the States* (2002).

43. See above, pp. 45–46, 61–62.

44. *Cantwell,* 310 U.S. at 303–304, 310.

45. Ibid., 304, 308.

46. See W. Glen How and Philip Brumley, "Religious Perspectives on Human Rights, Evangelism, and Proselytism: The Jehovah's Witnesses," in Witte and Martin, eds., *Sharing the Book*, 276.

47. 318 U.S. 413, 414 (1943); 319 U.S. 105, 110 (1943).

48. *Marsh v. Alabama*, 326 U.S. 501 (1946); *Tucker v. Texas*, 326 U.S. 517 (1946).

49. *Murdock v. Pennsylvania*, 319 U.S. 105, 108–109, 111–112 (1943).

50. See *Jones v. Opelika [II]*, 319 U.S. 103 (1943), overruling *Jones v. Opelika [I]*, 316 U.S. 584 (1942); *Largent v. Texas*, 318 U.S. 418 (1943); *Follett v. McCormick*, 321 U.S. 473 (1944).

51. 340 U.S. 290 (1951).

52. 340 U.S. 268 (1951). See similar result in *Saia v. New York*, 334 U.S. 558 (1948).

53. 345 U.S. 67 (1953).

54. 345 U.S. 395, 398–408 (1953). See also *Cox v. New Hampshire*, 312 U.S. 569 (1941).

55. See summary of cases in *Heffron v. International Society* (1981).

56. 122 S.Ct. 2080 (2002).

57. 321 U.S. 158, 165–167 (1944).

58. *Jehovah's Witnesses v. King County Hospital*, 390 U.S. 598 (1968).

59. See above, pp. 42–43.

60. *Watson v. Jones*, 80 U.S. (13 Wall.) 679, 728 (1871).

61. *Reynolds*, 98 U.S. at 164.

62. See above, pp. 126–129.

63. See above, pp. 129–131.

64. *Cantwell*, 310 U.S. at 303.

65. *Minersville School District v. Gobitis*, 310 U.S. 586, 594, 597–598 (1940).

66. *Barnette*, 319 U.S. at 642.

67. *United States v. Ballard* (1944); *In re Summers*, 325 U.S. 561 (1945).

68. *Girouard v. United States*, 328 U.S. 61 (1946). This case also turned on the test oath clause of Article VI.

69. *First Unitarian Church v. County of Los Angeles*, 357 U.S. 545 (1957).

70. *Torcaso v. Watkins*, 367 U.S. 488 (1961).

71. *McDaniel v. Paty*, 435 U.S. 618, 626 (1978) (citing *Torcaso v. Watkins*).

72. *Sherbert*, 374 U.S at 401, 406.

73. *Thomas v. Review Board* (1981).

74. *Hobbie v. Unemployment Commission* (1987).

75. *Frazee v. Illinois Department* (1989).

76. *Thomas v. Review Board*, 450 U.S. at 717–718. This same principle had earlier been denied to Jewish groups that sought free exercise exemptions from Sunday blue laws. Their argument was that while state law prohibited Sunday work, religious law prohibited Saturday work. This put Jewish merchants and workers at a general commercial disadvantage and required kosher establishments to be closed to Jewish communities for two days instead of one. The Court was not convinced that such regulations burdened "Jewish religion" per se. See cases in Chap. 7, note 12; Barbara J. Redman, "Sabbatarian Accommodation in the Supreme Court,"

Journal of Church and State 33 (1991):495–523; Jerome A. Barron, "Sunday in North America," *Harvard Law Review* 79 (1965):42–54.

77. See above, pp. 54–56.

78. *McDaniel v. Paty,* 435 U.S. at 622–626.

79. See above, pp. 132–134.

80. *Presbyterian Church in the United States v. Mary Elizabeth Blue Hull Presbyterian Church,* 393 U.S. 440, 447 (1969).

81. *Kedroff,* 344 U.S. at 94, 110, 116 (1952).

82. *Presbyterian Church,* 393 U.S. at 449. See further *Maryland & Virginia Churches v. Sharpsburg Church,* 396 U.S. 367 (1970).

83. *Milivojevich,* 426 U.S. at 713–715, 724–725; Kent Greenawalt, "Hands Off! Civil Court Involvement in Conflicts over Religious Property," *Columbia Law Review* 98 (1998):1843–1907.

84. 268 U.S. 510 (1925).

85. 440 U.S. 490 (1979).

86. 483 U.S. 327 (1987).

87. 406 U.S. at 216–218.

88. *Cantwell,* 319 U.S. at 310.

89. *Gobitis,* 310 U.S. at 593.

90. *Everson v. Board of Education,* 330 U.S. 1, 16 (1947) (emphasis in original).

91. *Sherbert,* 374 U.S. at 411 (Douglas, J., concurring).

92. 443 U.S. 595, 603, 605 (1979).

93. Bassett, *Religious Organizations and the Law,* secs. 7.32–36; Louis Sirico, "Church Property Disputes: Churches as Secular and Alien Institutions," *Fordham Law Review* 55 (1986):335–362.

94. 475 U.S. 503 (1986).

95. 476 U.S. 693, 696, 699, 707–708 (1986).

96. 482 U.S. 342, 350, 352 (1987).

97. 485 U.S. 439 (1988).

98. 42 U.S.C. sec. 1996 (1978); Ann E. Beeson, "Dances with Justice: Peyotism in the Courts," *Emory Law Journal* 41 (1992):1121.

99. *Lyng,* 485 U.S. at 447. See also ibid., 451 (recognizing "devastating effects on traditional Indian religious practices").

100. Ibid., 451–452 (citations omitted).

101. 493 U.S. 378, 389, 391 (1990) (emphasis added).

102. 494 U.S. 872 (1990).

103. Ibid., 879.

104. 508 U.S. 520 (1993).

105. *Locke v. Davey* (2004).

106. The phrase is from *Waltz v. Tax Commission,* 397 U.S. 664, 669 (1970), where it was used to defend the principle of neutrality in a disestablishment case.

107. *Gitlow v. New York,* 268 U.S. 652 (1925).

108. See, e.g., *Lovell v. City of Griffin,* 303 U.S. 444 (1938) (also decided on freedom of press grounds); *Schneider v. State of New Jersey,* 308 U.S. 147 (1939).

109. Equal access principles also were somewhat at work in *Capitol Square Review and Advisory Board v. Pinette,* 115 S.Ct. 2440 (1995) and *McDaniel v. Paty* (1978) discussed below, pp. 222–224.

110. 454 U.S. 263, 270, 273 (1981).

111. 508 U.S. 384, 387, 394 (1993) (citations omitted).

112. 115 S.Ct. 2510, 2517–2518, 2520 (1995).

113. Ibid., 2535 (Souter, J., dissenting).

114. 533 U.S. 98 (2001).

115. See below, pp. 199–201, 213–220.

116. *Locke v. Davey* (2004).

117. See summary in Thomas C. Berg, *The State and Religion in a Nutshell* (1998), 131–147.

118. See *United States v. Seeger* (1965).

119. 343 U.S. 306, 313–314 (1952).

120. 397 U.S. 664 (1970).

121. 432 U.S. 63 (1977). But cf. *Estate of Thornton v. Caldor, Inc.*, 472 U.S. 703 (1985) (striking down statute that gave employees a categorical right not to work on their sabbath); *Ansonia Board of Education v. Philbrook*, 479 U.S. 60 (1986) (employer is not required to accept the employee's preferred form of religious accommodation).

122. 483 U.S. 327 (1987).

123. *Brandon v. Board of Education of Guilderland School District*, 635 F.2d. 971 (1980), cert. denied, 454 U.S. 1123 (1981), rehearing denied, 455 U.S. 983 (1982).

124. 20 U.S.C. secs. 4071–4074.

125. 496 U.S. 226 (1990). See further below, pp. 222–224.

126. 10 U.S.C. sec. 774.

127. See *Texas Monthly, Inc. v. Bullock*, 489 U.S. 1 (1989) (striking down special state exemption for religious periodicals); *Board of Education of Kiryas Joel v. Grumet*, 496 U.S. 226 (1990) (creation of public school district that follows boundaries of religious village violates disestablishment clause).

128. 42 U.S.C. sec. 1996 (1978).

129. *Lyng*, 485 U.S. at 455.

130. See above, pp. 150–152.

131. Only Justice Stevens touched on this issue in his concurrence, finding that RFRA violated the disestablishment clause. *Boerne*, 117 S.Ct. at 2172 (Stevens, J., concurring).

132. See Kathleen Brady, "The Push to Private Religious Expression: Are We Missing Something?" *Fordham Law Review* 70 (2002):1147; see multiple perspectives in "Conference on Law and Religion," *Loyola University Chicago Law Journal* 33 (2001):1; Symposium, "Religious Liberty at the Dawn of a New Millennium," *Indiana Law Journal* 75 (2000):1.

133. See Derek H. Davis, "Equal Treatment: A Christian Separationist Perspective," in *Equal Treatment of Religion in a Pluralistic Society*, ed. Stephen V. Monsma and J. Christopher Soper (1998), 136; Michael W. McConnell, "Equal Treatment and Religious Discrimination," in ibid., 30.

134. See wide-ranging perspectives in Symposium, "State and Federal Religious Liberty Legislation," 415.

135. 508 U.S. at 559 (Souter, J., concurring) (expressing "doubts about whether the *Smith* rule merits adherence"); 508 U.S. at 578 (Blackmun, J., and O'Connor, J., concurring) (*"Smith* was wrongly decided").

136. 117 S.Ct. at 2176 (O'Connor, J., dissenting) (*"Smith* was wrongly decided"); 2186 (Souter, J., dissenting) (expressing "serious doubts" about *Smith*); 2186 (Breyer, J., dissenting) (calling for briefing and argument on the propriety of *Smith*).

137. *Watchtower Bible and Tract Society v. Village of Stratton* (2002) and *Locke v. Davey* (2004) used the *Smith* formulation without objection.

8

MODERN

DISESTABLISHMENT LAW

Modern free exercise law has moved from a multiprincipled to a single-principled reading of the "essential rights and liberties of religion" incorporated into the First Amendment. In its early free exercise cases, the Court applied the principles of liberty of conscience, freedom of religious expression, religious pluralism and equality, and separation of church from state. Since the mid-1980s, the Court has reduced the free exercise clause to the single principle of neutrality, which Congress is now struggling mightily to unmake.

Modern disestablishment law has moved in the opposite direction. In its early disestablishment cases, the principle of separation of church and state dominated the Court's reasoning. Since the mid-1980s, however, individual justices have slowly imported into their analysis new principles of religious equality and liberty of conscience, which the Court is now struggling mightily to integrate.

Following the style of Chapter 7, this chapter first maps the cases from 1947 onward following the terminology and methodology of the Supreme Court. It then reviews the Court's treatment of the first principles of the American experiment in the more than fifty cases that have addressed the meaning of the phrase: "Congress shall make no law respecting an establishment of religion."

Mapping Modern Disestablishment Doctrine

The Challenge

At the heart of a modern disestablishment case is a claimant's challenge that the government has made a law establishing religion or "respecting" the same. The challenged government entity or official can be at the federal, state, or local level. The law at issue can involve the exercise of executive, legislative, or regulatory power.

The claimant's challenge is that the government has improperly funded, supported, or endorsed religion. It has coerced parties to participate in religious worship, indoctrination, or education. It has made improper use of religious sanctuaries, symbols, or services. It has improperly allied itself with religious causes, clerics, or corporations. It has discriminately favored or preferred some religious interests, individuals, or institutions over others. In brief, government has taken one or more steps down the road toward the establishment of religion.

As in free exercise cases so in disestablishment cases, claimants must meet the usual requirements for pressing any constitutional case. In particular, claimants must state an actual "case or controversy" justiciable by a court, and they must have "standing" to bring the suit. But the Supreme Court has softened these threshold requirements considerably for disestablishment cases.

In free exercise and other cases, the Court has read the "case and controversy" rules strictly: "It is a fundamental rule of judicial restraint, that this Court will not reach constitutional questions in advance of the necessity of deciding them."[1] But in modern disestablishment cases, the Court has not always shown such restraint. In *Epperson v. Arkansas* (1968), for example, a schoolteacher challenged a state criminal law that prohibited the teaching of evolution in a public school or state university. The law had not been enforced against the teacher. Stating that the teacher "faced at least a literal dilemma" of whether the state law established the teaching of creationism, the *Epperson* Court addressed the constitutional issue and found that the state law violated the disestablishment clause.[2]

In *Zobrest v. Catalina Foothills School District* (1993), the Court also relaxed the case and controversy rule, this time to find no constitutional violation. A student attending a religious high school challenged a state decision not to afford him disability services. The case below turned largely on interpretation of applicable state and federal disability statutes. On appeal, the student raised the question whether a state's furnishing him with disability services in a religious high school would constitute an establishment of religion. Four dissenters argued that the Court "should vacate and remand this case for consideration of various threshold questions, statutory and regulatory, that may moot the constitutional question."[3] The majority judged otherwise: "The fact that there may be buried in the record a nonconstitutional ground for decision is not by itself enough to invoke this rule."[4] The Court addressed the constitutional question and found no establishment of religion.

Not only "case and controversy" rules but also "standing" rules have been relaxed in modern disestablishment cases. The Court's traditional standing rules, formulated in 1923, required that a party pressing a constitutional case "must be able to show that he has sustained or is in immediate danger of sustaining some direct injury as a result of the statute's enforcement and not merely that he suffers in some indefinite way in common with people generally."[5] In its early disestablishment cases, the Court applied this traditional rule.[6] In 1963, however, the Court declared that "the requirements for standing to challenge state action under the Establishment Clause, unlike those relating to the Free Exercise Clause, do not include proofs that particular *religious freedoms* are infringed."[7] In 1968, the Court held further that federal taxpayers could challenge any government programs that involved taxing and spending in aid of religion—opening federal courts to an ample tide of disestablishment cases.[8] In 1982, the Court stemmed this tide somewhat by holding that a religious liberty organization by itself lacked standing to challenge a federal agency's action that caused it no direct and obvious injury.[9] But it remains relatively easy for taxpaying citizens to challenge government actions under the disestablishment clause.

Some critics charge that these unique standing rules effectively empower a single secular party to "veto" popular laws touching religion that cause him or her only the most tangential injury. Such criticisms have become more pointed now that the Court no longer reads the free exercise clause to grant individual exemptions from neutral and generally applicable laws. Today, a secular claimant can use the disestablishment clause to overturn a carefully calibrated local law that happens to touch religion too favorably.[10] But a religious claimant cannot use the free exercise clause to claim an individual exemption from a discretionary regulatory decision that happens to "virtually destroy" its religion.[11]

Defenders of these unique rules counter that such open standing is precisely what the disestablishment clause requires. "History makes it clear," Justice Brennan has argued, "that the federal taxpayer is a singularly 'proper and appropriate party to invoke a federal court's jurisdiction' to challenge a federal bestowal of largesse as a violation of the Establishment Clause. Each, and indeed every, federal tax payer suffers precisely the same injury: . . . a continuing and intolerable burden on his pocketbook, his conscience, and his constitutional rights."[12] All such parties, whether religious or secular, must be given their day in court. To grant them standing is not necessarily to find an establishment of religion. But to deny them standing is to defy a cardinal purpose of the First Amendment: to enable citizens of any religion or of no religion to keep legislative majorities from taking a single step toward the establishment of religion.

Resolving the Conflict

The government claims the constitutional power to make or enforce a law. A citizen challenges the law as a form of religious establishment. How does the Court resolve this basic constitutional conflict?

We saw in Chapter 7 that in its modern free exercise cases, the Court used three interrelated methods: (1) "case-by-case balancing," which led to factually and logically related clusters of free exercise cases; (2) "definitional balancing," which led to shifting standards of judicial review under the free exercise clause and groups of cases under each of them; and (3) "principled balancing," which led to varying treatment of the first principles of liberty of conscience, freedom of religious expression, religious equality and plurality, and separation of church from state.

These three methods avail us rather little in mapping modern disestablishment law. The only factual cluster in which the Court has kept a rather steady line of logic concerns the role of religion in public education; even in this cluster, the Court's rationale of late has begun to shift. The only formal "standard of review" the Court has developed is the so-called *Lemon* test of 1971, newly modified as the *Agostini* test in 1997. The only "first principle" that the Court has consistently invoked is that of "separation of church and state," a phrase that has become stretched to the point of cliché. Indeed, in the minds of many today, "separation of church and state" is a synonym for "disestablishment of religion."

To address disestablishment challenges, the Court has developed a number of unique, and often sharply juxtaposed, approaches. From 1947 to the mid-1980s, these approaches were respectively labeled: (1) "separationism," (2) "accommodationism," and (3) "neutrality." Since the mid-1980s, the Court has added several new formulas to test for establishment, respectively labeled: (4) "endorsement," (5) "coercion," and (6) "equal treatment." For each of these formulas, one or more justices has offered lengthy historical and jurisprudential apologiae. But history has also become something of a "wild card" in modern disestablishment contests. In one case, the Court upheld on purely historical grounds a state legislature's hiring of a Presbyterian chaplain to offer prayers at the General Assembly; the Court's precedents would have easily outlawed this as an establishment of religion.[13] Figure 8.1 roughly illustrates the main shifts and juxtapositions of these approaches and a few of the main cases upholding them.

Separationism

One of the main principles at work in modern disestablishment law is that of separation of church and state. This formula has firm historical roots, especially in the writings of eighteenth-century Enlightenment and Evangeli-

FIGURE 8.1   Trends in Modern Disestablishment Law

Finding of Establishment	Finding of No Establishment
Separationism	Accommodationism
McCollum (1948)	*Zorach* (1952)

Wholesome Neutrality
Schempp (1963)

Strict Neutrality	Benevolent Neutrality
Lemon (1971)	*Walz* (1970)
Aguilar (1985)	*Mueller* (1983)
Texas Monthly (1989)	*Kendrick* (1988)

Endorsement
Mergens (1990)

Neutrality	Coercion
Kiryas Joel (1994)	*Weisman* (1992)

Equal Treatment
Rosenberger (1995)
Good News Club (2001)

Neutrality
Zelman (2002)

cal groups. Both these groups of founders had called for religious and political authorities to end their alliances and rivalries, and to distinguish their forms and functions. The state, they argued, should not give special aid, support, privilege, or protection to religious doctrines or groups—through special tax appropriations or government donations of lands and goods. The state should not predicate its laws on religious premises nor direct them to religious purposes. The state should not draw on the services of religious groups nor seek to interfere in their order, organization, or orthodoxy. Religion should be left alone to flourish in the conscience of each individual and in the voluntary assemblies that individuals convene.

   Enlightenment formulations of this separationist doctrine emphasized the need to protect politics and the state from the intrusions of religion and the church. Evangelical formulations emphasized the need to protect religion and the church from the intrusions of politics and the state. Both views were united, however, in their opposition to the traditional interlacings of religion and politics and the traditional alliances of church and state. Both had a formidable influence on the development of eighteenth-century state and federal laws on religious liberty. Both views came to special prominence in some states during the later nineteenth and early twentieth centuries—particularly in state constitutional provisions prohibiting governmental aid to religious causes and religious aid to public schools.[14]

The Supreme Court's first modern formulation of this separationist doctrine was offered by Justice Black in *Everson v. Board of Education* (1947):

> The "establishment of religion" clause of the First Amendment means at least this: Neither a state nor the Federal Government can set up a church. Neither can pass laws which aid one religion, aid all religions, or prefer one religion over another. Neither can force nor influence a person to go or to remain away from church against his will or force him to profess a belief or disbelief in any religion. No person can be punished for entertaining or professing religious beliefs or disbeliefs, for church attendance or non-attendance. No tax in any amount, large or small, can be levied to support any religious activities or institutions, whatever they may be called, or whatever form they may adopt to teach or practice religion. Neither a state nor the Federal Government can, openly or secretly, participate in the affairs of any religious organizations or groups, or vice versa. In the words of Jefferson, the clause against establishment of religion by law was intended to erect "a wall of separation between church and state."[15]

In later cases, Justice Black stressed that "a union of government and religion tends to destroy government and to degrade religion." "Religion is too personal, too sacred, [and] too holy, to permit its 'unhallowed perversion' by a civil magistrate."[16] Religion is also too powerful, too sinister, and too greedy to permit its unhindered pervasion of a civil magistracy. "[T]he same powerful religious propagandists" who are allowed to succeed in making one inroad on the state and its laws, Justice Black wrote, "doubtless will continue their propaganda, looking toward complete domination and supremacy of their particular brand of religion. And it is nearly always by insidious approaches that the citadels of [religious] liberty are more successfully attacked."[17] "The First Amendment has erected a wall of separation between church and state. That wall must be kept high and impregnable. We could not approve the slightest breach."[18]

Separationist logic found its strongest and most consistent application in a long series of cases outlawing religious officials, texts, ceremonies, and symbols from public schools. Separationism has also had an influence on other areas of government and religion, notably in cases dealing with tax support and tax exemption for religious organizations and religious causes.[19] Until 1971, separationist logic was applied directly. Since then, it has often expressed itself in a "separationist reading" of the *Lemon* test (discussed below).

Accommodationism

Accommodationists are the modern heirs of eighteenth-century Puritan and Civic Republican groups. Both these groups of founders had argued that every polity must support some form of public religion, some common morals and mores to undergird and support the plurality of protected private religions. Both groups supported state appointment of chaplains for the legislature, military, and prison, state sanctions against blasphemy, sacrilege, and iconoclasm, state administration of tithe collections, test oaths, and clerical appointments, state sponsorship of religious schools, charities, and other societies.

Puritan exponents of this accommodationist doctrine were inclined to a more specifically Christian public religion; Civic Republicans were inclined to be less denominationally rigorous. Puritan exponents tended to be more churlish in their toleration of private religions that strayed far from the mainstream; Civic Republicans were generally more tolerant of diverse religious groups. Both formulations had a formidable influence on state and federal constitution-making in the eighteenth century and on both state and federal constitutional decisions in the nineteenth and early twentieth centuries.

The Court's first modern formulation of this accommodationist doctrine came in *Zorach v. Clauson* (1952), which upheld the constitutionality of granting students release time from public schools to attend religious education or services. Justice Douglas wrote for the Court:

> We are a religious people whose institutions presuppose a Supreme Being. We guarantee the freedom to worship as one chooses. We make room for as wide a variety of beliefs and creeds as the spiritual needs of man deem necessary. We sponsor an attitude on the part of government that shows no partiality to one group and that lets each group flourish according to the zeal of its adherents and the appeal of its dogma. When the state encourages religious instruction or cooperates with religious authorities by adjusting the schedule of public events to sectarian needs, it follows the best of our traditions. For it then respects the religious nature of our people and accommodates the public service to their spiritual needs. To hold that it may not would be to find in the Constitution a requirement that government show a callous indifference to religious groups. That would be preferring those who believe in no religion over those

who do believe. Government may not finance religious groups nor undertake religious instruction nor blend secular and sectarian education nor use secular institutions to force one or some religion on any person. But we find no constitutional requirement which makes it necessary for government to be hostile to religion and to throw its weight against efforts to widen the effective scope of religious influence. The government must be neutral when it comes to competition between sects. It may not thrust any sect on any person. It may not make a religious observance compulsory. It may not coerce anyone to attend church, to observe a religious holiday, or to take religious instruction.[20]

Later formulations of this accommodationist doctrine counseled against too zealous an application of separationist logic.[21] To restrict all religious exercises in the public school and public square, Justice Stewart wrote, "is seen, not as the realization of state neutrality, but rather as the establishment of a religion of secularism, or at the least, as government support of beliefs of those who think that religious exercises should be conducted only in private."[22] Justice Rehnquist added: "The 'wall of separation between church and state' is a metaphor based on bad history, a metaphor that has proved useless as a guide to judging." The disestablishment clause was designed only to prohibit government "from asserting a preference for one religious denomination or sect over others." It does not mandate "government to be strictly neutral between religion and irreligion, nor does the Clause prohibit Congress or the States from pursuing legitimate secular ends through non-discriminatory sectarian means."[23]

Accommodationists share ample common ground with separationists. Both forbid formal government alliances with religious groups. Both forbid government coercion of religious teaching or observance. Both agree that a plurality of religions must stand equal before the law. Both agree that government must not discriminate on religious grounds.

But separationists and accommodationists differ at crucial points. Separationists forbid any government aid to religion; accommodationists allow aid that is equally or nonpreferentially distributed among religions. Separationists forbid any government participation in religious worship, education, or charity. Accommodationists allow such participation so long as citizens are not coerced into participation. Separationists forbid religious and political institutions from cooperating; accommodationists allow for such cooperation in the delivery of charity, education, and other social services.

Accommodationist logic found its strongest hold in some of the Court's pre-*Everson* cases on the place and role of government in religious schools. The Court repeated the logic and holdings of these cases a few times after *Everson*, although these early cases stood in rather awkward juxtaposition to the Court's more dominant separationist tendencies. Since the mid-1980s, this accommodationist logic has returned in the form of a "benevolent neutrality" reading of the *Lemon* test and in cases upholding various legislative accommodations and uses of religious services and symbols.

Neutrality

After a generation of vacillation between these juxtaposed separationist and accommodationist formulas, the Supreme Court in the early 1960s sought a middle way between them. In both its separationist and accommodationist opinions in these early years, the Court spoke intermittently about the need for government to adhere to a policy of religious neutrality. Separationists tended to formulate this as government neutrality between religion and nonreligion, accommodationists as governmental neutrality among religions. But they held this concern for neutrality in common.

Beginning in the early 1960s, the Court made neutrality the new operative principle of disestablishment. Strict separation between church and state, the Court argued, is impossible in today's society, even if it could have been possible in the eighteenth century. But evenhanded accommodation and acknowledgment of religion is impossible in today's religiously heterogeneous society, even if it could have been permitted in the more religiously homogeneous eighteenth century.

"Wholesome 'neutrality,'" Justice Clark announced for the Court in *Abington Township School District v. Schempp* (1963), is now the watchword. The disestablishment clause forbids the exercise of "all legislative power respecting religious belief or the expression thereof." Hereafter, if the stated purpose or primary effect of a law "either is the advancement or the inhibition of religion then the enactment exceeds the scope of legislative power as circumscribed by the Constitution."[24]

In *Walz v. Tax Commission* (1970) and *Lemon v. Kurtzman* (1971), the Court sharpened this "neutrality" approach into a formal test. In order to pass constitutional muster, Chief Justice Burger wrote in the *Lemon* case, a challenged law (1) must have a secular purpose, (2) must have a primary effect that neither advances nor inhibits religion, and (3) must foster no excessive entanglement between church and state. Incidental religious "effects" or modest "entanglements" of church and state are tolerable. But defiance of any of these three criteria is constitutionally fatal.

The "three main evils," Chief Justice Burger declared, are "sponsorship, financial support, and active involvement of the sovereign in religious activity." These are categorically forbidden. But beyond that, the "line of separation, far from being a 'wall,' is a blurred, indistinct and variable barrier depending on all the circumstances of a particular relationship."[25]

From the start, the *Lemon* test proved itself amenable to both accommodationist and separationist readings. For all of its seeming formalism, the test left ample room for interpretation. The "secular purpose" of a statute could be determined by its words alone or by a full review of its legislative history.[26] The "*primary* effect" of the statute could be determined from the perspective of the plaintiff alone or by a full inquiry into the law in action. Whether an "entanglement" between church and state proved *excessive* depended very much upon what Chief Justice Burger called "all the circumstances of a particular relationship." In the hands of skillful counsel, the *Lemon* test was subject to a variety of readings and applications.

In *Walz v. Tax Commission* (1970), the Court gave this test an accommodationist reading and upheld a state law granting tax exemption to church property. "The course of constitutional neutrality in this area cannot be an absolutely straight line," Chief Justice Burger wrote for the *Walz* Court. "The general principle" is that "we will not tolerate either governmentally established religion or government interference with religion. Short of those expressly proscribed government acts, there is ample room for play in the joints productive of a *benevolent neutrality* which will permit religious exercise to exist without sponsorship and without interference." Neutrality demands that we outlaw "the kind of involvement that would tip the balance toward government control of churches or government restraint on religious practice."[27] A general state policy of granting tax exemptions for the properties of churches, alongside charities, schools, and other public institutions, involves no such government control or restraint of the religious bodies that are exempt. To the contrary, it reflects a spirit of benevolent neutrality toward religion, which also ensures the separation of church and state. It is not a religious establishment.

This "accommodationist reading" of the *Lemon* test fell into desuetude for much of the 1970s and early 1980s. But it began to reappear in the Court's cases on government and religious education, beginning with *Mueller v. Allen* (1983).[28] Its most forceful exposition came in *Bowen v. Kendrick* (1988), which upheld federal funding of Catholic counseling centers for pregnant teenagers, in implementation of the Adolescent Family Life Act.[29]

In *Lemon v. Kurtzman* (1971) itself, the Court gave the *Lemon* test a separationist reading and struck down a state policy that reimbursed religious schools for some of the costs of teaching secular subjects that the state prescribed. The challenged state policy was restricted to religious schools that served students from lower-income families. Reimbursements were allowed only for clearly specified secular subjects and were limited to 15 percent of the costs. The Court declared that this policy fostered an "excessive entanglement between church and state." The Catholic schools in question were notably religious—closely allied with nearby parish churches, filled with religious symbols, and staffed primarily by nuns who were under "religious control and discipline." "[A] dedicated religious person, teaching at a school affiliated with his or her faith and operated to inculcate its tenets,

will inevitably experience great difficulty in remaining religiously neutral."
She will be tempted to teach secular subjects with a religious orientation in
violation of state policy. "A comprehensive, discriminating, and continuing
state surveillance will inevitably be required to ensure that these restrictions
are obeyed and the First Amendment otherwise obeyed." This is precisely
the kind of excessive entanglement between church and state that the disestablishment clause outlaws.[30]

This "separationist reading" of the *Lemon* test guided most of the
Court's disestablishment cases for the next fifteen years—not only for religion and education cases but also for cases raising other issues. The Court's
most forceful expositions came in *Wallace v. Jaffree* (1985), which outlawed moments of silence in public schools, and in *Texas Monthly v. Bullock* (1989), which outlawed state tax exemptions for the sale of religious
periodicals.[31]

In *Agostini v. Felton* (1997)[32] the Court reformulated the *Lemon* test—at
least for cases that challenged the constitutionality of government aid to religion. To pass constitutional muster under the disestablishment clause,
Lemon had required that such government aid programs: (1) have a secular
purpose; (2) have a primary effect that neither advances nor inhibits religion; and (3) not foster an excessive entanglement between church and
state. *Agostini* distilled *Lemon* and its progeny into a two-pronged inquiry:
(1) "whether the government acted with the purpose of advancing or prohibiting religion"; and (2) "whether the aid has the effect of advancing or
inhibiting religion." The second inquiry into the religious effect of the government aid should be guided by three criteria: (a) whether the aid results
in governmental indoctrination of religion; (b) whether the aid program defines its recipients with reference to religion; and (c) whether the aid creates
an excessive entanglement between government and religion.

The *Agostini* test was intended to be a less rigorous constitutional inquiry than the traditional *Lemon* test and has to date proved less amenable
to strict separationist readings. Significantly, by rendering "excessive entanglement" a simple factor in assessing the overall religious effect of a governmental program, rather than a separate inquiry, *Agostini* has allowed for
greater cooperation between religious and political officials in discharging
social and educational services funded by the government.

The *Agostini* Court used its new test to overturn *Aguilar v. Felton*
(1985),[33] a controversial case that had enjoined state educators from using
religious school buildings to deliver federal remedial educational services to
poor children, because such use fostered an excessive entanglement between church and state. The *Agostini* Court held that the mere presence of
state educators delivering these remedial services at religious schools was
not per se unconstitutional. The inquiry was not whether there was simply
an "excessive entanglement" of government and religion but whether such

entanglement evinced the fatal effect of advancing religion. The Court found no such impermissible religious effect and lifted the injunction against use of religious schools for delivery of Title I services to eligible indigent students.

In *Mitchell v. Helms* (2000),[34] a plurality of the Court used this same *Agostini* reformulation of the *Lemon* test to uphold a federally funded program that enabled states to lend educational materials directly to both public and private religious schools to implement "secular, neutral, and ideological programs." The *Mitchell* Court also overruled two earlier cases, *Meek v. Pittinger* (1975)[35] and *Wolman v. Walter* (1977),[36] that had read the *Lemon* test to outlaw all such "direct aid" to religious schools.

The increasingly wide disparities of logic and results in the Court's cases in the later 1970s and 1980s undercut the rationale for devising the *Lemon* test in the first place—to strike a more predictable middle way between separationism and accommodationism. Since the mid-1980s, individual justices have begun to experiment with alternative approaches to disestablishment. Three such approaches—"endorsement," "coercion," and "equal treatment"—have emerged, as well as a reformulation of the neutrality approach. None of these approaches has consistently captured a majority of the Court. But each has attracted considerable support among the justices, and each has led the Court in at least one recent case.

Endorsement

The endorsement approach is largely the creation of Justice O'Connor. The disestablishment clause, she argues, forbids governmental endorsement or disapproval of religion. "We live in a pluralistic society. Our citizens come from diverse religious traditions or adhere to no particular religious beliefs at all."[37] "[G]overnment may generally not treat people differently based on the God or gods they worship, or don't worship."[38] It may not "make adherence to religion relevant to a person's standing in the political community. Direct government action endorsing religion or a particular religious practice is invalid under this approach because it 'sends a message to nonadherents that they are outsiders, not full members of the political community, and an accompanying message to adherents that they are insiders, favored members of the community.'"[39]

Government accommodations of religion, if indiscriminately applied, are acceptable, Justice O'Connor writes. "What makes accommodation permissible, even praiseworthy, is not that the government is making life easier for some particular religious group as such. Rather, it is that the government is accommodating a deeply held belief."[40] This fosters equal protection for all, religious and nonreligious alike.[41]

Justice O'Connor has applied this endorsement reasoning in more than a dozen opinions since 1984. This approach came to strongest expression in Justice O'Connor's plurality opinion for the Court in *Board of Education v. Mergens* (1990), where the Court upheld the constitutionality of the Equal Access Act.[42] It was also invoked in part by Justice Blackmun in his majority opinion in *County of Allegheny v. ACLU* (1989), and again by Justice Stevens in the majority opinion of *Santa Fe Independent School District v. Doe* (2000). The endorsement test also played an important part in the plurality opinions of *Capitol Square Review and Advisory Board v. Pinette* (1995) and of *Mitchell v. Helms* (2000). Governmental support of religious symbols prominently displayed on its own buildings signals endorsement, she has argued.[43] But governmental accommodation of private religious displays in public parks and squares does not.[44] Governmental programs that give religious students equal access to state funding or facilities, or that support the secular functions of religious organizations, or that accommodate the special core needs of religious individuals or groups are necessary protections against outright hostility to religion.[45] But equality and accommodation give way to endorsement when the boundary of a public school district follows exactly the boundary of an exclusively religious community. In such an instance, religion does affect a person's standing in the political community.[46]

Justice O'Connor's endorsement approach is the most original of the Court's latest disestablishment offerings. Justice O'Connor's early formulations of this approach were criticized for inviting judicial inquiry into an elusive "legislative intent respecting religion" and for substituting rigorous judicial analysis of the constitutionality of governmental action with the "perceptions" of a "reasonable outsider" or "objective observer."[47] Her later formulations soften these inquiries into "legislative intent" and the "objective observer."[48] But by removing these inquiries, some critics now charge, her approach invites judges to make an abstract, subjective inquiry whether a government policy happens to favor religion. Such an approach is, at minimum, unpredictable. But, without requiring close inquiry into the context in which a law was made, the endorsement approach might now well require judges to outlaw the very legislative accommodations for religion that Justice O'Connor has so strongly favored.[49]

Coercion

Justice Kennedy regards "coercion" as the central concern of the disestablishment clause. In his view, "government may not coerce anyone to support or participate in any religion or its exercise; and it may not, in the guise of avoiding hostility or callous indifference, give direct benefits to religion in such a degree that it in fact 'establishes a religion or religious faith, or tends to do so.'"[50]

The disestablishment clause is designed to protect liberty of conscience and the autonomy of religious groups, Justice Kennedy argues, not to purge the public square or public policy of all religion. "[P]reservation and transmission of religious beliefs and worship is the responsibility and a choice committed to the private sphere, which itself is promised freedom to pursue its mission."[51] "Government policies of accommodation, acknowledgement or support for religion are an accepted part of our political and cultural heritage" and should be maintained in a pluralistic manner.[52] Only where such accommodations of religion effectively coerce public participation in religious exercises such as prayer or merge "political and religious lines" and institutions should they be struck down.[53] These latter policies invariably invite the kind of religious stigmatizing that impairs true liberty of conscience and autonomy of religious governance. Parties will choose to participate in the prayer or to abide by the religious line-drawing not out of voluntary conviction but because of the civil and social advantages attached to them.

A majority of the Court used this coercion test in *Lee v. Weisman* (1992) to outlaw prayers at a public middle school graduation ceremony. In this case, the school principal engaged a local rabbi to offer the prayers—instructing him to be "nonsectarian" and furnishing him with published guidelines to illustrate an appropriate prayer. The graduation ceremony took place on public school grounds. The prayer followed the public recitation of the pledge of allegiance, while the participants stood. Although students were not required to participate in the graduation ceremony, or in the prayer, most did.

Speaking for the Court, Justice Kennedy found the state's action doubly coercive. The state was dictating to the rabbi the content of his prayer. It was also effectively coercing all students to participate in its recitation. Although he adduced earlier cases that outlawed prayer in schools, Justice Kennedy did not dwell on their separationist reasoning. Although he did not apply the *Lemon* test, he explicitly rejected the recommendation of the parties and the dissent to bury it.[54] This concern to avoid coercion of religion was also at work in *Santa Fe Independent School District v. Doe* (2000), which outlawed student prayer at public high school football games.[55]

Neutrality

According to Justice Souter, the endorsement approach is not predictable enough, and the coercion approach is not embracive enough to outlaw more subtle forms of religious discrimination or favoritism. In Justice Souter's view, the disestablishment clause mandates "governmental neutrality" among religions and between religion and nonreligion. The *Lemon* test can be a helpful guide, but it is no dispositive method for judging whether government has acted neutrally.

Justice Souter's neutrality approach would outlaw a variety of forms of governmental accommodation of religion or cooperation with religious officials in the public school or the public square, for such actions favor religion over nonreligion.[56] Religiously neutral policies that afford an incidental benefit to religious beliefs or bodies are acceptable.[57] Governmental programs that support secular institutions along with religious institutions delivering secular services are also acceptable—so long as there is "a searching enquiry to ensure that the institution kept the secular activities separate from its sectarian ones, with any direct aid flowing only to the former and never the latter."[58] But direct government funding of any religious activities is "categorically prohibited," for taxpayers either of different or of nonreligious persuasion are being forced to pay for the religious activities of another.[59]

Justice Souter's neutrality approach carried a plurality of the Court in *Kiryas Joel Village School District v. Grumet* (1994). That case outlawed New York's creation of a new public school district that followed exactly the boundaries of a Hasidic Jewish community. The state had created this special school district in order to offer handicapped students in the Hasidic community the remedial services mandated by federal and state law, without forcing these students into the gentile world. All students in these remedial programs were Hasidic, and the school officials could respect the community's religious laws, particularly those mandating separate sex education. Writing for the Court, Justice Souter found this policy in violation of the disestablishment clause. It favors religious over nonreligious students. It subordinates and delegates the state's educational responsibility to the religious leadership and preferences of the community. Both features of the program fail to meet the neutrality required by the disestablishment clause.[60]

Equal Treatment and Neutrality

An emerging fourth approach to disestablishment has been called "equal treatment."[61] This approach, preferred especially by Chief Justice Rehnquist and Justices Thomas and Scalia, overlaps heavily in terminology and interpretation with the neutrality approach and is also consistent somewhat with the endorsement approach and the *Agostini* reformulation of *Lemon*.[62] But whereas Justice Souter's formulation of neutrality forbids government funding or alliances with religion, equal treatment exponents allow such funding and alliances so long as nonreligious parties similarly situated receive comparable treatment.[63]

Equal treatment of religion, of course, is no recent invention and is no monopoly of the disestablishment clause. Already in 1899, the Court upheld a federal grant to a religious hospital alongside others.[64] More recently, the Court has upheld construction grants to religious schools and religious charities as part of broader programs that fund nonreligious institutions as well.[65] The Court has upheld school bus transportation and textbook loans for religious students alongside nonreligious students.[66] It has upheld tax exemptions to church properties alongside those of schools, charities, and other associations.[67] And it has said that it is no establishment of religion for religious workers to receive the same access to unemployment compensation benefits afforded other workers.[68] The Court's rationale for these earlier holdings, however, was not stated in terms of "equality." These were forms of religious accommodation, protections of free exercise, expressions of benevolent neutrality, or suitable means of implementing secular policy.

In recent cases, however, the Court has said more explicitly that religious institutions and individuals are not "disabled by the First Amendment" from equal access to forums open to others, or from equal participation in government programs in which nonreligious parties participate.[69] Thus, in *Capitol Square v. Pinette* (1995), the Court upheld the private display of a cross in a public square that was "open to all on *equal terms.*"[70] In *Rosenberger v. University of Virginia* (1995), the Court upheld the equal access of a voluntary religious student group to the same state university funding for its publication that was available to more than 100 nonreligious student groups similarly situated. And in *Good News Club v. Milford Central School* (2001), the Court insisted that religious groups be given equal access to public school classrooms that were open to other groups offering extracurricular civics instruction.

In the plurality opinion in *Mitchell v. Helms* (2000) and in the majority opinion of *Zelman v. Simmons-Harris* (2002), the Court cast these concerns of equal treatment into a new two-step inquiry into "even-handed neutrality." A court must inquire whether a challenged statute is (1) religiously neutral on its face, and (2) religiously neutral in application. This latest inquiry flattens the *Agostini* concerns for religious indoctrination, line-drawing, or excessive entanglement into a more generic inquiry into neutrality in application.

This latest neutrality formulation of the disestablishment clause runs closely parallel to the *Smith* neutrality formulation of the free exercise clause—and it is no coincidence that Justice Scalia and Chief Justice Rehnquist have been leading architects of both formulations. Under the *Smith* test, as we saw, a challenged law will satisfy the free exercise clause if it is (1) neutral; and (2) generally applicable. Under the *Zelman* test, a law will satisfy the disestablishment clause if it is: (1) neutral on its face; and (2) neutral in application. There is some distinction between these two inquiries, especially in their second prongs. But they run closely parallel. It might well be that this latest establishment clause test will help the Court achieve what many justices have long coveted: a more integrated jurisprudence of the First Amendment religion clauses. But the cost of this inquiry has been a substantial weakening of both clauses.[71]

Endorsement, coercion, neutrality, and equal treatment—these are the four main alternative approaches that the Court has recently imported into its disestablishment clause calculus. All of these approaches have aimed to replace the *Lemon* neutrality test and to nuance the underlying separationist and accommodationist approaches that antedate and inform the *Lemon* test. None of these approaches has, as yet, commanded a consistent majority of the Court, and none has interred the *Lemon* test entirely, let alone its reformulation in *Agostini*.

The Dominant Principle of Separation of Church and State

The Supreme Court's modern disestablishment cases are not only forums for the contestation of rival judicial approaches. They are also laboratories for the application of the first principles of the American experiment in religious rights and liberties. In the foregoing section, I have used the Court's terms of art and forms of analysis to map modern disestablishment doctrine. In this section, I trace the Court's interpretation and application of the first principles of the American experiment in its more than fifty disestablishment cases issued since 1947.

The founders viewed the disestablishment clause as both a source and a summary of religious freedom. At minimum, disestablishment of religion meant foreclosing government from defining and enforcing by law the religion of the community—its religious texts and traditions, its doctrines and liturgies, its lectionaries and prayers—as European ecclesiastical laws had done for centuries. More fully conceived, disestablishment of religion meant foreclosing government from coercing citizens to participate in religious exercises and affiliations in violation of the principle of liberty of conscience. It foreclosed government from discriminating among its citizens on religious grounds in violation of the principle of equality of plural religions before the law. It foreclosed government from involving itself in the offices and activities of religious bodies, in violation of the principle of separation of church and state. The guarantee of disestablishment of religion, like the guarantee of free exercise of religion, was an umbrella term. It protected at once the principles of liberty of conscience, equality of a plurality of religions, and separation of church and state.[72]

There was ample debate, both in the founding era and in the generations to follow, about the relative rigor and priority of each of these constitutive principles of disestablishment. One issue that was particularly divisive was whether all government aid to religion was categorically forbidden or whether governmental aid could be given nonpreferentially among religions. Both interpretations could be plausibly drawn from the debates surrounding the formation of the religion clauses.[73] Both interpretations came to vigorous expression in nineteenth- and early twentieth-century state constitutions.[74]

The Emergence of Separationism

In *Everson v. Board of Education* (1947), the case that opened the modern era of disestablishment, the Supreme Court reiterated each of the first principles that the founders had incorporated into the disestablishment clause. This can be seen if one parses phrase by phrase Justice Black's famous summary in *Everson*: "The 'establishment of religion' clause of the First Amendment means at least this," Justice Black wrote. No federal or state government (1) "can set up a church"—a violation of the core disestablishment principle; (2) "can force or influence a person to go or to remain away from church against his will or force him to profess a belief or disbelief in any religion"—a violation of liberty of conscience; (3) can "punish [a person] for entertaining or professing religious beliefs or disbeliefs, for church attendance or non-attendance"—a violation of both liberty of conscience and religious equality; (4) "can, openly or secretly, participate in the affairs of any religious organizations or groups, or *vice versa*"—a violation of the principle of separation of church and state.[75] Justice Black also underscored the founders' principle of religious pluralism, declaring that government may not exclude "individual Catholics, Lutherans, Mohammedans, Baptists, Jews, Methodists, Nonbelievers, Presbyterians, or the members of any faith, *because of their faith, or lack of it,* from receiving the benefits of public welfare legislation."[76] Liberty of conscience, religious equality, religious pluralism, and separation of church and state were all considered part of the disestablishment clause in the Court's initial formulation.

On the perennially contested issue of government aid to religion, however, the *Everson* court came down foursquare against it and linked its "no-aid" formulation to the principle of separation of church and state. Government, Justice Black wrote, may pass no laws "which aid one religion, aid all religions, or prefer one religion over another. No tax in any amount, large or small, can be levied to support any religious activities or institutions, whatever they may be called, or whatever form they may adopt to teach or practice religion." "[T]he clause against establishment of religion by law was intended to erect a wall of separation between church and state."[77]

It was this latter move by the *Everson* Court that set the tone for much of the Court's early interpretation and application of the disestablishment clause. Disestablishment of religion meant no government aid to religion. No government aid to religion was best accomplished by separating government from religion altogether. Disestablishment, separation, and no aid were increasingly linked in the Court's opinions under the general rubric of "separationism." The other founding principles of disestablishment were increasingly lost in the Court's opinions for the next forty years.

Religion and Public Education

In its first generation of cases in the modern era, the Court enforced this separationist reading of the disestablishment clause repeatedly in the context of education. This was not so unusual a first forum for separationist logic. By 1947, thirty-three state constitutions prohibited state and local governments from granting funds and other aid to religious schools. Fifteen state constitutions insisted further that state schools remain free from "sectarian influence" or from the control of religious officials and institutions.[78] At the turn of the century, and thereafter, various Protestant, Catholic, and other religious constituencies had led campaigns to reinvigorate the religion of the public schools—calling for the enhancement of biblical teaching, the appointment of Christian teachers, the reinvigoration of religious ceremonies and symbols, and much else. By 1947, these issues had occupied state courts and constitutional conventions for more than a half century—with widely varying results.

After 1947, the Supreme Court took firm control of these controversies and systematically outlawed the use of religious teachers, texts, ceremonies, and symbols in the public schools. In its early cases, the Court developed a general logic that was specific to the issue of government support of religion in public education. The public school is one of the most visible and well-known arms of the state in any community, the cases repeatedly argued. One primary purpose of the public school is to stand as a model of constitutional democracy and to provide a vehicle for the communication of democratic values and abilities to its students. The state compels its students to be at schools. These students are perforce young and impressionable. As a consequence, the public schools must cling closely to core constitutional and democratic values. One such core value is the separation of church and state taught by the disestablishment clause. Some relaxation of constitutional values, even disestablishment values, might be possible in other public contexts—where mature adults can make informed assessments of the values being transmitted. But no such relaxation can occur in public schools with their impressionable youths who are compelled to be there. In public schools, the constitutional values of the disestablishment clause must be vigorously protected.

The case that opened this series was *McCollum v. Board of Education* (1948). The state action at issue was a "release time" program, adopted by a local public school board for fourth- through ninth-grade students. For thirty to forty-five minutes once a week, students were released from their regular classes to be able to participate in religious classes, if their parents consented to their participation. Students could choose among three such religious classes, taught respectively by qualified Protestant, Catholic, or Jewish teachers. These religious teachers were not employed by the school but were approved by its superintendent. Students whose parents did not consent to their participation continued their "secular studies" during this release time period.

A parent of one student challenged the release time program as a violation of the disestablishment clause. The *McCollum* Court agreed. Writing for the majority, Justice Black declared that this was precisely the kind of conflation of church and state that *Everson* sought to outlaw—using "tax-supported property for religious instruction and the close cooperation between school authorities and the religious council in promoting religious education."

> The operation of the State's compulsory education system thus assists and is integrated with the program of religious instruction carried on by separate religious sects. Pupils compelled by law to go to school for secular education are released in part from their legal duty upon the condition that they attend the religious classes. This is beyond all question a utilization of the tax-established and tax-supported public school to aid religious groups to spread their faith. And it falls squarely under the ban of the First Amendment [that] . . . had erected a wall of separation between Church and State.[79]

In a strongly worded concurrence, Justice Frankfurter underscored the importance of rigorous application of the principle of separationism in the realm of public education. After lamenting that public schools of late had become "hostage" to "sectarian control," Justice Frankfurter wrote:

> Separation means separation, not something less. Jefferson's metaphor in describing the relation between Church and State speaks of a "wall of separation," not of a fine line easily overstepped. The public school is at once the symbol of our democracy and the most pervasive means for promoting our common destiny. In no activity of the State is it more vital to keep out divisive influences than in its schools, to avoid confusing, not to say fusing, what the Constitution sought to keep strictly apart. "The great American principle of eternal separation"—Elihu Root's phrase bears repetition—is one of the vital reliances of our Constitutional system for assuring unities among our people

stronger than our diversities. It is the Court's duty to enforce this principle in its full integrity.[80]

In *Engel v. Vitale* (1962), the Court extended this separationist reasoning to outlaw prayer in schools. The State Board of Regents of New York had adopted a nondenominational prayer to be recited by public school teachers and their students at the commencement of each day: "Almighty God, we acknowledge our dependence upon Thee, and we beg Thy blessings upon us, our parents, our teachers, and our Country." Students who did not wish to participate in the prayer could remain silent or be excused from the room during its recitation. The parents of ten students challenged both the state's creation of the prayer and its use in the public school classroom, as violations of the disestablishment clause.

The *Engel* Court agreed. Again Justice Black wrote for the majority:

> It is no part of the business of government to compose official prayers for any group of the American people to recite as part of a religious program carried on by government. . . . There can be no doubt that New York's state prayer program officially establishes the religious beliefs embodied in the Regents prayer. . . . Neither the fact that the prayer may be denominationally neutral nor the fact that its observance on the part of the students is voluntary can serve to free it from the Establishment Clause. . . . When the power, prestige, and financial support of government is placed behind a particular religious belief, the indirect coercive pressure upon religious minorities to conform to the prevailing officially approved religion is plain.

This is plainly unconstitutional, Justice Black concluded. It violates the "first and most immediate" principle of the disestablishment clause: "[A] union of government and religion tends to destroy government and to degrade religion."[81] This prohibition on prayer in public schools remains the law, as the Court underscored more recently in *Lee v. Weisman* (1992) and again in *Santa Fe Independent School District v. Doe* (2000).[82]

In *Abington Township School District v. Schempp* (1963), the Court extended this reasoning to outlaw Bible reading in the public schools.[83] Following general state law, a public school district mandated that each school open its day with the reading of ten Bible verses. Either a teacher or a student who volunteered would read the text. Each reader was permitted to choose the text of the day. No commentary or discussion of the Bible reading was allowed. In some schools, a common reading was broadcast throughout the school; in other schools, the reading was done in individual classrooms. In some schools, this reading was followed by public recitation of the Lord's Prayer and of the Pledge of Allegiance. Students whose parents did not consent could again refuse to participate or leave the room during these religious exercises.

Against the backdrop of *Engel v. Vitale*, the *Schempp* Court found this case an easy violation of the disestablishment clause. The policy in question was an overtly religious exercise, mandated by the state, for impressionable youths required to be in school, with no realistic opportunity for the average student to forgo participation. "[I]t is no defense that the religious practices here may be relatively minor encroachments on the First Amendment," Justice Clark wrote for the Court. "The breach of neutrality that is today a trickling stream may all too soon become a raging torrent."

Justice Clark emphasized that to ban religion from the public school was not to ban it from society altogether:

> The place of religion in our society is an exalted one, achieved through a long tradition of reliance on the home, the church, and the inviolable citadel of the individual heart and mind. We have come to recognize through bitter experience that it is not within the power of government to invade that citadel, whether its purpose or effect be to aid or oppose, to advance or retard. In the relationship between man and religion, the state is firmly committed to a position of neutrality.[84]

Responding to Justice Stewart's sharply worded dissent that the Court's neutrality stance effectively established "secularism" as the religion of the public school, Justice Clark offered a conciliatory word about the objective value of religion in public education:

> We agree of course that the State may not establish a "religion of secularism" in the sense of affirmatively opposing or showing hostility to religion. . . . We do not agree, however, that this decision in any sense has that effect. In addition, it might well be said that one's education is not complete without a study of comparative religion or the history of religion and its relationship to the advancement of civilization. It certainly may be said that the Bible is worthy of study for its literary and historic qualities. Nothing we have said here indicates that such study of the Bible or of religion, when presented objectively as part of a secular program of education, may not be effected consistently with the First Amendment.[85]

In two subsequent cases, however, the Court closed the door firmly against symbolic and objective forms of religion in the public school. In *Stone v. Graham* (1980), the Court struck down a state statute that required the posting of a plaque bearing the Ten Commandments on the wall of each public school classroom. The plaques were donated and hung by private groups in the community. There was no public reading of the commandments nor any evident mention or endorsement of them by teachers or school officials. Each plaque bore a small inscription that sought to immunize it from charges of religious establishment: "The secular application of the Ten Commandments is clearly seen in its adoption as the fundamental legal code of Western Civilization and the Common Law of the United States."

The Court struck down the displays as a form of religious establishment. It found the statute mandating the Decalogue display had no "secular legislative purpose" but was "clearly religious." The Ten Commandments are sacred in Jewish and Christian circles, and they command "the religious duties of believers." It made no constitutional difference, said the Court, that the Ten Commandments were passively displayed rather than formally read or that they were privately donated rather than purchased with state money. The very display of the Decalogue served only a religious purpose and was thus per se unconstitutional.[86]

In *Edwards v. Aguillard* (1987), the Court pressed this logic further to strike down a Louisiana act requiring a "Balanced Treatment for Creation-Science and Evolution-Science in Public School Instruction." The statute mandated that a public school teacher could not teach "evolution-science" without teaching "creation-science" and vice versa. Teachers were not required to teach a theory of origins, but if they did, they had to give equal time to "the scientific evidences" for both evolutionary and creationist accounts of origins. The stated legislative purpose of the act was "to promote academic freedom" in allowing teachers to explore various theories of origins, including religious theories.

The *Edwards* Court declared the act unconstitutional. After rehearsing the legislative history at length, the Court concluded that the act had no real secular purpose but was a thinly veiled attempt to import religious teachings into the curriculum. The act evinced a "discriminatory preference for the teaching of creation and against the teaching of evolution," Justice Brennan wrote for the Court. Its "preeminent purpose" was "clearly to advance the religious viewpoint that a supernatural being created humankind. The term 'creation science' was defined as embracing this particular religious doctrine. . . . In this case, the purpose of the Creationism Act was to restructure the science curriculum to conform with a particular religious viewpoint." This was not a proper objective teaching of religion but an unconstitutional establishment of religion.[87]

In *Wallace v. Jaffree* (1985), the Court stretched its separationist logic to its furthest point. At issue in the case was a state statute that authorized a moment of silence at the beginning of each school day for "meditation or voluntary prayer." On rehearsing the legislative history, the Court found that the statute revealed no secular purpose but a "legislative intent to return prayer to the public schools." "The addition of 'or voluntary prayer'" to the statute, Justice Stevens wrote for the Court, "indicates that the State intended to characterize prayer as a favored practice. Such an endorsement is not consistent with the established principle that Government must pursue a course of complete neutrality toward religion."[88]

Government and Religious Education

From the start, the principle of separation of church and state dominated the Court's opinions on the role of religion in public education. This principle came only to more gradual application in the Court's opinions on the role of government in religious education.

In the decades before *Everson,* the Court had already several times countenanced general protection and support for religious schools.[89] In *Quick Bear v. Leupp* (1908), the Court upheld the allocation of federal funds to Catholic schools that offered education to Native Americans. In *Meyer v. Nebraska* (1923), the Court held that states could not forbid religious schools from teaching or reading the Bible in a foreign language. In *Pierce v. Society of Sisters* (1925), the Court held that a state government could not mandate that all students attend public schools; religious schools were a vital and viable alternative form of education that was constitutionally protected. In *Farrington v. Tokushige* (1927), the Court held that states could not impose unduly intrusive and stringent accreditation and regulatory requirements on religious and other private schools. In *Cochran v. Board of Education* (1930), the Court held that a state policy of supplying textbooks to all students could also supply them to religious school students.[90]

This accommodation of religious schools and students initially continued in the modern disestablishment cases. *Everson* itself, for all its sweeping separationist dicta, nonetheless held that it was no establishment of religion for states to provide school bus transportation to religious and public school children alike. Moreover, it was no establishment of religion for the state to reimburse the parents of religious and public school children alike for the costs of using school bus transportation. "[C]utting off church schools [and their students] from these services, so separate and indisputably marked off from the religious function, would make it far more difficult for the schools to operate," Justice Black wrote. "But such obviously is not the purpose of the First Amendment. The Amendment requires the State to be neutral in its relations with groups of religious believers and non-believers; it does not require the state to be their adversary."[91]

The Court struck a similar tone in *Board of Education v. Allen* (1968). The State of New York had a policy of lending prescribed textbooks in science, mathematics, and other "secular subjects" to all students in the state, whether attending public or private schools. Many of the private school recipients of the textbooks were religious schools. A taxpayer thus challenged the policy as a violation of the disestablishment clause. Citing the 1930 *Cochran* case, the Court upheld this policy, emphasizing that it was the students and parents, not the religious schools, that directly benefited. "Perhaps free books make it more likely that some children choose to attend a sectarian school," Justice White wrote for the Court, "but that was true of the state-paid bus fares in *Everson,* and does not alone demonstrate an unconstitutional degree of support for a religious institution."[92]

The Court continued this accommodationist tone in a trio of cases upholding the payment of government construction grants and revenue bonds to religious colleges and universities.[93] In *Tilton v. Richardson* (1971), the Court rebuffed a challenge to federal grants that supported construction of library, science, and arts buildings at four church-related colleges. The grants were made as part of the federal Higher Education Facilities Act (1963), which sponsored new college and university buildings throughout the nation. Chief Justice Burger wrote for the Court: "The Act itself was carefully drafted to ensure that the federally-subsidized facilities would be devoted to the secular and not the religious functions of the recipient institution."[94] This feature, together with the reality that most funding was directed to state, not religious, universities and colleges was sufficient to save them from charges of religious establishment.

In *Roemer v. Board of Public Works* (1977), the Court upheld a state construction grant program that aided five church-related schools among its seventeen grant recipients. The Court counseled against too zealous an application of separationist principles. In Justice Blackmun's words:

> A system of government that makes itself felt as pervasively as ours could hardly be expected never to cross paths with the church. In fact, our State and Federal Governments impose certain burdens upon, and impart certain benefits to, virtually all our activities, and religious activity is no exception. The Court has enforced a scrupulous neutrality by the State, as among religions, and also as between religious and other activities, but a hermetic separation of the two is an impossibility [and] it has never been required. . . . [R]eligious institutions need not be quarantined from public benefits that are neutrally available to all. . . . Just as *Bradfield [v. Roberts* (1899)] dispels any notion that a religious person can never be in the State's pay for a secular purpose, so *Everson* and *Allen* put to rest any argument that the State may never act in such a way that has the incidental effect of facilitating religious activity.[95]

Outside of these cases, however, the Court's accommodationist tones ended abruptly in 1971. With its adoption of the *Lemon* test that year, the Court began to apply the separationist logic of its public education cases to the religious education cases as well. *Lemon v. Kurtzman* (1971) itself, as we saw, used the separationist policy of the "no excessive entanglement between church and state" prong to strike down a state policy that reimbursed religious schools for up to 15 percent of the costs of teachers' salaries, plus the costs of textbooks and other instructional materials for prescribed secular subjects.

Lemon left open the question whether the state could give aid directly to religious students or to their parents—as the Court had allowed in earlier cases. Two years later, the Court closed this door tightly. In *Committee for Public Education v. Nyquist* (1973) and *Sloan v. Lemon* (1973), the Court struck down state policies that allowed low-income parents to seek reimbursements from the state for some of the costs of religious school tuition. *Nyquist* further struck down a state policy that allowed low-income parents to take tax deductions for the costs of sending their children to nonpublic schools. In *Nyquist,* Justice Powell characterized such policies as just another "of the ingenious plans of channelling state aid to sectarian schools." Responding to the state argument that "grants to parents, unlike grants to [religious] institutions, respect the 'wall of separation' required by the Constitution," the Court declared that "the effect of the aid is unmistakeably to provide desired financial support for non-public, sectarian institutions."[96] This violates the second prong of the *Lemon* test that outlaws any policy whose primary effect is to advance religion.

Lemon also left open the question of whether the state could give textbooks, educational materials, or other aid to religious schools for the teaching of mandatory secular subjects, or the administration of state-mandated tests and other programs. The Court struck down most such policies, save the lending of textbooks, which had been upheld since the 1930 *Cochran* case. In a long series of increasingly tedious cases, from 1973 to 1985, the Court held that states could not reimburse religious schools for most costs incurred to administer standardized tests or to prepare mandated state records[97]—although the "actual costs" for certain tests could be recouped.[98] States could loan textbooks on secular subjects to religious schools, but not if those schools discriminated on racial grounds.[99] States could not loan or furnish religious schools with various supplies and films, and various counseling and other personnel, even if those were mandated by state policy.[100] States could not use public school teachers to hold remedial educational programs for indigent children in classrooms leased from religious schools.[101] States could not lend public school personnel to teach remedial and enrichment courses in religious schools.[102]

By 1985, these cases on the relationship between government and religious schools began increasingly to "partake of the prolixity" of a bizarre byzantine code. Justice Rehnquist summarized the law:

[A] State may lend to parochial school children geography textbooks that contain maps of the United States, but the State may not lend maps of the United States for use in geography class. A State may lend textbooks on American colonial history, but it may not lend a film of George Washington, or a film projector to show it in history class. A State may lend classroom workbooks, but may not lend workbooks in which the parochial school children write, thus rendering them nonreusable. A State may pay for bus transportation to religious schools, but may not pay for bus transportation from the parochial school to the public zoo or natural history museum for a field trip. A State may pay for diagnostic services conducted in the parochial school but therapeutic services must be given in a different building; speech and hearing "services" conducted by the State inside the sectarian school are forbidden, but the State may conduct speech and hearing testing inside the sectarian school. Exceptional parochial school students may receive counseling, but it must take place outside of the parochial school, such as in a trailer parked down the street. A State may give cash to a parochial school to pay for administration of State-written tests and State-ordered reporting services, but it may not provide funds for teacher-prepared tests on secular subjects. Religious instruction may not be given in public school, but the public school may release students during the day for religion classes [in the sectarian school], and may enforce attendance of those classes with its truancy laws.[103]

Already in a 1948 education case, Justice Jackson had warned his brethren that if the Court did not set strict limits to federal jurisdiction over these local education cases, it would soon have "to accept the role of a super board of education for every school district in the nation." "And more importantly," he warned, "we are likely to make the legal 'wall of separation between church and state' as winding as the famous serpentine wall designed by Mr. Jefferson for the University he founded."[104] Within four decades, such warnings had proved painfully prescient.

Religion and the Public Square

The Court's separationist logic in its education cases set the tone for adjudicating other disestablishment cases as well. The Supreme Court itself heard very few disestablishment cases that did not involve questions of religion and education. But many lower federal and state courts did. These courts used the Supreme Court's separationist logic to outlaw all manner of traditional government subsidies for religious charities, social services, and mission works; government use of religious services, facilities, and publications; government protections of Sundays and holy days; government enforcement of blasphemy and sacrilege laws; government participation in religious rituals and religious displays.

It often did not take lawsuits to implement this separationist logic. Particularly local governments, sensitive to the costs of constitutional litigation, often voluntarily ended their prayers, removed their Decalogues, and closed their coffers to religion long before any case was filed against them. This voluntary "First Amendmentization" of religion and politics seemed to be what the Court's separationist reading of the disestablishment clause required.

The few Supreme Court disestablishment cases outside the realm of education underscored this popular impression. *Larkin v. Grendel's Den* (1982) was a good case in point. A Massachusetts law required that no facility within 500 feet of a school or church could receive a liquor license if "the governing body of such school or church files written objection thereto." Grendel's Den was denied a liquor license because a neighboring church had objected. Grendel's Den appealed, claiming that the licensing law was an establishment of religion. The Court agreed. "Jefferson's idea of a 'wall,'" Chief Justice Burger wrote for the Court, "was a useful figurative illustration to emphasize the concept of separateness. Some limited and incidental entanglement between church and state authority is inevitable in a complex modern society, but the concept of a 'wall' of separation is a useful signpost. Here that 'wall' is substantially breached by vesting discretionary governmental power in religious bodies."[105]

Writing in lonely dissent, Justice Rehnquist termed this "a silly case." This is a sound and sensible zoning law, he argued, not an establishment of religion. Massachusetts could have, like many states, simply banned altogether the serving of liquor within stated distances of schools and religious institutions—and this ban would easily pass constitutional muster. Instead of imposing this flat ban, the state here chose to leave it to schools or churches to decide whether they wanted to have this common protection from the sale of liquor in their immediate surroundings. Here, one church simply said that it wanted such protection, and the state gave it to them. This is hardly a "fusion of governmental and religious functions" or a "delegation of essential governmental powers" to religious bodies, Justice Rehnquist wrote, but an equitable application of a valid rule of law. The Massachusetts law in question "does not encourage, much less compel anyone to participate in religious activities or to support religious organizations." "The heavy First Amendment artillery that the Court fires at this sensible and unobjectionable Massachusetts statute is both unnecessary and unavailing."[106]

Toward Multiple Principles of Disestablishment

Justice Rehnquist's lonely 1982 dissent against too strict a separationist reading of the disestablishment clause increasingly became the norm for the

Court in the later 1980s and thereafter. While holding fast to separationism in most of its public education cases, the Court has been slowly retreating from this principle in other cases.

The Court's retreats have often been rather clumsy exercises—featuring inventive twists of the *Lemon* test in some cases, tendentious distinctions of precedent in others, and the rather haphazard introduction of new approaches and terms, such as endorsement, coercion, neutrality, and equal treatment. Moreover, in this process of retreat, the Court has issued a number of blatantly contradictory decisions. In successive years, the Court upheld the constitutionality of federal funding of Catholic teenage pregnancy counseling centers but struck down a state tax exemption for sales of religious periodicals.[107] The Court upheld the constitutionality of a federal law exempting religious employers from Title VII prohibitions on religious discrimination but struck down the constitutionality of a state law allowing religious employees to claim exemptions from working on their Sabbath.[108] The Court upheld the constitutionality of state funding of a legislative chaplain who opened each General Assembly session with prayer but struck down a county's policy of allowing a privately funded Christmas display in the foyer of its courthouse.[109] The Court required a local public school to allow a Christian club to lead its elementary students in prayer and Bible reading in its classrooms but prohibited a public high school student elected by his peers from offering a brief prayer at a football game.[110] While some of these decisions can be partially explained by close attention to their facts, they collectively betray ample evidence of "a jurisprudence of doubt."[111]

Yet, in the midst of all this confusion, the Court of late has shown some signs of developing a more integrative law of disestablishment. In *Everson,* as we saw, the Court had read into the disestablishment clause a number of other first principles of the American experiment besides separation of church and state—notably liberty of conscience and the equality of plural faiths before the law. In several recent cases, the Court seems to be importing these principles, alongside separationism, into its disestablishment calculus.

Liberty of Conscience, Equality, and Religious Education

The court's recent cases on the role of government in religious education provide a good example of this new trend. *Lemon v. Kurtzman* (1971) and its immediate progeny, as we saw, had outlawed most forms of government aid to and cooperation with religious schools. The core holdings of these cases have not changed: Government still may not directly fund, endorse, or cooperate in the religious teachings of religious schools. But in several recent cases, the Court has upheld various government programs that grant to religious students or their parents the same general benefits afforded to others. The common rationale of these cases is that students and their parents must be protected in their choices to attend religious schools—even if this results in indirect government funding of religious education. Too zealous an application of separationism intrudes on these parties' liberty of conscience to choose religious education and on equality of treatment in the choices they make.

In *Mueller v. Allen* (1983), the Court upheld a Minnesota law that allowed parents of private school children to claim tax deductions from state income tax for the costs of "tuition, transportation, and textbooks." Ninety-five percent of the private school children in the state attended religious schools. Most of their parents availed themselves of this tax deduction. A taxpayer in the state challenged the law as an establishment of religion.

Using the *Lemon* test, the *Mueller* Court upheld the law. The tax deduction policy had a secular purpose of fostering quality education, Justice Rehnquist wrote for the Court. The motives of the legislature should not be considered: Laws should be upheld against charges of establishment "when a plausible secular purpose for the state's program may be discerned from the face of the statute." The law fostered no entanglement between church and state.

The "more difficult" question for the *Mueller* Court was whether the law had "the primary effect of advancing the sectarian aims of the non-public schools"—the principal ground on which the *Nyquist* Court a decade before had struck down such tax deduction policies. The *Mueller* Court distinguished *Nyquist* rather tendentiously. The saving features of the Minnesota law, Justice Rehnquist argued, were that this was a deduction for educational costs, not religious education; that it allowed deductions for the costs of "private" education, not "nonpublic" education; and that the deductions for religious education allowed by this law were sufficiently diluted by the many other deductions, for medical, charitable, and other causes. The *Nyquist* Court had characterized all such arguments as "ingenious schemes." The *Mueller* Court found that these features sufficiently "reduced the Establishment Clause objections" to the law. The state aid to sectarian schools, Justice Rehnquist concluded, "becomes available only as a result of numerous, private choices of individual parents of school-age children." This saves it from constitutional infirmity.[112]

In *Witters v. Washington Department of Services for the Blind* (1986), the Court upheld a state program that furnished aid to a visually impaired student attending a Christian college. The program provided funds "for special education and/or training in the professions, business or trades" for the visually impaired. Money was to be paid directly to eligible recipients, who were entitled to pursue education in the professional schools of their choice. Mr. Witters's condition qualified him for the funds. His profession of choice was the Christian ministry. He sought funds to attend a Christian college in preparation for the same. The state agency denied funding, on grounds that this was a direct funding of religious education prohibited by *Lemon* and its progeny.

The *Witters* Court disagreed. Applying the *Lemon* test, the Court found the policy, and its application to Mr. Witters, constitutional. The policy served a secular purpose of fostering educational and professional choice for all, including the handicapped. It involved no entanglement of church and state. Its primary purpose was to facilitate this student's professional education, which happened to be religious. This "is not one of 'the ingenious plans for channeling state aid to sectarian schools that periodically reach this Court,'" Justice Marshall wrote. "It creates no financial incentive for students to undertake sectarian education. It does not provide greater or broader benefits for recipients who apply their aid to religious education. . . . In this case, the fact that aid goes to individuals means that the decision to support religious education is made by the individual not by the State."[113]

In *Zobrest v. Catalina Foothills School District* (1993), the Court extended this logic from a college student to a high school student. Both federal and state disability acts required that a hearing-impaired student be furnished with a sign-language interpreter to accompany him or her to classes. The state furnished the interpreters at its own cost. Mr. Zobrest's hearing impairment qualified him for an interpreter's services. But he enrolled at a Catholic high school. The state refused to furnish him with an interpreter, on grounds that this would violate the *Lemon* rule that the state could give no direct aid to a religious school; moreover, the presence of a state-employed interpreter in a Catholic high school would foster an excessive entanglement between church and state.

Following *Mueller* and *Witters,* the *Zobrest* Court upheld the act as "a neutral government program dispensing aid not to schools but to handicapped children." "If a handicapped child chooses to enroll in a sectarian school," Chief Justice Rehnquist wrote for the Court, "we hold that the Establishment Clause does not prevent the school district from furnishing him with a sign-language interpreter."[114]

In *Agostini v. Felton* (1997), the Court extended this logic from the high school to the grade school, overturning the controversial case of *Aguilar v. Felton* (1985). In the earlier *Aguilar* case, the Court had declared unconstitutional New York City's program that sent public school teachers into religious schools to offer remedial services to disadvantaged students. The remedial services in question in *Aguilar* were authorized and funded by Congress in the Elementary and Secondary Education Act (1965), known as the Title I program. The act set detailed standards both for student eligibility and for the education to be offered eligible students. More than 20,000 students in Catholic, Jewish, Protestant, and other religious schools in the city annually availed themselves of these Title I services. Lacking sufficient space in existing public buildings, and lacking sufficient land to build new public buildings adjacent to religious schools, New York City had chosen to offer the remedial services on site to eligible religious school students. State-funded public school teachers with materials were sent into the religious schools to teach the eligible religious school students. Field supervisors were sent out monthly to ensure compliance with the law, in particular to ensure that the Title I funds were directed to remedial, not religious, education in these schools. The program had been in place for nineteen years.

In the early 1980s, local taxpayers challenged the program as a violation of the disestablishment clause. The *Aguilar* Court agreed. Though "well-intentioned," Justice Brennan wrote for the Court in 1985, the program fosters an excessive entanglement of church and state. The religious schools receiving the Title I instructors are "pervasively sectarian," having as a "substantial purpose, the inculcation of religious values." Because of this, "ongoing inspection is required to ensure the absence of a religious message. In short, the scope and duration of New York's Title I program would require a permanent and pervasive State presence in the sectarian schools receiving aid." This, Justice Brennan concluded, is precisely the kind of excessive entanglement between church and state that the disestablishment clause outlaws.[115]

Four justices wrote bitter dissents in *Aguilar*. Justice Rehnquist charged that the Court "takes advantage of the 'Catch 22' paradox of its own creation, whereby aid must be supervised to ensure no entanglement, but the supervision itself is held to cause an entanglement."[116] Justice O'Connor denounced the majority opinion as "wooden," "formalistic," and "lacking in common sense." In the nineteen years of the program, she wrote, quoting the record, "there has never been a single incident in which a Title I instructor 'subtly or overtly' attempted to 'indoctrinate the students in particular religious tenets at public expense.'" The real losers, she wrote, are disadvantaged children who happen to live "in cities where it is not economically or logistically feasible to provide public facilities for remedial education adjacent to the parochial school. . . . For these children, the Court's decision is tragic."[117]

In 1997, the *Agostini* Court, led by Justice O'Connor, overruled *Aguilar*. The ample procedural subtleties of the case aside, the *Agostini* Court declared that its disestablishment law had changed sufficiently to offset the *Aguilar* holding. Citing *Zobrest,* Justice O'Connor wrote that the mere presence of a state employee in a religious institution is not a per se unconstitutional means of state inculcation of religion or the kind of "symbolic union of church and state" that violates the excessive entanglement prong.

Citing *Witters,* she wrote that "we have departed from the rule . . . that all government aid that directly aids the educational functions of religious schools is invalid." The *Aguilar* Court had been "unduly zealous and mechanical" in its application of the *Lemon* test, the Court concluded. In particular, it had used the "excessive entanglement prong" to enforce a form of separationism that could not be squared with other constitutional values. Children in religious schools are just as entitled to Title I benefits as children in public schools. They cannot be denied these benefits simply for the sake of upholding "the abstract principle" of separation of church and state.[118]

In *Mitchell v. Helms* (2000),[119] the Court extended *Agostini* to uphold the constitutionality of direct government aid to religious schools. Chapter 2 of the federal Education Consolidation and Improvement Act (1981) channels federal funds to state and local education agencies for the purchase of various educational materials and equipment. The act permits states to loan such materials directly to public and private elementary and secondary schools, provided that the state retain title in those materials and that the recipient schools use them only for programs that are "secular, neutral, and nonideological." The amount of aid for each participating school depends on the number of students it matriculates. In accordance with the act, Louisiana distributed materials and equipment to public and private schools within various school units in the state. In one such school unit, the Jefferson Parish (i.e., County), some 30 percent of the Chapter 2 aid was allocated to private schools, most of which were Catholic. The aid was distributed properly per the federal formula. There was no allegation that the private religious schools used the aid for anything but "secular, neutral, and nonideological" programs. Local taxpayers brought suit, however, arguing that such "direct aid" to such "pervasively sectarian" schools constituted an establishment of religion.

The *Mitchell* Court disagreed and held the Chapter 2 program constitutional both on its face and as applied in this case. Six justices found that the act did not advance religion using the three criteria that *Agostini* had distilled: There was no governmental indoctrination of religion because the aid was "offered to a broad range of groups or persons without regard to their religion" and was used for "secular, neutral, and nonideological programs." The act did not define its recipients by reference to religion; all accredited public and private schools and students were eligible. And there was no excessive entanglement between religious and governmental officials in the administration of the program. Accordingly, the Court upheld Chapter 2. The Court also overruled two earlier cases that had held unconstitutional similar aid programs distributing materials directly to religious schools, acknowledging that the separationist principles at work in these decisions had become unworkably rigid.

Writing for three others, Justice Thomas went beyond the *Agostini* reformulation of the *Lemon* test and stressed that the principle of neutrality alone was sufficient to uphold the constitutionality of the Chapter 2 program. He dismissed the distinction between direct and indirect aid, reasoning that even direct aid did not impermissibly indoctrinate religion so long as it was neutrally available and its allocation was subject to the choices of private citizens. Allocating aid on the basis of enrollment is a "neutral, secular criteri[on] that neither favor[s] nor disfavor[s] religion, and is made available to both religious and secular beneficiaries on a nondiscriminatory basis." In such a per capita system, "[i]t is the students and their parents—not the government—who, through their choice of school, determine who receives Chapter 2 funds." As a result, "[t]he ultimate beneficiaries of Chapter 2 aid are the students who attend the schools that receive the aid." Justice Thomas also noted that "nothing in the Establishment Clause requires the exclusion of pervasively sectarian schools from otherwise permissible aid programs"—even if there is a risk that the aid may be diverted to religious purposes. Since "the eligibility for aid is determined in a constitutionally permissible manner, any use of that aid to indoctrinate cannot be attributed to the government."

In a concurring opinion, Justice O'Connor, joined by Justice Breyer, rejected the plurality's heavy reliance on the principle of "neutrality" and insisted that the *Agostini* test should remain the test of choice for this and future cases involving government aid to religion. The Court has "never held that a government-aid program passes constitutional muster *solely* because of the neutral criteria it employs as a basis of distributing aid," Justice O'Connor argued. Moreover, there was no reason in the current case to dismiss the traditional distinction between direct and indirect aid or to be unconcerned whether aid to religious recipients is used for religious purposes. In this case, "no funds ever reached the coffers of a religious school" and no aid directly served the school's "religious purposes," and thus Chapter 2 did not have the fatal effect of advancing religion. For the two concurring justices, this was enough to render Chapter 2 constitutional, and it was best left to another case to determine the survival of traditional concerns for direct versus indirect aid.

In *Zelman v. Simmons-Harris* (2002), the majority of the Court took the step on which the *Mitchell* plurality had divided—upholding another form of state aid to religious schools on the grounds of neutrality alone.[120] In a 5–4 opinion, with Justice O'Connor now in the majority, the Court upheld the constitutionality of a school voucher program. At issue in *Zelman* was the State of Ohio's pilot project scholarship program, which Ohio had adopted to address a "crisis of magnitude" in its public school system. The program gave parents a choice to leave their children in the local Cleveland public school district or to enroll them in another public or private school that participated in the school voucher program. For those parents who chose to remove their children, the program provided them with a voucher to defray tuition costs at the private school to which they chose to send their children. In the 1999–2000 academic year, 82 percent of the private schools participating in the voucher program were religiously affiliated; 96 percent of the students participating in the voucher program enrolled in these private religious schools.

The Court concluded that there was no dispute that the program was enacted for a "valid secular purpose of providing educational assistance to poor children in a demonstrably failing public school system." Thus the Court addressed the sole issue of whether the Ohio program had the "effect" of advancing religion in violation of the disestablishment clause. Writing for the majority, Chief Justice Rehnquist drew a distinction between government programs that provide aid directly to religious schools *(Mitchell, Agostini, Rosenberger)*, and programs of "true private choice" *(Mueller, Witters and Zobrest)*. To the Court, the latter trio of cases "make clear that where a government aid program is *neutral* with respect to religion, and provides assistance directly to a *broad class of citizens*, who, in turn, direct government aid to religious schools wholly as a result of their own genuine and independent *private choice*, the program is not readily subject to challenge under the Establishment Clause. A program that shares these features permits government aid to reach religious institutions only by way of the deliberate choices of numerous individual recipients. The incidental advancement of a religious mission, or the perceived endorsement of a religious message is reasonably attributable to the individual, not the government, whose role ends with the disbursement of the funds."

The Court found that the Ohio voucher program is one of "true private choice" that is neutral to religion, and is thus constitutional. As in *Mitchell*, the majority stressed that there is a broad range of educational choices and the program did not define its recipients by reference to religion. Moreover, the Court distinguished its holding from that in *Nyquist*, where the program provided incentives for students to attend religious schools and prohibited public schools from participating. Rehnquist noted that here there are no financial incentives for parents to choose a religious school; rather there are disincentives for choosing religious schools since under the program private schools receive only a portion of the government assistance that public community and magnet schools receive.

Given the majority's characterization of this as an "indirect aid" case, it is not surprising that Justice O'Connor joined the majority. However, she wrote separately to elaborate on the broad array of nonreligious options inherent in this voucher program and to clarify that the support it provides religious institutions "is neither substantial nor atypical of existing government programs."

Justice Souter dissented, denouncing what he maintained is now the majority's "evenhandedness" neutrality test. Joined by Justices Ginsburg, Stevens, and Breyer, Souter accused the majority of applying its "twin standards of neutrality and free choice" in a way that renders them meaningless: "the espoused criteria of neutrality in offering aid, and private choice in directing it, are shown to be nothing but examples of verbal formalism." Most significant to Souter were the facts that the private schools predominated the program, and that 96.6 percent of the current voucher money goes to religious schools. For Souter, these statistics reveal that the program is not neutral, and that parents do not in fact have a "true private choice." Fundamentally, they confirm that the voucher program betrays the disestablishment objectives as expressed by James Madison—to ensure that "the minds of men always be wholly free" and "to save religion from its own corruption." In Souter's view, "the reality is that in the matter of education aid the Establishment Clause has largely been read away."

Locke v. Davey (2004) suggests that the Court may have not entirely "read away" its concerns for religious establishment.[121] In *Locke*, the Court upheld the State of Washington's decision to exclude theology majors from a general scholarship program in implementation of its state constitutional prohibitions on religious establishment. The state constitution provided: "No public money or property shall be appropriated for or applied to any religious worship, exercise, or instruction, or the support of any religious establishment." The holding of *Locke v. Davey* was that the exclusion of theology majors from this general scholarship program was not a violation of the First Amendment free exercise clause. But the implications of the case are that equal treatment and equal access have a limit, if not a stopping point, in constitutional prohibitions on religious establishments.

Liberty of Conscience and Public Education

One of the Court's common concerns in the foregoing cases on religious education was to protect liberty of conscience—the right of students and their parents to be free to choose a religious education without discrimination and deprivation by the state and without penalties for the choices they made.

The Court's concern for liberty of conscience is also reflected in the public education case of *Lee v. Weisman* (1992), which we encountered in analyzing the Court's new "coercion" approach to the disestablishment clause.[122] The *Weisman* Court could easily have outlawed the state sponsorship of a rabbi's public school graduation prayers with a simple recitation of principle and precedent on the separation of church and state. After all, prayer in public schools has been banned since 1962. Though perennially controversial, the ban is one of the few hard and fast rules left in the Court's modern disestablishment law.

The *Weisman* Court's concern, however, was not so much the principle of separation of church and state as the principle of liberty of conscience. Justice Kennedy wrote:

> The undeniable fact is that the school district's supervision and control of a high school graduation ceremony puts public pressure, as well as peer pressure, on attending students to stand as a group, or at least maintain respectful silence during the Invocation and Benediction. The pressure, though subtle and indirect, can be as real as any overt compulsion. . . . *[F]or the dissenter of high school age, who has a reasonable perception that she is being forced by the State to pray in a manner her conscience will not allow, the injury is no less real.* . . . [T]he embarrassment and the intrusion of the religious exercise cannot be refuted by arguing that these prayers, and similar ones said in the future, are of a *de minimis* character. To do so would be an affront to the Rabbi who offered them and to all those for whom the prayers were an essential and profound recognition of divine authority. And for the same reason, we think that the intrusion is greater than the two minutes or so of time consumed for prayers like these. Assuming, as we must, that the prayers were offensive to the student and the parent who now object, the intrusion was both real and, in the context of a secondary school, a violation of the objector's rights.[123]

In *Santa Fe Independent School District v. Doe* (2000) the Court held firm to the principle that liberty of conscience of the listener must be vigilantly protected during school-sponsored events.[124] The Santa Fe School District instituted a "Prayer at Football Games" policy that authorized students to participate in a referendum to determine first whether "invocations" should be given at the school's football games. Ninety-one percent of the students voted in favor of such invocations. One student was elected by his peers to deliver these invocations for all the home football games that year. The district offered several secular justifications for the pre-game invocation, including their purpose and effect "to solemnize the event, to promote good sportsmanship and student safety, and to establish the appropriate environment for the competition." Students and their parents brought suit, alleging that the district's policies and practices constituted an establishment of religion.

The Court agreed and declared unconstitutional the policy and practice of student-led invocations at high school football games. Justice Stevens, writing for a 6–3 majority, reiterated the principle set forth in *Lee v. Weisman* that "at a minimum, the Constitution guarantees that government may not coerce anyone to support or participate in religion or its exercise."

The Court was not convinced that the private student speech implicated no coercion, noting that the invocations were "authorized by a government policy . . . on government property at government-sponsored school-related events" and attendance was mandatory for some students, including cheer-leaders, band members, and the football players themselves. The Court further rejected the student election process as a "circuit-breaker" to the constitutional challenge. "[F]undamental rights may not be submitted to vote; they depend on the outcome of no elections."

Not only was the Santa Fe policy an unconstitutional coercion of religion in violation of the principle of liberty of conscience, it was also an impermissible state endorsement of religion masquerading as a concern for the student's freedom of speech: "The District . . . asks us to pretend that we do not recognize what every High School student understands clearly—that this policy is about prayer. The District further asks us to accept what is obviously untrue: that these messages are necessary to 'solemnize' a football game and that this single-student, year-long position is essential to the protection of student speech. We refuse to turn a blind eye to the context in which this policy arose, and that context quells any doubt that this policy was implemented with the purpose of endorsing school prayer." The Court further noted that the principle of equal access does not ultimately trump disestablishment clause concerns when it is countermajoritarian: "[T]he fact that only one student is permitted to give a content-limited message suggests this policy does little to 'foste[r] free expression.'"

Equality and Religious Expression

These recent religion and education cases reflect the Court's new concern in disestablishment cases for the principle of liberty of conscience—the right freely to choose or to forgo religious instruction and ceremony. These cases also hint at the Court's new concern for the principle of religious equality— the right of persons of all faiths and of no faith to receive equal protection and treatment under the law.

The principle of religious equality has long informed the Court's free exercise and free speech cases, as we saw.[125] But this principle has also come to fuller expression in the Court's disestablishment cases respecting religious expression.

In two earlier cases, the Court had already used the principle of religious equality to buffer the principle of separation of church and state. In *McDaniel v. Paty* (1978), the Court outlawed a Tennessee constitutional prohibition on ministers serving in political office. The stated purpose for the prohibition was to "assure" "the separation of church and state." The Court outlawed this prohibition as a violation of a clergy's free exercise rights to participate on equal terms in politics. Tennessee's concern for separation, Chief Justice Burger wrote for the Court, cannot "overbalance legitimate claims to the free exercise of religion." "The essence of the rationale underlying the Tennessee restriction on ministers is that if elected to public office they will necessarily exercise their powers and influence to promote the interests of one sect or thwart the interests of another thus pitting one against the others, contrary to the anti-establishment principle." "However widely that view may have been held in the 18th century," Chief Justice Burger concluded, today, "American experience provides no persuasive support for the fear that clergymen in public office will be less careful of anti-establishment interests or less faithful to their oaths of civil office than their unordained counterparts."[126]

In *Widmar v. Vincent* (1981), the Court declared that granting religious student groups equal access to state university facilities for voluntary meetings is "not incompatible with the Court's Establishment Clause cases." "It is possible—perhaps even foreseeable—that religious groups will benefit from access to University facilities," Justice Powell wrote. "But this Court has explained that a religious organization's enjoyment of merely 'incidental' benefits does not violate" the disestablishment clause.[127] Both religious and nonreligious students alike must be guaranteed equal access to public university forums. The religious speech in question is voluntary and private. In this instance, the principle of separation of church and state must give way to the principle of equality.

The Court has made ample use of this logic of equality in its most recent disestablishment cases. In *Board of Education v. Mergens* (1990), the Court used this principle to uphold the constitutionality of the Equal Access Act. The act mandated that voluntary groups of religious high school students be granted the same access to public high school facilities as is granted to nonreligious groups. "[T]he Act's prohibition of discrimination on the basis of 'political, philosophical, or other' speech," Justice O'Connor wrote for the Court:

> is a sufficient basis for meeting the secular purpose prong of the *Lemon* test. Congress' avowed purpose—to prevent discrimination against religious and other types of speech—is undeniably secular. Even if some legislators were motivated by a conviction that religious speech in particular was valuable and worthy of protection, that alone would not invalidate the Act, because what is relevant is the legislative *purpose* of the statute, not the possible religious *motives* of the legislators who enacted the law.

Moreover, the primary effect of the statute is not to endorse religion, but to protect equality.

[T]here is a crucial difference between *government* speech endorsing religion, which the Establishment Clause forbids, and *private* speech endorsing religion, which the Free Speech and Free Exercise Clauses protect. We think the secondary school students are mature enough and are likely to understand that a school does not endorse or support student speech that it merely permits on a nondiscriminatory basis.[128]

In *Rosenberger v. University of Virginia* (1995), the Court extended this equality principle from public forums to public funds. Voluntary groups of religious students at a state university were just as entitled to funding for their publications as voluntary groups of nonreligious students. To do otherwise, said the Court, would "select for disfavored treatment those student journalistic efforts with religious editorial viewpoints." It would entitle government "to scan the publication to ferret out views that principally manifest a belief in a divine being." This would manifest not equality of treatment but hostility to religion.[129]

In *Capitol Square v. Pinette* (1995), the Court extended this equality principle to protect even the religious expression of a notably unpopular group. The City of Columbus, Ohio, had for more than a century made a ten-acre square surrounding the State House available "for use by the public . . . for free discussion of public questions, or for activities of a broad public purpose." All manner of public and private groups could use the square for meetings, speeches, and displays, so long as they applied for a permit and adhered to stated standards of sanitation and security. One December, the city put up its own Christmas tree. It granted a rabbi's application to put up a menorah in the square. But the city denied the application from the Ku Klux Klan to put up its trademark cross. The Klan leader appealed.

The *Pinette* Court held that the free speech clause protected the Ku Klux Klan's display of the cross and that the disestablishment clause did not prevent it. Citing *Widmar* and its progeny, Justice Scalia wrote that such private expression of religion "is as fully protected under the Free Speech clause as secular private expression." Indeed, "a Free Speech clause without religion would be *Hamlet* without the prince." Moreover, for the state to open its public forum to private religious expression is no establishment of religion. "Religious expression cannot be said to violate the Establishment Clause where it (1) is purely private and (2) occurs in a traditional or designated public forum, publicly announced, and open to all on *equal terms.*"[130]

Conclusions

In 1986, constitutional historian Leonard Levy wrote that "the Court has managed to unite those who stand at polar opposites on the results that the

Court reaches; a strict separationist and a zealous accommodationist are likely to agree that the Supreme Court would not recognize an establishment of religion if it took life and bit the Justices."[131]

While some of the Court's cases since 1986 have shown hopeful signs of a more integrated law of disestablishment, this description remains largely apt. Few areas of law today are so riven with wild generalizations and hairsplitting distinctions, so given to grand statements of principle and petty applications of precept, so rife with selective readings of history and inventive renderings of precedent. Few areas of law hold such a massive jumble of juxtaposed doctrines and rules. Even a sympathetic reader of the Court's modern disestablishment decisions is tempted to apply to it the definition that Oliver Wendell Holmes Jr. once applied to the common law: "chaos with an index."

It is apt, in this context, to be reminded of the founders' original vision of the disestablishment clause. In the founders' view, the disestablishment clause was designed to complement the free exercise clause in the protection of religious liberty. The free exercise clause outlawed government *proscriptions* of religion—actions that unduly burdened the conscience, restricted religious expression and action, discriminated against religion, or invaded the autonomy of churches and other religious bodies. The disestablishment clause outlawed government *prescriptions* of religion—actions that unduly coerced the conscience, mandated forms of religious expression, discriminated in favor of religion, or improperly allied the state with churches or other religious bodies. Both the free exercise and the disestablishment clauses thereby provided complementary protections to the first principles of the American experiment—liberty of conscience, freedom of religious expression, equality of plural faiths before the law, and separation of church and state.

In *Everson v. Board of Education* (1947), the Court effectively read each of these first principles into modern disestablishment law. But in most of its cases in the next forty years, the Court focused on the single principle of separation of church and state—yielding secularist dicta and decisions that seemed strangely out of place in a nation so widely devoted to a public religion and a religious public. Since the mid-1980s, the Court has begun to widen its disestablishment calculus, introducing new lines of cases that attempt, albeit awkwardly, to strike new balances among the principles of separation of church and state, equality of plural religions, and liberty of conscience.

This emerging multiprincipled reading of the disestablishment clause holds considerable promise. To be sure, a strong reading of the principle of separation of church and state, evident in some modern First Amendment cases, remains essential. Government officials have no constitutional business interfering in the internal affairs of religious groups. Religious officials have no constitutional business converting the offices of government into instruments of their mission and ministry. Government has no business funding, sponsoring, or actively involving itself in the religious exercises of a particular religious group or religious official. Religious groups have no business drawing on government sponsorship or funding for their core religious exercises. Religious groups have no constitutional business insisting that government cede or delegate to them some of the core political responsibilities. All such conduct violates the principle of separation of church and state and should be outlawed by the disestablishment clause.

But a categorical insistence on the principle of separation of church and state avails us rather little. James Madison warned in 1833 that "it may not be easy, in every possible case, to trace the line of separation between the rights of Religion and the Civil authority, with such distinctness, as to avoid collisions & doubts on *unessential points.*"[132] This caveat has become even more salient today. The modern welfare state, and now the modern security state, for better or worse, reaches deeply into virtually all aspects of modern life—through its network of education, charity, welfare, child care, health care, construction, zoning, workplace, taxation, security, and sundry other regulations. Madison's solution was "an entire abstinence of the Government from interference [with religion] in any way whatever, beyond the necessity of preserving public order, & protecting each sect against trespasses on its legal rights by others."[133] This traditional understanding of a minimal state role in the life of society in general, and of religious bodies in particular—however alluring it may be in theory—is no longer realistic in practice.

It is thus even more imperative today than in Madison's day that the principle of separation of church and state not be pressed to reach, what Madison called, the "unessentials." It is one thing for the Court to outlaw daily Christian prayers and broadcasted Bible readings from the public school, quite another thing to ban moments of silence and private displays of the Decalogue in the same schools. It is one thing to bar direct tax support for religious education, quite another thing to bar tax deductions for parents who wish to educate their children in the faith. It is one thing to prevent government officials from delegating their core police powers to religious bodies, quite another thing to prevent them from facilitating the charitable services of voluntary religious and nonreligious associations alike. It is one thing to outlaw governmental prescriptions of prayers, ceremonies, and symbols in public forums, quite another thing to outlaw governmental accommodations of private prayers, ceremonies, and symbols in public forums. To press separationist logic too deeply into "unessentials" not only "trivializes" the place of religion in public and private life, as Stephen Carter argues.[134] It also trivializes the power of the Constitution, converting it from a coda of cardinal principles of national law into a codex of petty precepts of local life.

Too zealous an interpretation of the principle of separation of church and state also runs afoul of other constitutive principles of the disestablishment clause—particularly the principles of liberty of conscience and religious equality. The Court must be at least as zealous in protecting religious conscience from secular coercion as protecting secular conscience from religious coercion. The Court should be at least as concerned to ensure the equal treatment of religion as to ensure the equality of religion and nonreligion. It is no violation of the principle of separation of church and state when a legislature or court accommodates judiciously the conscientious scruples of a religious individual or the cardinal callings of a religious body. It is also no violation of this principle when government grants religious individuals and institutions equal access to forums, facilities, or funds that are open to nonreligionists similarly situated. To do otherwise is, indeed, to move toward what Justice Stewart once called "the establishment of a religion of secularism."[135]

Notes

1. *Zobrest v. Catalina Foothills School District*, 509 U.S. 1, 24 (1993) (O'Connor, J., dissenting), quoting *Three Affiliated Tribes of Fort Berthold Reservation v. Wold Engineering*, P.C., 467 U.S. 1. See also *McCollum v. Board of Education*, 333 U.S. 203, 232, 235 (Jackson, J., concurring) (expressing doubt whether the Court had jurisdiction over a local case involving religious instruction in public schools, and urging the Court to devise strict limits to jurisdiction over these cases).

2. 393 U.S. 97, 100 (1968).

3. *Zobrest*, 504 U.S. at 24 (O'Connor, J., dissenting).

4. Ibid., 8.

5. *Frothingham v. Mellon*, 262 U.S. 447 (1923).

6. See, e.g., *Doremus v. Board of Education*, 342 U.S. 429 (1952).

7. *Abington School District v. Schempp*, 374 U.S. 203, 224, n. 9 (1963) (emphasis added).

8. *Flast v. Cohen*, 392 U.S. 83 (1968). See also *Larson v. Valente*, 456 U.S. 228, 238–244 (1982); and 456 U.S. at 264–272 (Rehnquist, J., dissenting) (detailed discussion of Article III standing in disestablishment cases).

9. *Valley Forge Christian College v. American United for Separation of Church and State*, 454 U.S. 464, 487 (1982). See also *Karcher v. May*, 484 U.S. 72 (1987); *Elk Grove Unified School District v. Newdow*, 124 S.Ct. 2301 (2004).

10. See, e.g., *Kiryas Joel Village School District v. Grumet*, 114 S.Ct. 2481 (1994).

11. *Lyng v. Northwest Indian Cemetery Protective Association*, 485 U.S. 439, 451 (1988); see Michael W. McConnell, "Equal Treatment and Religious Discrimi-

nation," in *Equal Treatment of Religion in a Pluralistic Society,* ed. Stephen V. Monsma and J. Christopher Soper (1998), 30.

12. *Valley Forge,* 454 U.S. at 509–510 (Brennan, J., dissenting) (references omitted).

13. *Marsh v. Chambers,* 463 U.S. 783 (1983) (upholding state appointment of legislative chaplains exclusively on historical grounds). See also *McGowan v. Maryland,* 366 U.S. 420 (1961) (upholding Sunday blue laws largely on historical grounds); *Walz v. Tax Commission,* 397 U.S. 664 (1970) (upholding tax exemptions of church property, in part, on historical grounds).

14. See above, pp. 26–33, 112–113.

15. *Everson,* 330 U.S. at 15–16.

16. *Engel v. Vitale,* 370 U.S. 421, 430–432 (1962).

17. *Board of Education v. Allen,* 392 U.S. 236, 251–252 (1968) (Black, J., dissenting).

18. *Everson,* 330 U.S. at 18.

19. See *Walz v. Tax Commission* (1970); *Texas Monthly v. Bullock,* 489 U.S. 1 (1989).

20. 343 U.S. 306, 312–314 (1952).

21. *Engel v. Vitale,* 370 U.S. at 421, 445–446 (Stewart, J., dissenting).

22. *Schempp,* 374 U.S. at 313 (Stewart, J., dissenting).

23. *Wallace v. Jaffree,* 472 U.S. 38, 107, 113 (Rehnquist, J., dissenting).

24. 374 U.S. at 222. See also ibid., 243–244, 299–305 (Brennan, J., concurring) (expounding and illustrating the principle of neutrality).

25. *Lemon v. Kurtzman,* 403 U.S. 602, 612–614 (1973), quoting in part, *Walz v. Tax Commission,* 397 U.S. at 670, 674–675. See also Burger's comments in *Tilton v. Richardson,* 403 U.S. 672, 677 (1971).

26. Compare, e.g., *Wallace v. Jaffree* (1985) (offering a searching inquiry into legislative history); *Mueller v. Allen,* 463 U.S. 388 (1983) (spurning inquiry into the motives of the legislature or the history of the statute). See also *Board of Education of the Westside Community Schools v. Mergens,* 496 U.S. 226, 248–250 (1990).

27. 397 U.S. at 669–670 (1970) (emphasis added).

28. 463 U.S. 388 (1983).

29. 487 U.S. 589 (1988).

30. 403 U.S. at 619–620, 622 (1971), rehearing denied, 404 U.S. 876 (1971).

31. 472 U.S. 38 (1985) and 489 U.S. 1 (1989), respectively.

32. 521 U.S. 203 (1997).

33. 473 U.S. 402 (1985), overruled by *Agostini v. Felton,* 521 U.S. 203, 235 (1997).

34. 530 U.S. 793 (2000).

35. 421 U.S. 349 (1975), overruled by *Mitchell v. Helms,* 530 U.S. at 808.

36. 433 U.S. 229 (1977), overruled by *Mitchell v. Helms,* 530 U.S. at 808.

37. *Allegheny County v. American Civil Liberties Union,* 492 U.S. 573, 627 (O'Connor, J., concurring).

38. *Kiryas Joel,* 114 S.Ct. at 2497 (O'Connor, J., concurring).

39. *Wallace v. Jaffree,* 472 U.S. at 69 (O'Connor, J., concurring), quoting in part *Lynch v. Donnelly* (1984).

40. *Kiryas Joel,* 114 S.Ct. at 2497 (O'Connor, J., concurring).

41. *Mergens*, 496 U.S. at 248–50.

42. Ibid.

43. *Allegheny County*, 492 U.S. at 623–637 (O'Connor, J., concurring).

44. *Lynch v. Donnelly*, 465 U.S. 668, 687–694 (O'Connor, J., concurring); see also *Capitol Square v. Pinette*, 115 S.Ct. 2440, 2451–2457 (1995) (O'Connor, J., concurring).

45. *Mergens*, 110 S.Ct. at 2356; *Rosenberger v. University of Virginia*, 115 S.Ct. at 2525–2528 (1995) (O'Connor, J., concurring).

46. *Kiryas Joel*, 114 S.Ct. at 2481, 2497 (O'Connor, J., concurring).

47. Michael W. McConnell, "Religious Freedom at a Crossroads," *University of Chicago Law Review* 59 (1992):115, 147ff.

48. See, e.g., *Rosenberger*, 115 S.Ct. at 2525–2528 (O'Connor, J., concurring) (including only a passing quotation about the "reasonable observer"); *Mergens*, 110 S.Ct. at 2356 (rejecting inquiry into legislative intent, and not referring to the "reasonable observer" standard).

49. See Jesse H. Choper, "The Endorsement Test: Its Status and Desirability," *Journal of Law and Politics* 18 (2002):499, 510ff.

50. *Allegheny County*, 492 U.S. at 659, quoting in part, *Lynch v. Donnelly* (1984).

51. *Lee v. Weisman*, 505 U.S. 577, 586–587, 592–594 (1992).

52. *Allegheny County*, 492 U.S. at 657 (Kennedy, J., concurring in judgment in part, dissenting in part).

53. *Kiryas Joel*, 114 S.Ct. at 2501–2505 (Kennedy, J., concurring).

54. 505 U.S. at 587, 589–592.

55. 530 U.S. 290 (2000).

56. See Justice Souter's illustrations in *Lee v. Weisman*, 112 S.Ct. at 618–619 (Souter, J., concurring); *Kiryas Joel*, 114 S.Ct. at 2491–2492.

57. *Kiryas Joel*, 114 S.Ct. at 2491–2492.

58. *Rosenberger*, 115 S.Ct. at 2539 (Souter, J., dissenting).

59. Ibid., 2534–2539. See Douglas Laycock, "Formal, Substantive, and Disaggregated Neutrality Toward Religion," *DePaul Law Review* 39 (1990):993.

60. *Kiryas Joel*, 114 S.Ct. at 2487–2493.

61. Monsma and Soper, eds., *Equal Treatment of Religion in a Pluralistic Society.*

62. See, e.g., Justice O'Connor's explicit concerns for "equal protection of religion" in *Mergens*, 496 U.S. at 235–238, 248–252; *Kiryas Joel*, 114 S.Ct. at 2497.

63. See esp. the contrast between Justice Kennedy's and Justice Souter's reading of "neutrality" in *Rosenberger v. University of Virginia* (1995).

64. *Bradfield v. Roberts*, 175 U.S. 291 (1899).

65. See, e.g., *Tilton v. Richardson*, 403 U.S. 672 (1971); *Roemer v. Board of Public Works*, 426 U.S. 736 (1976); *Bowen v. Kendrick*, 487 U.S. 589 (1988).

66. *Everson v. Board of Education* (1947); *Board of Education v. Allen*, 392 U.S. 236 (1968).

67. *Walz v. Tax Commission* (1970).

68. See *Sherbert v. Verner*, 374 U.S. 398, 409–410 (1963) (defending the free exercise exemption on grounds of neutrality but explicitly forgoing analysis of the equal protection issue); repeated in *Thomas v. Review Board*, 450 U.S. 707,

719–720 (1981); *Hobbie v. Unemployment Appeals Commission*, 480 U.S. 136, 144–145 (1987).

69. Quoting *Bowen v. Kendrick*, 487 U.S. at 609.

70. *Pinette*, 115 S.Ct. at 2440, 2450 (emphasis added).

71. See multiple perspectives in Symposium, "Shifting into Neutral? Emerging Perspectives on Separation of Church and State," *Boston College Law Review* 43 (2002):1009; Symposium, "Beyond Separatism: Church and State," *Journal of Law and Politics* 18 (2002):1; Ira C. Lupu and Robert W. Tuttle, "*Zelman's* Future: Vouchers, Sectarian Providers, and the Next Round of Constitutionanl Battles," *Notre Dame Law Review* 78 (2003):917.

72. See above, pp. 57–61.

73. See above, pp. 59–61, 94–96.

74. See above, pp. 111–118.

75. *Everson*, 330 U.S. at 15–16.

76. Ibid., 16 (emphasis in original).

77. Ibid., 15–16.

78. See above, pp. 111–113, and Appendix 2.

79. 333 U.S. 203, 209–211 (1948).

80. Ibid., 231 (Frankfurter, J., concurring).

81. 370 U.S. at 421, 430–432 (1962).

82. See also *Treen v. Karen B.*, 455 U.S. 913 (1982) (affd. memo) (striking down statute authorizing student volunteers to lead prayer in public school classroom).

83. 374 U.S. 203 (1963). *Schempp* also involved a companion case, *Murray v. Curlett*. The Court, in a per curiam opinion, extended the *Schempp* holding in *Chamberlain v. Public Instruction Board*, 377 U.S. 402 (1964).

84. 374 U.S. 203, 221, 226 (1963).

85. Ibid., 225.

86. 449 U.S. 39 (1980) (per curiam).

87. 482 U.S. 578, 591–593 (1987).

88. 472 U.S. 38, 59–60 (1985).

89. Except when quoting, I shall use the generic term "religious school." The conventional term "parochial" school not only has a deprecatory tone in common parlance but also when used properly means "parish" school. This term is not inclusive enough, since it does not cover the range of Jewish, Muslim, Protestant, and other schools affiliated with religious groups. The other conventional term, "sectarian" school, is even more deprecatory, even in technical parlance, and I have sought to avoid it herein as well.

90. See further discussion of these cases above, pp. 131–132, 135–136.

91. *Everson*, 330 U.S. at 16, 18.

92. 392 U.S. at 243–244.

93. Respectively, *Tilton v. Richardson*, 403 U.S. 672 (1971); *Hunt v. McNair*, 413 U.S. 734 (1973); *Roemer v. Maryland Public Works Board*, 426 U.S. 736 (1977).

94. 403 U.S. at 679–682.

95. 426 U.S. at 746.

96. *Committee for Public Education v. Nyquist*, 413 U.S. 756, 783, 785 (1973).

97. *Levitt v. Committee for Public Education*, 413 U.S. 472 (1973); *New York v. Cathedral Academy*, 434 U.S. 125 (1977).

98. *Committee for Public Education v. Regan*, 444 U.S. 646 (1980).

99. *Norwood v. Harrison*, 413 U.S. 455 (1973); see also *Wolman v. Walter*, 433 U.S. 229 (1977), overruled by *Mitchell v. Helms* (2000).

100. *Meek v. Pittinger*, 421 U.S. 349 (1975), overruled by *Mitchell v. Helms* (2000); for exceptions, see *Wolman v. Walter* (1977), also overruled by *Mitchell v. Helms* (2000).

101. *Aguilar v. Felton*, 473 U.S. 402 (1985), overruled by *Agostini v. Felton* (1997).

102. *Grand Rapids School District v. Ball*, 473 U.S. (1985).

103. *Wallace v. Jaffree*, 482 U.S. at 110–111 (Rehnquist, J., dissenting).

104. *McCollum*, 333 U.S. at 237–238 (Jackson, J., concurring).

105. *Larkin v. Grendel's Den*, 459 U.S. 116, 122–123 (1982).

106. Ibid., 127–130 (Rehnquist, J., dissenting).

107. *Bowen v. Kendrick*, 487 U.S. 589 (1988); *Texas Monthly, Inc. v. Bullock*, 489 U.S. 1 (1989).

108. *Corporation of the Presiding Bishop v. Amos*, 483 U.S. 327 (1987); *Estate of Thornton v. Caldor, Inc.*, 472 U.S. 703 (1985).

109. *Marsh v. Chambers*, 463 U.S. 783 (1983); *Allegheny County v. ACLU* (1989).

110. *Good News Club v. Milford Central School* (2001); *Santa Fe Independent School District v. Doe* (2000).

111. The phrase is Justice O'Connor's in *Planned Parenthood v. Casey*, 505 U.S. 833 (1992).

112. 463 U.S. 388, 394–399 (1983).

113. 474 U.S. 481, 488 (1986).

114. 509 U.S. 1, 13–14 (1993).

115. 473 U.S. 402, 411–413 (1985).

116. Ibid., 420–421 (Rehnquist, J., dissenting).

117. Ibid., 424, 430–431 (O'Connor, J., dissenting).

118. *Agostini v. Felton*, 521 U.S. at 206.

119. 530 U.S. 793 (2000).

120. 122 S.Ct. 2460 (2002).

121. See above, pp. 168–169.

122. See above, pp. 197–198.

123. 505 U.S. at 593–594 (emphasis added).

124. 530 U.S. 290 (2000).

125. See above, pp. 153–157, 169–176.

126. 435 U.S. 622, 628–629 (1978), quoting in part *Wisconsin v. Yoder*, 406 U.S. 205 (1972).

127. 454 U.S. 263, 271, 273 (1981).

128. 496 U.S. at 248–250.

129. *Rosenberger*, 115 S.Ct. at 2517, 2524.

130. Ibid., 2444, 2446, 2450 (emphasis added).

131. Levy, *The Establishment Clause*, 163.

132. James Madison, Letter to Rev. Adams (1833), in Dreisbach, *Religion and Politics*, 120 (emphasis added).

133. Ibid.

134. Stephen L. Carter, *The Culture of Disbelief: How American Law and Politics Trivializes Religious Devotion* (1993).

135. *Schempp*, 374 U.S. at 313 (Stewart, J., dissenting).

9

TOWARD AN INTEGRATION OF RELIGIOUS LIBERTY

The American Experiment in International Context

Methods and Measures of Integration

The ample vacillations in the Supreme Court's First Amendment cases can be explained, in part, on factual grounds. The application of a sixteen-word guarantee to dozens of diverse and complex issues over the course of a century and more has inevitably led to conflicting decisions. "The life of the law has not been logic: it has been experience," Oliver Wendell Holmes Jr. reminds us.[1] The American law of religious rights and liberties is no exception.

These vacillations, however, also betray the failure of the Court to develop a coherent framework for interpreting and applying the First Amendment. The Court has tended to rely too heavily on its mechanical tests of free exercise and establishment and to use these tests as substitutes, rather than as guides to legal analysis. The Court has tended to pit the disestablishment and free exercise clauses against each other, rather than treating them as twin guarantees of religious rights and liberties. The Court has been too eager to reduce the religion clauses to one or two principles, thereby often ignoring the range of interlocking first principles of the American experiment. The accumulation of these interpretive shortcomings, particularly in the past two decades, has brought the American experiment to a state of acute crisis—both of law and of faith in the law.

The Court needs to develop a more integrated approach to First Amendment questions that incorporates the first principles of religious rights and liberties on which the American experiment was founded and integrates them into the resolution of specific cases. Such a framework is easy enough to draw up on the blackboard or in the pages of a treatise—and a number of important integrative methodologies and frameworks have been offered of late. In the context of the ongoing constitutional experiment in religious liberty—with the thickly entangled work of federal and state courts and legislatures—deliberate and provisional steps are essential to reaching any type of coherent new framework or methodology. There is ample wisdom in Justice O'Connor's caveat in *Kiryas Joel v. Grumet* (1994):

> It is always appealing to look for a single test, a Grand Unified Theory that would resolve all the cases that might arise under a particular [First Amendment] clause. . . . But the same constitutional principle may operate very differently in different contexts. . . . And setting forth a unitary test for a broad set of cases may do more harm than good. Any test that must deal with widely disparate situations risks being so vague as to be useless. . . . I think a less unitary approach provides a better structure for analysis. If each test covers a narrower and more homogeneous area, the tests may be more precise and therefore easier to apply. . . . Perhaps eventually under this structure we may indeed distill a unified, or at least a more unified [approach].[2]

Whatever interim steps are taken, the Supreme Court—with the help of Congress, the states, and the academy—must strive for this "more unified approach." Such an approach might come in a variety of forms—in another grand synthetic case in the series of *Watson, Cantwell, Everson, Sherbert,* and *Lemon,* or through comprehensive restatements, congressional statutes, or even another constitutional amendment on religious rights and liberties.

Any integrative approach to the First Amendment must certainly embrace "the long-standing traditions of *our people*," as Justice Scalia urged in response to Justice O'Connor in *Kiryas Joel.*[3] Such traditions are, to my mind, best captured in the roll of "essential rights and liberties" first incorporated into the First Amendment. The task of this volume has been, in part, to lay out some of the rich resources of this American tradition, both in its genesis and its exodus, which can be profitably drawn into a more integrated understanding of religious liberty today.

An integrative approach to the First Amendment must also consider the emerging traditions of *other people.* The way of integration is not only the way of the past, the original intent of the eighteenth-century founders of the American experiment. It is also the way of the future, the intent of the emerging world system of law and human rights, in which American law has played and must continue to play a vital part.

Resort to international legal and human rights norms of religious liberty might seem a rather unpromising path to developing a more integrated American constitutional law of religious liberty. Not only are Americans better at exporting their constitutional ideas and institutions than importing those of other peoples. But the budding international norms on religious rights and liberties seem, by conventional wisdom, to have rather little that is worth importing. The canon of applicable international human rights norms has developed only slowly and sporadically since World War II. Even as more fully developed in the 1980s and 1990s, these international norms are often seen to affect America's foreign diplomatic relations, not its domestic constitutional law. Very few international cases are at hand, and those that have been reported do not follow the conventional form and format of American constitutional law. International human rights norms would thus seem to be better left outside the ambit of First Amendment inquiry.

To keep this parochial veil drawn shut, however, is to deprive the American experiment of a rich source of instruction and inspiration. Comparative legal analysis is always edifying—if for no other reason than to have confirmation, from a fresh perspective, of the validity and utility of one's own legal norms and practices and to gain an idea or two about reforming them.[4] But especially at this time of transition, if not turmoil, in First Amendment law, comparative legal analysis is particularly necessary and salutary. Some members of the Court have drawn on international norms and customs in its adjudication of other highly contested claims of sexual liberty. The same methodology is warranted in the adjudication of cases of religious liberty.

Several principles and teachings of international human rights help to confirm, refine, and integrate prevailing First Amendment principles and cases. For example, the prioritizing of the principles of liberty of conscience, free exercise, and religious equality in international human rights instruments suggests a prototype for the integration of American free exercise and disestablishment values. The insistence of international human rights instruments that governmental abridgments of religious rights and liberties be both "necessary" and "proportionate" confirms the strict scrutiny test of American free exercise jurisprudence—demanding both a "compelling state interest" (necessity) and the "least restrictive alternative" of achieving that interest (proportionality). The heavy emphasis on group religious rights in recent international instruments both confirms the American protection of corporate free exercise rights and one core understanding of the doctrine of separation of church and state. The international doctrine of granting "a margin of appreciation" for local religious and political practices could be put to particularly effective use in our federalist system of government.[5] The international debate over the "universalism versus relativism" of human rights has profound implications for the American debate concerning federal and state jurisdiction over religious rights.[6]

Moreover, a good deal of what appears in modern international human rights instruments captures the best of American, and other Western, constitutional learning on religious liberty. Both the Universal Declaration of 1948 and the great Covenants of 1966 encapsulate and elaborate President Roosevelt's famous "four freedoms"—including religious freedom.[7] More recent international provisions on religious rights were forged, in no small measure, by the efforts of American politicians, jurists, and theologians. To compare First Amendment law with international norms is, in a real sense, to judge American law by an international standard that it has helped to shape.[8] It is also to judge America by the same international standard that the U.S. State Department and Office and Commission of International Religious Freedom now use each year to judge the laws and policies on religion of all 195 nations on earth. [9]

Religious Rights and Liberties in International Context

Three international instruments contain the most critical protections of religious rights and liberties: (1) the International Covenant on Civil and Political Rights (1966) (the 1966 Covenant);[10] (2) the United Nations Declaration on the Elimination of All Forms of Intolerance and of Discrimination Based on Religion or Belief (1981) (the 1981 Declaration);[11] and (3) the Concluding Document of the Vienna Follow-up Meeting of Representatives of the Participating States of the Conference on Security and Co-operation in Europe, which was promulgated in 1989 (the 1989 Vienna Concluding Document).[12] Viewed collectively, these three documents confirm most of the "essential rights and liberties" of religion embodied in the American experiment but prioritize them quite differently.

1966 Covenant

The 1966 International Covenant on Civil and Political Rights largely repeats the capacious guarantee of religious rights and liberties first announced in the 1948 Universal Declaration of Human Rights. Article 18 reads:

> 1. Everyone shall have the right to freedom of thought, conscience and religion. This right shall include freedom to have or to adopt a religion or belief of his choice, and freedom, either individually or in community with others and

in public or private, to manifest his religion or belief in worship, observance, practice and teaching.

2. No one shall be subject to coercion which would impair his freedom to have or to adopt a religion or belief of his choice.

3. Freedom to manifest one's religion or beliefs may be subject only to such limitations as are prescribed by law and are necessary to protect public safety, order, health, or morals or the fundamental rights and freedoms of others.

4. The States Parties to the present Covenant undertake to have respect for the liberty of parents and, when applicable, legal guardians to ensure the religious and moral education of their children in conformity with their own convictions.

Article 18 distinguishes between the right to freedom of religion and the freedom to manifest one's religion—what at American law are called liberty of conscience and free exercise of religion, respectively. The right to freedom of religion—the freedom to have, to alter, or to adopt a religion of one's choice—is an absolute right from which no derogation may be made and which may not be restricted or impaired in any manner. Freedom to manifest or exercise one's religion—individually or collectively, publicly or privately—may be subject only to such limitations as are prescribed by law and are necessary to protect public safety, order, health, or morals or the fundamental rights and freedoms of others. The latter provision is an exhaustive list of the grounds allowed to limit the manifestation of religion. Legislatures may not limit the manifestation of religion on any other grounds.

The requirement of necessity implies that any such limitation on the manifestation of religion must be proportionate to its aim to protect any of the listed state interests. Such limitations must not be applied in a manner that would vitiate the rights guaranteed in Article 18. In American law terms, Article 18 upholds the requirement that to pass constitutional muster, a law burdening the exercise of religion must be in service of a compelling state interest and use the least restrictive alternative to achieve that interest.

Articles 2 and 26 of the 1966 Covenant require equal treatment of all persons before the law and prohibit discrimination based, among other grounds, on religion. According to international case law, unequal treatment of equal cases is allowed only if that treatment serves an objective and reasonable purpose and the inequality is proportionate to that purpose.

The Human Rights Committee, established under the 1966 Covenant, has made it explicit in its General Comment No. 22 (48) concerning Article 18 that:

The terms belief and religion are to be broadly construed. Article 18 is not limited in its application to traditional religions or to religions and beliefs with institutional characteristics or practices analogous to those of traditional religions. The Committee therefore views with concern any tendency to discriminate against any religion or belief for any reasons, including the fact that they are newly established, or represent religious minorities that may be the subject of hostility by a predominant religious community.

In this same General Comment, the Human Rights Committee has further clarified that the freedom to manifest one's religion

includes acts integral to the conduct by religious groups of their basic affairs, such as, *inter alia*, the freedom to choose their religious leaders, priests and teachers, the freedom to establish seminaries or religious schools and the freedom to prepare and distribute religious texts or publications.[13]

1981 Declaration

The 1981 Declaration elaborated what the 1966 Covenant adumbrated. The Declaration includes (1) prescriptions of religious rights for individuals and groups; (2) proscriptions on religious discrimination, intolerance, or abuse; (3) provisions specific to the religious rights of parents and children; and (4) explicit principles of implementation. Like the 1966 Covenant, the 1981 Declaration on its face applies to "everyone," whether "individually or in community," "in public or in private."

Articles 1 and 6 of the 1981 Declaration set forth a lengthy illustrative catalogue of rights to "freedom of thought, conscience, and religion"—illustrating more concretely the ambit of what American law calls "liberty of conscience" and "free exercise of religion." Such rights include the right (1) to worship or assemble in connection with a religion or belief and to establish and maintain places for these purposes; (2) to establish and maintain appropriate charitable or humanitarian institutions; (3) to make, to acquire, and to use to an adequate extent the necessary articles and materials related to the rites or customs of a religion or belief; (4) to write, to publish, and to disseminate relevant publications in these areas; (5) to teach a religion or belief in places suitable for these purposes; (6) to solicit and receive voluntary financial and other contributions from individuals and institutions; (7) to train, to appoint, to elect, or to designate by succession appropriate leaders called for by the requirements and standards of any religion or belief; (8) to observe days of rest and to celebrate holy days and ceremonies in accordance with the precepts of one's religion or belief;

and (9) to establish and maintain communications with individuals and communities in matters of religion and belief at the national and international levels.

Like the 1966 Covenant, the 1981 Declaration allows the "manifestation of religion" to be subjected to "appropriate" state regulation and adjudication. The 1981 Declaration permits states to enforce against religious individuals and institutions general regulations designed to protect public safety, order, health, or morals, or the fundamental rights and freedoms of others. It is assumed, however, that in all such instances, the grounds for such regulation are enumerated and explicit and that such regulations abide by the international legal principles of proportionality and necessity.

The 1981 Declaration includes more elaborate provisions concerning the religious rights of children and their parents. It guarantees the rights of parents (or guardians) to organize life within the household and to educate their children in accordance with their religion or beliefs. Such parental responsibility, however, must be discharged in accordance with the "best interests of the child." At minimum, the parents' religious upbringing or education "must not be injurious to his physical or mental health or to his full development." Although the drafters debated at length the potential conflicts between the parents' right to rear and educate their children in accordance with their religion and the state's power to protect the best interests of the child, they offered no specific principles to resolve these disputes.

The 1981 Declaration includes suggested principles of implementation and application of these guarantees. It urges states to take all "effective measures to prevent and eliminate discrimination on the grounds of religion or belief in the recognition, exercise and enjoyment of human rights and fundamental freedoms in all fields of civil, economic, political, social and cultural life." It urges states to remove local laws that perpetuate or allow religious discrimination and to enact local criminal and civil laws to combat religious discrimination and intolerance.

The 1981 Declaration, though not a binding legal instrument, provides a principled reference for monitoring a nation's compliance with international standards of religious liberty. It sets a baseline for guiding diplomatic relations and treaties among nation-states. It provides a common ground for nongovernmental and intergovernmental organizations to report and register complaints of religious rights violations. It also provides the United Nations Special Rapporteur, appointed by the United Nations Commission on Human Rights, to provide a general survey and specific on-site evaluations of member states of the United Nations. The United States was among the states under evaluation in 1998.[14]

1989 Vienna Concluding Document

The 1989 Vienna Concluding Document extends these norms and their implementation, particularly for religious groups. Principles 16 and 17 provide a clear distillation of principles that is worth quoting in full:

16. In order to ensure the freedom of the individual to profess and practice religion or belief the participating States will, *inter alia,*

A. take effective measures to prevent and eliminate discrimination against individuals or communities, on the grounds of religion or belief in the recognition, exercise and enjoyment of human rights and fundamental freedoms in all fields of civil, political, economic, social and cultural life, and ensure the effective equality between believers and non-believers;

B. foster a climate of mutual tolerance and respect between believers of different communities as well as between believers and non-believers;

C. grant upon their request to communities of believers, practicing or prepared to practice their faith within the constitutional framework of their states, recognition of the status provided for them in their respective countries;

D. respect the right of religious communities to establish and maintain freely accessible places of worship or assembly; organize themselves according to their own hierarchical and institutional structure; select, appoint and replace their personnel in accordance with their respective requirements and standards as well as with any freely accepted arrangement between them and their State; solicit and receive voluntary financial and other contributions;

E. engage in consultations with religious faiths, institutions and organizations in order to achieve a better understanding of the requirements of religious freedom;

F. respect the right of everyone to give and receive religious education in the language of his choice, individually or in association with others;

G. in this context respect, *inter alia,* the liberty of parents to ensure the religious and moral education of their children in conformity with their own convictions;

H. allow the training of religious personnel in appropriate institutions;

I. respect the right of individual believers and communities of believers to acquire, possess, and use sacred books, religious publications in the language of their choice and other articles and materials related to the practice of religion or belief;

J. allow religious faiths, institutions and organizations to produce and import and disseminate religious publications and materials;

K. favorably consider the interest of religious communities in participating in public dialogue, *inter alia*, through mass media.

17. The participating States recognize that the exercise of the above mentioned rights relating to the freedom of religion or belief may be subject only to such limitations as are provided by law and are consistent with their obligations under international law and with their international commitments. They will ensure in their laws and regulations and in their application the full and effective implementation of the freedom of thought, conscience, religion or belief.

These are the basic international provisions on religious rights on the books. Regional instruments—notably the European Charter on Human Rights (1950), the American Convention on Human Rights (1969), and the African Charter on Human and People's Rights (1981)—elaborate some of these guarantees.[15] International treaties involving religious bodies—notably the recent Concordats between the Vatican and Italy, Spain, and Israel as well as the Universal Islamic Declaration of Human Rights (1981) and the Cairo Declaration on Human Rights in Islam (1990)—give particular accent to the religious concerns and constructions of their co-signers.[16] But the foregoing three instruments capture the common lore of current international human rights norms on religious rights and liberties.

International Norms and American Laws Compared

The United States has signed the 1966 Covenant. None of the fourteen reservations, understandings, or declarations that the United States put to the instrument seeks to avoid or evade the standards of strict scrutiny and nondiscrimination on religious grounds set out in Articles 18 and 26 of the document. The 1966 Covenant, however, is not self-executing. It "does not, by itself, create private rights enforceable in U.S. courts."[17] It requires implementing legislation to become effective, and no such legislation to date has been forthcoming.[18] Nonetheless, the 1966 Covenant holds out a high standard of religious liberty, which the United States has pledged to support.[19]

The 1981 Declaration and 1989 Vienna Concluding Document are not binding legal instruments—on the United States or any other nation-state. Nonetheless, as collective expressions of international opinion on the meaning and measure of religious rights and liberties, these two instruments also carry ample moral, intellectual, and diplomatic suasion.

The international human rights norms reflected in these three main instruments both confirm and prioritize several of the "essential rights and liberties of religion" that have long been part of the American experiment. The principles of liberty of conscience, individual and corporate free exercise of religion, and equality of religions before the law form the backbone of the international norms on religious rights and liberties. Liberty of conscience rights, with their inherent protections of voluntarism and prohibitions against coercion, are absolute rights from which no derogation can be made. The exercise of religion can be regulated only to protect either other fundamental rights or public health, safety, and welfare and only when the religious intrusion is "proportionate" to achieving that narrowly stated need. Equality of religions before the law is not only to be protected but to be affirmatively fostered by the state. To achieve the mandated goals of equality and nondiscrimination on grounds of religion, exemptions from generally applicable laws and policies are sometimes necessary, as are affirmative state actions to protect religion or to undo past religious repression.

International human rights norms assume a vast pluralism of confessions and faiths. Multiple forms of religious belief and expression are deserving of special religious rights protection—whether ancient or new, individual or communal, internal or external, private or public, permanent or transient. The special religious functions of parents, teachers, and religious officials are given particular attention and protection in international human rights instruments. The rights of religious minorities and nontraditional religions are given special weight, and states are obligated to be particularly solicitous of their peculiar needs.

The Vienna Concluding Document particularly protects the principle of structural pluralism. It also protects the basic autonomy of various religious organizations, which is assumed in the American principles of corporate free exercise and of separation of the institutions of church and state. Religious associations have rights to function in expression of their founding religious beliefs and values, which the state cannot compromise except on stated grounds that are necessary and proportional. Churches, synagogues, temples, mosques, tribes, and other religious groups thus have rights to organize, assemble, worship, and enforce certain religious laws against their voluntary members (at least up to the limits of endangering the safety of their members in violation of criminal laws). Parents and families have rights to rear, educate, and discipline children in expression of their religious convictions (again with some limitation against endangering the safety of children). Religious publishers and suppliers have rights to produce the particular products needed for their religious cultus. Religious schools have rights to educate and discipline children in accordance with the basic norms and habits of their religious traditions.

Conspicuously absent from international human rights instruments are the more radical demands for separationism, rooted in certain strains of Enlightenment reasoning and reified in the popular American metaphor of a "wall of separation between church and state." *Everson, McCollum, Engel,* and other early disestablishment cases assumed that religious liberty requires the separation of church and state and the cessation of state support for religion. Only the secular state can guarantee religious liberty, it was argued, and only separation can guarantee its neutrality on religious matters.

Such strict separationist logic is not reflected in international human rights instruments nor, indeed, widely shared by nation-states around the world. International norms and many domestic laws regard the material and moral cooperation of religion and state as conducive, and sometimes essential, to the achievement of both religious liberty and national identity. Indeed, today a number of religious groups in the former Soviet bloc and in sub-Saharan Africa regard restitution and affirmative state action toward religion as a necessary feature of any religious rights regime—if nothing else, to undo and overcome past confiscation and repression of religion by the state. Similarly, some Catholic groups in Italy, Iberia, and Latin America urge cooperation of religious and political bodies to preserve the "Catholicization" of public life and culture. Islamic revivalists in various countries urge similar arrangements to enhance the "Islamicization" of the community. Jewish groups argue similarly to protect the Jewish character of the state of Israel. Absolute separationists in this country have fewer allies abroad than is conventionally assumed.

If hypothetically applied in the United States, the international provisions on liberty of conscience would confirm the "strict scrutiny" test for free exercise claims, elaborated in *Sherbert, Yoder,* and the Religious Freedom Restoration Act. It would confirm the "noncoercion" reading of the disestablishment clause reflected in *Lee v. Weisman* and *Santa Fe Independent School District v. Doe.* It would confirm the multiple forms of religious accommodation for individual believers upheld under both religion clauses of the First Amendment and in various statutes.

Conversely, the international principle that liberty of conscience is a nonderogable right runs directly counter to the wooden reading of the free exercise clause introduced in the late nineteenth-century Mormon polygamy cases—*Reynolds* and *Davis*—and resurrected in the later 1980s and 1990s in *Roy, Lyng, Smith,* and their many lower court progeny.

The international norms on equality would applaud the "equal access" and "equal treatment" cases from *Paty* to *Zelman* as necessary protections of equality. It would confirm the various statutes, regulations, and cases that foster religious equality in the workplace, in the school, and in public facilities. It would likewise uphold the application of general taxing, licensing, parading, reporting, and other statutes and regulations to religious groups, finding no ready violation of free exercise rights if such regulations are equally and indiscriminately applied to all like groups.

Conversely, international norms would have little patience with the patently discriminatory treatment of certain religious minorities in America. The United States Supreme Court's failure to accommodate the distinctive theology of polygamous marriage among Mormons, the special sabbatarian needs of Jews, the religious worship patterns of Muslims, and the nontraditional sites and rites of Native Americans would run directly counter to the cardinal principle of equality and nondiscrimination mandated by a number of international human rights instruments. International human rights norms demand not only general toleration of religious minorities but special solicitude for their religious needs that often are not accommodated in majoritarian laws and policies. The Supreme Court's rather cavalier interpretations of both the free exercise and disestablishment clauses under the rubric of neutrality will not do. The kinds of special accommodations and exemptions afforded to Adventist sabbatarianism in *Sherbert* and to Amish communitarianism in *Yoder* come much closer to the solicitude mandated by international human rights norms.

The international principle of structural pluralism would endorse the lines of cases protecting the forms and functions of religious bodies, whether worship centers, religious schools, or religious charities, among others. Cases upholding general regulation of these bodies in furtherance of health, safety, and welfare, and in exercise of taxing and police power would likewise pass muster. Similarly cases upholding general and generically available governmental support for religion—in the form of tax exemptions or equal access to public facilities or state benefits—would find ample support under international human rights norms.

The principle of structural pluralism, especially as elaborated in the Vienna Concluding Document, would look askance, however, at a case like *Jones v. Wolf,* which permitted government resolution of intrachurch disputes involving "neutral principles" of law. The "deference test" of *Watson, Kedroff,* and *Milivojevich* would find greater favor under international human rights instruments, as would the *Catholic Bishop* and *Amos* holdings that religious employers be allowed to discriminate in favor of their coreligionists in their employment decisions.

This same principle of structural pluralism might also look askance at a case like *Bob Jones University v. United States,* which withheld tax exempt status from a religious university that engaged in racial discrimination on the basis of religious convictions. The holding of the *Bob Jones* case is intuitively attractive, given the tragic history of slavery and discrimination against African Americans—just as holdings in modern Germany outlawing any private discrimination against Jews are intuitively attractive, given that county's tragic history of anti-Semitism. But international norms of religious rights protect even unpopular and prejudicial policies of a religious body that are firmly grounded and sincerely held—so long as such policies do not threaten or violate the life or limb of its members or impair any party's liberty of exit from the religious body.[20]

The absence of a principle of "disestablishment" in international human rights norms would not call into question the entire line of disestablishment clause cases. Many of these cases, as we have seen, serve to protect the principles of liberty of conscience, equality, and pluralism in a manner consistent with prevailing international norms. But when there is a clash between such principles and the principle of religious establishment, international norms would give preference to the former—as do American cases upholding the principle of accommodation.

According to international human rights norms, the realm of education—where parental religious rights and preferences receive especially strong protection—is not the ideal place for undue zealotry in application of disestablishment values. To be sure, international norms would not countenance any more than American law coerced religious exercises in school classrooms—such as mandatory participation in prayers, pledges, confessions of faith, Bible reading, and the like—however strong the countervailing parental preferences. But the constitutional purging of tax-supported public schools of virtually all religious symbols, texts, and traditions—in favor of purportedly neutral and secular tropes—stands in considerable tension with international principles of religious equality and of parental religious rights.

Finally, the absence of a universal definition, or common method of defining, religion in American law would meet with harsh criticism under international norms. The current system of leaving such definitions to individual states and statutes, courts and agencies has introduced a bewildering array of legal definitions of "religion." Some courts and legislatures make a simple "common sense" inquiry as to the existence of religion. Others defer to the good faith self-declarations of religion by the claimant. Others seek to find sufficient analogies between existing religions and new religious claimants. Others insist on evidence of a god or something transcendent that stands in the same position as a god. Others analyze the motives for formation of the religious organization or adoption of a religious belief, the presence and sophistication of a set of doctrines explicating the beliefs, the practice and celebration of religious rites and liturgies, the degree of formal training required for the religious leaders, the strictures on the ability of members to practice other religions, the presence and internal enforcement of a set of ethical rules of conduct, and other factors.[21] All this results in considerable inequality and potentially discriminatory treatment of religious claims and claimants.

It may not be apt to adopt the capacious definition of religion set out in international human rights instruments—particularly given that under the First Amendment, one definition of religion must be usefully applied to both religion clauses. But the term "religion" must be assigned some consistent boundaries to be useful, at least for a constitutional rights regime. No universal definition can easily embrace every religious dimension of modern culture. No bright line tests can readily resolve all penumbral cases. Fairness commands as broad a legal definition of religion as possible, so that no legitimate religious claim is excluded. Prudence commends a narrower definition, so that not every claim becomes religious (and thus no claim becomes deserving of special religious rights protection). To define "religion" too closely is to place too much trust in the capacity of the lexicon or the legislature. To leave the term undefined is to place too much faith in the self-declarations of the claimant or the discernment of local judges and administrators.

In my view, the functional and institutional dimensions of religion deserve the strongest emphasis in defining the constitutional realm of religious rights and liberties in America. Of course, religion viewed in its broadest terms embraces all beliefs and actions that concern the ultimate origin, meaning, and purpose of life, of existence. It involves the responses of the human heart, soul, mind, conscience, intuition, and reason to revelation, to transcendent values, to what Rudolf Otto once called the "idea of the holy."[22] But such a definition applied at modern constitutional law would render everything (and thus nothing) deserving of constitutional protection.

Viewed in a narrower institutional sense, religion embraces a creed, a cult, a code of conduct, and a confessional community.[23] A creed defines the accepted cadre of beliefs and values concerning the ultimate origin, meaning, and purpose of life. A cult defines the appropriate rituals, liturgies, and patterns of worship and devotion that give expression to those beliefs. A code of conduct defines the appropriate individual and social habits of those who profess the creed and practice the cult. A confessional community defines the group of individuals who embrace and live out this creed, cult, and code of conduct, both on their own and with fellow believers. By this definition, a religion can be traditional or very new, closely confining or loosely structured, world-avertive or world-affirmative, nontheistic, polytheistic, or monotheistic. Religious claims and claimants that meet this definition, in my view, deserve the closest consideration.

Notes

1. Oliver Wendell Holmes Jr., *The Common Law* (1881), 1.

2. *Kiryas Joel Village School District v. Grumet*, 114 S.Ct. 2481, 2498–2499 (O'Connor, J., concurring). See also *Rosenberger v. University of Virginia*, 115 S.Ct. 2510, 2525–2526 (O'Connor, J., concurring).

3. *Kiryas Joel*, 114 S.Ct. at 4683 (Scalia, J., dissenting) (emphasis added).

4. See, e.g., "International Law and Religion Symposium," *Brigham Young Law Review* (2001):413, (2002):205; van der Vyver and Witte, eds., *Religious Human Rights: Legal Perspectives.*

5. Clovis C. Morrisson Jr., "Margin of Appreciation in European Human Rights Law," *Revue des droits de l'homme* 6 (1973):263–286.

6. John D. Kelsay and Sumner B. Twiss, eds., *Religion and Human Rights* (1998 [1994]).

7. See "Roosevelt's Eighth Annual Message to Congress (January 6, 1941)," in *State of the Union Messages of the Presidents, 1790–1966*, ed. F. Israel (1966), 3:1; Louis B. Sohn, *The Human Rights Movement: From Roosevelt's Four Freedoms to the Interdependence of Peace, Development, and Human Rights* (1982).

8. Louis Henkin, "Rights, American and Human," *Columbia Law Review* 79 (1979):405.

9. International Religious Freedom Act of 1998, 112 Stat. 2787, 22 U.S.C.A. 6401. The act affirms the importance of religious freedom, as reflected in American history and law, and in various international human rights instruments. The act further decries the fresh rise of religious repression and persecution around the world and applies religious freedom standards in its assessment of diplomatic relations with foreign nations. An Office of International Religious Freedom, with an ambassador-at-large for International Religious Freedom, publishes annual reports on the state of religious freedom on each of the 195 countries of the world, as well as in-depth studies of selected countries. The office also makes recommendations to Congress and the executive branch on responses, including the imposition of economic sanctions, on countries that fall short of international standards.

10. International Covenant on Civil and Political Rights, G.A. Res. 2200A, U.N. GAOR, 21st Sess., Supp. No. 16, U.N. Doc. A/6316 (1968), 999 U.N.T.S. 171 (1976) (hereafter cited as ICCPR), reprinted in *Religion and Human Rights: Basic Documents*, ed. Tad Stahnke and J. Paul Martin (1998), 69–82.

11. Declaration on the Elimination of All Forms of Intolerance and of Discrimination Based on Religion or Belief, adopted November 25, 1981, G.A. Res. 55, 36 U.N. GAOR Supp. (No. 51), U.N. Doc. A/RES/36/55 (1982) (hereafter cited as 1981 Declaration), reprinted in Stahnke and Martin, eds., *Religion and Human Rights*, 102–104.

12. Concluding Document of the Vienna Meeting 1986 of Representatives of the Participating States of the Conference on Security and Co-operation in Europe, Held on the Basis of the Provisions of the Final Act Relating to the Follow-Up to the Conference, January 17, 1989, 28 I.L.M. 527 (hereafter cited as Vienna Concluding Document), reprinted in Natan Lerner, *Religion, Beliefs, and International Human Rights* (2000), 139.

13. U.N. Doc. CCPR/C/21/Rev.1/Add.4 (1993), reprinted in Stahnke and Martin, eds., *Religion and Human Rights*, 92–95.

14. See "Report Submitted by Mr. Abdelfattah Amor . . . Addendum: Visit to the United States," E/CN.4/1999/58/Add.1. While Professor Amor's Report is generally very commendatory of American protections of religious freedom for multiple faiths, it includes some useful criticisms and recommendations. At ibid., nos. 70–88, the Special Rapporteur criticizes the reductionism of the "new" free exercise jurisprudence of *Smith* and its progeny; the "absence of a consistent and detailed framework within which the two constitutional clauses on 'non-establishment' and free exercise of religion could be interpreted and applied" (ibid., no. 72); the unduly fragmentary protections of religious freedom in the workplace; and the need for better protection of the religious rights of children, prisoners, and religious minorities (most notably Native Americans). See also Abdelfattah Amor, "The Mandate of the UN Special Rapporteur," *Emory International Law Review* 12 (1998):945–950.

15. In Lerner, *Religion, Beliefs*, 140–149.

16. In ibid. and Stahnke and Martin, eds., *Religion and Human Rights*, 185–189, 221–244.

17. David P. Stewart, "United States Ratification of the Covenant on Civil and Political Rights: The Significance of the Reservations, Understandings, and Declarations," *DePaul Law Review* 42 (1993):1183, 1202ff.

18. Louis Henkin, "U.S. Ratification of Human Rights Conventions: The Ghost of Senator Bricker," *American Journal of International Law* 89 (1995):341; Natalie H. Kaufman and David Whiteman, "Opposition to Human Rights Treaties in the United States Senate: The Legacy of the Bricker Amendment," *Human Rights Quarterly* 10 (1988):309–337.

19. Gerald Neumann, "The Global Dimension of RFRA," *Constitutional Commentary* 14 (1997):33.

20. See Natan Lerner, *Group Rights and Discrimination in International Law*, 2d. ed. (2002).

21. See sources and analysis in the first edition of this volume, pp. 203–208. For more recent studies see T. Jeremy Gunn, "The Complexity of Religion and the Definition of 'Religion' in International Law," *Harvard Human Rights Journal* 16 (2003):189; Lerner, *Religion, Beliefs*.

22. Rudolf Otto, *The Idea of the Holy: An Inquiry into the Non-Rational Factor of the Idea of the Divine and Its Relation to the Rational*, 2d ed. (1950).

23. See Leonard Swidler, ed., *Religious Liberty and Human Rights in Nations and Religions* (1986), vii.

CONCLUDING REFLECTIONS

Writing in the context of the United States Constitutional Convention of 1787, John Adams, the great Massachusetts jurist and future American president, offered a robust appraisal of the new American experiment:

> The people in America have now the best opportunity and the greatest trust in their hands, that Providence ever committed to so small a number, since the transgression of the first pair [Adam and Eve]; if they betray their trust, their guilt will merit even greater punishment than other nations have suffered, and in the indignation of Heaven. . . . The United States have exhibited, perhaps, the first example of governments erected on the simple principles of nature; and if men are now sufficiently enlightened to disabuse themselves of artifice, imposture, hypocrisy, and superstition, they will consider this event as a [new] era in history. Although the detail of the formation of the American governments is at present little known or regarded either in Europe or in America, it may hereafter become an object of curiosity [for it is] destined to spread over the northern part of . . . the globe. The institutions now made in America will not wholly die out for thousands of years. It is of the last importance, then, that they should begin right. If they set out wrong, they will never be able to return, unless it be by accident to the right path.[1]

More than two centuries later, Adams's sentiments prove remarkably prescient. The eighteenth-century American founders did, indeed, begin on the right path of liberty. And today, we enjoy ample freedom of religion as a consequence. American models of religious liberty have had a profound influence around the globe, and they now figure prominently in a number of national constitutions and international human rights instruments.

To be sure, as Adams predicated, there has always been "a glorious uncertainty in the law" of religious liberty and a noble diversity of understandings of its details.[2] This was as true in Adams's day as in our own. In Adams's day, there were competing models of religious liberty more overtly theological than his—whether Puritan, Evangelical, or Anglican in inspiration. There were also competing models more overtly philosophical than his—whether Classical, Republican, or Enlightenmentarian in inclination. Today, these and other founding models of religious liberty have born am-

ple progeny, and the great rivalries among them are fought out in the
courts, legislatures, and academies throughout the land.

Prone as he was to a dialectical model of religious liberty, Adams would
likely approve of our rigorous rivalries of principle—so long as all rivals remain committed to constitutional ideals of democracy, liberty, and rule of
law. But Adams would also likely insist that we reconsider his most cardinal insights about the necessary dialectical nature of religious freedom and
religious establishment. Too little religious freedom, Adams had insisted, is
a recipe for hypocrisy and impiety. But too much religious freedom is an invitation to depravity and license. Too firm a religious establishment breeds
coercion and corruption. But too little religious establishment allows secular prejudices to become constitutional prerogatives. Somewhere between
these extremes, Adams believed, a society must find its balance.

The balance that Adams and other founders often struck between the
freedom of all private religions and the establishment of one public Christian religion can no longer serve in our day. But the balance that the
Supreme Court has often struck between the freedom of all private religions and the establishment of one public secular religion also can no
longer serve. Somewhere between these extremes, our society must now
find a new constitutional balance.

One key to restriking this constitutional balance today lies in the eighteenth-century founders' most elementary and most essential insight—that
religion is special and is accorded special protection in the Constitution.
"[W]e cannot repudiate that decision," Douglas Laycock has written,
"without rejecting an essential feature of constitutionalism, rendering all
constitutional rights vulnerable to repudiation if they go out of favor."[3]
The founders' vision was that religion is more than simply a peculiar form
of speech and assembly, privacy and autonomy. Religion is a unique source
of individual and personal identity, involving "duties that we owe to our
Creator, and the manner of discharging them," as Madison put it.[4] Religion
is also a unique form of public and social identity, involving a vast plurality
of sanctuaries, schools, charities, missions, and other forms and forums of
faith. Individual and corporate, private and public entities and exercises of
religion—in all their self-defined varieties—properly deserve the protection
of the First Amendment.

A second key to restriking this constitutional balance today lies in the
founders' insight that to be enduring and effective, the constitutional
process must seek to involve all voices and values in the community—religious, areligious, and antireligious alike. Constitutionalism ultimately demands ecumenism to be effective and enduring. Thus in creating the state
and federal constitutions, the founders stretched the roll of delegates and
ratifiers to the furthest edges of conscience and credulity. Believers and
skeptics, churchmen and statesmen, Protestants and Catholics, Republicans

and *Philosophes,* Quakers and Jews—many of whom in decades and centuries past had slandered and slaughtered each other with a vengeance—now came together in a rare moment of solidarity. The founders understood that to create a proper law of religious liberty required that all religions have liberty to participate both in its creation and its unfolding.

A third key to restriking this constitutional balance today lies in repristinating anew the six basic principles of religious liberty that the founders set forth. The founders designed the First Amendment free exercise and disestablishment clauses as twin guarantees of religious liberty for all. The free exercise clause outlawed government *proscriptions* of religion—actions that unduly burdened the conscience, restricted religious expression and activity, discriminated against religion, or invaded the autonomy of churches and other religious bodies. The disestablishment clause outlawed government *prescriptions* of religion—actions that unduly coerced the conscience, mandated forms of religious expression and activity, discriminated in favor of religion, or improperly allied the state with churches or other religious bodies. Both the free exercise and the disestablishment clauses thereby provided complementary protections to the other constitutive principles of the American experiment—liberty of conscience, freedom of religious expression, equality of plural faiths before the law, and separation of church and state.

These three key insights of the American experiment were not only part of the original vision of the eighteenth-century founders. They were also part of the original vision of the Supreme Court justices when they founded the modern national law of religious liberty. All three of these insights recur in *Cantwell v. Connecticut* (1940) and *Everson v. Board of Education* (1947), the two cases that first applied the First Amendment religion clauses to the states and inaugurated the modern era of religious liberty in America.

Cantwell and *Everson* declared anew that religion had a special place in the Constitution and deserved special protection in the nation. In a remarkable countertextual reading, the Court took it upon itself to enforce the First Amendment religion clauses against all levels and branches of government in the nation—whether federal, state, or local, whether executive, legislative, or regulatory. "*Congress* shall make no law" now became, in effect, "*Government* shall make no law respecting an establishment of religion or prohibiting the free exercise thereof."

Cantwell and *Everson* declared anew that all religious voices were welcome in the modern constitutional process concerning religious liberty. These two cases themselves welcomed hitherto marginal voices: *Cantwell* welcomed a devout Jehovah's Witness who sought protections for his unpopular mission work. *Everson* welcomed a skeptical citizen who sought protection from paying taxes in support of religious schoolchildren. Subsequent cases have drawn into the constitutional dialogue a whole host of rival religious and antireligious groups—Catholics, Protestants, and Orthodox, Jews, Muslims, and Native Americans, Mormons, Quakers, and Krishnas, alongside a variety of skeptics, cynics, and secular iconoclasts.

Cantwell and *Everson* declared anew the efficacy of the six founding principles of the American experiment. The free exercise clause, the *Cantwell* Court declared, protects "freedom of conscience and freedom to adhere to such religious organization or form of worship as the individual may choose." It "safeguards the free exercise of the chosen form of religion," the "freedom to act" on one's beliefs. It protects a "plurality of forms and expressions" of faith, each of which deserves equal protection under the law. "The essential characteristic of these liberties is, that under their shield many types of life, character, opinion and belief can develop unmolested and unobstructed."[5] The disestablishment clause, the *Everson* Court echoed, means that no government "can set up a church"; "can force or influence a person to go or to remain away from church against his will or force him to profess a belief or disbelief in any religion"; can "punish [a person] for entertaining or professing religious beliefs or disbeliefs, for church attendance or non-attendance"; "can, openly or secretly, participate in the affairs of any religious organizations or groups, or vice versa." Government may not exclude "individual Catholics, Lutherans, Mohammedans, Baptists, Jews, Methodists, Nonbelievers, Presbyterians, or the members of any faith, because of their faith, or lack of it, from receiving the benefits of public welfare legislation" or participating in the American public arena.[6] Such was the original vision of the eighteenth-century founders and the original vision of the United States Supreme Court at the start of the modern era of religious liberty.

A good deal of this volume has been devoted to documenting the Supreme Court's repeated departures from these original insights in both its free exercise and disestablishment cases. Far from being special and specially protected, religion has often become a suspect category at modern constitutional law. The free exercise clause no longer accords religious individuals or groups special exemptions from general laws that burden core claims of conscience or central commandments of the faith. Such religious exemptions now come only from the legislature, and even then the Court has sometimes ignored them or struck them down. The disestablishment clause does not include religious individuals or religious groups among those naturally eligible for government benefits, forums, and programs. Such religious entitlements come only if they are sufficiently buffered by nonreligious entitlements and so long as they are not directed to "sectarian" ends.

Far from openly engaging and valuing all religious voices and values in modern constitutional dialogue, the Supreme Court has often been notorious in its harsh treatment of some religious groups. No Jew, no Muslim, and no Native American has ever won a free exercise case before the Supreme Court, despite numerous efforts. And when Christians have sought to inject their concerns for equal treatment into neutral legislation, the Supreme Court has often struck down these laws as "ingenious and self-serving schemes" that violate the disestablishment clause.

Far from judiciously balancing the multiple principles on which the American religious experiment was founded, the modern Supreme Court has often taken more reductionist approaches. In its early free exercise cases, the Court applied the principles of liberty of conscience, freedom of religious expression, religious pluralism and equality, and separation of church from state. Beginning in the mid-1980s, however, the Court has reduced the free exercise clause to the single principle of neutrality. In its early disestablishment cases, the single principle of separation of church and state dominated the Court's reasoning. Since the mid-1980s, individual justices have slowly imported into their analyses new principles of religious equality and liberty of conscience, but the most recent trend has likewise been toward a simple neutrality standard.

Such criticisms, and the ample volumes of others that can be found in the literature, have not been lost on the Supreme Court. In the past two decades, the Court seems to be charting something of a new constitutional course to offset some of these criticisms and to return to some of the original vision of the First Amendment. The Court has, in effect, taken up again the challenge of John Adams with which we started these concluding reflections: how to balance the freedom of all religions with the maintenance of a public religion that is neither a newly established secularism nor a traditionally established Christianity. The Court has not yet crafted a coherent new First Amendment logic, let alone a consistent new test, to address this question. But some of these recent cases hold signposts of a new way to protect religious freedom: Both private and public forms of religion deserve constitutional freedom and support, though neither may be established nor preferred.

Tradition has become one strong vector in the Court's recent First Amendment cases. The Court had used arguments from tradition a few times before, as part of broader rationales for upholding religious tax exemptions and Sabbath Day laws. In *Marsh v. Chambers* (1983), however, this argument from tradition became the exclusive basis for upholding a state legislature's practice of funding a chaplain and opening its sessions with his prayers. Writing for the Court, Chief Justice Burger defended such practices as a noble survival of the traditional public role of religion in American life and law:

In light of the unambiguous and unbroken history of more than 200 years, there can be no doubt that the practice of opening legislative sessions with prayer has become part of the fabric of our society. To invoke Divine guidance on a public body entrusted with making the laws is not, in these circumstances, an "establishment" of religion [but] simply a tolerable acknowledgement of beliefs widely held among the people of this country. . . . [W]e are a religious people whose institutions presuppose a Supreme Being.[7]

Arguments from tradition, though by themselves rarely convincing, can sometimes bolster a broader rationale for upholding traditional features of a public religion and a religious public. Tradition can sometimes serve effectively as something of a "null hypothesis"—to be overcome by strong constitutional arguments rather than discarded by simple invocations of principle. As Holmes once put it: "If a thing has been practised for two hundred years by common consent, it will need a strong case for the Fourteenth Amendment to affect it."[8] Innocuous long-standing practices, therefore, such as religious tax exemptions, military and prison chaplains, public displays of Decalogues, religious artwork and literature in state museums and libraries, and official coinage, oaths, proclamations, and pledges that invoke the name of God and other religious language might well be justified—particularly when private parties are not coerced into participating in or endorsing this language.[9]

There are limits and dangers to arguments from tradition, which the Court itself betrayed the following year. In *Lynch v. Donnelly* (1984) the Court upheld a municipality's traditional practice of maintaining a manger scene (a crèche) in a public park as part of a large holiday display in a downtown shopping area. "There is an unbroken history of official acknowledgment by all three branches of government of the role of religion in American life," Chief Justice Burger wrote, repeating his *Marsh* argument and now giving an ample list of illustrations.

There is another reason to uphold this display, however, Burger continued. Crèches, while of undoubted religious significance to Christians, are merely "passive" parts of "purely secular displays extant at Christmas." They "engender a friendly community spirit of good will" that "brings people into the central city and serves commercial interests and benefits merchants."[10] The prayers that are occasionally offered at the crèche, Justice O'Connor wrote in concurrence, merely "solemnize public occasions, express confidence in the future, and encourage the recognition of what is worthy of appreciation in society."[11] Governmental participation in and support of such "ceremonial deism," the Court concluded, cannot be assessed by "mechanical logic" or "absolutist tests" of establishment. "It is far too late in the day to impose a crabbed reading of the [Disestablishment] Clause on the country."[12]

A crabbed reading of establishment would have been better than such a crass rendering of religion. For the Court to suggest that crèches are mere advertisements, prayers mere ceremony, and piety mere nostalgia is to create an empty "American Shinto"—a public religion that is perhaps purged enough of its confessional identity to pass constitutional muster but too bleached and too bland to be religiously efficacious, let alone civilly effective.[13]

Arguments from tradition, while helpful, are thus inherently limited in their ability to define and defend the public place of religion today. Such arguments perforce assume a traditional definition of what a public religion is—namely, a common system of beliefs, values, and practices drawn eclectically from the multiple denominations within a community. In the religiously homogeneous environment of John Adams's day, a public religion of the common denominator and common denomination still had the doctrinal rigor, liturgical specificity, and moral suasion to be effective. In the religiously heterogeneous environment of our day—with more than 1,000 incorporated denominations on the books—no such effective common religion can be readily devised or defended.

More recent cases suggest a budding new way of defining and defending the legal place of public religion. The Court has numerous times upheld government policies that support the public access and activities of religious individuals and groups—so long as these religious parties act voluntarily, and so long as nonreligious parties also benefit from the same government support. Under this logic, Christian clergy were just as entitled to run for state political office as nonreligious candidates.[14] Church-affiliated pregnancy counseling centers could be funded as part of a broader federal family counseling program.[15] Religious student groups could have equal access to state university and public school classrooms that were open to nonreligious student groups.[16] Religious school students were just as entitled to avail themselves of general scholarships, remedial, and disability services as public school students.[17] Religious groups were given equal access to public facilities or civic education programs that were already opened to other civic groups.[18] Religious parties were just as entitled as nonreligious parties to display their symbols in public forums.[19] Religious student newspapers were just as entitled to public university funding as those of nonreligious student groups.[20] Religious schools were just as entitled as other private schools to participate in a state-sponsored educational improvement or school voucher or educational program.[21]

These holdings were defended on wide-ranging constitutional grounds—as a proper accommodation of religion under the disestablishment clause, as a necessary protection of religion under the free speech or free exercise clauses, as a simple application of the equal protection clause, among other arguments.

One theme common to many of these cases, however, is that public religion must be as free as private religion. Not because the religious groups in these cases are really nonreligious. Not because their public activities are really nonsectarian. And not because their public expressions are really part of the cultural mainstream. To the contrary, these public groups and activities deserve to be free, just because they are religious, just because they engage in sectarian practices, just because they sometimes take their stands above, beyond, and against the mainstream. They provide leaven and leverage for the polity to improve.[22]

A second theme common to these cases is that the freedom of public religion sometimes requires the support of the state. Today's state is not the distant, quiet sovereign of Jefferson's day from whom separation was both natural and easy. Today's modern welfare state, whether for good or ill, is an intensely active sovereign from whom complete separation is impossible. Few religious bodies can now avoid contact with the state's pervasive network of education, charity, welfare, child care, health care, family, construction, zoning, workplace, taxation, security, and other regulations. Both confrontation and cooperation with the modern welfare state are almost inevitable for any religion. When a state's regulation imposes too heavy a burden on a particular religion, the free exercise clause should provide a pathway to relief. When a state's appropriation imparts too generous a benefit to religion alone, the establishment clause should provide a pathway to dissent. But when a general government scheme provides public religious groups and activities with the same benefits afforded to all other eligible recipients, disestablishment clause objections are not only "crabbed" but corrosive.

A third theme common to these cases is that a public religion cannot be a common religion. If the religious gerrymandering of *Lynch v. Donnelly* and its progeny had not already made this clear, these more recent cases underscore the point. Today, our public religion must be a collection of particular religions, not the combination of religious particulars. It must be a process of open religious discourse, not a product of ecumenical distillation. All religious voices, visions, and values must be heard and deliberated in the public square. All public religious services and activities, unless criminal or tortious, must be given a chance to come forth and compete, in all their denominational particularity.

Some conservative Evangelical and Catholic groups today have seen and seized on this insight better than most. Their rise to prominence in the public square in recent years should not be met with glib talk of censorship or habitual incantation of Jefferson's mythical wall of separation. The rise of the so-called Christian right should be met with the equally strong rise of the Christian left, of the Christian middle, and of many other Jewish, Muslim, and other religious groups who test and contest its premises, prescriptions, and policies. That is how a healthy democracy works. The real challenge of the new Christian right is not to the integrity of American politics but to the apathy of American religions. It is a challenge for peoples of all faith and of no faith to take their place in the marketplace.

A fourth teaching of these cases is that freedom *of* public religion also requires freedom *from* public religion. Government must strike a balance between coercion and freedom. The state cannot coerce citizens to participate in religious ceremonies and subsidies that they find odious. But the state cannot prevent citizens from participation in public ceremonies, programs, and forums, just because they are religious. It is one thing to prevent government officials from delegating their core police powers to religious bodies, quite another thing to prevent them from facilitating the charitable services of voluntary religious and nonreligious associations alike. It is one thing to outlaw governmental prescriptions of prayers, ceremonies, and symbols in public forums, quite another thing to outlaw governmental accommodations of private prayers, ceremonies, and symbols in these same public forums.

Individuals should exercise a comparable prudence in seeking protection from public religion. In the public religion schemes of nineteenth-century America, it was not so much the courts as the frontier that provided this freedom—a place away from it all, where one could escape with one's conscience and coreligionists. Today, the frontier still provides this freedom—if not physically in small towns and wild mountains, then virtually in our ability to sift out and shut out the public voices of religion that we do not wish to hear.

Both modern technology and modern privacy make escape to the frontier considerably easier than in the days of covered wagons and mule trains. Just turn off the Christian television channel. Block religious e-mails and faxes. Turn away the missionary at your door. Close your eyes to the city crucifix that offends. Cover your ears to the public prayer that you can't abide. Forgo the military chaplain's pastoral counseling. Skip the legislative chaplain's prayers. Walk by the town hall's menorah and star. Don't read the Decalogue in the courthouse. Don't join the religious student group. Don't vote for the collared candidate. Don't visit the military chaplain. Don't browse the Evangelicals' newspapers. Avoid the services of the Catholic counselors. Shun the readings of the Scientologists. Turn down the trinkets of the colporteurs. Turn back the ministries of the hate mongers. All these escapes to the virtual frontier, the law does and will protect—with force if necessary. Such voluntary self-protections from religion will ultimately provide far greater religious freedom for all than pressing yet another tired constitutional case.

Notes

1. Adams, *Works*, 4:290, 292–293, 298. See also James Madison in *Federalist Paper, No. 37*, writing of the formation of the Constitution: "It is impossible for the man of pious reflection not to perceive in it a finger of the Almighty hand."

2. Adams, *Works*, 9:629–632, at 630.

3. Douglas Laycock, "Religious Liberty as Liberty," *Journal of Contemporary Legal Issues* 7 (1996):313–356, at 314. Michael E. Smith, "The Special Place of Religion in the Constitution," *Supreme Court Review* (1983):83–123.

4. For a moden reflection on this, see Stephen G. Post, *Human Nature and the Freedom of Public Religious Expression* (2003).

5. *Cantwell v. Connecticut*, 310 U.S. at 303–304, 310 (1940).

6. *Everson v. Board of Education*, 330 U.S. 1, 16 (1947).

7. *Marsh v. Chambers*, 463 U.S. 783 (1983), quoting, in part, *Zorach v. Clauson*, 343 U.S. 306 (1952).

8. *Jackman v. Rosenbaum*, 260 U.S. 22, 31 (1922).

9. Chief Justice Rehnquist offered this reading of tradition in his concurrence in the Pledge of Allegiance case, *Elk Grove Unified School District v. Newdow*, 124 S.Ct. 2301, 2311 (2004). After quoting at length from Presidential speeches and other official historical documents that recognized and recited the name of God, the Chief Justice concluded: "All of these events strongly suggest that our national culture allows public recognition of our Nation's religious history and character. In the words of the House Report that accompanied the insertion of the phrase 'under God' in the Pledge: 'From the time of our earliest history our peoples and our institutions have reflected the traditional concept that our Nation was founded on a fundamental belief in God.'"

The free exercise clause prevents Congress and California from requiring a student to recite this pledge, the Chief Justice noted, citing *West County Board of Education v. Barnette* (1943). The disestablishment clause, in turn, cannot be read to give any citizen "veto power over the decision of the public schools that willing participants should pledge allegiance to the flag in the manner prescribed by Congress.... Only if it can be said that the phrase "under God" somehow tends to the establishment of a religion in violation of the First Amendment can respondent's claim succeed....The recital, in a patriotic ceremony pledging allegiance to the flag and to the Nation, of the descriptive phrase 'under God' cannot possibly lead to the establishment of a religion, or anything like it." (Internal citations omitted).

10. *Lynch v. Donnelly*, 465 U.S. 668, 680–686 (1984).

11. Ibid., 693 (O'Connor, J. concurring). Twenty years after Lynch, concurring in *Elk Grove Unified School District v. Newdow*, 124 S.Ct. at 2317, Justice O'Connor elaborated her theory of "ceremonial deism": "I believe that government can, in a discrete category of cases, acknowledge or refer to the divine without offending the Constitution. This category of 'ceremonial deism' most clearly encompasses such things as the national motto ('In God We Trust'), religious references in traditional patriotic songs such as the Star-Spangled Banner, and the words with which the Marshal of this Court opens each of its sessions ('God save the United States and this honorable Court'). These references are not minor trespasses upon the Establishment Clause to which I turn a blind eye. Instead, their history, character, and context prevent them from being constitutional violations at all."

Justice O'Connor then specified four criteria by which to judge whether a governmental action or practice "constitutes an instance of such ceremonial deism":

(1) History and Ubiquity: "The constitutional value of ceremonial deism turns on a shared understanding of its legitimate nonreligious purposes. That sort of understanding can exist only when a given practice has been in place for a significant portion of the Nation's history, and when it is observed by enough persons that it can fairly be called ubiquitous."

(2) Absence of Worship or Prayer: "Any statement that has as its purpose placing the speaker or listener in a penitent state of mind, or that is intended to create a spiritual communion or invoke divine aid, strays from the legitimate secular purposes of solemnizing an event and recognizing a shared religious history."

(3) Absence of Reference to Particular Religion:

"[N]o religious acknowledgment could claim to be an instance of ceremonial deism if it explicitly favored one particular religious belief system over another."

(4) Minimal Religious Content: "[T]he brevity of a reference to religion or to God in a ceremonial exercise can be important for several reasons. First, it tends to confirm that the reference is being used to acknowledge religion or to solemnize an event rather than to endorse religion in any way. Second, it makes it easier for those participants who wish to 'opt out' of language they find offensive to do so without having to reject the ceremony entirely. And third, it tends to limit the ability of government to express a preference for one religious sect over another." (Internal citations omitted).

12. Ibid., 687.

13. The phrase is from John T. Noonan Jr., *The Lustre of Our Country: The American Experience of Religious Freedom* (1998), 230–231. For critical analysis of these cases, see Winnifred Fallers Sullivan, *Paying the Words Extra: Religious Discourse in the Supreme Court of the United States* (1994); Stephen B. Epstein, "Rethinking the Constitutionality of Ceremonial Deism," *Columbia Law Review* 96 (1996):2083.

14. *McDaniel v. Paty*, 435 U.S. 618 (1978).

15. *Bowen v. Kendrick*, 487 U.S. 589 (1988).

16. *Widmar v. Vincent*, 454 U.S. 263 (1981); *Board of Education of the Westside Community Schools v. Mergens*, 496 U.S. 226 (1990).

17. *Witters v. Washington Department of Services for the Blind*, 474 U.S. 481 (1986); *Zobrest v. Catalina Foothills School District*, 509 U.S. 1 (1993).

18. *Lamb's Chapel v. Center Moriches Union Free School District*, 508 U.S. 384 (1993); *Good News Club v. Milford Central School District*, 533 U.S. 98 (2001).

19. *Capitol Square Review and Advisory Board*, 515 U.S. 753 (1995).

20. *Rosenberger v. University of Virginia*, 515 U.S. 819 (1995).

21. *Mitchell v. Helms*, 530 U.S. 793 (2000); *Zelman v. Simmons-Harris*, 122 S.Ct. 24690 (2002).

22. See Michael J. Perry, *Under God? Religious Faith and Liberal Democracy* (2003), 20–54, who argues for the constitutional propriety, and sometimes priority, of religious arguments in public policy debates.

DRAFTS OF THE FEDERAL RELIGION CLAUSES, 1787–1789

Drafts in the Constitutional Convention, 1787

1. *"The Legislature of the United States shall pass no Law on the subject of Religion."*—Proposal by Charles Pinckney, May 29, 1787. Proposal died in Committee, without recorded discussion.

2. *"[N]o religious test shall ever be required as a qualification to any office or public trust under the authority of the U[nited] States."*—Motion by Charles Pinckney, August 30, 1787. Motion passed with one dissent.

3. *"The Congress shall have power . . . to establish an University, in which no preferences or distinctions should be allowed on account of religion."*—Motion by James Madison and Charles Pinckney on September 14, 1787. Motion failed 6–4.

Drafts Proposed to the First Congress by the State Ratification Conventions, 1788

1. *"Congress shall make no laws touching religion, or to infringe the rights of conscience."*—New Hampshire Proposal, June 21, 1788.

2. *"That religion, or the duty which we owe to our creator, and the manner of discharging it, can be directed only by reason and conviction, not by force or violence, and therefore all men have an equal, natural and unalienable right to the free exercise of religion according to the dictates of conscience, and that no particular religious sect or society ought to be favored or established by law in preference to others."*—Virginia Proposal, June 26, 1788.

3. *"That the people have an equal, natural, and unalienable right freely and peaceably to exercise their religion, according to the dictates of conscience; and that no religious sect or society ought to be favored or established by law in preference to others."*—New York Proposal, July 26, 1788.

4. *"That any person religiously scrupulous of bearing arms ought to be exempted, upon payment of an equivalent to employ another to bear arms in his stead. That religion, or the duty which we owe to our Creator, and the manner of discharging it, can be directed only by reason and conviction, not by force or violence; and therefore all men have an equal, natural, and unalienable right to the free exercise of religion according to the dictates of conscience, and that no particular religious sect or society ought to be favored or established by law in preference to others."*—North Carolina Proposal, August 1, 1788; repeated by Rhode Island, June 16, 1790.

Drafts Debated in the First Congress, 1789

5. *"The civil rights of none shall be abridged on account of religious belief or worship, nor shall any national religion be established, nor shall the full and equal rights of conscience be in any manner, or any pretext infringed."*—Draft proposed to the House by James Madison, June 8, 1789.

6. *"No state shall violate the equal rights of conscience, or the freedom of the press, or the trial by jury in criminal cases."*—Draft proposed to the House by James Madison, June 8, 1789.

7. *"[N]o religion shall be established by law, nor shall the equal rights of conscience be infringed."*—Draft proposed to the House by Committee of Eleven, July 28, 1789.

8. *"[N]o person religiously scrupulous shall be compelled to bear arms."*—Draft proposed to the House by Committee of Eleven, July 28, 1789.

9. *"[N]o State shall infringe the equal rights of conscience, nor the freedom of speech or of the press, nor of the right of trial by jury in criminal cases."*—Draft proposed to the House by Committee of Eleven, July 28, 1789.

10. *"Congress shall make no laws touching religion, or infringing the rights of conscience."*—Draft proposed by Charles Livermore on August 15, 1789; passed by the House.

11. *"[T]he equal rights of conscience, the freedom of speech or of the press, and the right of trial by jury in criminal cases, shall not be infringed by any State."*—Draft proposed by Charles Livermore on August 17, 1789; passed by the House.

12. *"Congress shall make no law establishing religion, or to prevent the free exercise thereof, or to infringe the rights of conscience."*—Revised draft proposed by Fisher Ames on August 20, 1789; passed by the House.

13. *"No person religiously scrupulous shall be compelled to bear arms in person."*—Revised draft passed by the House, August 20, 1789.

14. *"Congress shall make no law establishing religion, or prohibiting the free exercise thereof, nor shall the rights of conscience be infringed."*—Final draft proposed by the Style Committee, passed by the House and sent to the Senate, August 25, 1789.

15. *"Congress shall make no law establishing One Religious Sect or Society in preference to others, nor shall the rights of conscience be infringed."*—Draft proposed and defeated in the Senate, September 3, 1789.

16. *"Congress shall not make any law, infringing the rights of conscience, or establishing any Religious Sect or Society."*—Draft proposed and defeated in the Senate, September 3, 1789.

17. *"Congress shall make no law establishing any particular denomination of religion in preference to another, or prohibiting the free exercise thereof, nor shall the rights of conscience be infringed."*—Draft proposed and defeated in the Senate, September 3, 1789.

18. *"Congress shall make no law establishing religion, or prohibiting the free exercise thereof."*—Draft proposed and passed by the Senate, September 3, 1789.

19. *"Congress shall make no law establishing articles of faith or a mode of worship, or prohibiting the free exercise of religion."*—Draft proposed and passed by the Senate, and sent to the House, September 9, 1789.

20. *"Congress shall make no Law respecting an establishment of Religion, or prohibiting the free exercise thereof."*—Draft proposed by Joint House-Senate Committee on September 24, 1789; passed by the House and Senate on September 25, 1789.

For detailed discussion of and full citations to these drafts, see Chapter 4.

STATE CONSTITUTIONAL PROVISIONS ON RELIGION (AS OF 1947)

APPENDIX 2
State Constitutional Provisions on Religion as of 1947

State and Year of Constitution	does preamble use "God" or other religious language?	a liberty or right of conscience clause?	a free exercise clause?	a clause against coercion or compulsion to religion or religious support?	a conscientious objection to arms or pacifism clause?	an equality of religion clause?	a clause indicating no state preference for or among religions?	a disestablishment clause?	a clause prohibiting the mandatory payment of money or tithes?	a prohibition on religious test oaths for holding public office?	a prohibition on religious tests or oaths for serving on a jury or as a witness?	a prohibition on religious tests or oaths for voting?	is a tax exemption given to religious property or bodies?	a prohibition against state funding for religious education?	a prohibition against state funding of religion more generally?
Alabama (1901)[1]	yes	yes		yes			yes	yes	yes	yes	—	—	yes	yes	yes
Arizona (1912)	yes	yes						yes	yes	yes	yes	—	yes	yes	yes
Arkansas (1874)	yes	yes		yes			yes			no	no	yes	yes		
California (1879)	yes	yes	yes		yes		yes			—	yes	—	yes	yes	yes
Colorado (1876)	yes	yes	yes	yes			yes			—	—	—		yes	yes
Connecticut (1818)	yes	yes	yes	yes		yes	yes		yes	—	—	—	yes	yes	
Delaware (1897)	yes	yes	yes	yes			yes		yes	yes	—	—	yes	yes	

NOTE: These provisions are drawn, in large measure, from Chester James Antieus, Phillip Mark Carroll, and Thomas Carroll Burke, *Religion Under the State Constitutions* (Brooklyn, 1965), 173–239, with some corrections and refinements drawn from the state constitutions in F. Thorpe, ed., *The Federal and State Constitutions*, 7 vols. (Washington, 1909), and *Constitutions of the United States: National and State* (New York, 1962). As this list depicts only the status of the state constitutions in 1947, Alaska and Hawaii are omitted, as they were not yet states.

[1]The year listed for each state constitution is the year of adoption. Some state constitutions were amended between the year of adoption and 1947. This table incorporates such changes and thus provides a statement of the status of religious liberty in the states in the year 1947.

(continues)

(continues)

APPENDIX 2 *(continued)*

State and Year of Constitution	does preamble use "God" or other religious language?	a liberty or right of conscience clause?	a free exercise clause?	a clause against coercion or compulsion to religion or religious support?	a conscientious objection to arms or pacifism clause?	an equality of religion clause?	a clause indicating no state preference for or among religions?	a disestablishment clause?	a clause prohibiting the mandatory payment of money or tithes?	a prohibition on religious test oaths for holding public office?	a prohibition on religious tests or oaths for serving on a jury or as a witness?	a prohibition on religious tests or oaths for voting?	is a tax exemption given to religious property or bodies?	a prohibition against state funding for religious education?	a prohibition against state funding of religion more generally?
Florida (1887)	yes	yes	yes		yes		yes				yes	—	yes	yes	yes
Georgia (1945)	yes	yes	yes	yes	yes				yes	yes	—	—	yes	yes	yes
Idaho (1890)	yes	yes	yes	yes	yes		yes			—	—	—		yes	yes
Illinois (1870)	yes	yes	yes	yes	yes		yes			—	—	—	yes	yes	yes
Indiana (1851)	yes	yes	yes	yes	yes					yes	yes	—	yes	yes	
Iowa (1857)	yes	yes	yes	yes	yes			yes	yes	yes	yes	—			
Kansas (1861)	yes	yes	yes	yes		yes	yes			yes	yes	yes	yes	yes	
Kentucky (1891)	yes	yes				yes	yes	yes		—	—	—	yes	yes	
Louisiana (1921)	yes	yes				yes	yes	yes		—	—	—	yes	yes	
Maine (1820)	yes	yes							yes	no	no	—			
Maryland (1867)	yes	yes	yes	yes	yes		yes		yes	yes	—	—			
Massachusetts (1780)	yes	yes	yes	yes	yes				yes	—	—	—			yes
Michigan (1890)	yes	yes		yes					yes	yes	yes	—	yes	yes	yes
Minnesota (1857)	yes	yes		yes			yes		yes	yes	yes	yes	yes	yes	yes

(continues)

APPENDIX 2 (continued)

State and Year of Constitution	does preamble use "God" or other religious language?	a liberty or right of conscience clause?	a free exercise clause?	a clause against coercion or compulsion to religion or religious support?	a conscientious objection to arms or pacifism clause?	an equality of religion clause?	a clause indicating no state preference for or among religions?	a disestablishment clause?	a clause prohibiting the mandatory payment of money or tithes?	a prohibition on religious test oaths for holding public office?	a prohibition on religious tests or oaths for serving on a jury or as a witness?	a prohibition on religious tests or oaths for voting?	is a tax exemption given to religious property or bodies?	a prohibition against state funding for religious education?	a prohibition against state funding of religion more generally?
Mississippi (1890)	yes	yes					yes			no				yes	yes
Missouri (1945)	yes	yes					yes			yes	yes		yes	yes	yes
Montana (1889)	yes	yes	yes	yes			yes						yes	yes	yes
Nebraska (1875)	yes	yes		yes							yes		yes	yes	
Nevada (1864)	yes	yes	yes	yes		yes	yes			yes	yes			yes	yes
New Hampshire (1784)	yes	yes	yes		yes				yes				yes		
New Jersey (1947)	yes	yes	yes	yes			yes		yes	yes	yes		yes	yes	yes
New Mexico (1913)	yes	yes		yes			yes			yes	yes	yes	yes	yes	
New York (1895)	yes	yes	yes			yes		yes					yes		
North Carolina (1868)	yes	yes			yes					no	yes		yes	yes	yes
North Dakota (1889)	yes	yes	yes		yes		yes			yes	yes		yes	yes	
Ohio (1851)	yes	yes		yes			yes			yes	yes		yes		
Oklahoma (1907)	yes									yes	yes	yes	yes	yes	yes
Oregon (1859)	yes	yes	yes		yes					yes			yes	yes	yes

APPENDIX 2 *(continued)*

State and Year of Constitution	does preamble use "God" or other religious language?	a liberty or right of conscience clause?	a free exercise clause?	a clause against coercion or compulsion to religion or religious support?	a conscientious objection to arms or pacifism clause?	an equality of religion clause?	a clause indicating no state preference for or among religions?	a disestablishment clause?	a clause prohibiting the mandatory payment of money or tithes?	a prohibition on religious test oaths for holding public office?	a prohibition on religious tests or oaths for serving on a jury or as a witness?	a prohibition on religious tests or oaths for voting?	is a tax exemption given to religious property or bodies?	a prohibition against state funding for religious education?	a prohibition against state funding of religion more generally?
Pennsylvania (1874)	yes	yes	yes	yes	yes		yes		yes	no			yes	yes	yes
Rhode Island (1843)	yes	yes	yes	yes	yes					yes				yes	yes
South Carolina (1895)	yes				yes			yes		no			yes	yes	
South Dakota (1889)	yes	yes	yes	yes	yes		yes		yes		yes		yes	yes	yes
Tennessee (1870)	yes	yes	yes	yes	yes		yes		yes	yes	yes		yes	yes	
Texas (1876)	yes	yes	yes	yes	yes	yes	yes			no	yes		yes	yes	yes
Utah (1896)	yes	yes		yes	yes			yes	yes	yes	yes	yes		yes	yes
Vermont (1793)		yes	yes	yes	yes				yes						
Virginia (1902)		yes	yes				yes			yes	yes	yes	yes	yes	yes
Washington (1889)	yes	yes			yes								yes	yes	yes
West Virginia (1872)	yes	yes	yes	yes			yes		yes	yes	yes	yes			
Wisconsin (1848)	yes	yes	yes	yes			yes		yes	yes	yes		yes	yes	yes
Wyoming (1890)	yes	yes	yes				yes			yes	yes		yes	yes	yes

UNITED STATES SUPREME COURT DECISIONS RELATING TO RELIGIOUS LIBERTY

APPENDIX 3
United States Supreme Court Decisions Relating to Religious Liberty

Issue	Case	Citation	Ratio[1]	Author of Opinion	Holding
Church Property	Terrett v. Taylor	13 U.S. (9 Cranch) 43 (1815)	7-0	Story, J.	State may not rescind the properly obtained charter of the Episcopal Church and expropriate the church's lands.
Charitable Bequest	Vidal v. Girard's Executors	43 U.S. (2 How.) 127 (1844)	7-0	Story, J.	Testamentary bequest for establishment of school for orphans is valid notwithstanding provisions derogatory of Christianity.
Federalism	Permoli v. First Municipality of New Orleans	44 U.S. (3 How.) 589 (1844)	8-0	Catron, J.	United States Constitution does not protect citizens' religious liberties in regards to the respective states.
Church Property	Goesele v. Bimeler	55 U.S. (14 How.) 589 (1852)	8-0	McLean, J.	Heirs of member of communitarian religious group cannot recover share of property from the religious society.
Church Property: Civil Court Relief	Smith v. Swormstedt	57 U.S. (16 How.) 288 (1853)	9-0	Nelson, J.	A court may sit in equity and divide jointly held property to carry out a voluntarily reached agreement of the church.

NOTE: This chart is modeled, in part, after Carl Esbeck's chart, "Table of United States Supreme Court Decisions Relating to Religious Liberty, 1789–1994," *Journal of Law and Religion* 10 (1994): 573–588.

[1] The "ratio" listed below usually includes two numbers only: the majority and the dissenters. If justices concur in the judgment but not in the opinion, they are listed following the number of the majority, designated by a "/". I have not differentiated among dissenting opinions but listed them all together. Similarly, concurring opinions are not listed at all unless they concur in the judgment only. As a shorthand way of denoting the ratio in more complicated cases, I have simply designated the ratio as "Pluralities." In such cases, if the author is listed as "opinion of the Court," then the opinion garnered a majority of votes, and there was disagreement only beyond the majority. If the author is listed as "for the plurality," then there was no clear majority, though there was sufficient consensus for a judgment, and the named author rendered the judgment of the Court.

(continues)

APPENDIX 3 *(continued)*

Issue	Case	Citation	Ratio[1]	Author of Opinion	Holding
Church Property	*Baker v. Nachtrieb*	60 U.S. (19 How.) 126 (1856)	9-0	Campbell, J.	Defecting member of communitarian religious group may not recover share of property from the religious society.
Mandatory Oath	*Cummings v. Missouri*	71 U.S. (4 Wall.) 277 (1866); dissent attached to *Ex parte Garland*, 71 U.S. (4 Wall.) 397 (1866)	5-4	Field, J.	State may not deprive priest of the right to preach for failure to take a mandatory oath disavowing support/sympathy for the cause of the Confederate states.
Church Property	*Watson v. Jones*	80 U.S. (13 Wall.) 679 (1871)	6-2	Miller, J.	Civil courts should defer to the judgment of the highest religious authority in determining which of two internal religious factions is entitled to disputed property.
Church Property: Internal Church Governance	*Bouldin v. Alexander*	82 U.S. (15 Wall.) 131 (1872)	9-0	Strong, J.	Courts have no power to question acts of internal church discipline or excommunication; the rule of the church's highest internal tribunal must govern property disputes dependent on doctrine.
Polygamy; First Application of Free Exercise Clause	*Reynolds v. United States*	98 U.S. 145 (1879)	9-0	Waite, C.J.	Upheld federal criminal law prohibiting polygamy and denied a Mormon's free exercise claim to the practice, stating that beliefs could not be regulated but actions could.
Polygamy	*Murphy v. Ramsey*	114 U.S. 15 (1885)	9-0	Matthews, J.	Upheld laws disenfranchising known and suspected bigamists.

(continues)

APPENDIX 3 *(continued)*

Issue	Case	Citation	Ratio[1]	Author of Opinion	Holding
Tax Exemptions	Gibbons v. District of Columbia	116 U.S. 404 (1886)	9-0	Gray, J.	Allowed property tax scheme that exempted "church buildings, and grounds actually occupied by such buildings" but not land owned by but not used for the church.
Church Property	Speidel v. Henrici	120 U.S. 377 (1887)	9-0	Gray, J.	Defecting member of communitarian religious group may not recover share of property from the religious group.
Polygamy	Davis v. Beason	133 U.S. 333 (1890)	9-0	Field, J.	Upheld a conviction for falsely taking a (mandatory) oath renouncing polygamy.
Polygamy	The Late Corporation of the Church of Jesus Christ of Latter Day Saints v. United States	136 U.S. 1 (1890)	6-3	Bradley, J.	Upheld government's dissolution of the Mormon Church's corporate charter and the confiscation of its property for continued advocacy of polygamy.
Church Staff Hiring	Church of the Holy Trinity v. United States	143 U.S. 457 (1892)	9-0	Brewer, J.	Refused to apply a new federal law forbidding contracts with foreign aliens to a church seeking to hire a foreign cleric.
Building Grants; First Application of Disestablishment Clause	Bradfield v. Roberts	175 U.S. 291 (1899)	9-0	Peckham, J.	Upheld, against disestablishment clause challenge, the allocation and distribution of federal funds to build religious hospital.
Religious School Funding; Indian Trust Disbursement	Quick Bear v. Leupp	210 U.S. 50 (1908)	9-0	Fuller, C.J.	Upheld federal distribution of funds (under an Indian treaty) to Catholic schools that offered education to Native Americans.

(continues)

APPENDIX 3 *(continued)*

Issue	Case	Citation	Ratio[1]	Author of Opinion	Holding
Treaty; Church Property	*Ponce v. Roman Catholic Apostolic Church*	210 U.S. 296 (1908)	9-0	Fuller, C.J.	Confirmed church's title to property acquired from Spanish government before the U.S. annexation of Puerto Rico.
Church Property	*Order of St. Benedict v. Steinhauser*	234 U.S. 640 (1914)	9-0	Hughes. J.	Upheld communal ownership of property within monastic order and granted the Order title to the estate of deceased life-long member.
Conscientious Objection	*Selective Draft Law Cases (Arver v. United States)*	245 U.S. 366 (1918)	9-0	White, C.J.	Upheld as constitutional Congress's power to define conscientious objector status and Congress's restriction of the status to ordained ministers, theology students, and members of well-recognized pacifist sects.
Religious School Curriculum	*Meyer v. Nebraska*	262 U.S. 390 (1923); dissent attached to *Bartels v. Iowa*, 262 U.S. 412 (1923)	7-2	McReynolds, J.	State statute mandating English-only instruction in all grade schools held unconstitutional, as applied to private religious school.
Religious School Attendance	*Pierce v. Society of Sisters*	268 U.S. 510 (1925)	9-0	McReynolds, J.	Invalidated state law mandating attendance at public schools as violation of rights of private schools and of parents.
Religious School Regulation	*Farrington v. Tokushige*	273 U.S. 284 (1927)	9-0	McReynolds, J.	States may not impose unduly intrusive and stringent accreditation and regulatory requirements on religious and other private schools.
Naturalization Qualifications; Conscientious Objection	*United States v. Schwimmer*	279 U.S. 644 (1929)	6-3	Butler, J.	Permitted the denial of citizenship to pacifist who refused to swear an oath to take up arms in defense of the country.

(continues)

APPENDIX 3 *(continued)*

Issue	Case	Citation	Ratio[1]	Author of Opinion	Holding
Religious School Subsidization: Textbooks	*Cochran v. Louisiana Board of Education*	281 U.S. 370 (1930)	9-0	Hughes, C.J.	Upheld state policy of furnishing textbooks to public and religious school students over objection of taxpayer that this constituted a taking of his private property in violation of the Fourteenth Amendment due process clause.
Naturalization Qualifications	*United States v. Bland*	283 U.S. 636 (1931)	5-4	Sutherland, J.	Refusal to bear arms in defense of the United States is a valid reason to bar a person's naturalization as a U.S. citizen.
Conscientious Objection	*Hamilton v. Regents of the University of California*	293 U.S. 245 (1934)	9-0	Butler, J.	Due Process Clause of Fourteenth Amendment, though to be construed broadly, confers no right to exemption for pacifists from mandatory R.O.T.C. training at state university.
Federal Jurisdiction; Distribution of Religious Literature	*Coleman v. City of Griffin*	302 U.S. 421 (1937), letting stand 189 S.E. 427 (Ga. Ct. App. 1936)	9-0	Per curiam	No federal question presented in appeal of city ordinance prohibiting distribution of religious literature on religion grounds; same ordinance addressed substantively in *Lovell v. City of Griffin*, 303 U.S. 444 (1938).
Distribution of Religious Literature	*Lovell v. City of Griffin*	303 U.S. 444 (1938)	8-0	Hughes, C.J.	Invalidated city ordinance prohibiting distribution of religious literature for violating freedom of the press.
Distribution of Religious Literature	*Schneider v. State of New Jersey (Town of Irvington)*	308 U.S. 147 (1939)	7-1	Roberts, J.	Invalidated local ordinance prohibiting distribution of religious literature for violating freedom of speech and freedom of the press.
Licensing; Free Exercise Clause Incorporated	*Cantwell v. Connecticut*	310 U.S. 296 (1940)	9-0	Roberts, J.	Free exercise clause expressly applied to the states through the Fourteenth Amendment; city licensing law, requiring religious groups to procure a license in advance but giving discretion to local administrators to deny such licenses, held unconstitutional.

(continued)

APPENDIX 3 *(continued)*

Issue	Case	Citation	Ratio[1]	Author of Opinion	Holding
Flag Salute	*Minersville School Board v. Gobitis*	310 U.S. 586 (1940)	7/1-1	Frankfurter, J.	Providing no free exercise exemption from public school requirement of saluting and pledging allegiance to the American flag.
Licensing	*Cox v. New Hampshire*	312 U.S. 569 (1941)	9-0	Hughes, C.J.	City may require all groups to obtain a license/permit and pay a reasonable fee, consonant with the expense incurred by the city to administer the license and maintain public order during and after the parade/procession.
Fighting Words	*Chaplinsky v. New Hampshire*	315 U.S. 568 (1942)	9-0	Murphy, J.	Cursing a police officer is not the exercise of "religion" nor speech protected by the First Amendment.
Distribution of Religious Literature	*Jones v. Opelika (I)*	316 U.S. 584 (1942)	5-4	Reed, J.	Local ordinance requiring license fee on distribution of all literature, and reserving discretion of revocation, may constitutionally be applied to distributors of religious literature.
Distribution of Religious Literature	*Jamison v. Texas*	318 U.S. 413 (1943)	8-0	Black, J.	Local ordinance prohibiting distribution of religious pamphlets in the public square and door to door is unconstitutional.
Licensing	*Largent v. Texas*	318 U.S. 418 (1943)	8-0	Reed, J.	City ordinance that requires permit to solicit orders for books but reserves to city official discretion to deny permits is unconstitutional as applied to religious publications.

(continues)

APPENDIX 3 *(continued)*

Issue	Case	Citation	Ratio[1]	Author of Opinion	Holding
Distribution of Religious Literature	*Jones v. Opelika (II)*	319 U.S. 103 (1943); dissents attached to *Murdock v. Pennsylvania (City of Jeannette)*, 319 U.S. 117 (1943), and *Douglas v. City of Jeannette*, 319 U.S. 166 (1943)	5-4	Per curiam (relying on Justice Douglas's opinion in *Murdock v. Pennsylvania (City of Jeannette)*, 319 U.S. 105 (1943), and Chief Justice Stone's dissent in *Jones v. Opelika (I)*, 316 U.S. 600 (1942))	Explicitly overruled *Jones v. Opelika (I)*, 316 U.S. 584 (1942); state may not prohibit distribution of religious literature; even if ordinance is "nondiscriminatory" on its face, the liberties guaranteed by the First Amendment are in a preferred position.
Distribution of Religious Literature; Flat License Tax	*Murdock v. Pennsylvania (City of Jeannette)*	319 U.S. 105 (1943); additional dissent attached to *Douglas v. City of Jeannette*, 319 U.S. 166 (1943)	5-4	Douglas, J.	A flat tax on all persons soliciting or selling goods is a "prior restraint" on those exercising their constitutional right to exercise their religion through distributing tracts and is thus unconstitutional.
Distribution of Religious Literature	*Martin v. Struthers*	319 U.S. 141 (1943); additional dissent attached to *Douglas v. City of Jeannette*, 319 U.S. 166 (1943)	5-4	Black, J.	Ordinance forbidding door-to-door distribution of religious pamphlets and circulars is unconstitutional because it violates free speech and press.

(continues)

APPENDIX 3 *(continued)*

Issue	Case	Citation	Ratio[1]	Author of Opinion	Holding
Federal Jurisdiction; Flat License Tax	*Douglas v. City of Jeannette*	319 U.S. 157 (1943)	7/2-0	Stone, C.J.	Case not properly in federal court; same ordinance addressed substantively in *Murdock v. Pennsylvania (City of Jeannette)*, 319 U.S. 105 (1943).
Flag Salute	*West Virginia State Board of Education v. Barnette*	319 U.S. 624 (1943)	6-3	Jackson, J.	Overruled *Minersville School Board v. Gobitis*, 310 U.S. 586 (1940); First Amendment provides exemption from mandatory participation in rituals that parties conscientiously oppose—including saluting the flag in a public school classroom.
Parent/Guardian Rights	*Prince v. Massachusetts*	321 U.S. 158 (1944)	5-4	Rutledge, J.	State criminal law regulating child labor, applied to guardian of nine-year-old girl distributing religious tracts on the public streets in the evening, is not a denial or abridgment of free exercise rights.
Flat License Tax; Distribution of Religious Literature	*Follett v. Town of McCormick*	321 U.S. 573 (1944)	5/1-3	Douglas, J.	City may not impose flat license tax on minister distributing religious literature.
Religious Fraud	*United States v. Ballard*	322 U.S. 78 (1944)	5-4	Douglas, J.	Truth of religious belief is not subject to the scrutiny of a jury, but jury may be called upon to decide the sincerity of defendant's belief.
Conscientious Objection	*In re Summers*	325 U.S. 561 (1945)	5-4	Reed, J.	Refusal of bar admission to conscientious objector who refused to swear oath that he would serve in military not a free exercise violation.

(continues)

APPENDIX 3 (continued)

Issue	Case	Citation	Ratio[1]	Author of Opinion	Holding
Polygamy	Chatwin v. United States	326 U.S. 455 (1946)	7/1-0	Murphy, J.	Defendant who persuaded minor female to join him in "celestial" marriage not guilty of violating Federal Kidnapping Act.
Distribution of Religious Literature	Marsh v. Alabama	326 U.S. 501 (1946)	5-3	Black, J.	Statute imposing criminal penalties for distribution of religious literature in company-owned town is unconstitutional, per free exercise and speech clauses.
Distribution of Religious Literature	Tucker v. Texas	326 U.S. 517 (1946)	5-3	Black, J.	Statute imposing criminal penalties for distributing religious literature in government-owned town is unconstitutional, per free exercise and speech clauses.
Naturalization Qualifications; First Application of Article VI Test Oath Clause	Girouard v. United States	328 U.S. 61 (1946)	5-3	Douglas, J.	Government may not require a party who is conscientiously opposed to swear a military test oath before receiving naturalized citizenship status, per free exercise clause and Article VI ban on religious test oaths.
Polygamy	Cleveland v. United States	329 U.S. 14 (1946)	5/1-3	Douglas, J.	Upheld convictions of members of polygamous sect for transporting plural wives across state lines in violation of the Mann "White Slave" Act.
Conscientious Objection	Eagles v. Samuels	329 U.S. 304 (1946)	9-0	Douglas, J.	Civilian panel could properly determine that defendant failed to establish right to pre-ministerial deferment under Selective Service Act.

(continues)

APPENDIX 3 *(continued)*

Issue	Case	Citation	Ratio[1]	Author of Opinion	Holding
School Transportation; Disestablishment Clause Incorporated	Everson v. Board of Education	330 U.S. 1 (1947)	5-4	Black, J.	Expressly applied disestablishment clause to the states through the Fourteenth Amendment; but it is not establishment of religion for states to provide school bus transportation to religious and public school children alike.
Polygamy	Musser v. Utah	333 U.S. 95 (1948)	5/1-3	Jackson, J.	Conviction for polygamy vacated and remanded for consideration of state law questions.
Public School On-Campus Release Time	McCollum v. Board of Education	333 U.S. 203 (1948)	6/1/1-1	Black, J.	Disallowed public school "release time" program, wherein students were released from regular classes once a week to be able to participate in religious classes, which were held on campus.
Religious Speech	Saia v. New York	334 U.S. 558 (1948)	5-4	Douglas, J.	City ordinance prohibiting sound amplification, reserving discretion to police chief but giving no criteria for exercising that discretion, violates free speech because it operates as a prior restraint.
Conscientious Objection	Gara v. United States	340 U.S. 857 (1950), affirming, by an equally divided Court, 178 F.2d 38 (6th Cir. 1949)	4-4	Per curiam	Upheld conviction for counseling another person conscientiously to object to draft registration and for actively opposing Selective Service Act.
Licensing	Niemotko v. State of Maryland	340 U.S. 268 (1951)	7/1/1-0	Vinson, C.J.	City may not deny a permit to use a public park for religious purposes when the applicable statute lacks clear criteria for such denials.

(continues)

APPENDIX 3 *(continued)*

Issue	Case	Citation	Ratio[1]	Author of Opinion	Holding
Licensing	*Kunz v. New York*	340 U.S. 290 (1951); concurrence attached to *Niemotko v. Maryland*, 340 U.S. 273 (1951)	6/1/1-1	Vinson, C.J.	City may not deny a license to a Baptist minister to preach in a public park because the licensing regulation improperly gave local officials discretion to deny licenses.
Standing	*Doremus v. Board of Education*	342 U.S. 429 (1952)	6-3	Jackson, J.	Party lacks standing to challenge Bible reading in public school when the student has already graduated.
Release Time from Public Schools	*Zorach v. Clauson*	343 U.S. 306 (1952)	6-3	Douglas, J.	Upheld the constitutionality of granting students release time from public schools to attend religious education or services.
Censorship	*Joseph Burstyn, Inc. v. Wilson*	343 U.S. 495 (1952)	6/2/1-0	Clark, J.	State law requiring permit for commercial showing of films but allowing censorship of films that are "sacrilegious" is a prior restraint and thus an unconstitutional violation of freedoms of speech and press.
Church Property; Regulation of Churches; Internal Church Governance	*Kedroff v. Saint Nicholas Cathedral*	344 U.S. 94 (1952)	8-1	Reed, J.	State religious incorporation law may not prohibit foreign religious authority from selecting church leaders and shift control to local church authorities; internal church law must be allowed to decide who makes such a decision.
Public Forum	*Fowler v. Rhode Island*	345 U.S. 67 (1953)	7/1/1-0	Douglas, J.	Struck down ordinance that prohibited religious speech but allowed for religious services in a public park because it was religiously discriminatory.

(continues)

APPENDIX 3 *(continued)*

Issue	Case	Citation	Ratio[1]	Author of Opinion	Holding
Licensing	*Poulos v. New Hampshire*	345 U.S. 395 (1953)	6/1-2	Reed, J.	Ordinance that leaves officials no discretion in granting permits but nevertheless requires payment of a sliding-scale fee to pay for city expenses incurred because of the permitted activity is constitutional.
Conscientious Objection	*United States v. Nugent*	346 U.S. 1 (1953)	5-3	Vinson, C.J.	Conscientious objector refusing to submit to induction into armed services has not shown the statute to be unconstitutional; Selective Service not required to disclose full FBI file on claimants.
Conscientious Objection	*Sicurella v. United States*	348 U.S. 385 (1955)	7-2	Clark, J.	Willingness to fight in "theocratic" wars does not disqualify a Jehovah's Witness who would otherwise qualify for exemption as a conscientious objector.
Conscientious Objection	*Simmons v. United States*	348 U.S. 397 (1955)	5/2-2	Clark, J.	Reversed conviction of defendant who was denied fair conscientious objection hearing because of government's failure to supply him "fair resume" of materials from his FBI files.
Conscientious Objection	*Gonzales v. United States*	348 U.S. 407 (1955)	6-3	Clark, J.	Reversed conviction of defendant who was denied fair conscientious objection hearing because of government's failure to supply him "fair resume" of materials from his FBI files.

(continues)

APPENDIX 3 *(continued)*

Issue	Case	Citation	Ratio[1]	Author of Opinion	Holding
Loyalty Oath	*First Unitarian Church v. County of Los Angeles*	357 U.S. 545 (1958); concurrence and dissent attached to *Speiser v. Randall*, 357 U.S. 529, 538 (1958)	7/1-1	Brennan, J.	Government may not require a party who is conscientiously opposed to swear a loyalty oath as a prerequisite to receiving a tax exemption.
Sunday Laws	*McGowan v. Maryland*	366 U.S. 420 (1961)	6/2-1	Warren, C.J.	Upheld state law proscribing certain business and commercial activity on Sunday against disestablishment clause challenge.
Sunday Laws	*Two Guys from Harrison Allentown, Inc. v. McGinley*	366 U.S. 582 (1961); concurrence and dissent attached to *McGowan v. Maryland*, 366 U.S. 459, 561 (1961)	6/2-1	Warren, C.J.	Sunday closing law does not violate disestablishment clause.
Sunday Laws	*Braunfeld v. Brown*	366 U.S. 599 (1961); other opinions attached to *McGowan v. Maryland*, 366 U.S. 459, 561 (1961)	Pluralities	Warren, C.J. (for the plurality)	Statute disallowing sales on Sunday does not violate free exercise rights of Jewish appellant, who is a strict Saturday sabbatarian.
Sunday Laws	*Gallagher v. Crown Kosher Super Market of Massachusetts*	366 U.S. 617 (1961); other opinions attached to *McGowan v. Maryland*, 366 U.S. 459, 561 (1961), and to *Braunfeld v. Brown*, 366 U.S. 610, 616 (1961)	Pluralities	Warren, C.J. (for the plurality)	Sunday closing law does not violate free exercise rights of owner of kosher supermarket, Orthodox Jewish customers, or rabbis with a duty to inspect kosher markets per Jewish dietary laws.
Mandatory Public Office Oath	*Torcaso v. Watkins*	367 U.S. 488 (1961)	7/2-0	Black, J.	Requirement of mandatory oath affirming belief in God as a prerequisite for holding public office is unconstitutional.

(continues)

APPENDIX 3 *(continued)*

Issue	Case	Citation	Ratio[1]	Author of Opinion	Holding
Prayer in Public School	*Engel v. Vitale*	370 U.S. 421 (1962)	6-1	Black, J.	Disallowed state program of daily (nondenominational) prayer in public school classrooms.
Federal Jurisdiction; Sunday Laws	*Arlan's Department Store v. Kentucky*	371 U.S. 218 (1962), letting stand 357 S.W.2d 708 (Ky. 1962)	8-1	Per curiam	Dismissed for lack of federal question; state court decision allowed to stand, upholding regulation that provided exemption from Sunday closing law only for those whose religion required rest on another day.
Bible Reading in Public School	*Abington School District v. Schempp*	374 U.S. 203 (1963)	8-1	Clark, J.	Mandatory Bible reading in public school classrooms violates disestablishment clause.
Unemployment Compensation Benefits	*Sherbert v. Verner*	374 U.S. 398 (1963)	6/1-2	Brennan, J.	Free exercise clause forbids state to deny unemployment compensation to claimant discharged from a job that would require her to work on her sabbath.
Bible Reading in Public School	*Chamberlain v. Public Instruction Board*	377 U.S. 402 (1964)	6-3	Per curiam	Reading of Bible and recitation of Lord's Prayer in public school is unconstitutional.
Prisoner's Rights	*Cooper v. Pate*	378 U.S. 546 (1964)	9-0	Per curiam	Muslim prisoner entitled to hearing on the merits that he was denied access to religious publications.

(continues)

APPENDIX 3 *(continued)*

Issue	Case	Citation	Ratio[1]	Author of Opinion	Holding
Conscientious Objection	*United States v. Seeger*	380 U.S. 163 (1965)	9-0	Clark, J.	Section 6(j) of Selective Service Act should be construed broadly, such that claimants may qualify for conscientious objector status if their belief is "sincere and meaningful" and occupies in their life "a place parallel to that filled by the God of those admittedly qualifying for the exemption."
Medical Care; Parent/Guardian Rights	*Jehovah's Witnesses v. King County Hospital*	390 U.S. 598 (1968); affirming 278 F.Supp. 488 (W.D. Wash.)	7-2	Per curiam	Blood transfusions may be administered to children, even if the parents are religiously opposed.
Standing	*Flast v. Cohen*	392 U.S. 83 (1968)	8-1	Warren, C.J.	Federal taxpayer has standing to challenge appropriation of federal funds for religious schools under the disestablishment clause.
Religious School Subsidization: Textbooks	*Board of Education v. Allen*	392 U.S. 236 (1968)	6-3	White, J.	Upheld state law requiring textbooks of "secular subjects" be provided to all students in the state, whether attending public or private (religious or other) schools.
Teaching Evolution in Public School	*Epperson v. Arkansas*	393 U.S. 97 (1968)	8/1-0	Fortas, J.	State criminal law which prohibited the teaching of evolution in a public school or state university violates the disestablishment clause.
Internal Church Governance; Church Property	*Presbyterian Church in the United States v. Mary Elizabeth Blue Hull Memorial Presbyterian Church*	393 U.S. 440 (1969)	9-0	Brennan, J.	Internal church disputes, including property disputes, should be governed by internal church law; civil courts may not use "departure from doctrine" standard, and should defer to the highest internal church authority.

(continues)

APPENDIX 3 *(continued)*

Issue	Case	Citation	Ratio[1]	Author of Opinion	Holding
Church Property	*Maryland and Virginia Churches v. Sharpsburg Church*	396 U.S. 367 (1970)	9-0	Per curiam	Civil courts may resolve church property disputes as long as they do not involve inquiry into church doctrine.
Tax Exemption	*Walz v. Tax Commission*	397 U.S. 664 (1970)	8-1	Burger, C.J.	Upheld state property tax exemption for church property against disestablishment clause challenge.
Conscientious Objection	*Welsh v. United States*	398 U.S. 333 (1970)	4/1-3	Black, J. (for the plurality)	Section 6(j) must be construed broadly; persons whose consciences, "spurred by deeply held moral, ethical, or religious beliefs," do not allow them to be an "instrument of war" are entitled to conscientious objector status.
Conscientious Objection	*Gillette v. United States*	401 U.S. 437 (1971)	7/1-1	Marshall, J.	Congress may exempt persons opposed to participating in all wars, but not those objecting to participation in a particular war, from military service without violating the First Amendment.
Employment	*Dewey v. Reynolds Metals Co.*	402 U.S. 689 (1971); affirming, by an equally divided Court, 429 F.2d 324 (6th Cir. 1970)	4-4	Per curiam	Rejected free exercise claim of a Sabbatarian who claimed he was wrongfully discharged on the basis of his religious beliefs.
Religious School Subsidization	*Lemon v. Kurtzman (I)*	403 U.S. 602 (1971)	6/1/1-0	Burger, C.J.	Disestablishment clause requires laws to have (1) a secular purpose; (2) primary effect that neither advances nor inhibits religion; and (3) no excessive entanglement of church and state; statute that reimbursed religious schools for costs of teaching secular subjects violates (3).

(continues)

APPENDIX 3 *(continued)*

Issue	Case	Citation	Ratio[1]	Author of Opinion	Holding
Construction Grants	Tilton v. Richardson	403 U.S. 672 (1971); additional opinions attached to Lemon v. Kurtzman (I), 403 U.S. 642, 661 (1971)	Pluralities	Burger, C.J.	Upheld federal grants that supported construction of library, science, and arts buildings at religious colleges as well as secular colleges.
Prisoner's Rights	Cruz v. Beto	405 U.S. 319 (1972)	6/1/1-1	Per curiam	Buddhist prisoner must be given "reasonable" opportunities to free exercise of religion.
Compulsory Education	Wisconsin v. Yoder	406 U.S. 205 (1972)	6-1 (but dissenting opinion concurred in part)	Burger, C.J.	Granted free exercise exemption to Amish, which exempted them from full compliance with compulsory school attendance law.
Religious School Subsidization	Lemon v. Kurtzman (II)	411 U.S. 192 (1973)	4/1-3	Burger, C.J. (for the plurality)	Lemon v. Kurtzman (I), 403 U.S. 602 (1971), should not be applied retroactively.
Religious School Subsidization: Textbooks	Norwood v. Harrison	413 U.S. 455 (1973)	7/2-0	Burger, C.J.	State may loan textbooks on secular subjects to religious schools, but not if those schools discriminate on racial grounds.
Religious School Subsidization	Levitt v. Committee for Public Education and Religious Liberty	413 U.S. 472 (1973)	5/3-1	Burger, C.J.	States may not reimburse religious schools for most costs incurred to administer standardized tests and to prepare mandated state records.
Revenue Bonds	Hunt v. McNair	413 U.S. 734 (1973)	6-3	Powell, J.	Upheld issuance of revenue bonds for religious colleges.

(continues)

APPENDIX 3 *(continued)*

Issue	Case	Citation	Ratio[1]	Author of Opinion	Holding
Religious School Subsidization	Committee for Public Education and Religious Liberty v. Nyquist	413 U.S. 756 (1973)	Pluralities	Powell, J. (opinion of the Court)	Disallowed state reimbursement for low-income parents for part of religious school tuition; disallowed tax deduction for low-income parents whose children attended religious schools; disallowed direct grants to private schools serving low-income students for maintenance and repair costs.
Religious School Subsidization	Sloan v. Lemon	413 U.S. 825 (1973); additional opinions attached to Committee for Public Education and Religious Liberty v. Nyquist, 413 U.S. 798, 813 (1973)	6-3	Powell, J.	Disallowed state reimbursement to parents for portion of religious school tuition.
Education Benefits; Conscientious Objection	Johnson v. Robinson	415 U.S. 361 (1974)	8-1	Brennan, J.	Statute which grants educational benefits to military draftees but not to draftees who perform civilian alternative service is not unconstitutional.
Education Benefits; Conscientious Objection	Hernandez v. Veterans' Administration	415 U.S. 391 (1974)	8/1-0	Brennan, J.	Vacated a Ninth Circuit dismissal, for lack of jurisdiction, of a former conscientious objector's challenge to the statute at issue in Johnson v. Robinson, 415 U.S. 361 (1974) and remanded for reconsideration in light of that case.
Title I; Religious School Subsidization	Wheeler v. Barrera	417 U.S. 402 (1974)	6/1/1-1	Blackman, J.	State receiving Title I funds must provide "comparable" but "not identical" services to disadvantaged students in both public and private schools, or forfeit Title I funds.

(continues)

APPENDIX 3 *(continued)*

Issue	Case	Citation	Ratio[1]	Author of Opinion	Holding
Conscientious Objection; Taxes	*United States v. American Friends Service Committee*	419 U.S. 7 (1974)	8-1	Per curiam	Upheld collection of taxes from those conscientiously opposed to having their taxes support the military.
Religious School Subsidization: Textbooks	*Meek v. Pittenger*	421 U.S. 349 (1975) overruled by *Mitchell v. Helms*, 530 U.S. 793 (2000)	Pluralities	Stewart, J. (for the plurality)	State may loan textbooks, but not other various supplies and film, nor various counseling and other personnel, even if those were mandated by state policy.
Internal Church Governance	*Serbian Orthodox Diocese v. Milivojevich*	426 U.S. 696 (1976)	6/1-2	Brennan, J.	Internal church law must govern internal church matters, including removal from ecclesiastical posts; civil courts may not give marginal review to ecclesiastical decisions, even if they appear arbitrary, collusive, or fraudulent.
Construction Grants	*Roemer v. Maryland Public Works Board*	426 U.S. 736 (1976)	3/2-4	Blackmun, J. (for the plurality)	Upheld a state construction grant program that aided religious colleges alongside secular colleges.
Title VII; Employment	*Parker Seal Company v. Cummins*	429 U.S. 65 (1976), affirming, by an equally divided Court, 516 F.2d 544 (6th Cir. 1975)	4-4	Per curiam	Employer did not make sufficient effort to accommodate Sabbatarian.
State Motto	*Wooley v. Maynard*	430 U.S. 705 (1977)	Pluralities	Burger, C.J. (opinion of the Court)	State cannot require, upon pain of criminal sanctions, display of state motto upon vehicle license plates that violates owner's religious convictions.

(continues)

APPENDIX 3 *(continued)*

Issue	Case	Citation	Ratio[1]	Author of Opinion	Holding
Title VII; Employment Accommodation	*Trans World Airlines, Inc. v. Hardison*	432 U.S. 63 (1977)	7-2	White, J.	Employer's attempted accommodation of employee's religious beliefs was reasonable; no obligation to violate union contracts or incur additional costs without express congressional intent.
Religious School Subsidization	*Wolman v. Walter*	433 U.S. 229 (1977), overruled by *Mitchell v. Helms*, 530 U.S. 793 (2000)	Pluralities	Blackmun, J. (for the plurality)	State may provide various personnel, diagnostic services, and standardized testing but may not loan instructional materials to private schools or to parents or provide transportation for field trips by private schools.
Title VII; Employment Accommodation	*Parker Seal Company v. Cummins*	433 U.S. 903 (1977), vacating 429 U.S. 65 (1976)	8-0	Vacated and remanded	Vacated and remanded for consideration in light of *Trans World Airlines, Inc. v. Hardison*, 432 U.S. 63 (1977).
Religious School Subsidization	*New York v. Cathedral Academy*	434 U.S. 125 (1977)	6-3	Stewart, J.	Disallowed reimbursement of religious schools for state-mandated record keeping.
Clergy Disqualified from Public Office	*McDaniel v. Paty*	435 U.S. 618 (1978)	4/2/1-0	Burger, J. (for the plurality)	State constitutional prohibition against clergy holding political office is unconstitutional.
Labor Law	*National Labor Relations Board v. Catholic Bishop of Chicago*	440 U.S. 490 (1979)	5-4	Burger, C.J.	Denied jurisdiction to the NLRB over a Catholic school's teachers, based on the rights of a religious group to function separately from the state.

(continues)

APPENDIX 3 *(continued)*

Issue	Case	Citation	Ratio[1]	Author of Opinion	Holding
Church Property; Internal Church Governance	*Jones v. Wolf*	443 U.S. 595 (1979)	5-4	Blackmun, J.	Courts may decide intrachurch property disputes using "neutral principles of law," and thus avoid deferring all decisionmaking to internal church authorities.
Religious School Subsidization	*Committee for Public Education and Religious Liberty v. Regan*	444 U.S. 646 (1980)	5-4	White, J.	Upheld reimbursement of religious schools for "actual costs" of state-mandated tests and reporting.
Abortion and Religion	*Harris v. McRae*	448 U.S. 297 (1980)	5-4	Stewart, J.	Upheld congressional restrictions on Medicaid-funded abortions.
Ten Commandments in Public School	*Stone v. Graham*	449 U.S. 39 (1980)	5-4	Per curiam	Struck down state statute that required the posting of a plaque bearing the Ten Commandments on the wall of each public school classroom.
Unemployment Compensation Benefits	*Thomas v. Review Board, Indiana Employment Security Division*	450 U.S. 707 (1981)	7/1-1	Burger, C.J.	Government may not deny unemployment benefits to claimant who refused to accept employment, based on individual religious beliefs, at a job that produced parts that would be used in military armaments.
Religious Schools and Unemployment Compensation Taxes	*St. Martin Evangelical Lutheran Church v. South Dakota*	451 U.S. 772 (1981)	8/1-0	Blackmun, J.	The word "church" in the Federal Unemployment Tax Act exempting service performed in the employ of a church applies to schools that have no separate legal existence from a church.

(continues)

APPENDIX 3 *(continued)*

Issue	Case	Citation	Ratio[1]	Author of Opinion	Holding
Distribution of Religious Literature; Charitable Solicitation Law	*Heffron v. International Society for Krishna Consciousness*	452 U.S. 640 (1981)	Pluralities	White, J. (opinion of the Court)	Regulation requiring all persons and groups wishing to sell, exhibit, or distribute materials at a fair do so from a rented booth does not violate First Amendment rights of itinerant religious group.
Equal Access	*Widmar v. Vincent*	454 U.S. 263 (1981)	7/1-1	Powell, J.	When a state university creates a limited public forum open to voluntary student groups, religious groups must be given "equal access" to that forum.
Standing	*Valley Forge Christian College v. Americans United for Separation of Church and State*	454 U.S. 464 (1982)	5-4	Rehnquist, J.	Religious liberty litigant, as federal taxpayer, lacked standing to challenge federal donation of property to religious organizations.
Tax Exemption	*United States v. Lee*	455 U.S. 252 (1982)	8/1-0	Burger, C.J.	Denied free exercise exemption from social security taxes for Amish employer.
Prayer in Public School	*Treen v. Karen B.*	455 U.S. 913 (1982); affirming 653 F.2d 897 (5th Cir. 1981)	9-0	Affirmed on appeal	Affirmed, without comment, a Fifth Circuit opinion which struck down a statute authorizing student volunteers to lead prayer in public school classrooms.
Charitable Solicitation Law	*Larson v. Valente*	456 U.S. 228 (1982)	5-4	Brennan, J.	Disallowed state law requiring only certain religious organizations to make revenue reports.

(continues)

APPENDIX 3 (continued)

Issue	Case	Citation	Ratio[1]	Author of Opinion	Holding
Charitable Solicitation Law	Rusk v. Espinoza	456 U.S. 951 (1982); affirming 634 F.2d 477 (10th Cir. 1980)	7-2	Affirmed on Appeal	Affirmed, without comment, a Tenth Circuit opinion which struck down ordinance that required officials to distinguish between "religious" and "secular" religious activities of religious bodies for licensing and regulation purposes.
Federal Jurisdiction; Unemployment Tax	California v. Grace Brethren Church	457 U.S. 393 (1982)	7-2	O'Connor, J.	Federal District Court did not have jurisdiction to hear case involving state tax.
Zoning; Delegation of Civil Power	Larkin v. Grendel's Den	459 U.S. 116 (1982)	8-1	Burger, C.J.	States may not grant veto power to churches over whether a liquor license will be granted to a facility within 500 feet from the church property.
Tax Exempt Status	Bob Jones University v. United States	461 U.S. 574 (1983)	7/1-1	Burger, C.J.	Upheld IRS decision to remove federal tax exempt status from religious university that engaged in racial discrimination, on the basis of its religious convictions, in matriculation and employment decisions.
State Income Tax Deduction	Mueller v. Allen	463 U.S. 388 (1983)	5-4	Rehnquist, J.	Upheld state law that allowed parents of private school children to claim state income tax deductions for the costs of "tuition, transportation, and textbooks."
Legislative Prayer	Marsh v. Chambers	463 U.S. 783 (1983)	6-3	Burger, C.J.	Upheld, against disestablishment clause challenge, the state practice of appointing legislative chaplains to offer prayers at the General Assembly.

(continues)

APPENDIX 3 *(continued)*

Issue	Case	Citation	Ratio[1]	Author of Opinion	Holding
Religious Display	Lynch v. Donnelly	465 U.S. 668 (1984)	5-4	Burger, C.J.	Upheld government practice of displaying nativity scene as part of holiday display in city park.
Conscientious Objection	Wayte v. United States	470 U.S. 598 (1985)	7-2	Powell, J.	"Passive enforcement policy" and "beg policy" of Selective Service System do not violate First (or Fifth) Amendment.
Religious Display	Village of Scarsdale v. McCreary	471 U.S. 83 (1985); affirming, by an equally divided Court, 739 F.2d 716 (2d Cir. 1984)	4-4	Per curiam	Accommodation of displaying a nativity scene, at no expense to city, is not a violation of disestablishment clause.
Fair Labor Standards Act	Tony and Susan Alamo Foundation v. Secretary of Labor	471 U.S. 290 (1985)	9-0	White, J.	Application of Fair Labor Standards Act does not obstruct core religious functions of a foundation.
Moment of Silence in Public School	Wallace v. Jaffree	472 U.S. 38 (1985)	5/1-3	Stevens, J.	Struck down state law providing for moments of silence (for prayer or meditation) in public schools.
Driver's License Photograph	Jensen v. Quaring	472 U.S. 478 (1985), affirming, by an equally divided Court, 728 F.2d 1121 (8th Cir. 1984)	4-4	Per curiam	Struck down requirement that applicant submit to having color photograph taken to affix on driver's license as an unconstitutional burden on applicant's free exercise of her sincerely held religious beliefs.
Sabbath Laws	Estate of Thornton v. Caldor	472 U.S. 703 (1985)	8-1	Burger, C.J.	Struck down state law that allowed private sector employees to pick their Sabbath, which employers must accommodate.

(continues)

APPENDIX 3 (continued)

Issue	Case	Citation	Ratio[1]	Author of Opinion	Holding
Religious School Subsidization: Shared Time Programs	Grand Rapids School District v. Ball	473 U.S. 373 (1985)	Pluralities	Brennan, J. (opinion of the Court)	States may not lend public school personnel to teach remedial and enrichment courses in religious schools.
Title I Remedial Services	Aguilar v. Felton	473 U.S. 402 (1985), overruled by Agostini v. Felton 521 U.S. 203 (1997)	5-4	Brennan, J.	States may not use public school teachers to hold remedial educational programs to indigent children in classrooms leased from religious schools.
State Aid for Vocational Education at Religious College	Witters v. Washington Department of Services for the Blind	474 U.S. 481 (1986)	8/1-0	Marshall, J.	Upheld state program furnishing aid to a visually impaired student attending a Christian college for vocational education.
Standing	Bender v. Williamsport Area School District	475 U.S. 534 (1986)	5-4	Stevens, J.	School board member has no standing, in his capacity as a parent, to appeal a board decision affecting the religious rights of his child in the school.
Military Regulations	Goldman v. Weinberger	475 U.S. 503 (1986)	5-4	Rehnquist, J.	Military officer does not have free exercise right to wear his yarmulke on duty.
Social Security Number Requirement	Bowen v. Roy	476 U.S. 693 (1986)	Pluralities	Burger, C.J. (for the plurality)	Agency's use of social security number does not violate free exercise rights of native American, who believes such use would impair his child's spirit.

(continues)

APPENDIX 3 *(continued)*

Issue	Case	Citation	Ratio[1]	Author of Opinion	Holding
Federal Jurisdiction	*Ohio Civil Rights Commission v. Dayton Christian Schools*	477 U.S. 619 (1986)	5/4-0	Rehnquist, J.	Federal District Courts should abstain from adjudicating pending state proceedings as long as federal plaintiff has opportunity to litigate his constitutional claim.
Title VII; Employment Accommodation	*Ansonia Board of Education v. Philbrook*	479 U.S. 60 (1986)	Pluralities	Rehnquist, C.J. (opinion of the Court)	Employer not required to accept employee's preferred religious accommodation.
Unemployment Compensation Benefits	*Hobbie v. Unemployment Appeals Commission of Florida*	480 U.S. 136 (1987)	6/1/1-1	Brennan, J.	Government may not deny unemployment benefits to claimant, a new religious convert, who was discharged for refusal to work on her Sabbath.
Religious Discrimination	*Shaare Tefila Congregation v. Cobb*	481 U.S. 615 (1987)	9-0	White, J.	Jews may rely on racial clause of civil rights statute for cause of action against desecrators of synagogue.
Prisoner's Rights	*O'Lone v. Estate of Shabazz*	482 U.S. 342 (1987)	5-4	Rehnquist, C.J.	Denying free exercise accommodation for Muslim prisoner to engage in collective Friday worship.
Overbreadth Doctrine	*Airport Commissioners of Los Angeles v. Jews for Jesus*	482 U.S. 569 (1987)	9-0	O'Connor, J.	Airport regulation banning all "first amendment activities" within a public (or nonpublic) forum is a violation of the free speech clause.
Creationism in Public School	*Edwards v. Aguillard*	482 U.S. 578 (1987)	6/1-2	Brennan, J.	Struck down state statute that required, in public schools, teaching of both creation and evolution, if a theory of origins was taught at all.

(continues)

APPENDIX 3 *(continued)*

Issue	Case	Citation	Ratio[1]	Author of Opinion	Holding
Employment Discrimination	*Corporation of the Presiding Bishop of the Church of Jesus Christ of Latter-Day Saints v. Amos*	483 U.S. 327 (1987)	5/2/1/1-0	White, J.	Upheld exemption of religious school from Civil Rights prohibition against religious discrimination; religious employer not required to retain employee who has lapsed from its faith.
Standing	*Karcher v. May*	484 U.S. 72 (1987)	8/1-0	O'Connor, J.	State legislators cannot appeal a disestablishment case involving a moment of silence law for which they voted, but which the legislature has chosen not to appeal.
Native American Rights	*Lyng v. Northwest Indian Cemetery Protective Association*	485 U.S. 439 (1988)	5-3	O'Connor, J.	Construction of road through section of national forest regarded as sacred ground by three tribes does not violate free exercise clause; American Indian Religious Freedom Act provides no cause of action.
Unemployment Compensation Benefits	*Employment Division, Oregon v. Smith (I)*	485 U.S. 660 (1988)	5-3	Stevens, J.	State must determine whether religious use of peyote is legal under state law.
Standing	*United States Catholic Conference v. Abortion Rights Mobilization*	487 U.S. 72 (1988)	8-1	Kennedy, J.	A nonparty witness held in contempt had standing to challenge federal court's jurisdiction over case.
Religious Social Agency Subsidization	*Bowen v. Kendrick*	487 U.S. 589 (1988)	5-4	Rehnquist, C.J.	Upheld federal funding of Catholic counseling centers for pregnant teenagers, in implementation of the Adolescent Family Life Act.

(continues)

APPENDIX 3 *(continued)*

Issue	Case	Citation	Ratio[1]	Author of Opinion	Holding
Tax Exemption	*Texas Monthly v. Bullock*	489 U.S. 1 (1989)	3/2/1-3	Brennan, J. (for the plurality)	State sales tax exemption exclusively for religious periodicals violates disestablishment clause.
Unemployment Compensation Benefits	*Frazee v. Illinois Department of Employment Security*	489 U.S. 829 (1989)	9-0	White, J.	State may not deny unemployment benefits to claimant who refused to take a job that might require him to work on Sunday.
Tax Deductions	*Hernandez v. Commissioner of Internal Revenue*	490 U.S. 680 (1989)	5-2	Marshall, J.	Upheld denial of charitable deduction for contributions to the Church of Scientology, given in return for religious services.
Religious Display	*County of Allegheny v. ACLU*	492 U.S. 573 (1989)	Pluralities	Blackmun, J. (for the plurality)	Disallowed county's practice of allowing a privately funded nativity scene in front of its courthouse but upheld the display of a menorah on courthouse grounds.
Tax Exemption	*Jimmy Swaggart Ministries v. Board of Equalization of California*	493 U.S. 378 (1990)	9-0	O'Connor, J.	Levy of state sales and use taxes on religious articles is not a prior restraint.
Unemployment Compensation Benefits	*Employment Division v. Smith (II)*	494 U.S. 872 (1990)	5/1-3	Scalia, J.	Denial of unemployment compensation benefits to Native American who was discharged for sacramental use of peyote, a proscribed narcotic, does not violate free exercise clause.

(continues)

APPENDIX 3 *(continued)*

Issue	Case	Citation	Ratio[1]	Author of Opinion	Holding
Public Safety Exemption	*Minnesota v. Hershberger*	495 U.S. 901 (1990)	7-2	Vacating and remanding on appeal	Vacated a state supreme court holding that Amish were entitled to free exercise exemption from a law requiring them to place reflective triangles on their buggies for public safety reasons and remanded for reconsideration in light of *Employment Division v. Smith (II)*, 494 U.S. 872 (1990).
Tax Deductions	*Davis v. United States*	495 U.S. 472 (1990)	9-0	O'Connor, J.	Upheld denial of charitable deduction for contribution in return for religious services.
Equal Access	*Board of Education of the Westside Community Schools v. Mergens*	496 U.S. 226 (1990)	4/2/2-1	O'Connor, J. (for the plurality)	Equal Access Act, which applies *Widmar v. Vincent*, 454 U.S. 263 (1981) rule to public high schools, does not violate disestablishment clause.
Title VII; Employment Discrimination	*EEOC v. Arabian American Oil Co.*	499 U.S. 244 (1991)	5/1-3	Rehnquist, C.J.	Nondiscrimination in employment rules of Title VII do not apply outside U.S. to U.S. employers who employ U.S. citizens abroad.
Graduation Prayers in Public School	*Lee v. Weisman*	505 U.S. 577 (1991)	5-4	Kennedy, J.	Ecumenical prayer by Jewish rabbi at a public middle school graduation ceremony violates disestablishment clause.
Forum Analysis; Religious Solicitation	*International Society for Krishna Consciousness v. Lee*	505 U.S. 672 (1992)	Pluralities	Rehnquist, C.J. (opinion of the Court)	An airport terminal operated by a public authority is a nonpublic forum, and therefore a ban on distribution of religious literature and solicitation need only satisfy a reasonableness standard; the ban on solicitation here is reasonable.

(continues)

APPENDIX 3 *(continued)*

Issue	Case	Citation	Ratio[1]	Author of Opinion	Holding
Distribution of Religious Literature	Lee v. International Society for Krishna Consciousness	505 U.S. 830 (1992)	5-4	Per curiam	Ban on distribution of religious materials in airport terminals is invalid under First Amendment, as it does not satisfy a reasonableness standard.
Mootness; IRS Summons	Church of Scientology of California v. United States	506 U.S. 9 (1992)	9-0	Stevens, J.	Compliance with an enforcement order to surrender taped conversations does not render moot an appeal concerning the lawfulness of the search claim.
Equal Access	Lamb's Chapel v. Center Moriches Union Free School District	508 U.S. 384 (1993)	6/2/1-0	White, J.	Public school that opens its school facilities, during nonschool time, to various voluntary community groups may not exclude only those with religious viewpoint; equal access must be given.
Ritual Sacrifice of Animals	Church of the Lukumi Babalu Aye, Inc. v. City of Hialeah	508 U.S. 520 (1993)	9-0, but concurring opinions	Kennedy, J. (opinion of the Court, except as to Part II.A.2)	Local ordinance discriminating against ritual sacrifice of animals violates the free exercise clause.
Religious School Subsidy: Interpreter	Zobrest v. Catalina Foothills School District	509 U.S. 1 (1993)	5-4	Rehnquist, C.J.	State's provision of an interpreter to disabled student at religious high school does not violate disestablishment clause.
Delegation of Civil Power	Board of Education of Kiryas Joel Village School District v. Grumet	512 U.S. 687 (1994)	4/1/1-3	Souter, J. (for the plurality)	State's creation of a single public school district within an exclusively Satmar Hasidic community violates disestablishment clause.

(continues)

APPENDIX 3 *(continued)*

Issue	Case	Citation	Ratio[1]	Author of Opinion	Holding
Religious Display	*Capitol Square Review and Advisory Board v. Pinette*	515 U.S. 753 (1995)	4/3-2	Scalia J. (for the plurality)	City may not ban private display of KKK cross in an otherwise open public forum.
Equal Access	*Rosenberger v. University of Virginia*	515 U.S. 819 (1995)	5-4	Kennedy, J.	State university must grant equal access to funding for voluntary religious student groups as for voluntary nonreligious student groups.
Title I Remedial Services	*Agostini v. Felton*	521 U.S. 203 (1997)	5-4	O'Connor, J.	Overturned *Aguilar v. Felton*, (1985); the mere presence of a state employee in a religious institution is not per se unconstitutional, and thus the state may provide Title I remedial services to students at religious schools.
Free Exercise Standard of Review	*City of Boerne v. Flores*	521 U.S. 507 (1997)	5/1-3	Kennedy, J.	Religious Freedom Restoration Act (1993), which required use of the compelling state interest test for free exercise cases, declared unconstitutional, as applied to the state.
Religious School Subsidy	*Mitchell v. Helms*	530 U.S. 793 (2000)	4/2/3	Thomas, J.	Federally-funded state policy to lend educational materials directly to public and private schools does not violate the disestablishment clause simply because many of the private schools receiving aid are religiously affiliated; *Meek v. Pittinger* (1975) and *Wolman v. Walter* (1977) overruled.
Student Prayer at Public School Football Games	*Santa Fe Independent School District v. Doe*	530 U.S. 290 (2000)	6-3	Stevens, J.	School policy instituting student-led, student-initiated "invocations" prior to public high school football games violates the disestablishment clause.

(continues)

APPENDIX 3 *(continued)*

Issue	Case	Citation	Ratio[1]	Author of Opinion	Holding
Equal Access	Good News Club v. Milford Central School	533 U.S. 98 (2001)	4/1/1/2	Thomas J.	Public middle school's exclusion of Christian children's club from meeting on school property after hours was unconstitutional viewpoint discrimination, and was not required to avoid establishment of religion.
Licensing	Watchtower Bible and Tract Society v. Village of Stratton	122 S. Ct. 2080 (2002)	6-2/1	Stevens, J.	Ordinance requiring door-to-door solicitors and canvassers to obtain a permit containing one's name violates constitutional free speech and free exercise rights because of its breadth and unprecedented nature, and is not narrowly enough tailored to the stated interest of preventing fraud, crime, and privacy intrusion.
Religious School Subsidy: Voucher	Zelman v. Simmons-Harris	122 S.Ct. 2460 (2002)	5-4	Rehnquist, C.J.	School voucher program, enacted for valid secular purpose of providing educational assistance to poor children in demonstrably failing public school system, does not violate the disestablishment clause, because program was neutral toward religion and government aid to religious schools was the result of parents' "true private choices."
State Scholarship Program	Locke v. Davey	124 S.Ct. 1307 (2004)	7-2	Rehnquist, C.J.	State scholarship program established to assist payment of academically-gifted students' post-secondary education expenses for all students, except those pursuing a theology degree, does not violate the free exercise clause.
Pledge of Allegiance/ Standing	Elk Grove Unified School District v. Newdow	124 S. Ct. 2301 (2004)	5/1/1/1-0	Stevens, J	Non-custodial father lacked standing to bring disestablishment case on behalf of his minor daughter challenging school district's policy that required teacher-led recitation of the Pledge of Allegiance, with phrase "One Nation Under God."

INDEX

Abington Township School District v. Schempp, 189f, 193, 205, 206, 285

Abortion rights, 292

Absolute monarchy, 14

Accommodationism or accommodation of religion, xxi, xxii, xxiv, 34, 44, 46, 47, 60, 121, 174–175, 188, 191–193, 197, 198–199, 208–209, 245, 291, 293, 296. *See also* Disestablishment of religion; Religious pluralism

Act of 1649, 16–17

Act of Succession, 11

Adams, Jaspar, 31

Adams, John, xv, 3, 14, 22, 26, 33, 34–35, 42, 47–48, 49, 54, 55, 63n1, 67n102, 248, 250, 253, 255

Adams, Zabdiel, 25

Adolescent Family Life Act, 194, 298

African and African-American religions, 60, 100, 118, 119–120, 145, 244–245

African Charter on Human and People's Rights (1981), 241

Agostini test, 188, 199, 200, 201, 217–218

Agostini v. Felton, 195, 215–216, 219, 302

Aguilar v. Felton, 189, 189f, 195–196, 215–217, 296

Aid to religion, 24, 31, 112, 113, 118, 138, 187, 189, 190, 192, 195, 196, 199, 202–203, 206, 209–210, 213–220. *See also* Disestablishment of religion; Free exercise of religion

AIRFA. *See* American Indian Religious Freedom Act

Airport Commissioners of Los Angeles v. Jews for Jesus, 297

Alabama, Constitution of, 15–16, 109, 114, 267

Alfred, King, 6

Ambrose, Bishop of Milan, 6

American Convention on Human Rights, 241

American Indian Religious Freedom Act (AIRFA), 166, 175–176

American Protective Association, 113

American Protestant Association, 113

American Revolution, 16, 28, 29

American Secular Union, 113

Ames, Fisher, 86, 87, 91, 263

Amish, 11, 162, 288, 293, 300

Amor, Abdelfattah, 248

Anabaptism and Anabaptists, 1, 11–12, 15–16, 19n38, 26, 27, 52, 55, 132. *See also* Evangelicalism

Anastasius, Emperor, 6

Anglicanism or Anglicans, 11, 15–17, 22, 25, 32, 58, 64n19, 72, 93, 105n73, 117, 120, 120t, 124n37, 249

Annals of Congress, 80

Ansonia Board of Education v. Philbrook, 182n121, 297

Antifederalists, 83

Arizona, Constitution of, 110, 123n28, 267

Arkansas, Constitution of, 111, 267
Arlan's Department Store v. Kentucky, 285
Arms, right to bear, 86. *See also* Pacifism
Arthur, Thomas C., xiii
Articles of Confederation (1787), 72, 74, 75
Arver v. United States, 129, 149, 174, 273
Assemblies of God, 168
Atheism and atheists, 30, 35, 47, 145, 159
Augustine, Bishop of Hippo, 5–6
Avignon, 9

Backus, Isaac, 21, 22, 27, 28, 29, 37n32, 47, 49, 61
Bacon, Francis, xxi, xxii
Baker v. Nachtrieb, 271
Baltimore, Lord, 16
Bankruptcy, 151
Baptism, 8, 12
Baptist Declaration (1776), 29
Baptists, 11, 22, 23, 25, 27, 28–29, 34, 49, 52, 56, 61, 67n85, 112, 117, 119, 120, 121, 155, 159, 163, 167, 202. *See also* Evangelicalism
Becket, Thomas, 1
Bender v. Williamsport Area School District, 296
Benefit of clergy, 9, 48, 55, 62, 82–83, 105n73
Benefits, state, 23, 28–29, 34, 159, 163, 167, 202, 292
Benson, Charles, 85, 94, 99, 130–131
Berg, Thomas C., xiii
Berman, Harold J., xiii
Bible, 1, 6, 8, 11, 25, 28–29, 34, 35, 51, 52, 58, 67n85, 72, 74, 93, 112, 115, 118, 135, 155, 158, 172, 205, 226, 280, 282, 285
Bigamy, 12, 110, 127, 140n8. *See also* Mormonism and Mormons
Bigotry, 2, 44, 54, 73, 140

Bill for the Establishment of Religious Freedom, 93, 108–109. *See also* Jefferson, Thomas
Bill of Rights, 77, 79, 81, 86, 88–89, 91, 101, 130, 136, 147. *See also* First Amendment; U.S. Constitution
Blackstone, William, 1–2
Blaine Amendment, 107, 113, 121n1, 138. *See also* Education
Board of Education of Kiryas Joel Village School District v. Grumet, 189f, 199, 234, 301
Board of Education of the Westside Community Schools v. Mergens, 189f, 197, 223, 300
Board of Education v. Allen, 208–209, 286
Bob Jones University v. United States, 244–245, 294
Bodin, Jean, 14
Boniface VIII, Pope, 8
Book of Commandments (Smith, J.), 126. *See also* Mormonism and Mormons
The Book of Common Prayer (Church of England), 11, 58
Book of Mormon (Smith, J.), 126. *See also* Mormonism
Boudinot, Elias, 87, 92, 98, 99
Bouldin v. Alexander, 134, 271
Bowen v. Kendrick, 189f, 194, 298
Bowen v. Roy, 165, 167, 176, 243, 296
Bradfield v. Roberts, 125, 131, 132, 138, 209, 272
Braunfeld v. Brown, 284
Brethren, 73
Buddhism, 69n130, 100, 120
Burgh, James, 52–53
Burke, Aedanus, 92, 104n45

Cairo Declaration on Human Rights in Islam (1990), 241
California, Constitution of, 267
California v. Grace Brethren Church, 294
Calvin, John, 1, 10, 12, 52

Calvinism and Calvinists, 11–12, 14, 16, 22, 23, 25, 67n102, 120, 120t, 124n37. *See also* Puritanism
Canon law. *See* Catholicism
Cantwell v. Connecticut, xix, 107, 126, 136–137, 138, 149, 152–155, 157, 158, 160, 161, 162, 163, 169, 177, 234, 251–252, 274
Capitol Square Review and Advisory Board v. Pinette, 197, 200, 224, 302
Carr, Spencer, xiii
Carroll, Charles, 88
Carroll, Daniel, 82, 97
Carter, Stephen, 226
Catherine of Aragon, 11
Catholicism (Roman) and (Roman) Catholics, 1, 2
  campaign against, 113, 117, 121
  canon laws/courts for, 7–9, 14
  federal office for, 78–79, 160, 222–223, 255, 291
  as frontier settlers, 119, 257
  Henry VIII's break with, 11
  heresy under, 4, 9
  influence of, 2, 52, 119, 120, 256
  as a minority, 121
  papal authority for, 9, 14
  Peace of Westphalia for, 14
  persecution under, 2–3, 35, 47, 69n132
  population as, 120t, 124n37
  Quebec Act for, 73
  religious education for, 135
  separatism for, 53, 204–205
  state benefits for, 23, 28–29, 34, 159, 163, 167, 202
  subordination of, 9–10
  tyranny of, 54
Cato's Letters, 42, 54
Chamberlain v. Public Instruction Board, 285
Chaplains, 34, 38n41, 61, 72, 74, 78, 92, 93, 95, 96, 117, 118, 191, 213, 254. *See also* Disestablishment of religion
Chaplinsky v. New Hampshire, 275

Chapter 2. *See* Education Consolidation and Improvement Act
Charitable Solicitation Law, 293, 294
Charlemagne, Emperor, 6
Charles I, King of England, 15
Chatwin v. United States, 278
Chauncy, Charles, 23
Checks and balances, 35, 47, 77
Christianity and Christians, xix, 2, 3–4, 5–6, 8, 37n32, 47, 52, 60, 82–83, 117, 120
Church autonomy, xx–xxi, xxiii, 28, 38n41, 46, 53–54, 166–167, 169
Church of England, 11, 15, 16
Church of Jesus Christ of Latter-Day Saints. *See* Mormonism
Church of Lukumi Babalu Aye, Inc. v. City of Hialeah, 167–168, 177, 301
Church of Scientology of California v. United States, 301
Church of the Holy Trinity v. United States, 272
Citizenship, naturalized, 129
City of Boerne v. Flores, 150, 176, 177, 183n131, 302
City of God (Augustine), 5
Civic ceremony, 158. *See also* Jehovah's Witness
Civic Republicans. *See* Republicanism
Civil religion. *See* Public religion
Civil rights, 28, 45, 46, 48, 49, 62, 75, 77, 81, 91, 133, 160, 210. *See also* First Amendment
Civil Rights Act, 174
Civil War, 134
Clergy, political office for, 78–79, 160, 222–223, 255, 291
Cleveland v. United States, 278
Cloud, A. Morgan, xiii
Cochran v. Board of Education, 208, 209, 210
Cochran v. Louisiana Board of Education, 274
Coercion/compulsion of religion, xxi, xxiv, 28, 53, 58, 62, 109, 186,

188, 192, 197–198, 201,
221–222. *See also*
Disestablishment of religion
Coleman v. City of Griffin, 274
Colorado, Constitution of, 109, 267
Commerce clause, 151
*Committee for Public Education and
Religious Liberty v. Regan*, 292
*Committee for Public Education v.
Nyquist*, 210, 214, 289
Concordat of Bologna, 9
Condorcet, Marquis de, 29, 53
Confessional pluralism, 46–47, 110.
See also Religious pluralism
Confucianism, 120
Congregationalism, 51
Connecticut, Constitution of, 61, 76,
110, 111, 117, 122n12, 267
Conscientious objection, 138, 273, 274,
277, 278, 279, 281, 283, 286,
287, 289, 290, 292, 295. *See also*
Pacifism
Constantine the Great, 2, 4
Constitutional Convention (1787), xv,
22, 35, 49, 50, 61, 71, 76–102,
249
Constitutionalism, 250–251
Continental Congress (1774-1789), xv,
34, 71–76, 79, 91, 92, 93, 99, 130
Contractarian political philosophy,
31–32
Cooper v. Pate, 285
Corporate free exercise, 235. *See also*
Religious group rights
*Corporation of the Presiding Bishop of
the Church of Jesus Christ of
Latter-Day Saints v. Amos*, 162,
174–175, 244, 298
Corpus Iuris Civilis (Roman law), 5
Cotton, John, 23
County of Allegheny v. ACLU, 197,
299
Cox v. New Hampshire, 275
Cranmer, Thomas, 10
Creationism Act, 207
Cruz v. Beto, 288

Cuius regio eius religio (whose region,
his religion), 10–11
Cumings, Henry, 43, 64n19
Cummings v. Missouri, 134, 271
Cummins, Francis, 59, 68n121

Danbury Baptist Association, 56
Davis v. Beason, 127–128, 272
Davis v. United States, 300
Decalogues, 206, 207, 212, 213, 254,
257, 259n9, 292
Declaration of Independence, 22, 34,
76
*A Defense of the Constitutions of
Government in the United States
of America* (Adams), 3
Deists and Deism, 2, 35, 47, 100
Delaware, Constitution of, 44, 49–50,
51, 58, 109, 111, 117, 267
Dewey v. Reynolds Metals Co., 287
Dickinson, John, 74–75
The Dictates of the Pope (Gregory VII),
7
Disciples, 119
Disestablishment of religion, xx, 17,
27, 41, 57–61, 61–62, 71, 89, 90,
94, 100, 101, 102, 105n68, 125,
131, 138, 139, 144, 160,
185–227, 189t, 252, 272. *See also*
Establishment of religion; Liberty
of conscience
accommodations and, xxiv, 34, 44,
60, 121, 174–176, 183n121, 188,
189, 191–194, 196–201,
208–209, 225–226, 243,
244–245, 255, 257, 290, 291, 301
aid to religion, 24, 31, 112, 113,
118, 138, 187, 189, 190, 192,
195, 196, 199, 202–203, 206,
209–210, 213–220, 288, 296
Bible reading and, 1, 6, 8, 11, 25,
28–29, 34, 35, 51, 58, 67n85, 72,
74, 93, 112, 115, 118, 135, 145,
155–156, 158, 172, 205, 206,
208, 213, 226, 245, 280, 282, 285
Blaine Amendment for, 107, 113,
121n1

case and controversy requirements, 145

chaplains, 34, 38n41, 61, 72, 74, 78, 92, 93, 95, 96, 117, 118, 191, 213, 254

coercion/compulsion and, xxi, xxiv, 28, 53, 58, 62, 109, 186, 188, 192, 197–198, 201, 221–222

equal access doctrine for, xxi, 170–174, 175, 182n106, 182n109, 197, 222, 223, 293, 300, 301, 302, 303

moment of silence and, 195, 207, 226, 227n9, 295, 298

neutrality and, xxi–xxii, xxiv, 152, 163–169, 182n106, 185, 188, 193–196, 198–199, 206, 208, 218–220

public schools and, 76, 92–93, 109, 112, 117–118, 121, 121n1, 123, 203–211

racial discrimination and, 244–245

release time and, 174, 191, 203, 204, 279, 281, 282

religious employers and, xx, 162, 174, 183n121, 213, 244, 272

religious schools and, 4–5, 14, 24, 34, 43, 47, 60, 61, 73, 111, 119, 162, 203–211, 230n89

religious symbols, 9, 118, 194, 197, 245

remedial education and, 195, 199, 210, 215–216, 255

school prayer and, 172, 173, 197, 198, 205, 207–208, 212, 213, 220–222, 226, 230n82, 245, 258n9, 285, 293, 300

school transportation for, 112, 123n20, 200, 208, 279, 281

separationism for, 5, 25, 121, 202–203, 204–205, 209, 212–213, 214, 243

social services and, 62, 192, 211

tax exemption and, 34, 55, 61, 113, 118, 123n26, 146, 159, 166–167, 174, 179nn21–22, 187, 190–191, 194, 195, 200, 213, 214, 244, 253, 272, 287, 293, 294, 299

tax subsidies and, 61, 118, 187, 190–191, 202, 211–212, 287, 288, 289, 290, 291, 292, 296, 301, 302

teaching creationism/evolution for, 186, 207, 286, 297

textbook loan and, 200, 208–211, 274, 286, 288, 290

Dissent, Christian, 9, 11, 14–16, 28, 29, 43, 57, 58, 60, 64n19, 93, 121

Dissertation on the Canon and the Feudal Law (Adams), 54

Doremus v. Board of Education, 280, 282

Douglas v. City of Jeannette, 277

Dreisbach, Daniel L., xiii, 56

Dutch Pietists, 12

Dutch Protestants, 13

Dwight, Timothy, 33

Eagles v. Samuels, 278

Eastern Europe, 120

Edict of Fontainebleau, 14–15

Edict of Milan, 4

Edict of Nantes, 14

Education. *See also* Separation of church and state
discrimination in, 109, 298
disestablishment clause for, 203–208
exemptions for, 113
government aid to, 188, 199, 200, 201, 217–219, 296
government sponsorship of, 24, 34, 35, 60, 68n121, 95, 96, 112, 114, 116
international norms for, 245
Northwest Ordinance for, 34, 75–76, 92–93, 112
religion and, 4, 7, 9, 11, 46, 73, 93, 112, 117, 118, 121, 135, 143, 162, 168, 185, 188, 203–208, 210, 213–220, 230n89
right to, 12
separatism in, 53, 204–205
for Sioux Indians, 131–132

transportation for, 112, 123n20, 200, 208, 279, 281

Education Consolidation and Improvement Act, 217–218

Edwards, Jonathan, 22

Edwards v. Aguillard, 207, 297

EEOC v. Arabian American Oil Co., 300

Elementary and Secondary Education Act (Title I), 196, 215–217, 289, 296, 302. *See also* Education; Schools

Elk Grove Unified School Dist. v. Newdow, 227n.9, 258–259nn.9,11, 303

Ellsworth, Oliver, 33, 34, 88

Employment Division, Oregon v. Smith, 96, 149–150, 151, 164, 167, 168, 169, 174, 175, 176, 177, 200–201, 243, 248n14, 298, 299

Endorsement, 196–197. *See also* Accommodationism; Disestablishment of religion

Engel v. Vitale, 205, 206, 285

England or Great Britain, xxi, 11, 14, 15, 29, 58, 71–72, 73, 74, 75, 101, 120

English Levellers, 1

Enlightenment, xxi, 22–23, 29–33, 35, 41, 43, 46, 47, 52, 55, 60, 71, 101, 113, 139, 188–190, 249

Enthusiasts, 25, 27

Episcopalianism and Episcopalians. *See* Anglicanism

Epperson v. Arkansas, 186, 286

Equal Access Act, 175, 197, 223

Equal access doctrine, xxi, 170–174, 175, 182n106, 182n109, 197, 222, 223, 293, 300, 301, 302, 303. *See also* Freedom of Speech

Equal Employment Opportunity Commission, 145, 300

Establishment of religion, 56, 57–61, 71, 81, 82, 83, 86, 87, 88, 89–90, 91, 93, 94, 95, 96, 102, 107, 114, 121n1, 123n28, 138–139, 157,

174, 185–190, 206–207, 214–215, 219–222, 245. *See also* Blaine Amendment; Disestablishment of religion

Estate of Thornton v. Caldor, 295

European Charter on Human Rights, 241

Evangelicalism and Evangelicals, xxi, 22, 23, 26–29, 32, 33, 35, 37n32, 41, 42, 43, 46–47, 52, 55, 60, 68n103, 71, 73, 88, 101, 113, 117, 119, 120, 120t, 121, 124n37, 139, 188–190, 249, 256. *See also* Enlightenment

Evans, Israel, 28

Everson v. Board of Education, xix, 107, 123n20, 126, 138–139, 190, 202, 204, 208, 213, 225, 234, 251–252, 279, 281

Fair Labor Standards Act, 295

Family, importance of, 13, 47–48, 65n50

Farrington v. Tokushige, 208, 273

Federal Fair Housing Act, 174–175

Federal Unemployment Tax Act, 292

Federalism, xx, xxii, 56, 139, 144, 151, 152, 270

Federalist Papers (Hamilton; Madison), 48

Fifteenth Amendment, 119–120

First Amendment
  application of, to states, 251
  civil rights under, 48, 81, 91
  Constitutional protection of, xxii, 13, 17, 32, 50, 100, 152, 250–251, 255
  drafting of, xxi, xxiii, 46, 50, 76–102, 261–264
  enforcement of, xxiii, 137
  federalism under, xx, xxii, 56, 139, 144, 151
  guarantees/principles of, xix, xxi, xxii, xxiii, xxiv, 45, 51, 59, 61, 91, 98, 101, 102, 185
  interpretation of, xix, 89, 91, 233

religion clause of, 21–22, 45, 71,
  87–93
First Session of Congress (1789), 21,
  59, 71, 79, 80, 81, 92, 93, 94, 95,
  97, 98, 99, 100, 102, 263–264
*First Unitarian Church v. County of
  Los Angeles,* 284
Flag salute, 138, 158, 258, 275, 277
Florida, Constitution of, 122n7, 268
Follett v. Town of McCormick, 277
Fourteenth Amendment, xix, 102,
  119–120, 126, 143, 147, 151, 153
Fowler v. Rhode Island, 155, 280, 282
France, 29
  Concordat of Bologna, 9
  Edict of Fontainebleau, 14–15
  Edict of Nantes, 14
Franklin, Benjamin, 29, 34, 42, 77–78
*Frazee v. Illinois Employment Security
  Department,* 167, 299
Free Church Evangelicals, 12, 22, 52,
  67n85
Free exercise of religion, 4, 9, 12, 16,
  17, 21, 29, 32, 41, 42, 44, 45–46,
  48, 50, 51, 54, 56, 58, 71, 73, 74,
  75, 80, 83, 86, 87, 88, 89, 90,
  96–97, 98–99, 100, 101, 102,
  107–110, 114, 117, 121n1,
  126–129, 144–178, 148f, 150,
  295, 296
  case and controversy requirements
    for, 145
  child labor and, 156
  compulsory school attendance and,
    162
  equal access doctrine for, xxi,
    170–174, 175, 182n106,
    182n109, 197, 222, 223, 293,
    300, 301, 302, 303
  flag salute and, 138, 158, 258, 275,
    277
  intrachurch disputes over property
    under, 11, 13, 14, 53, 133, 161,
    164, 286, 287, 292
  neutrality in, xxi–xxii, xxiv, 152,
    163–169, 182n106, 185, 188,
    193–196, 198–199, 206, 208,
    218–220
  pledge of allegiance and, 158, 198,
    205–206, 258n9, 303
  political participation under, 1,
    78–79, 160, 222–223, 255, 274,
    275, 276, 277, 278, 291, 293,
    300, 301
  prisoner's rights for, 143, 145, 146,
    151, 165, 178n3, 248n14, 285,
    288, 297
  proselytism as, 146, 153, 173
  racial discrimination and, 244–245
  religious attire and, 145
  religious expression and, xxiii, 62,
    146, 152–157, 177, 185, 188,
    222–224,
  ritual slaughter and, 167–168, 177,
    301
  sincerity test for, 146
  standing requirements for, 280, 282,
    286, 293, 298
  tax exemption and, 34, 55, 61, 113,
    118, 123n26, 146, 159, 166–167,
    174, 179nn21–22, 187, 190–191,
    194, 195, 200, 213, 214, 244,
    253, 272, 287, 293, 294, 299
  tax subsidies and, 61, 118, 187,
    190–191, 202, 211–212, 287,
    288, 289, 290, 291, 292, 296,
    301, 302
  tests for, xx, 36, 49, 57, 60, 66n56,
    75, 78, 101, 104nn33, 109–110,
    124n34, 129, 130, 138, 152, 159,
    191, 254, 271, 278, 284
  unemployment compensation and,
    145, 146, 149, 151, 159, 167,
    179n22, 200, 285, 292, 297, 298,
    299
Freedom of assembly, 28, 46, 61, 88,
  97, 99, 117, 149, 152, 177
Freedom of press, 46, 62, 63n1, 79, 81,
  85, 86, 88, 97, 98, 99, 103n29,
  117, 136, 152, 177
Freedom of speech, 9, 46, 62, 81, 85,
  86, 88, 97, 99, 101, 117, 136,
  149, 152, 156, 169–174,

176–177, 224, 255, 275, 279, 280, 281, 282, 297. *See also* Liberty of conscience
French Huguenots, 12
French Revolution, 53
Fundamental liberty under Fourteenth Amendment, 135–140

Gallagher v. Crown Kosher, 284
Gallicanism, 14–15
Gara v. United States, 279, 281
Gaustad, Edwin, 119
Gedicks, Frederick Mark, xiii
Gelasius, Pope, 6
Georgia, Constitution of, 46, 49–50, 107, 268
Germany, 9, 10, 11, 15, 74, 120, 139–140
    Peace of Augsburg, 10–11, 14
    Peace of Westphalia, 14
Gerry, Eldridge, 77, 82, 83, 84, 91, 95, 99
Gibbons v. District of Columbia, 272
Gillette v. United States, 287
Girouard v. United States, 130, 278
Goesele v. Bimeler, 272
Goldman v. Weinberger, 164–165, 167, 175, 296
Gonzales v. United States, 283
Good News Club v. Milford Central School, 172, 175, 189f, 200, 259n9, 303
Grand Rapids School District v. Ball, 295
Great Awakening (ca. 1720-1780), 26–27
Great Law of 1682, 17. *See also* Penn, William
Gregory VII, Pope, 7
Gunn, T. Jeremy, xiii

Hamburger, Philip, 57
Hamilton, Alexander, 77, 104n33
Hamilton v. Board of Regents, 136
Hamilton v. Regents of the University of California, 274
Harmony Society, 132–133

Harris v. McRae, 292
Heffron v. International Society for Krishna Consciousness, 293
Henry VIII, 11
Heresy, 4, 6, 11, 43, 134, 157
Hernandez v. Commissioner of Internal Revenue, 299
Hernandez v. Veterans' Administration, 289
Higher Education Facilities Act, 209
Hinduism, 69n130, 120
Hobbie v. Unemployment Appeals Commission, 297
Holiness Church, 119, 120
Holland. *See* Netherlands
Holmes, Oliver Wendell, Jr., 225, 233, 254
Holocaust, 139
Human rights, xxii, 62, 235–237, 241, 244
Hume, David, 29
Hunt v. McNair, 288
Huntington, Benjamin, 50, 82, 94, 95, 97–98, 100
Hus, John, 1
Hutchinson, Anne, 25
Hutterites, 11

Idaho, Constitution of, 109, 110, 123n28, 268
Illinois, Constitution of, 112–113, 268
Immigration, 25, 120
In God We Trust, 118
In re Summers, 277
Incorporation doctrine, 28, 31, 60, 102, 111, 117, 132, 135–140, 143, 151
Indiana, Constitution of, 108, 109, 268
Integration of religious liberty, xiii, xxii, 1–2
International Covenant on Civil and Political Rights (1966), 236–238, 241
International norms of religious liberty, xxii, 62, 235, 241–246
International Society for Krishna Consciousness v. Lee, 300

Intrachurch disputes over property, 11, 13, 14, 53, 133, 161, 164, 286, 287, 292
Iowa, Constitution of, 109, 114, 268
Iredell, James, 2, 49, 76–77
Ireland, 11, 120
Islam and Muslims, 2, 7, 9–10, 23, 28–30, 34, 69n130, 78–79, 100, 118, 145, 146, 151–152, 159, 163, 165, 167, 202, 244, 253

James I, 15
Jamison v. Texas, 154, 275
Jay, John, 54
Jefferson, Thomas, xv, xix, 2, 9, 21, 22, 29, 32, 33, 38n36, 47, 56–57, 59, 62, 93, 108–109, 127, 139, 204, 211, 212, 256. *See also* Enlightenment
Jehovah's Witness, 119, 121, 136–138, 145, 153, 154, 155, 156, 157, 158, 251
Jehovah's Witnesses v. King County Hospital, 286
Jensen v. Quaring, 295
Jesuits, 15
Jewish and Roman Catholic Emancipation Acts of 1829 and 1833, 15
Jimmy Swaggart Ministries v. Board of Equalization of California, 166–167, 179nn21–22, 299
Johnson v. Robinson, 289
Jones v. Opelika (I), 275
Jones v. Opelika (II), 276
Jones v. Wolf, 164, 167, 244, 292
Joseph Burstyn, Inc. v. Wilson, 280, 282
Journal of the Senate, 87
Judaism and Jews, 5, 7, 8, 9–10, 15, 23, 25, 28–29, 34, 47, 49, 50, 51, 60, 69n130, 100, 118, 120, 121, 145, 146, 151–152, 159, 163–165, 167, 179n24, 181n76, 202, 244–245, 253

Kansas, Constitution of, 111, 268
Karcher v. May, 298

Kedroff v. Saint Nicholas Cathedral, 161, 164, 244, 280, 282
Kentucky, Constitution of, 50, 109, 268
King James Version. *See* Bible
Know-Nothing Party, 113
Ku Klux Klan, 113, 302
Kunz v. New York, 155, 280, 282

Lamb's Chapel v. Center Moriches Union Free School District, 170–172, 173, 301
Largent v. Texas, 275
Larkin v. Grendel's Den, 212, 294
Larson v. Valente, 293
The Late Corporation of the Church of Jesus Christ of Latter Day Saints v. United States, 127, 128, 272
Laycock, Douglas, xiii, 250
Lee v. International Society for Krishna Consciousness, 301
Lee v. Weisman, 189f, 198, 205, 220–222, 243, 259n9, 300
Leland, John, 27, 42–43, 61, 68n103
Lemon test, 188, 191, 192–195, 198, 199, 201, 209–210, 213, 217, 218, 223. *See also* Accommodationism; *Agostini* test; Separation of church and state
Lemon v. Kurtzman, 189f, 193, 194–195, 209–210, 213, 215, 234, 287, 288
Letter Concerning Toleration (Locke), 29–30, 36, 38n34, 64n21
Levitt v. Committee for Public Education and Religious Liberty, 288
Levy, Leonard, 224–225
Liberty of conscience, xxi, xxii, xxiii, xxiv, 10, 12, 16, 17, 21, 25–34, 41–45, 47–51, 55–56, 58, 61–62, 63n1, 64n19, 71, 74–75, 79–91, 97–102, 107–110, 113–117, 126, 127, 137, 144, 152–153, 157–160, 163, 169, 177, 185, 188, 189, 198, 201, 202, 213–222, 245. *See also*

Disestablishment of religion; Free exercise of religion
Licensing, 136, 154–155, 212, 244, 275, 277, 279, 280, 281, 282, 283, 303
Line of separation, 31, 193, 226
Livermore, Charles, 83, 86, 91, 95, 263
Livingston, Henry, 46
Lloyd, Thomas, 80
Locke, John, 1–2, 29–31, 36, 38n34, 52, 64n21, 174, xxivn1
Locke v. Davey, 168, 189f, 220, 303
Lord of the Netherlands. *See* Philip II
Louis XIV, 14
Louisiana, Constitution of, 107, 111, 114, 268
Lovell v. City of Griffin, 136, 274
Lupu, Ira, 146
Luther, Martin, 1, 10, 52
Lutheranism and Lutherans, 10, 12, 14, 15, 16, 23, 28–29, 34, 119, 120, 120t, 124n37, 159, 163, 167, 202
Lying v. Northwest Indian Cemetery Protective Association, 165–166, 167, 176, 243, 298
Lynch v. Donnelly, 254, 256, 295

Madison, James, xvi, 2, 8, 9, 17, 21–22, 29, 31, 32, 36n1, 38n41, 41–42, 45, 47, 48–49, 50, 51, 55–56, 58–59, 60–61, 63n1, 69n132, 76, 77, 81–83, 86, 88, 91, 94, 95, 96, 98, 100–101, 139, 160, 226, 250, 262, 263. *See also* Enlightenment
Mahometanism. *See* Islam
Maine, Constitution of, 111, 114, 268
Marbury v. Madison, 125
Margin of appreciation, xxii, 235–236
Marsh v. Alabama, 278
Marsh v. Chambers, 253–254, 294
Martin, Luther, 50
Martin v. Struthers, 154, 276
Maryland and Virginia Churches v. Sharpsburg, 287
Maryland, Constitution of, 17, 51, 61, 109, 111, 117, 268

Mason, George, 77, 103n29
Massachusetts Bay Colony, 16, 23, 25
Massachusetts, Constitution of, 26, 27, 34–35, 51, 61, 107, 111, 114–117, 122n12, 212, 268
Mather, Cotton, 23
Mayflower Compact, 115
Mayflower Pilgrims, 14
Mayhew, Jonathan, 23
McCollum v. Board of Education, 189f, 204, 279, 281
McConnell, Michael, 98
McDaniel v. Paty, 111, 160, 222–223, 243–244, 291
McGowan v. Maryland, 284
Meek v. Pittinger, 196, 290
Mennonites, 11, 73
Methodism and Methodists, 23, 27–29, 34, 112, 117, 119, 120, 121, 159, 163, 167, 202
Mexico, 120
Meyer v. Nebraska, 135, 208, 273
Michigan, Constitution of, 268
Military protection, 4, 6, 24, 129, 149. *See also* Pacifism
Minersville School Board v. Gobitis, 158, 163, 275
Minnesota, Constitution of, 214, 268
Minnesota v. Hershberger, 300
Mississippi, Constitution of, 269
Missouri, Constitution of, 112, 269
Mitchell v. Helms, 196, 197, 200, 217, 218, 219, 302
Monasticism, 5
Montana, Constitution of, 110, 123n28, 269
Montesquieu, Baron, 1–2, 29
Moravians, 27, 49, 84, 100
Mormonism and Mormons, 110, 112, 118, 119, 120, 121, 126–129, 149, 150, 158, 243, 244
Movements, political/theological, xxi
Mueller v. Allen, 189f, 194, 214, 219, 294
Murdock v. Pennsylvania (City of Jeannette), 154, 166, 276

Murphy v. Ramsey, 271
Muslims. *See* Islam
Musser v. Utah, 279, 281

*National Labor Relations Board v.
    Catholic Bishop of Chicago*, 162,
    244, 291
National Liberal League, 113
National Reform Association, 113
Native Americans, xx, 60, 100, 118,
    131–132, 151–152, 165, 167,
    175–176, 208, 244, 253, 272,
    296, 298
Naturalization, 273, 274, 278
Nebraska, Constitution of, 135, 269
Nero, Emperor, 3–4
Netherlands, 17, 75, 101
Nevada, Constitution of, 112, 269
New Deal, 139
New Hampshire, Constitution of, 61,
    107, 111, 122n12, 269
New Jersey, Constitution of, 44–45, 51,
    59, 109, 112, 114, 116–117,
    123n20, 269
New Mexico, Constitution of, 110,
    111, 123n28, 269
New York, Constitution of, 44, 51, 59,
    97, 112, 123n20, 269
New York v. Cathedral Academy, 291
Niemotko v. State of Maryland, 155,
    281
Ninety-Five Theses, 10
Nonbelievers, 23, 28–29, 34, 159, 163,
    167, 202
Nonpreferentialism, 60, 96, 113, 192.
    See also Disestablishment of
    religion
Noonan, John, xxiii
North Carolina, Constitution of,
    76–77, 97, 269
North Dakota, Constitution of,
    123n28, 269
Northwest Ordinance (1787), 34,
    75–76, 92–93, 112
Norwood v. Harrison, 288
Novels (Roman law), 5

Oaths. *See* Religious tests
Office and Commission of International
    Religious Freedom, 236
*Ohio Civil Rights Commission v.
    Dayton Christian Schools*, 297
Ohio, Constitution of, 269
Oklahoma, Constitution of, 109, 269
O'Lone v. Estate of Shabazz, 165, 167,
    297
Order of St. Benedict v. Steinhauser,
    133, 273
Oregon, Constitution of, 109, 135,
    168, 269
Orthodox Christianity, 4, 100, 120,
    121
Orthodox Diocese v. Milivojevich,
    161–162, 244
Otto, Rudolf, 246

Pacifism, 44, 45, 49, 50, 73, 80, 81,
    84–87, 97, 99, 100, 109, 121,
    122n7, 129–131, 136, 152, 158,
    159, 174. *See also* First
    Amendment
Paine, Thomas, 21, 29, 31, 53, 59
Palko v. Connecticut, 136
Parent/guardian rights, 277, 286, 296
Parker Seal Company v. Cummins, 290,
    291
Patterson, William, 88
Peace of Augsburg, 10–11, 14
Peace of Westphalia, 14
Penn, William, 17, 45, xxivn1
Pennsylvania, Constitution of, 44, 50,
    58, 270
Pentecostals, 119, 120
*Permoli v. First Municipality of New
    Orleans*, 270
Philip II, 13
Pierce v. Society of Sisters, 135, 162,
    208, 273
Pinckney, Charles, 77, 78, 262
Pledge of Allegiance, 158, 198,
    205–206, 258n9, 303
Plymouth Colony (1620), 16

Polygamy, 110, 118, 126–129, 149,
    158, 243, 244, 271, 272, 278,
    279, 281. *See also* Mormonism
*Ponce v. Roman Catholic Apostolic
    Church*, 273
Postmodernism, xxiii
Poulos v. New Hampshire, 155, 283
Pragmatic Sanction of Bourges, 9
Prayer
    in political body, 34, 72, 73, 77–78,
        93, 95, 118, 188, 213, 294
    in school, 172, 173, 197, 198, 205,
        207–208, 212, 213, 220–222,
        226, 230n82, 245, 258n9, 285,
        293, 300, 302
*Presbyterian Church in the United
    States v. Mary Elizabeth Blue Hull
    Memorial Presbyterian Church*,
    161, 286
Presbyterians, 23, 28–29, 34, 159, 163,
    167, 202
Prince v. Massachusetts, 147, 156, 277
Prisoner's rights, 143, 145, 146, 151,
    165, 178n3, 248n14, 285, 288,
    297
Protestantism, 10–12, 61, 100, 120,
    121
Providence Plantation, 16
Prussia, 75
Public religion, 34–35, 117, 118, 119,
    120, 256–257, 294
Puritanism and Puritans, xxi, 12, 15,
    16, 22, 23–26, 27, 28, 33, 35,
    37n32, 41, 42, 43, 47, 49, 52, 55,
    57, 61, 71, 88, 101, 116, 139,
    191, 249. *See also* Calvinism;
    Republicanism; Separation of
    church and state

Quakerism and Quakers, 1, 17, 25, 44,
    45, 49, 55, 60, 73, 84–85, 100,
    117, 120
Quebec Act (1774), 73
Quick Bear v. Leupp, 131–132, 138,
    208, 272. *See also* Native
    Americans

Racial discrimination, 244–245
Randolph, Edmund, 59
The Reasonableness of Christianity,
    (Locke), 30–31
Religion
    abolishment of, 81–82, 100
    action/expression of, xxiii, 62, 146,
        152–157, 177, 185, 188, 222–224
    Blaine Amendment for, 107, 113,
        121n1
    censorship in, 282, 280
    Constitutional protection for, xxii,
        13, 17, 50, 100, 152, 250–251,
        255
    definition of, 41, 100, 245–246
    education in, 4, 7, 9, 11, 46, 73, 93,
        112, 117, 118, 135, 143, 162,
        168, 185, 188, 203–208,
        213–220, 230n89
    equal access for, xxi, 170–174, 175,
        182n106, 182n109, 197, 222,
        223, 293, 300, 301, 302, 303
    European laws on, 1
    fraud in, 277
    free exercise of, xx, xxi, xxii, xxiv,
        41, 45–46, 48, 61–62, 71, 74,
        79–80, 83, 87, 88, 90, 96–97,
        98–99, 101, 102, 107–110, 114,
        117, 121n1, 126–129, 144–178,
        148f, 150, 222, 224, 255
    funding of, 112–113
    government aid to, 21 3–220, 24, 31,
        34, 112, 113, 118, 138, 187–189,
        190, 192, 196, 199, 200–203,
        206, 209–210
    government regulation of, 149
    land grants for, 61
    patronage for, 6, 60, 117, 120
    political pluralism and, 120–121
    school transportation for, 112,
        123n20, 200, 208, 279, 281
    state benefits and, 23, 28–29, 34,
        159, 163, 167, 202, 292
    substantive neutrality in, xxi–xxii,
        xxiv, 152, 163–169, 182n106,
        185, 188, 193–196, 198–199,
        206, 208, 218–220

tax exemption of, 34, 55, 61, 113, 118, 123n26, 146, 159, 166–167, 174, 179nn21–22, 187, 190–191, 194, 195, 200, 213, 214, 244, 253, 272, 287, 293, 294, 299

tax subsidies for, 61, 118, 187, 190–191, 202, 211–212, 287, 288, 289, 290, 291, 292, 296, 301, 302

U.S. Supreme Court review of, 125, 146

Religion, freedom of, 4, 10–12, 41–42. *See also* Religious liberty

Religious denominations, xx

Religious discrimination, xxiii, 2, 43, 44, 109, 150, 154–155, 158, 168, 174, 192, 297, 298

Religious display, 197, 295, 299

Religious dissension, 9, 11, 14–16, 28, 29, 43, 57, 58, 60, 64n19, 93, 121

Religious equality, xix, xxi, xxii, xxiv, 35, 41, 44, 48–51, 58, 61–62, 71, 79–80, 90, 99, 101, 110–111, 113–117, 134, 137, 144, 152, 153–157, 163, 167, 170, 176–177, 185, 188, 192, 199–201, 202, 213–220, 222–224, 227, 245. *See also* Disestablishment of religion; Free exercise of religion; Liberty of conscience

Religious establishments, 2, 17, 151

Religious exemptions, 29, 34, 55, 61, 113, 118, 123n26, 146, 159, 166–167, 174, 179nn21–22, 187, 190–191, 194, 195, 200, 213, 214, 244, 253, 293, 294, 299. *See also* Accommodationism; Free exercise of religion; Tax exemption of religion

Religious expression, 152–157, 177, 185, 188, 222–224

Religious freedom, xix–xxi, 130, 247n9, 248n14

Religious Freedom Restoration Act (RFRA), 150–151, 176, 177, 243, 302

Religious governance, 28, 161–162

Religious group rights and religious autonomy, xx–xxi, xxiii, 28, 38n41, 46, 53–54, 166–167, 169, 179nn21–22. *See also* Free exercise of religion

Religious incorporation, 28, 31, 60, 102, 111, 117, 132, 135–140, 143, 151

Religious Land Use and Institutionalized Persons Act (RLUIPA), 150–151, 176

Religious liberty. *See also* Disestablishment of religion
Bible passages for, 1
experimentation in, 17, 152
First Amendment for, xix, xxi, xxii, xxiii, xxiv, 45, 61, 91, 143, 185, 234–235
free exercise scrutiny for, 143–177, 148f, 179n24, 179n31, 243
international norm for, xxii, 62, 235, 241–246
Jefferson's bill for, 38n36
national law for, xix, 22, 75, 77, 139
neutralization of, xxi–xxii, xxiv, 152, 163–169, 182n106, 185, 188, 193–196, 198–199, 208, 218–220
pluralism guarantee for, 48
principles of, xxi, xxiii, 41
protection of, xxii, 13, 17, 32, 50, 152, 250–251, 255, 257
Protestant Reformation for, 10–12
revolution of, 3, 17
Rhode Island charter for, 27, 37n24
state laws for, xix, 76, 77, 79, 123n28, 135, 180n38
writings for, 19, 36n9, 43, 48, 55, 61–62, 64nn15, 139

Religious minorities, 117, 120–121, 167, 177, 244, 248n14

Religious neutrality, xxi–xxii, xxiv, 152, 163–169, 182n106, 185, 188, 193–196, 198–199, 206, 208, 218–220

Religious persecution, 2–3, 35, 47, 59, 61, 62, 69n132, 75, 76, 92–93

Religious pluralism, 10–11, 25, 26, 28, 29, 33, 34–35, 44, 46–48, 58–59, 61–62, 71, 77, 90, 99, 100, 101, 110–111, 126, 134, 137, 144, 152, 160, 162–163, 177, 185, 188, 192, 201, 202, 245

Religious property, 5, 24, 61, 74, 118, 127, 132–134, 151, 161, 194, 200, 270, 271, 272, 273, 280, 282, 286, 287, 292, 293

Religious relativism, xxii, 62, 236

Religious rights, xxii, 13, 17, 32, 50, 62, 135, 152, 235, 241–246, 250–251, 257

Religious tests or test oaths, xx, 36, 49, 57, 60, 66n56, 75, 78, 101, 104nn33, 109–110, 124n34, 129, 130, 138, 152, 159, 191, 254, 271, 278, 284. *See also* Free exercise of religion; Liberty of conscience

Religious tolerance, 14–17, 44, 101

Religious voluntarism, 28, 42, 205, 230n82

Religious warfare, 14

Republicanism or Civic Republicanism, xxi, 3, 22–23, 31, 33–35, 37n32, 41, 43, 47, 48, 51, 61, 71, 100, 139, 191, 249

Revolutionary War, 72, 73, 74

Reynolds v. United States, 125, 126, 127, 149, 157, 243, 271

RFRA. *See* Religious Freedom Restoration Act

Rhode Island, Constitution of, 37n24, 76, 83, 108, 270

RLUIPA. *See* Religious Land Use and Institutionalized Persons Act

Roemer v. Board of Public Works, 209, 290

Roman Empire, 3–6

Root, Elihu, 204–205

Rosenberger v. Rector and Visitors of the University of Virginia, 171, 173, 189f, 200, 219, 224, 302

Rush, Benjamin, 33, 48

Rusk v. Espinoza, 294

Russia, 120, 139

Russian Orthodoxy, 161

Sabbatarianism, 145, 159, 244, 287, 290

Sabbath beliefs/regulations, 24, 31, 33, 37n32, 60, 75, 76, 117, 118, 121, 145, 151–152, 159–160, 179n24, 211, 213, 244, 253, 284, 285, 295

Sacraments, Christian, 8

Saia v. New York, 279, 281

Santa Fe Independent School District v. Doe, 189f, 197, 205, 221–222, 243, 302

Santerians, 150, 167–168

Schneider v. State of New Jersey (Town of Irvington), 274

Schneider v. Town of Irvington, 136

School voucher program, 218–220, 303

Schools. *See also* Disestablishment of religion; Education; Equal Access Act; Free exercise of religion

  Bible teachings and, 1, 6, 8, 11, 25, 28–29, 34, 35, 51, 52, 58, 67n85, 72, 74, 93, 112, 115, 118, 135, 155, 158, 172, 205, 226, 280, 282, 285

  as public, 76, 92–93, 109, 112, 117–118, 121, 121n1, 123, 203–211, 292

  as religious, 4–5, 14, 24, 34, 43, 47, 60, 61, 73, 111, 119, 162, 203–211, 230n89, 270, 272, 273, 287, 288, 290, 291

  remedial education for, 195, 199, 210, 215–216, 255

  voucher program for, 218–220, 303

Scientology, Church of or Scientologists, 117, 119, 120, 258, 299, 301

Scottish Presbyterians, 12

Second Great Awakening (1820-1860), 119, 126, 127

Secularism, 192, 206

Selective Draft Act (1917), 129, 173–174

Selective Draft Law Cases (Arver v. United States), 273

Separation of church and state, xx–xxii, xxiv, 5–6, 17, 23–25, 27, 28–29, 29–30, 31, 33, 41, 51–57, 59, 61–62, 71, 90, 99, 101, 111–113, 121, 126, 128, 134, 139, 144, 152, 160–162, 163, 170, 177, 185, 188–191, 201–202, 222–223, 225–236. *See also* Disestablishment of religion; Free exercise of religion; Wall of separation

Separationism, 5, 25, 121, 202–203, 204–205, 209, 212–213, 214, 243. *See also* Separation of church and state; Wall of separation

Serbian Orthodox Diocese v. Milivojevich, 290

Sermons, political, 1

Seventh-day Adventists, 117, 119, 120, 121, 159–160, 244

Shakers, 73

Shalom Tefila Congregation v. Cobb, 297

Sherbert v. Verner, 149, 150, 159, 160, 163, 167, 175, 229n68, 234, 243

Sherman, Roger, 82, 84–85, 88, 91, 92, 95, 99

Sicurella v. United States, 283

Sigismund, Emperor, 9

Simmons v. United States, 283

Simons, Menno, 10

Sin, doctrine of, 13

Sincerity test, 146

Slavery, 119–120, 244–245

Sloan v. Lemon, 210, 289

Smith, Adam, 29

Smith, Joseph, 126, 127. *See also* Mormonism

Smith v. Swormstedt, 270

Social pluralism, 47, 110–111. *See also* Confessional pluralism; Religious liberty; Religious pluralism

Society of Sisters, 135

South Carolina, Constitution of, 55, 59, 109, 114, 270

South Dakota, Constitution of, 123n28, 270

Spaight, Richard, 49

Speidel v. Henrici, 272

State constitutions and religion, xix, xxi–xxii, xxii, 135, 256, 290. *See also* Disestablishment of religion; Federalism; Free exercise of religion; *individual state names*

State ratification conventions
First Amendment drafts from, 262–263
proposals for, 22, 32, 35, 49, 58–59, 76–80, 262–263

States' rights, 30, 84, 85, 88–89, 92, 94, 101, 102, 107, 135, 251, 256

Stiles, Ezra, xx, 43

Stone v. Graham, 206–207, 292

Strong, Nathan, 34

Suarez, Francisco, 1–2

Superstition, 2

Supremacy Act, 11

Sweden, 75

Tax deduction, 300

Tax exemption of religion, 34, 55, 61, 113, 118, 123n26, 146, 159, 166–167, 174, 179nn21–22, 187, 190–191, 194, 195, 200, 213, 214, 244, 253, 272, 287, 294, 299. *See also* Disestablishment of religion; Free exercise of religion

Tennessee, Constitution of, 50, 111, 160, 222–223, 270

Tenth Amendment, 94

Terrett v. Taylor, 132, 270

Texas, Constitution of, 270

Texas Monthly v. Bullock, 189f, 195, 299

Thanksgiving Day and proclamations, 33, 34, 57, 72–73, 92, 93, 95, 96, 118

Theodosian Code (Roman law), 5

Theodosius, Emperor, 6

Thirteenth Amendment, 119–120

The Thirty-Nine Articles of Religion (Church of England), 11

Thomas v. Review Board, Indiana Employment Security Division, 160, 181n76, 292

Thoughts on Education (Locke), 30–31

Tilton v. Richardson, 209, 288

Tithes or religious taxes, 11, 24, 25, 28, 31, 43–45, 50, 55, 57, 60, 74, 95, 101, 109, 139, 154, 191, 202

Title I. *See* Elementary and Secondary Education Act

Toleration Act (1689), 15, 25

Tony and Susan Alamo Foundation v. Secretary of Labor, 295

Torcaso v. Watkins, 109, 159, 284

Tradition, constitutional arguments from

Transworld Airlines v. Hardison, 174, 291

Treen v. Karen B., 293

Trial by jury, 81, 86, 103n29

Trinitarian Christianity, 4, 49, 72–73, 75

Tucker, Thomas, 85, 91, 92

Tucker v. Texas, 278

Two guys from Harrison Allenstown Ind. v. McGinley, 284

Two kingdoms doctrine, 10

Two swords doctrine, 7–8, 10

Union of Utrecht of 1579, 13–14

Unitarianism and Unitarians, 117, 119, 120

United Nations Declaration on the Elimination of All Forms of Intolerance and of Discrimination Based on Religion or Belief (1981), 218–220, 236, 238–239, 242, 303

United States Catholic Conference v. Abortion Rights Mobilization, 298

United States v. American Friends Service Committee, 290

United States v. Ballard, 277

United States v. Bland, 274

United States v. Lee, 293

United States v. Macintosh, 129, 130

United States v. Nugent, 283

United States v. Schwimmer, 129–130, 273

United States v. Seeger, 286

Universal Declaration of Human Rights (1948), 236

Universalism and Universalists, 119, 120

U.S. Congress, xv, xix, xxi–xxiiv, 45, 59, 61, 91, 150–151, 166, 175, 176, 188

U.S. Constitution, xix, 34, 36n9, 45, 49, 58, 82, 83, 90, 125, 158, 177, 188, 193, 250

state ratification proposals for, 22, 32, 35, 49, 58–59, 76–80, 262–263

U.S. Congress and, xix, 125

U.S. State Department, 236

U.S. Supreme Court

case-by-case balancing by, 146, 188

criticism of, 224–225, 233–234, 253

definitional balancing by, 146–147, 188

disestablishment cases for, 186, 211

endorsement approach by, 196–197

equal treatment by, 199–201

First Amendment and, xix, 89, 91, 233–234, 248n14

First Amendment neutralization by, xxi–xxii, xxiv, 152, 163–169, 182n106, 185, 188, 193–196, 198–199, 208, 218–220

free exercise scrutiny by, 143–177, 148f, 179n24, 179n31, 243

inconsistency of, xx–xxi, xxii, 146, 181n76, 188, 196, 213, 233, 252–253

incorporation doctrine for, 28, 31, 60, 102, 111, 117, 132, 135–140, 143, 151

Lemon/Agostini tests by, 188, 191, 192–193, 198, 199, 200, 201

as model for states, 143

powers of, 125

principled balancing, by, 188

reductionism by, 253

religious liberty and, xix, 251
review by, 125, 144–147, 152, 187
tradition and, 254–255
Utah, Constitution of, 110, 111, 112, 114, 128, 270

Valley Forge Christian College v. Americans United for Separation of Church and State, 293
Vatican, 34
Vermont, Constitution of, 49–50, 109, 270
Vidal v. Girard's Executors, 270
Vienna Concluding Document (1989), 236, 240–244
Vietnam War, 131. *See also* Pacifism
Village of Scarsdale v. McCreary, 295
Vining, John, 82, 85, 88
Virginia, Constitution of, 22, 32–33, 38n36, 46, 51, 58–59, 63n1, 111, 117, 132, 139, 270
Vitoria, Francisco de, 1–2, 19n37
Voltaire, François-Marie Arouet de, 29
Voluntarism in religion, 28, 42, 205, 230n82. *See also* Free exercise of religion; Liberty of conscience

Wall of separation, 1, 11, 12, 27, 52, 53, 56, 127, 192, 202, 204, 211, 212, 256. *See also* Burgh, James; Jefferson, Thomas; Line of separation; Luther, Martin; Separation of church and state; Simons, Menno; Williams, Roger; Wortman, Tunis
Wallace v. Jaffree, 195, 207–208, 295
Walz v. Tax Commission, 174, 189f, 193, 194, 287
Washington, Constitution of, 123n28, 270
Washington, George, 33, 44, 54, 72, 88, 92
Watchtower Bible and Tract Society of New York Inc. v. Village of Stratton, 156, 303

Watson v. Jones, 133–134, 157, 234, 244, 271
Wayte v. United States, 295
Welsh v. United States, 287
Wesley, Charles, 27
Wesley, John, 27
West Virginia, Constitution of, 32–33, 109, 111, 270
West Virginia State Board of Education v. Barnette, 158–159, 259n9, 277
Western (wailing) wall, 51
The Westminster Confession, 42
Westside Community Schools v. Mergens, 175
Wheeler v. Barrera, 289
White House, xv
Whitfield, George, 27
Wide Awake: A Christian Perspective at the University of Virginia (newspaper), 171, 173
Widmar v. Vincent, 169–170, 175, 223, 224, 293
Wiegman, Leo, xiii
Willard, Samuel, 25
Williams, Elisha, 25–26, 42, 53, 55, 63n1
Williams, Roger, xvi, 16, 22, 25, 27, 29, xxivn1
Wilson, James, 77
Winchester, Elhanan, xix–xx
Winthrop, John, 23, 24
Wisconsin, Constitution of, 270
Wisconsin v. Yoder, 162, 243, 288
Wise, John, 23
Witherspoon, John, 21, 22
Witters v. Washington Department of Services for the Blind, 214–215, 217, 219, 296
Wolman v. Walter, 196, 291
Woodruff, Wilford, 128
Wooley v. Maynard, 290
Wortman, Tunis, 54
Wycliff, John, 1
Wyoming, Constitution of, 123n28, 270

Young, Brigham, 126

Zelman test, 200–201
Zelman v. Simmons-Harris, 189f, 200,
    218–219, 243–244, 303

*Zobrest v. Catalina Foothills School
    District*, 186, 215, 216–217, 219,
    227n1, 301
Zorach v. Clauson, 174, 189f,
    191–192, 280, 282